THE BURDEN OF THE ANCIENTS

The Linda Schele Series in Maya and Pre-Columbian Studies

This series was made possible through the generosity of William C. Nowlin Jr. and Bettye H. Nowlin, the National Endowment for the Humanities, and various individual donors.

THE BURDEN OF THE ANCIENTS

Maya Ceremonies of World Renewal from the Pre-Columbian Period to the Present

ALLEN J. CHRISTENSON

UNIVERSITY OF TEXAS PRESS
Austin

Printed in the United States of America
First edition, 2016

All photographs by author unless otherwise noted.

Requests for permission to reproduce material from this work should be sent to:
Permissions
University of Texas Press
P.O. Box 7819
Austin, TX 78713-7819
http://utpress.utexas.edu/index.php/rp-form

♾ The paper used in this book meets the minimum requirements of ANSI/NISO Z39.48-1992 (R1997) (Permanence of Paper).

LIBRARY OF CONGRESS CATALOGING-IN-PUBLICATION DATA
Names: Christenson, Allen J., 1957- author.
Title: The burden of the ancients : Maya ceremonies of world renewal from the Pre-Columbian period to the present / Allen J. Christenson.
Series: Linda Schele series in Maya and pre-Columbian studies.
Description: First edition. Austin : University of Texas Press, 2016. Includes bibliographical references and index.
Identifiers: LCCN 2016003027
ISBN 9781477309957 (cloth : alk. paper)
ISBN 9781477310267 (pbk. : alk. paper)
ISBN 9781477309964 (library e-book)
ISBN 9781477309971 (non-library e-book)
Subjects: LCSH: Mayas—Rites and ceremonies. Mayas—Religion. Mayas—Religious life and customs. Tzutuhil Indians—Religion. Tzutuhil Indians—Rites and ceremonies. Santiago Atitlán (Guatemala)—Religious life and customs. Holy Week—Guatemala—Santiago Atitlán.
Classification: LCC F1435.3.R56 C48 2016
DDC 299.7/842—dc23
LC record available at http://lccn.loc.gov/2016003027

doi: 10.7560/309957

To the people of Santiago Atitlán—those living in this world and those now living with the ancients

CONTENTS

ACKNOWLEDGMENTS

My gratitude belongs first and last to the people of Santiago Atitlán who have so patiently and generously given of their time, hospitality, and wisdom over the many years when this project was gestating, beginning with my first visit there in 1977 as an ethnographer and linguist. This work could not have been done without the collaboration of the many Maya confraternity officials and members, *ajq'ijaa'* (traditional Maya priests) and other ritual specialists, municipal leaders, and citizens of the community. They have been extraordinarily kind in granting access to their ritual life, much of which is private and little known outside their own circles.

This book draws heavily on conversations that I have had with the people of Santiago Atitlán, known locally as Atitecos, and I have tried wherever possible to use their words rather than to paraphrase. It is after all their voice that matters. Because of the continued threat of violence against traditionalists in Santiago Atitlán, I have not included their names unless specifically told to do so. As one of those whose names I did include told me, "far more tragic than being threatened is being forgotten." I look forward to the day when circumstances in Guatemala will make it safe to acknowledge others.

This book would never have seen the light of day without the generous support and encouragement of Brigham Young University, particularly my mentors who have served as department chairs—George Tate, Roger Macfarlane, Stanley Benfell, Michael Call, and George Handley—and my dean, John Rosenburg. I am grateful to my colleagues who have offered invaluable advice on early drafts of the book—particularly Karen Bassie-Sweet, Garrett W. Cook, Shannon Dame, John D. Early, Juan José Guerrero Pérez, Stephen Houston, Ashley Kistler, Linda O'Brien-Rothe, Sandra Orellana, Jesper Nielsen, Camille Richey, Frauke Sachse, Garry Sparks, and Gabrielle Vail. I am deeply indebted to my friend Andrew Weeks. Beginning in 2001, we worked together on several occasions in Santiago Atitlán while he was making his beautiful film *Balancing the Cosmos*. His natural sympathy for the people and profound understanding of the changing Atiteco world are deeply inspiring. His influence may be found on most if not all of the better pages of this book. It has been a cherished privilege to work with him.

It is expected to recognize the love and support of an author's spouse at some point in the acknowledgments. With all my heart I do so for my wife, Janet. Not only would this book never have been written without her encouragement and help, but I would never have had the chance to do this kind of work at all without her. This book is as much hers as it is mine.

THE BURDEN OF THE ANCIENTS

INTRODUCTION

Nearly every major modern Maya ceremony is founded in one way or another on the concept of rebirth and renewal. In traditional Maya belief, everything passes through endless cycles of birth, maturation, dissolution, death, and rebirth. This includes not only the obvious life cycles of humans and the crops on which they depend, but also gods and the world itself. All have their beginnings in a creative act and ultimately weaken and die in an orderly succession of days that is both comforting in its predictability and terrifying in its unwavering finality. Traditional Maya today believe that it is the role of human beings to perpetuate this cycle through ritual offerings and ceremonies that have the power to rebirth the world at critical points during the calendar year. The most intense ceremonies of world renewal practiced by the ancient Maya took place during the final five days of their solar calendar year, a period known as the Wayeb'.

The first two chapters of this book outline what we know of these Pre-Columbian ceremonies of world renewal, focusing on the rituals tied to the Wayeb' days, a ritual cycle that apparently was observed throughout the Maya world, at least in the years immediately preceding the Spanish Conquest in the early sixteenth century. Much of this information is derived from the writings of the earliest Spanish missionaries to the Maya region, particularly Fray Diego de Landa in Yucatan, Mexico, and Fray Bartolomé de las Casas in the Guatemalan highlands. Albeit for very different reasons, both attempted to record the traditional beliefs and practices of the Maya prior to the arrival of the Spanish conquerors. Both Landa and Las Casas based their writings on firsthand accounts from surviving members of the Maya royal court and nobility that they either elicited directly or derived from the writings of fellow missionary priests who were living among the Maya during this period. Wherever possible I have supplemented these early Spanish accounts with those written by the Maya themselves, both before and soon after the Conquest. These indigenous texts describe many of the same ceremonies and refer to the actions of deities that clarify the theological underpinnings of world regeneration at important crisis points during the year. Chapter 3 addresses the impact of the Spanish Conquest on the Maya region. Its violence came to be interpreted by the Maya as a type of world death followed by rebirth, replicating in a tragically real way the type of world renewal that had previously been observed only conceptually through ritual. Chapter 4 attempts to reconstruct the process of syncretism in the early centuries of the Spanish colonial period whereby the Maya identified important elements of their ancient world renewal ceremonies with Roman Catholic observances, particularly those connected with the death of Christ at the Easter season, a period known as Semana Santa (Holy Week). This blending of traditional Maya beliefs and practices with those of European Christianity is an ongoing process that continues today in many Maya communities. The second half of the book is devoted to a detailed description of Holy Week observances in Santiago Atitlán, a traditional Tz'utujil-Maya community in the highlands of Guatemala, as a living example of this type of syncretic process.

In Santiago Atitlán the most elaborate ceremonies of world renewal take place during Holy Week, the days preceding Easter on the Christian calendar. In Guatemala Holy Week falls at the critical point in early spring when the long dry season finally comes to a close. Due to the extreme lack of rain in the months preceding Holy Week, the earth becomes barren and incapable of germinating new crops. Traditionalist Tz'utujils believe that the world dies during Holy Week and a complex cycle of ceremonies, processions, ritual offerings, and prayers must be carried out to give the sky the strength to generate rain so that it can sustain new crops and human life. If these actions are performed properly, the first heavy rains will fall soon afterward and farmers can plant their maize seeds in anticipation of a successful harvest. Significant elements of these world-renewing ceremonies during Holy Week echo those once carried out by their Pre-Columbian ancestors during the Wayeb' period.

The Tz'utujil Maya people of Santiago Atitlán believe that they occupy sacred land, the place of first creation, the navel of the earth and sky, and the very heart of the world. They are fiercely proud of their language, costumes, and traditions. The town is built on a narrow promontory of land at a point where the lower skirts of three great volcanoes come together to form a rocky and uneven foundation for its winding streets and buildings (fig. 1). On its southern, western, and northern sides, it is surrounded by a large bay of Lake Atitlán whose principal shores lie close by to the north. The Lake Atitlán area of highland Guatemala is reputed to be among the most beautiful places on earth. Far more important than the beauty of their community's location, however, is the profoundly held conviction on the part of traditionalist Tz'utujils that they live in a sacred place. The volcanoes and surrounding mountains are the abode of gods and powerful semideified ancestors. The lake

1. *Santiago Atitlán with two of the three volcanoes surrounding its bay*

contains the primordial waters of creation, suffused with power capable of regenerating and sustaining life as well as the capacity to destroy it.

Despite centuries of pressure by outsiders to abandon their ancestral traditions, sometimes through well-meaning persuasion but often through unthinkable violence, a significant number of Tz'utujils continue to practice centuries-old ceremonies whose core elements are often directly related to those once carried out by their ancient forebears. This religious and social conservatism may be explained in part by their history following the Spanish Conquest in 1524. The territory now occupied by Santiago Atitlán was once the capital of the ancient Tz'utujil kingdom, one of three great Pre-Columbian powers in the region, the others being the kingdoms of the K'iche's and the Kaqchikels. The highland Maya lords who ruled the major K'iche' and Kaqchikel lineages resisted Spanish dominion. These efforts at resistance were ruthlessly crushed, resulting in the torture and execution of the K'iche' and Kaqchikel kings. The capital of the K'iche's at Q'umarkaj was burned and its population depleted by warfare and enslavement. In contrast, the Tz'utujil ruling dynasty capitulated to the Spaniards after a brief battle and never rebelled openly against Spanish political authority once it was established. As a result, the Tz'utujils were subsequently allowed to administer their affairs much as they had done prior to the Conquest. The Tz'utujils undoubtedly considered this a sign of divine favor and were thus less susceptible to radical shifts in their indigenous worldview. In contrast to the fatalistic acceptance of defeat found in K'iche' and Kaqchikel accounts of the Conquest, most legends told by Atitecos about the arrival of the Spaniards emphasize the supernatural power of their ancient kings and gods in escaping the destruction that befell other highland Maya kingdoms. Even today the Tz'utujils consider themselves to be distinct from other highland Maya groups because their kings were never killed and their ancient communities were never destroyed.

For many Tz'utujils, the Spanish Conquest was not a catastrophic event that ended Maya culture but a kind of temporary death followed by rebirth that is not different in kind from other periodic world renewals that took place prior to the Conquest and continue to some degree today. Santiago Atitlán is somewhat exceptional in preserving a rich tradition of ritual practices that follow ancestral precedent, although they have certainly been adapted and altered to fit the changing needs of Tz'utujil society as it adopted elements of Roman Catholicism and other foreign influences over the next five centuries. The Spanish Conquest and subsequent evangelization efforts suppressed many of these traditions in other highland Maya communities.

René Acuña argues that the violence of the Spanish Conquest and subsequent imposition of Roman Catholic doctrine on the Maya populace of Guatemala effectively subsumed indigenous culture and belief. He contends that those remnants of Maya culture that survive today are primarily those chosen by the Spaniards themselves, who adapted them to help in their conversion efforts. As a result, he suggests, highland Maya religion is more a kind of Folk Catholicism with little if any authentically Maya components (Acuña 1975, 1983).

It is the more common assertion among scholars today that important elements of Maya belief and their public expressions in the form of ritual dances, prayers, and ceremonialism were never completely suppressed (B. Tedlock 1982; D. Tedlock, 1986; Farriss 1984; Watanabe 1992; Carlsen 1997; Cook 2000; Cook et al. 2013). Previous researchers have noted the prevalence of objects and practices in Santiago Atitlán that preserve significant elements of ancient Maya theology. E. Michael Mendelson described the Atiteco bundle ritual as one of many examples of fundamentally Maya practices that have no counterpart in orthodox Roman Catholic worship (Mendelson 1958a, 121). Robert S. Carlsen finds that a defining characteristic of Atiteco society is a "distinct and identifiable continuity with the pre-Columbian past" (Carlsen 1997, 5).

A certain degree of disjunction in meaning must be expected with regard to religious practices in Santiago Atitlán considering the lengthy time since the Spanish Conquest and the convulsive changes in Atiteco society, particularly in the twentieth century. Nevertheless, it is apparent that modern Tz'utujil

Maya continue to practice many rituals and relate mythic stories that bear a remarkable resemblance to similar cultural entities from their Pre-Columbian past. It is also probable that modern Tz'utujils are influenced to one degree or another by the original meaning of these practices. The Tz'utujils are a modern people—not a lost civilization somehow rediscovered from the ancient past. Like any living society they are well aware of the world beyond the borders of their community and readily adopt aspects of Western culture, art, and language that fit the needs of their people. The colonial Spanish past as well as the political and social turbulence of the present are integral to Atiteco ceremonial practices because they are at least as much a part of the Tz'utujil world as their Pre-Conquest heritage. How recognition of these ancient concepts and motifs in the religious life of the Tz'utujils informs the cultural heritage of Santiago Atitlán has only begun to be addressed. This book is an attempt to approach the problem of identifying possible Pre-Columbian and early colonial Maya antecedents to contemporary Tz'utujil Maya practices in a systematic way based on documentary evidence.

Brief references to the Tz'utujils appear in the writings of many of the early Roman Catholic missionaries in Guatemala, particularly Fray Bartolomé de las Casas, Fray Domingo de Vico, and Fray Luis Cancer. While valuable, these writings often describe the highland Maya in general terms without distinguishing one group from another. There are no extensive colonial period descriptions of early Tz'utujil ceremonialism that can compare with the wealth of ethnographic material on Yucatec Maya culture compiled by Fray Diego de Landa or on the Mexica culture in the extensive writings of Fray Bernardino de Sahagún and Fray Diego Durán. Further significant references to Tz'utujil history and society may be found in the writings of later colonial Spanish writers, particularly Francisco Antonio de Fuentes y Guzmán (1932–1933 [1699]), Fray Francisco Ximénez (1929–1931 [1722], 1967 [1722]), Fray Francisco Vásquez (1937–1944 [1714]), Pedro Cortés y Larraz (1958 [1770]), and Francisco de Paula García Peláez (1943 [1851]).

In contrast to the scarcity of material from the colonial period, the twentieth century offers a wealth of information concerning the modern Tz'utujil Maya thanks to the efforts of anthropologists and ethnographers. The first published documentation of Santiago Atitlán's ceremonial life was made by Samuel Lothrop following a two-month stay in various highland Guatemalan villages in the winter of 1927–1928 (Lothrop 1928, 1929). Lothrop's description of public rituals, including Holy Week, formed only a minor part of this report and was admittedly "superficial in nature," because the Maya people tended to be "suspicious and uncommunicative" around strangers (Lothrop 1929, 1). He urged that further work be carried out by observers who could remain longer in residence so as to win the confidence of the local population. Various travelers and ethnographers since that time have observed public ceremonies at Santiago Atitlán (McDougall 1955; Mendelson 1956, 1957, 1958a, 1958b, 1959, 1965; Termer 1957; Douglas 1969; O'Brien-Rothe 1975, 2015; Orellana 1981, 1984; Tarn and Prechtel 1986, 1990, 1997; Prechtel and Carlsen 1988; Carlsen and Prechtel 1991, 1994; Carlsen 1996, 1997; Christenson 2001; Stanzione 2003), making it one of the most intensively studied communities in Guatemala.

E. Michael Mendelson was the first to spend a significant amount of time in Santiago Atitlán, residing there a full year from 1951 to 1952 while conducting fieldwork for his doctorate under the direction of Robert Redfield. His dissertation (Mendelson 1956) and voluminous field notes available on microfilm (Mendelson 1957) contain a wealth of information concerning all phases of Atiteco culture, society, religious organizations, and worldview. Although Mendelson's work focused on contemporary Atiteco society, he suggested that many Tz'utujil religious practices may have had Pre-Columbian antecedents (Mendelson 1958a, 124–125). Sandra Orellana attempted to reconstruct ancient Tz'utujil culture from the pre-Hispanic era through the early colonial period based on archaeological and documentary sources as well as her own anthropological fieldwork in Santiago Atitlán (Orellana 1981, 1984). Her work suggests that the Tz'utujils preserved significant elements of their native culture despite enforced accommodation to European culture, particularly in the ritual cycles of the local confraternities. More recently, the anthropologist Robert Carlsen spent much of the 1990s investigating the social organization and political history of Santiago Atitlán, including the development of confraternities and their system of worship (Carlsen 1996, 1997).

My own experience in Santiago Atitlán began in 1977 when I was working in Guatemala as a linguist, preparing a dictionary of the K'iche' language. I paid a brief visit to Santiago Atitlán to determine the feasibility of writing a similar dictionary for Tz'utujil. While nothing ultimately came of this, I was struck that most men and nearly all women at the time still wore their traditional dress on a daily basis and most preferred to speak Tz'utujil rather than Spanish. This was somewhat unusual, as men in most communities, even traditional ones like Momostenango, tended to wear nonindigenous clothing. I returned to Santiago Atitlán in 1988 when I saw their celebration of Holy Week for the first time. From 1996 to 1998 I lived for extended periods in Santiago Atitlán for my doctoral work. My dissertation focused on the central altarpiece of the town's sixteenth-century Roman Catholic church, a remarkable work of art that was reconstructed in the 1970s by traditional Tz'utujil sculptors who carved new panels that combined both Maya and European

Christian motifs. Much of the iconography of the altarpiece refers to Holy Week observances (Christenson 2001). The artists saw this as the critical period when life is renewed through ceremonies that had been practiced in much the same way as far back as the oldest people in the community could remember. The altarpiece is to a certain extent a synthesis in monumental form of the kind of cultural interaction that has evolved over the centuries since the Spanish Conquest. I have since returned to Santiago Atitlán for Holy Week numerous times, often accompanied by Andrew Weeks, a British filmmaker and colleague who documented this important ceremonial cycle in a film called *Balancing the Cosmos*, completed in 2010.

The world of Santiago Atitlán has changed dramatically in the years since I first visited the town. Robert Carlsen (1996, 1997) as well as Nathaniel Tarn and Martín Prechtel (Tarn and Prechtel 1997) have documented sweeping shifts in nearly all aspects of Atiteco society. Santiago Atitlán has little room to grow, being wedged into a small area bounded on three sides by water and on the other by steep mountains. Lacking sufficient arable land to support their growing population, the people of Santiago Atitlán have tended to move from an agriculturally based economy toward an emphasis on mercantilism, with many Atitecos traveling each day into the capital and other cities to work as tradesmen or in other business ventures. Improved roads and increased boat traffic on the lake in the second half of the twentieth century brought an influx of tourists and non-Maya businesses into the community. This contact with outside influences has had a tremendous impact on the traditional life of the community. The ever-increasing popularity of evangelical Protestantism and orthodox Catholicism have steadily eroded older Atiteco religious beliefs to the point where traditionalists now constitute a small minority of the overall population. The relatively peaceful town that I first encountered in 1977 has given way to a bustling commercial center under nearly constant siege by the din of rumbling trucks and buses, Protestant services amplified to ear-splitting volume, and the ever-present sound of radios turned up as high as they can go.

The devastating civil war in Guatemala, particularly the period in the 1980s known simply as *la violencia* (the violence), has had the greatest recent impact on the social fabric of Santiago Atitlán. Atitecos suffered disproportionately among neighboring highland Maya communities during these years. The Committee of Campesino Unity (CUC) estimates that as many as 1,700 Atitecos were killed between 1980 and 1990 out of a population of approximately 20,000 (Carlsen 1997, 18). Those perceived as promulgating traditional Maya culture and religion were targeted specifically as dangerous threats to social stability by some factions of the military.

The violence culminated in an incident on December 2, 1990. The day before, the garrison commander and a group of his soldiers had terrorized the community, raping the daughter of a local store owner and committing numerous thefts and acts of vandalism. When several thousand unarmed Atiteco men and women, some with their children, gathered the next day to complain about recent abuses, soldiers from the nearby garrison opened fire. Thirteen died instantly and scores of others lay wounded. The incident drew immediate international condemnation, forcing the Guatemalan government to take the unprecedented step of withdrawing its military presence from the community.

Despite the treaty of peace that officially ended the civil war in early 1997, political and religious conflict still plagues Santiago Atitlán. That same year a dispute between political factions resulted in the destruction of the mayor's offices, which included the town's library and archives. A lingering atmosphere of religious and social tension within the community has created a level of mutual mistrust among many Atitecos that periodically erupts into open violence and even murder. Nevertheless, the town has enjoyed something of a population explosion since the war and now approaches 50,000 inhabitants, spilling out into new subsidiary communities to the north and south of the traditional municipal boundaries. Santiago Atitlán is now an affluent, vibrant community with a rapidly growing youthful population that knows little about the horrors of the civil war. The center of town has witnessed the recent appearance of trendy boutiques, beauty salons, and electronics superstores with the latest flat screen televisions and hand-held gadgets, sprouting up alongside the more traditional shops of the older generation.

TRADITIONAL MAYA PRACTICES AND ROMAN CATHOLICISM

The ceremonialism of Holy Week in Santiago Atitlán is a complex blend of Roman Catholic and traditional Maya ritual practices. The fundamental belief underlying the ceremonies of Holy Week is that all things, both animate and inanimate, require periodic renewal through ritual performance to reenact the origin of the world. This is a core Maya principle. But although the message it expresses is predominantly Maya, it is not a fossil of the Pre-Columbian past with a superficial gilding of Catholicism to hide its "true" nature. The Catholic components are integral to the overall message of Easter observances. E. Michael Mendelson, who worked as an anthropologist in Santiago Atitlán in the early 1950s, observed that the Tz'utujil people of Santiago Atitlán celebrate the death and rebirth of their old gods in the history of the Christian God (Mendelson 1965, 138). This is not because Atitecos perceive Maya gods as equivalent in all respects to Jesus Christ and the Roman Catholic saints but because the two sets of deities carry out similar roles in their society. It is these similarities that Tz'utujils choose to emphasize rather than the differences. Atitecos seldom consider whether the components of their myths or ritual actions are Christian or Maya. They believe that their traditions have existed much as they exist today since the beginning of time, as ordained by all the gods and saints, and must be continued according to the patterns set by their Tz'utujil ancestors.

The introduction of Spanish rule and Christianity in Guatemala in the early sixteenth century resulted in the abrupt suppression of many of the more public indigenous Maya ceremonies as they were practiced prior to the Conquest—particularly those linked with the worship of their ancient deities and human sacrifice. Christian missionaries systematically destroyed Pre-Columbian temples as well as the carved and painted images they contained in an effort to prevent the Maya from returning to their former beliefs and practices. European deities and saints replaced the older Maya gods. The Maya adopted these new deities as essential members of their community but gave them many of the attributes that once belonged to their ancestral gods.

In Santiago Atitlán, San Francisco watches over the souls of the dead in the underworld—a role that has little to do with the ministry of St. Francis of Assisi. The central altarpiece of the town's early colonial church contains two images of the Virgin Mary (fig. 2). They are considered distinct individuals. On the lower right corner of the altarpiece is María Dragón (Mary of the Dragon), a chaste, protective deity who commands the winged serpent beneath her to defend the town and keep it from harm. Opposite this image on the lower left corner of the same altarpiece is María Andolor (Mary of Sorrows), described as a young moon deity associated with fertility, sexual licentiousness, and childbirth. She is symbolically impregnated by St. John the Evangelist, the saint who occupies the niche just to her left, on Thursday night during Holy Week in order to give birth to a new world the following day.

None of this, of course, would be recognizable as Roman Catholicism by non-Atitecos. Occasionally orthodox Catholic priests attempt to weed out such irregularities, sometimes violently. One Sunday I attended Mass in Santiago Atitlán in which the subject of the priest's homily was the continued presence of "pagan idolatry" in the town. He angrily stabbed his finger at the congregation and said that if they didn't stop these practices themselves, and help to suppress them in others, they would burn in hell and God would be perfectly just in sending them there. A traditionalist friend of mine who had

2. *Lower tier of saints on the central altarpiece of the colonial era church, Santiago Atitlán*

also been at Mass told me afterward that this priest was just a "Protestant" (not a complimentary term, because he believes that the Protestants were responsible for most of the murders during the recent civil war) who did not understand their form of Catholicism and had no right or authority to interfere in the practice of their beliefs. He said that traditionalist Maya are the "only true Catholics" because their Catholicism was practiced by their ancient Maya ancestors long before the Spanish conquerors arrived. Roman Catholicism and the traditional Maya worldview are inextricably intertwined in Tz'utujil thought. Any attempt to distinguish between the two would ultimately lead to an artificial construct that is foreign to Atiteco thought. Mendelson noted that in his experience at Santiago Atitlán "Indians hardly ever separate the Indian and non-Indian elements in their religion" (Mendelson 1957, 497). It has been my experience in conversations with traditionalist Maya over many years that they have little interest in differentiating ancestral Maya elements in their ceremonies from Christian ones. To them their rituals are conducted as they have always been done and will always continue to be done.

This process of incorporating new gods and beliefs from foreign sources has been a characteristic of Maya society since its earliest beginnings. The lowland Maya of the Pre-Classic and Classic periods adopted elements of rituals and ideology from the Olmecs, Teotihuacanos, and other foreign cultures. Elite rulers of the highland Maya of the Late Post-Classic Period were multilingual and heavily influenced by ideas from beyond their borders, particularly those of Nahua speakers from central Mexico. Like any living society, modern Maya are also well aware of the world beyond the borders of their community and select those aspects of Western culture, art, and language that fit the needs of their people. Nevertheless, they are also proud of their ancestral heritage and tenaciously hold on to an essentially Maya view of the world.

Above the doorway on the west façade of the church in Santiago Atitlán is a red stained-glass window. Before sunset, the light passing through this window causes the saints arrayed along the side walls of the church to cast red, blood-like shadows (fig. 3). A few years ago the parish priest suggested that the window be replaced with a new one bearing the design of a white dove. There was significant opposition to this proposal in the community. As one traditionalist Maya parishioner said, "How then will the saints bleed for us each evening as they did for our mothers and our fathers?" The images of the saints are not seen as lifeless effigies but as ensouled figures capable of continuing the work of the sacred beings that they embody. Several times I have spoken with caretakers of the church who swear that they hear voices at night in the darkened nave and insist that the carved statues gather to discuss the affairs of the community after the doors are locked. The images of saints and gods are considered animate. They are a living part of the everyday lives of the people of Santiago Atitlán. They need each other in every sense of the word, particularly in times of crisis. Holy Week is the most critical of such

3. *Saints in the church, 1997. The shadows behind the saints are red at sunset.*

times during the course of the year. It is during this week that gods, saints, deceased ancestors, and their living descendants work hand in hand to give rebirth to the world.

ANCESTRAL TRADITION AND UNITY

In the late 1970s I worked as an anthropologist and linguist in the K'iche'-Maya area of the Guatemalan highlands. During that time I worked closely with a number of *ajq'ijab'* (they of the days/the sun—traditionalist Maya shaman-priests who use the ancient Maya calendar in divination ceremonies) over the years. Never once did I hear any of them lay out a set of theological principles concerning the nature of the gods, humanity's place in the universe, or the symbolism behind ritual performances. These are the questions that most Western religions seek to answer. But the Maya are for the most part unaccustomed to rhetorical methods of expressing this kind of information. As Evon Vogt noted in his work with the Tzotzils of Zinacantan, "the Maya are not articulate in describing, only in doing" (Vogt 1993, 2). The focus of their work is the correct performance of ritual actions and prayers at the proper time and in the proper place, thus achieving a kind of unity with their ancestors that gives authenticity and meaning to their lives. Ruth Bunzel, who worked in K'iche' areas from 1930 to 1932, noted that the people of Chichicastenango claimed that their prayers and ceremonies were based on ancestral precedent and that the repetition of ancient words and actions was a means of preserving the lives and knowledge of their ancestors: "And now this rite and custom belongs to the first people, our mothers and fathers. . . . This belongs to them; we are the embodiment of their rites and ceremonies" (Bunzel 1952, 232, 238). When performed at appropriate times and under appropriate circumstances, such ceremonies are perceived as a means for dead ancestors to manifest themselves among the living. To alter the actions of those ancestors would be to change the very fabric of their existence in potentially destructive ways. As mediators between this world and the world of the sacred, it is the Maya's obligation to continue the actions of their ancestors in as authentic a manner as possible: "It is our name and destiny to repeat and perpetuate these ceremonies before the world" (ibid., 242).

I worked for nearly a year in 1979 with a K'iche' *ajq'ij* named Vicente de León Abak in the mountains above Momostenango, Guatemala. He was a well-respected practitioner who was busy nearly every day conducting prayers and ceremonies on behalf of clients from all around the region. Don Vicente constantly reminded his apprentices that whenever he conducted a ceremony his heart and his thoughts had to be *saq* (pure, white) in order for him to be *junam* (united, one, same) with the gods and ancestors. He considered this unity to be essential to the successful outcome of the ceremony. On one occasion he told me that he could not do proper ceremonies if he had been involved in an argument with his wife or his son or a neighbor: "If my heart and my thoughts are red [meaning angry or envious] then the ceremony can only come out red. If my heart and my thoughts are black [tinged with death or evil] then the ceremony will come out black and I will be responsible for bringing blackness into the world."

By the same token participants in modern Tz'utujil-Maya Holy Week ceremonies in Santiago Atitlán are encouraged to be pure of heart and in unity with each other. In practical terms this prevents embarrassing conflicts during public observances. But it is also because the ultimate goal of Holy Week is to facilitate the renewal of life and initiate the rebirth of the world. If this were done in anger or hatred, the result would be a world burdened by anger or hatred.

Among my closest colleagues and friends in Santiago Atitlán is Nicolás Chávez Sojuel, a traditionalist Maya sculptor. His wife, Magdalena, is a master embroiderer. My wife, Janet, wanted to learn Maya embroidery techniques, so she asked Magdalena if she would be willing to teach her. Magdalena immediately took out her embroidery, said a brief prayer that the work would come out well, and worked silently for a half hour or so while my wife watched. She then handed the needle and the piece she was working on to Janet and told her to continue the stitching. After half a minute Magdalena gently took the embroidery back and without a word undid all of Janet's stitches and redid them properly. She never said what my wife had done wrong; nor did she explain how to do it right. This process was repeated again and again until Janet was able to work for ten or fifteen minutes without interruption. Though this was frustrating for my wife, who had hoped that she would get some kind of verbal instruction, it was a good lesson in how the Maya teach a skill or a principle—they do it properly according to the way things have always been done while apprentices watch until they can do it independently. After Janet did a particularly nice set of embroidered stitches, Magdalena smiled and, while pointing to her head, said: "Now we are one," meaning that they now had the same knowledge or thoughts. She then placed her hand over Janet's heart and said simply *junam* (same). For the Maya, embroidery is a sacred act in much the same way that conducting a ceremony is a sacred act—both repeat ancestral tradition in a spirit of accord and unity with the past.

Failure to follow tradition creates discord. In addition to being solicitous and benevolent, Maya deities and ancestors can be vindictive and even lethal. Each year after Holy Week is over, a common topic of conversation in Santiago Atitlán is comparing that year's observances with those of the past. Mostly these comparisons focus on the negative—this or that ceremony wasn't done the way it had been done in their youth. The worst laments are when a major ceremony failed to be done at all due to neglect, bad feelings among the participants, or simply a lack of money to fund it. If anything goes wrong in the days and weeks after Easter it is common to blame these oversights directly for the problems of the community. For example, the former *alcalde* (mayor, head) of the Cofradía Santa Cruz (Confraternity of the Holy Cross, one of ten traditionalist Maya religious societies in Santiago Atitlán) contracted a serious illness after he was charged with arranging for major portions of Holy Week in 2002. One of these was the annual procession of young men to the coast to retrieve fruit used in various important rituals. The tradition is for the young men to walk the entire way there and back, bearing the fruit on their backs in wooden pack frames adorned with flowers. Ceremonies and prayers are expected to be done along the way, and a drummer and flutist generally accompany them as they walk.

The *alcalde* claimed that he did not receive sufficient donations to fund such an expensive pilgrimage, so he simply had a truck bring the fruit into town. It became a major scandal, and many believed that the *alcalde* would be cursed for this gross neglect of tradition. Sure enough he did fall ill soon afterward. Every day for a month the *alcalde*'s health and sanity figured prominently in conversations that I heard around town. Many discussions centered on the latest grim details of the *alcalde*'s illness or rumors about additional curses that had recently been added. It came as a shock to most (and a disappointment to some) when he recovered. Still, the *alcalde*'s relationship with the town was never quite the same again. Whenever anything bad happened to him, including a debilitating stroke and eventual death a few years later, people recalled the fruit incident during Holy Week among other breaches of tradition as the cause of his misfortunes. Tradition and unity had been violated. More ominously, the maize harvest did not turn out well that year, and the perceived failures of the Holy Week ceremonies were often blamed.

THE BURDEN OF THE ANCIENTS

In the late 1970s I had the opportunity to read through the Maya view of creation as described in an ancient Maya book, the *Popol Vuh*, with a group of *aj-q'ijab'* in Canquixaja, a small K'iche'-Maya community near Momostenango. In the *Popol Vuh* account, the gods made several attempts to create beings that would be able to nourish and sustain the world. One of these attempts involved the formation of people made out of dry wood. This turned out to be a failure because the wood people did not "remember" their creators and thus failed to carry out their responsibilities to the gods (Christenson 2007, 83–84). In highland Maya belief, memory is a function of the blood not the brain. The dry flesh of the wood people lacked blood, so they did not have the capacity to fulfill their obligations. As a result, the gods destroyed them for their negligence (ibid.). Ultimately the gods succeeded in creating human beings from sacred maize dough and blood, giving them the ability to remember the gods and sustain them. When we had finished reading the passage in the *Popol Vuh* that recounts the gratitude of the first maize people and their extraordinary vision, an elderly *ajq'ij* stood and said that he had a word to say:

> I wonder if these words belong only to the ancient past. I think all of us pass through the various stages of creation. . . . I think Wood People are like teenagers. They can speak, they can reproduce, but they forget who they are. They do not remember their mothers and fathers or the ancient people. They don't know their purpose in life. *Wachalal* [Brothers], we bear a heavy, sweet burden on our backs and our shoulders, because we remember. And because we remember we must bear the burden of carrying out our work so that the ancestors may speak to us through our blood and our flesh. This is often very hard. But if we don't do this, who will? Everything would end.

The *ajq'ij* referred to his work as a "heavy, sweet burden," one that must be borne in the same way in which his ancestors performed their ceremonies in the past. For Maya traditionalists, bearing that burden is often overwhelmingly difficult both financially and physically, but in their minds it must be done and done properly if the world is to be renewed during times of crisis.

Chapter 1

PRE-COLUMBIAN RITUALS OF WORLD RENEWAL IN YUCATAN

The renewal of the world through ritual has been a characteristic of Maya religious practices throughout their history and across wide geographic boundaries. A major focus of rebirth ceremonialism among the ancient Maya who occupied the Yucatan Peninsula of what is today Mexico took place during period-ending observances when it was believed that the world passed through death in order to be reborn when the calendar cycle began again with the new year. This occurred over a five-day period at the end of the solar year that was considered dangerous and outside the regular flow of days and months. During these five days, the Yucatec Maya carried out a complex cycle of rituals in order to regenerate the life-bearing elements of their world. This period of five days was called the Wayeb'.

The Wayeb' was the single most important ritual period of the year among the Maya prior to the Spanish Conquest. It is illustrated in most of the Yucatec Maya texts that have come down to us from the Pre-Columbian era. Only four Maya bark paper hieroglyphic codices survived the flames of the Spanish Conquest. Because there are so few, each of these precious books is an invaluable record of the Maya world before it was confronted by the arrival of European conquerors and Christian missionaries who targeted such books for destruction. The Dresden Codex, one of these Pre-Columbian texts, contains four pages that illustrate New Year's observances with accompanying glyphic texts. The final page of the Dresden manuscript depicts the devastation of the world by flood that preceded the present age. The Wayeb' period commemorates this "death" of the world before its rebirth on New Year's day. Yucatec Maya scribes continued to record important aspects of their culture after the Spanish Conquest using the newly introduced Latin alphabetic script. Many of these writings also contain references to New Year's observances and the ancient gods that attended them.

In addition to primary indigenous Maya sources, much of what we know of Wayeb' ceremonies is derived from the accounts of Maya nobles who described Pre-Columbian cultural practices to Spanish explorers and Christian missionaries soon after the conquest of the Yucatan region. It is therefore important to recognize the state of affairs at the time of first contact between the Maya and the invading Spanish forces in order to understand the interaction. Unlike the empires of the Aztecs of central Mexico or the Inca of Peru, the Maya of the Yucatan Peninsula and adjacent Peten regions of Guatemala had no single center of political authority at the time of the Spanish Conquest. The region consisted of a network of independent city-states, characterized by a complex history of shifting alliances and internecine warfare. Although this political situation left the Maya relatively weak in the face of the Spanish invasion of their lands, it also made the permanent conquest of the Yucatan highly problematic. Each of the Maya states had to be dealt with individually, and many met the Spaniards with fierce resistance. Concerted efforts to conquer the region began under Francisco de Montejo in 1527, with major battles continuing over the next twenty years. In late 1546 an alliance of Maya kingdoms in the eastern provinces launched a final desperate offensive against Spanish forces. The defeat of this alliance sealed the conquest of at least the northern portion of the Yucatan Peninsula.

Nevertheless, the lack of gold and other resources of interest to the Spaniards made the Maya lowlands less appealing than the rich lands of central Mexico and the Andean region of South America. As a result, few Spanish settlers occupied the land, making their authority in the region rather tenuous. In part due to the lack of a strong Spanish presence, sporadic revolts broke out over the succeeding decades. The last Maya stronghold of Nojpeten, an island on Lake Peten to the south, remained an independent Maya state until as late as 1697.

FRAY DIEGO DE LANDA AND THE EARLY EVANGELIZATION OF YUCATAN

Soon after the conquest of northern Yucatan, the Spanish Crown granted to the Franciscan order the exclusive right to conduct missionary work among the Maya of that region. Among the first Franciscan friars to sail to the Yucatan was Fray Diego de Landa, who arrived in 1549 (fig. 4). From his base in the Mission of San Antonio in Izamal, Landa traveled extensively throughout the area, often entering lands only recently conquered and still dangerous. His willingness to walk into such territories, virtually defenseless, was a remarkable act of daring that could easily have cost him his life. According to Fray Diego López de Cogolludo, while passing through the community of Dzit Haas, Landa came upon a group of 300 Maya about to sacrifice a young boy. Enraged, Landa pushed his way through the crowd, released the boy, and smashed the idols arrayed around the ceremonial altar. He then

4. *Fray Diego de Landa, Izamal Monastery*

launched into an impassioned sermon on the evils of idolatry and human sacrifice that reportedly so impressed those present that they abandoned their former practices and requested instruction in Christianity (Cogolludo 2006, book 5, chapter 14, 416–417). While this account appears to be exaggerated, Landa was undoubtedly a zealous and at times incautious missionary.

Landa was intensely curious about the language, history, traditions, and religion of the Maya before the arrival of the Spanish conquerors. He had a scholar's obsession for detail and accuracy, making his writings the single most important source for lowland Maya culture composed in the sixteenth century. Landa was also a gifted linguist. He initiated an intensive study of the Yukatek Mayan language soon after his arrival in the region and rapidly achieved fluency. He became so proficient that for many years his Franciscan superiors gave him the task of training newly arrived missionaries in Maya linguistics and evangelization strategies. He also wrote a Yukatek grammar, now lost (Landa 1941, 74n332). In addition to his own observations, Landa worked closely with indigenous informants to elicit information on the Maya world prior to the arrival of the Spaniards. The names of at least two of Landa's advisors are known, Juan Nachi Cocom and Gaspar Antonio Chi, both important members of the old Maya nobility.

Yet Landa is principally remembered today for his tenacious and at times ruthless efforts to destroy what remained of Maya literature, artifacts, and ritual practices after the Spanish Conquest. The primary purpose of Landa's studies was to understand Maya language and ceremonies in order to combat what he considered to be pernicious errors that hindered his efforts to convert the Maya to Christianity. As a preface to his description of ancient Maya rituals observed at the close of the calendar year, he recorded these things for the benefit of his fellow missionaries so that they could better recognize their continued practice and eliminate them:

> I will speak of their fasts and of the ceremonies with which they made their wooden idols, as well as other things, all of which, as well as the rest which I have here related about this people, it is not my purpose that they should serve for anything more than as a cause of thanking the divine goodness who has tolerated such things, and who has thought well to remedy them in our time . . . , that they may not fail in what has been begun, and thus return to their wretchedness and vomitings of errors; and that worse things than before may not befall them, by the devils returning to the houses of their souls, from which we have tried with heavy care to drive them away, cleaning them and purifying them of their vices and of their habits of the past time. (Landa 1941, 150)

Landa could be patient while teaching unconverted Maya. However, once they had been baptized, he considered any return to traditional Maya faith to be heretical and subject to the harshest punishment. Later in his ministry he came to believe in the existence of an extensive underground network of Maya apostates dedicated to the overthrow of the church and Spanish authority. He became obsessed with the notion that it was his calling to expose the conspiracy and destroy it by any means necessary. In May 1562 missionaries in the town of Mani uncovered evidence that some of their Christian converts were performing traditional Maya ceremonies in secret. Upon investigation, it became apparent that this was much more widespread than they had at first expected. Many if not most of the nobles in the core area of Mani and its adjacent provinces were found to have been conducting rituals in honor of their old gods. Diego de Landa arrived in Mani a few weeks later. When confronted with the evidence he took control of the proceedings and initiated an episcopal inquisition.

Landa was disheartened to learn that these ancient Maya rites were being practiced in regions where it had been assumed that Christianity had taken firm root. When evidence came to light that Nachi Cocom, his now-deceased Maya advisor, was one of those who had practiced traditional Maya ceremonies after his baptism, Landa had his bones dug up from the churchyard and scattered in the fields (Cogolludo 2006, book 6, chapter 1, 449). Most distressing of all to Landa, some of the most egregious practices such as human sacrifice were reportedly conducted within consecrated Christian buildings, including sacrifices by crucifixion.

Like most Franciscans of the time, Landa believed in the millenarian doctrine that the Second Coming of Christ was imminent, necessitating the mass conversion of as many Maya souls as possible before the fiery purges of God's wrath condemned them to hell forever (Timmer 1997, 481–483). He deemed traditional Maya religious practices to be a hindrance to his conversion efforts and ruthlessly sought to extirpate any remnants of it. If this goal necessitated a measure of violence in the short term, such was the unavoidable price for the salvation of the Maya from damnation before the apocalypse and final judgment of God. Landa later insisted that although his actions technically circumvented the law, they were justified by the danger posed by the continued practice of idolatry among the Maya:

> All [the Indians] being idolators and culpable, it was not possible to proceed strictly according to the law against them . . . for if we had proceeded according to the order of the law in all things, it would have been impossible to complete our work in the aforementioned province of Mani in twenty years. Meanwhile they would all have become idolaters and gone to hell. (Scholes and Adams 1938, 1:171, translation by author)

In Landa's mind, the suffering of the few at the hands of the inquisitors paled in comparison with the eternal pain of many more souls who would otherwise be eternally damned. He suggested in the following prayer that the Maya willfully imposed upon themselves a measure of infernal torments in connection with their ritual observances prior to the arrival of the Europeans. These included prolonged fasting, abstinences, self-mortification, and human sacrifice, all of which are integral, as we shall see, to the celebration of the ancient Wayeb' rites:

> And so as I believe [God's] yoke to be easy and light, I may give thee thanks for finding myself placed under the soft skin of thy yoke and free from the yoke under which you see that such multitudes go and have gone, following the path to hell, which is such a heavy grief that I do not know anyone whose heart does not break upon seeing the fatal weight and intolerable burden by which the devil has always carried and still carries off idolaters to hell. And if this is a great cruelty on the part of the devil who manages it and does it, it is justly permitted on the part of God, so that, since they

> do not wish to rule themselves by the light of reason which he has given them, they may begin to be tormented in this life and to suffer a part of hell, which they deserve, with the wearisome services which they continually are giving to the devil with their very long fasts and abstinences and vigils; with incredible offerings and presents of their property and effects; with continual shedding of their own blood; with heavy pains and wounds of their bodies; and what is worse and more serious with the lives of their neighbors and brothers. (Landa 1941, 185)

Normally an inquisition such as that convened by Landa in Mani could only be authorized by a bishop. The first bishop of Yucatan, Francisco de Toral, had been consecrated two years before, but he had yet to arrive in country. As the highest-ranking ecclesiastical authority within the Franciscan order, Landa felt justified in taking matters into his own hands. He did so with unprecedented ruthlessness. He and his Franciscan brethren interrogated and tortured thousands of Maya converts suspected of reverting to paganism. Spanish ecclesiastical law forbade any interrogation techniques that caused bleeding or the loss of life or limb. Nevertheless, other forms of torture were permitted in order to elicit information from suspected heretics. Water torture was one of the more common techniques. In one version, the head of the witness was held under water for prolonged periods. In another, the accused heretic's mouth was propped open with sticks while large volumes of water were poured down his or her throat (fig. 5). The interrogators then stood on the victim's belly or administered a beating, causing fluid to issue from the nose and ears. Other techniques included scorching with wax tapers, splashing the body with boiling water, or binding the arms or thighs with cords and then tightening the knots with a stick. In their written complaints to the Spanish Crown, Maya lords particularly noted the despised practice of stretching or hanging in which witnesses were suspended with their wrists tied behind their backs for extended periods, often with stone weights attached to their feet, in order to force confessions or to implicate others (Scholes and Adams 1938, 1:25–68, 189–232, 294). John Chuchiak notes that this procedure was considered by jurists and inquisitors of the time to be the "queen of the torments" (Chuchiak 2012, 133). Those who were found guilty during these proceedings were given as many as two hundred lashes, were forced to wear a special yellow shirt marked with a red cross for up to three years, or were sold into slavery for as long as five years as penance (Landa 1941, 77n340).

Don Diego de Quijada, who reported the testimony obtained in many of these proceedings to the Spanish Crown, wrote that in 1562 alone 4,549 men

5. *Torture used by the Inquisition. (Féréal 1844, 204)*

and women were subjected to torture and an additional 6,330 were whipped, shorn, and fined (Scholes and Adams 1938, 2:213). Of these, he reported that 157 died as the result of interrogation and many more were maimed for life. During later hearings on the legality of these proceedings, Landa insisted that neither he nor his Franciscan brethren knew of anyone who might have died during these interrogations. He suggested that those few deaths that did occur were the result of suicide. Two or three hanged themselves "in order not to give up their idols nor abandon their evil ways." Two others struck themselves with stones, "having been driven to despair and not for any occasion which was given them by the said friars" (Landa 1941, 79n342). It is impossible to know where the truth lies so many centuries later, although it is beyond dispute that the Maya suffered greatly at the hands of the Franciscan interrogators during this period.

At the conclusion of the inquisition, Landa convened an *auto de fé* (an imposed ritual of public penance for condemned heretics) on July 12, 1562, in which he forced hundreds of Maya prisoners, primarily members of the nobility, to wear penitential ropes around their necks as they watched thousands of sculpted deity images and associated ritual paraphernalia burned in the public square at Mani. Along with these antiquities, Landa also burned at least twenty-seven ancient Maya hieroglyphic books: "We found a large number of books of these characters and, as they contained nothing in which there were not to be seen superstition and lies of the devil, we burned them all, which they regretted to an amazing degree and which caused them much affliction" (Landa 1941, 78).

Living Maya traditionalists echo their ancestors' lament at the tragic loss of their literary heritage. Landa and others were so effective in burning Maya hieroglyphic texts in the years that followed that only four books, some of which are fragmentary, are known to have survived the flames (Landa 1941, 77–78n340). Other Spanish clerics later regretted the loss of these books, which might have provided useful information on the history and traditions of the Maya people. As Bernardo de Lizana wrote in his *Historia de Yucatán*:

> Then [Landa] gathered the books and ancient writings and commanded that they should be bound up and burned. They burned many books regarding the history of the ancient Yucatan which contained the origins and history [of its people], which would be of much value if they had been translated in our own writing, because today there would be an original source. At present there is no great authority for the traditions of these Indians. (Lizana 1893, book 2, chapter 6, 5, translation by author)

Further trials and conflagrations continued until the first resident bishop of Yucatan, Francisco de Toral, arrived the following year. Shocked by the violence, Bishop Toral halted the proceedings, released hundreds of Maya prisoners, reduced the sentences of others, and had Landa recalled to Spain to face charges of exceeding his authority and exercising excessive cruelty against Maya "idolaters." Landa claimed at his trial that he was only acting in the best interest of the Maya themselves, who were still weak in the Christian faith and needed to be forcibly dissuaded from returning to paganism. He suggested that these incidents had to be dealt with quickly and severely lest the perpetrators and others influenced by them should die in their sins and suffer eternal damnation.

Ultimately Landa was cleared of all charges and returned to Yucatan in 1573 as the second bishop of the region. He replaced Bishop Toral, who had died two years earlier. As bishop, with full episcopal authority, Landa reconvened the inquisition and continued ruthlessly to root out any remnants of perceived paganism until his death in 1579. The final irony is that Landa's excessive zealotry persuaded the Spanish Crown as well as local secular authorities to wrest control of the inquisitions away from the Franciscan order after Landa's death, with the result that the Maya became freer to exercise their former religious practices than might otherwise have been possible. Chuchiak suggests that Landa unwittingly helped to preserve traditional Maya ceremonialism in the Yucatan, as subsequent generations of political administrators and clerics were loath to repeat Landa's cruelty (Chuchiak 2005, 644–645). As a result Spanish authorities instituted policies that tolerated the practice of some aspects of traditional Maya worship, allowing the survival of significant elements of ancient rituals and beliefs that persist to the present day. Subsequently, Franciscan missionaries could do little to punish the Maya for continuing to practice elements of their ancestral faith without risking a confrontation with secular authorities.

WORLD RENEWAL CEREMONIES AS DESCRIBED BY FRAY DIEGO DE LANDA

During his ministry Landa wrote extensively on the history and religion of the Maya, based in part on his own experiences and in part on the testimony of his Maya consultants. He may have intended to publish these findings himself, although this never occurred in his lifetime. According to recent research by Restall and Chuchiak, the only surviving version of Landa's research, now known as the *Relación de las cosas de Yucatan* (Account of the Things of Yucatan), was apparently the work of three or four compilers who redacted Landa's writings after his death in 1579. This compilation is unquestionably based on Landa's writings but may also have included information garnered from papers in Landa's possession containing firsthand accounts of ancient Maya practices that were elicited directly from Maya noblemen (Restall and Chuchiak 2002). The earliest known copy of this work was compiled about 1616 (Landa 1941, viii; Timmer 1997, 482). In the version that has come down to us Landa mentions chapters (and even an illustration) that do not appear in the extant copy, suggesting that the original book was much longer and included images. The abbreviated version was rediscovered in 1862 by the French antiquarian and cleric Charles Étienne Brasseur de Bourbourg, who published it along with a French translation two years later. The *Relación* is one of the few accounts of Pre-Columbian Maya culture composed at a time when survivors of the Spanish Conquest could still recall what the world was like before the arrival of the Europeans.

Considering the remarkable detail of Landa's account of the Yucatec Wayeb' rites, it is possible that he may have witnessed some part of these ceremonies himself in the early days of his ministry, although it is more likely that he recorded firsthand accounts given to him by his Maya consultants. As noted above, Landa named as one of his principal sources a man by the name of don Juan Nachi Cocom, a Maya nobleman "of remarkable discernment and well acquainted with native matters" who "told him many facts concerning the antiquities" (Landa 1941, 44). Nachi Cocom had in his possession ancient manuscripts. He showed at least two of them to Landa and explained their contents (ibid., 42–47). Landa noted that others also contributed to his knowledge of ancient Maya ritual practices but did not record their names other than Gaspar Antonio Chi, a nobleman from the town of Mani who often served as a translator for Spanish missionary priests and who worked closely with Landa for many years.

According to Landa's Maya consultants, the final five days of their ancient calendar are nameless, "since they considered them unlucky and bad" (Landa 1941, 134). Juan Pío Pérez wrote that the most common name for these days was Uayeb (Wayeb' in present-day orthography), although they were also called *xma kaba kin* (without name days) or *u yail kin* (unfortunate days) (Craine and Reindorp 1979, 39n27). Diego López de Cogolludo wrote that the five days of the Wayeb' period were also called "Utuz Kin [Days of Lies or Deception], as well as Ulobol Kin [Days of Harm or Ruin], which means time of lies, a bad time, because misfortune attends the five final days of the year." He added:

> The five days that fall at the close of the three hundred and sixty-five days [of the calendar] are called days without name (*ixma kaba kin*). They held these to be ill omened and on those days occurred miserable and sudden deaths: stings and bites from vipers and wild and venomous animals, as well as quarrels and dissensions, particularly on the first day. On these days they took care not to leave the house, arranging for necessary things beforehand so that they would not need to go into the fields or any other place. During these days they attend most to their pagan rites, praying to their idols to save them from the evil of those dangerous days so that they would give them a good new year, fertile and abundant. (Cogolludo 2006, book 4, chapter 5, 274; translation by author)

In addition to Spanish accounts, the Maya themselves composed texts following the Conquest that preserve important elements of their religious beliefs, ritual practices, and history. The books of *Chilam Balam* are particularly important as compilations of indigenous cultural information. At least nine versions of the *Chilam Balam* texts have survived, most named for the town in which they were written. The title of the texts is derived from the name of a Maya prophet (Chilam or Chilan means "prophet"; Balam is his surname), who lived just prior to the arrival of the Spaniards. Although the extant versions of these texts date from the early eighteenth through the nineteenth centuries, they clearly contain passages that were recopied over many years and reflect concepts and even phraseology that predate the Spanish Conquest (Roys 1967, 3–6, 186–187; Paxton 2009, 78). In the *Chilam Balam of Mani*, the Maya author writes: "The calendar of our ancestors is thus: twenty days in one month, eighteen months in a year, and at the end of the eighteen months the five nameless days begin. These five days are called fateful, or unlucky, because in them occur all kinds of misfortunes, such as sudden death, snakebites, and the piercing of the feet with stakes" (Craine and Reindorp 1979, 88).

During the five days of the Wayeb' normal life is suspended and the people become susceptible to disease, misfortune, and death, linked to the perceived death of the world preceding its rebirth on New Year's Day. The days of the Wayeb' are therefore marked with important ceremonies meant to overcome the powers of death, malignant forces that Landa associated with the devil. According to Landa's Maya consultants, if these ceremonies were not performed or were carried out in an improper manner, the malignity of the Wayeb' period would persist into the following year:

> And the devil, who deceived them in this as in everything else, informed them of the worships and offerings, which they were to make to him in order to escape the calamities. And so the priests said, when no calamity happened to them, that it was on account of the services, which they had offered to him; and in case misfortunes came, they made the people understand and believe that it was owing to some sin or fault in the services or in those who performed them. . . .
>
> In any festival or solemnity that this people celebrated in honor of their gods, they always began by chasing away from themselves the evil spirit, in order to perform the ceremony the better. And the driving him off was done sometimes by prayers and benedictions, which they had for this purpose; at other times by worship, offerings and sacrifices, which they offered for this purpose. For celebrating the festival of the New Year, this people with great rejoicing and with much dignity according to their unhappy ideas made use of the five unlucky days, which were regarded by them as such before the first day of the new year. (Landa 1941, 136, 138–139)

As a reflection of the ceremonial rebirth of the world during the Wayeb' period, the Maya of the Yucatan also renewed their personal belongings at the close of major calendric cycles:

> The first day of Pop, which is the first month of the Indians, was their new year and was a very solemn festival among them; as it was universal and all took part in it and so the whole town jointly made the feast to all the idols.

> To celebrate it with more solemnity, they renewed on this day all the objects which they made use of, such as plates, vessels, stools, mats and old clothes and the stuffs with which they wrapped up their idols. They swept out their houses, and the sweepings and the old utensils they threw out on the waste heap outside the town; and no one, even were he in need of it, touched it. (Landa 1941, 151–152)

This practice persists in other areas of the Maya world. In 1977 I lived in a small community called Kankixaja, located near Momostenango, Guatemala. At the close of the 260-day ritual calendar, each household ritually smashed its primary cooking vessel used for boiling maize prior to grinding. The larger fragments of the pot were then carried as a family to an ancestral shrine in the mountains and placed atop a great mound of other shards that had accumulated over the years (fig. 6). There an *ajq'ij* blessed each member of the family in turn to cleanse them from any corruption that they might have accumulated during the previous year. He then called upon various deities, saints, and their own sacred ancestors to give them a healthy and abundant new year. The families then returned to their homes, where they thoroughly washed themselves in the nearby river to remove any taint from the bad influences of the final days of the year. Immediately afterward they swept their homes clean and prepared a new cooking vessel as a token that the world had been reborn and would continue to provide nourishment for them in the coming year.

According to Landa, the Maya also underwent severe purification rituals to cleanse themselves at the same time that they cleansed their belongings. This included a period of fasting, sexual abstinence, ritual washings, and penitential bloodletting:

6. *Ancestral shrine, Canquixaja, 1977*

> For this festival, the lords and the priest, and the principal people began to fast and to abstain from their wives, as well as those who wished to do so on account of their devotion, for such time beforehand as they judged proper; for some set about it three months in advance, others only two, and still others as long as seemed good to them, but no one less than thirteen days and for these thirteen days besides abstaining from their wives, they did not eat salt or pepper with their food, which they regarded as a great penitence. . . . Those who once began these fastings did not dare to break them, because they believed some calamity to themselves or to their houses would befall them. New Year's day having then arrived, all the men assembled in the court of the temple, by themselves; since in no sacrifice or festival, which they celebrated in the temple, could women be present, except the old women who had to dance their dances. To the other festivals, which took place elsewhere women could go and be present there. Here now the men came clean and ornamented with their red ointment, after having cleaned themselves of the black soot with which they covered themselves when they fasted. (Landa 1941, 152)

THE RULE OF THE B'AKAB'S

In Landa's account four gods named Bacab (B'akab' in modern orthography), one for each of the cardinal directions, presided over the five "unlucky days" that fell at the close of the calendar year:

> Among the multitudes of gods which this nation worshipped they worshipped four, each of them called Bacab. They said that they were four brothers whom God placed, when he created the world, at the four points of it, holding up the sky so that it should not fall. They also said of these Bacabs that they escaped when the world was destroyed by the deluge. They gave other names to each one of them and designated by them the part of the world where God had placed him, bearing up the heavens. . . . And in these days [the five days of Wayeb'] they held many services for the Bacabs, of whom we have spoken above. (Landa 1941, 135–136, 139)

The B'akab's are associated with the primordial world that existed prior to the creation of the present age, "before the world was destroyed by the deluge" (Landa 1941, 139). Normally the role of the B'akab's is to support the vault of the sky from their positions at the four corners of the earth (Landa 1941, 135–142; Thompson 1970, 276–280). Presumably the destruction of the world occurs when the B'akab's cease to perform this function. Although this is not explicit in Landa's account of the Wayeb' rites, it implies that the B'akab's not only escaped the deluge but had a hand in its devastating effects. They are the principal deities of the Wayeb', a period marked by an array of misfortunes, including death. The malevolent side of the B'akab's is more explicitly stated in texts from the early colonial period written by the Maya themselves. The *Chilam Balam of Chumayel* states that the B'akab's caused the flood that destroyed the previous era of the world: "There would be a sudden rush of water when the theft of the insignia <of Oxlahun-ti-ku> occurred. Then the sky would fall, it would fall down upon the earth, when the four gods, the four Bacabs, were set up, who brought about the destruction of the world" (Roys 1967, 99–100).

The tradition of a destructive flood preceding the present age is widespread throughout the Maya world. The *Popol Vuh*, compiled by K'iche' noblemen in the Guatemalan highlands, describes the destruction of the previous age by flood, which killed its inhabitants who were made of wood: "Then came the end of the effigies carved of wood, for they were ruined, crushed, and killed. A flood was planned by Heart of Sky that came down upon the heads of the effigies carved of wood. . . . Thus they caused the face of the earth to be darkened, and there fell a black rain, a rain that fell both day and night" (Christenson 2007, 85–87).

Page 74 of the Dresden Codex (fig. 7) illustrates this world-devastating flood in a full-page image. The goddess Chak Chel is depicted as a powerful world destroyer pouring out streams of water from an inverted vase accompanied by a crocodilian sky creature with water gushing from his mouth and body, an event tied to the Wayeb' period at the close of the calendar year (Thompson 1972, 99; Taube 1992, 101; Knowlton 2004, 2010, 65–66; Vail and Hernández 2014, 155).

Thompson notes that on each of the New Year's pages in the Madrid Codex the glyph representing God N (whom he equates with Landa's Bacabs) appears over the *k'in* (sun, day, or festival) glyph. He interprets this as identifying the New Year ceremonies as the "festival of the Bacabs" or more literally "days of the Bacabs" (Thompson 1970, 278–279). David Stuart also associates the B'akab's in their manifestation as God N with period-ending rites in the earlier Classic period. He identifies four God Ns on the fragmentary Panel 1 from Pomona, each holding the day associated with the seating of the first month of the calendar year (Stuart 2004, 4). In his description of the New Year's observances Landa wrote that the Maya of Yucatan linked the B'akab's so closely to the five-day period of the Wayeb' that it became an alternative name for them:

7. *Dresden Codex, p. 74. (Förstemann 1880, pl. 53)*

> And in these days they held many services for the Bacabs, of whom we have spoken above, and for the god whom they called, as well as the Bacabs, by four other names, which are Kan u Uayeyab, Chac u Uayeyab, Sac u Uayeyab and Ek u Uayeyab. These services and feasts over, and the evil spirit chased away from them, as we shall see, they began the new year and its festivals.
>
> It was the custom in all the towns in Yucatan that there should be two heaps of stone, facing each other at the entrance of the town, on all four sides of the town, that is to say, at the East, West, North and South, for the celebration of the festivals of the unlucky days, which they observed in this way every year. In the year of which the dominical letter was Kan, the omen was Hobnil, and according to what they said, they both ruled in the region of the South. In this year then they made an image or hollow figure of the god of clay, which they called Kan u Uayeyab, and they carried it to the heaps of dry stone which they had raised at the southern side. (Landa 1941, 139–140)

These four alternate titles for the B'akab's all bear the name of the five-day period of the Wayeb' linked with the four colors associated with the cardinal directions—kan (*k'an*, meaning "yellow") for south, *chac* (*chak*, meaning "red") for east, *sac* (*sak*, meaning "white") for north, and *ek* (*ek'*, meaning "black") for west. The order of the names describes a counterclockwise rotation through the cardinal points, so that over a four-year period each of the four B'akab's has his turn reigning over the Wayeb' days linked to one of the four directions of the compass. In addition to color, each of the four B'akab's in Landa's account is linked to a Year Bearer:

> They gave other names to each of them [the B'akab's] and designated by them the part of the world where God had placed him, bearing up the heavens, and they appropriated to him and to the part where he stands one of the four dominical letters. . . . The first then of these dominical letters is Kan. . . . They assigned this one to the direction of the South. The second letter is Muluc. They assigned him to the East. . . . The third letter is Ix. . . . They assigned him to the direction of the North. The fourth letter is Cauac . . . they assigned him to the direction of the West. (Landa 1941, 136–138)

In addition to the solar calendar of 365 days, the Maya also used a sacred almanac of 260 days (the *tzolk'in*) used in divination and the timing of religious observances. The *tzolk'in* consists of twenty named days that follow one another in succession, each with a number prefix from one to thirteen. The dominical letters that Landa describes refer to the days of the 260-day calendar upon which the New Year can begin. When the two calendars are correlated, only four of the *tzolk'in* days can line up with the first day of the solar New Year: K'an, Muluk, Ix, and Kawak. These four days are called Year Bearers when they fall on the first day of the 365-day calendar. The Maya believed that each Year Bearer day had a certain character that influenced the year on which it began, for good or ill. In addition to a direction and a color, each of the Year Bearers is presided over by one of four gods who reigns in succession for a year at a time.

Unlike the B'akab's, who are quadripartite manifestations of the same god and reign only during the five days of the Wayeb', the four gods linked to the Year Bearers are separate and distinct entities who preside over the remaining 360 days of the year in succession. In Landa's account the four gods are Bolon Dzacab (a god of rain and regeneration) when the B'akab' is placed in the south; Kinich Ahau (K'inich Ajaw, a sun god) when the B'akab' is placed in the east; Itzamna (a sky god) when the B'akab' is in the north; and Uac Mitun Ahau (Wak Mitun Ajaw, an underworld deity) when the B'akab' is in the west. These gods have little in common with one another beyond being powerful deities that dominate their respective spheres of influence. The following is Landa's description of the years in which the B'akab' is located at the south entrance of the community and Bolon Dzacab is placed in a temporary shrine nearby prior to his ascension to rule on New Year's day: "They chose a chief of the town in whose house this festival was celebrated on these days, and to celebrate it they made the statue of a god, which they called Bolon Dzacab, which they placed in the house of the *principal*, adorned in a public place where everyone could go to it" (Landa 1941, 140).

Landa notes that this *principal* (important nobleman or lord) was chosen specifically to oversee the celebration of the Wayeb' festival for that year, suggesting that the office rotated on an annual basis, perhaps determined by the location of that lord's house in the appropriate quadrant of the community linked to the Year Bearer. As seen in the passage above, the god who oversees the year in which the B'akab' is in the south is Bolon Dzacab. *B'olon* means "nine" but is also a superlative meaning "many" or "very." Dzacab (Tz'akab' in modern orthography) is defined in the Motul dictionary as "generations, lineages" as well as *cosa sin fin* (thing without end, eternal) (Barrera Vásquez 1995, 871–872). Bolon Dzacab would thus mean "Nine/Many Generations" or simply "Eternal/Endless." The books of *Chilam Balam* associate this god with rain as well as with the regenerative power of the earth to produce abundant crops: "Then it was that the word of Bolon Dzacab descended to the tip of his tongue. Then the charge of the katun was sought; nine was its charge when it descended from heaven. Kan was the day when its burden was bound to it. Then the water descended, it came from the heart of the sky for the *rebirth* of the House of Nine Bushes" (Roys 1967, 104n6; emphasis added).

In the *Chilam Balam of Mani* Bolon Dzacab oversees growing vegetation and seeds (Craine and Reindorp 1979, 118). The *Chilam Balam of Tizimin* links his name with life-sustaining food and water, calling him "Bolon tz'acab maize food and Bolon tz'acab water" (Edmonson 1982, 62, lines 1391–1392; translation by author). Taube concurs with Seler in identifying this deity with God K (Taube 1992, 73), a god of rain and agricultural abundance as well as lightning, and royal power.

Once the god who presides over his designated year is placed in the house of a chosen nobleman for the days of Wayeb', the principal men of the community form a procession to bring offerings for the B'akab', who now assumes his temporary role as lord of the world, usurping the authority of the customary gods:

> This having been done, the lords and the priest and the men of the town assembled together and having cleaned and adorned with arches and green the road leading to the place of heaps of stone where the statue was [that of B'akab'], they went all together to it with great devotion. And when they came there the priest incensed it with forty-nine grains of maize ground up with their incense, and they distributed it in the brazier of the idol and perfumed him. They call the ground maize alone *sacah* and that of the Lords *chahalte*. The image having been incensed, they cut off the head of a hen and presented or offered it to him. This having been done, they placed the statue upon a standard called *kante*. (Landa 1941, 140–141)

The last sentence of this passage, as translated by Alfred M. Tozzer, notes that the Maya placed the image of the B'akab' on a "standard." The original Spanish word used by Landa is *palo*, which is simply a piece of wood—anything from a stick to a pole to a tree to a large-diameter log or mast. The name for this *palo* is given as *kante* (*k'ante'*, meaning "yellow tree") indicating that it was meant to represent a tree, whatever its size. It is yellow because that is the color that corresponds to the B'akab' of that year, when he occupies the south. In other years the *palo* bears the name of the same color as the cardinal direction that corresponds to that year's Wayeb' observances: *chacte* (*chakte'*, meaning "red tree") in the east; *sachia* (probably *sakche'*, meaning "white tree"), which Tozzer interprets as "white zapote tree" (Landa 1941, 141n664) in the north; and *yaxek* (*yaxek'*, meaning "new or first black") in the west.

With the B'akab' affixed to his effigy tree, the principal men of the city carry him to the lord's house, where the god linked to the Year Bearer has already been placed, in this case Bolon Dzacab:

> And thus they carried it [B'akab' on his effigy tree] with much rejoicing and dancing, to the house of the principal where the other statue of Bolon Dzacab was standing. . . . When they reached the dwelling of the chief, they placed this image opposite to the statue of the god, which they had there, and thus they made to it many offerings of food and drinks, of flesh and fish; and they divided these offerings among the strangers who were present and they gave the priest the leg of a deer. Others drew blood from themselves, cutting their ears, and anointing with it a stone which they had there of a god Kanal Acantun. (Landa 1941, 141)

During the final five days of the year, the customary statuses of the gods that reign over the year (in this case B'olon Tz'akab') are reversed, with the B'akab's receiving offerings that would normally belong to them. Instead they are displaced to temporary accommodations away from their temples or shrines. In the pages of the Pre-Columbian Maya Dresden Codex that depict the Wayeb' days, these presiding gods are clearly marked as dead (in the Maya conception of death, where gods die periodically only to be reborn when the cycle begins again), not just absent from their temples (Vail and Hernández 2014, 102, 113). Once the five days are over and the image of the B'akab' is taken away, the legitimate god returns to his accustomed place to carry out his role in the community during the course of the year.

THE RAISING OF THE WORLD TREE

From Landa's description it is clear that two effigy trees are venerated during the days of the Wayeb', both situated for a time in the same household of a principal lord of the community. The first is a "standard" or pole with tree associations on which the B'akab', or temporary god of the five-day period preceding New Year's day, is hung prior to carrying him in procession. This effigy tree is named for the color appropriate to the world direction linked to the B'akab' in a given year: *k'ante'* in the south, *chakte'* in the east, and so forth. Each of these monuments is spelled using a lowercase initial letter in Landa's description. The standard of the B'akab' receives an offering of incense and the head of a sacrificed turkey. Although it is unclear what happened to the rest of the sacrificed turkey, it is clear that only the heads were given to the B'akab' "tree" (Landa 1941, 144–146).

The second tree monument described by Landa is the Acantun (Akantun in current orthography), spelled with a capital letter, perhaps denoting its greater importance. In Landa's account of the Wayeb' observances, this is a completely separate entity from the B'akab's standard and is linked with the presiding deity for each successive year. Thus Landa describes the B'akab's standard as "opposite to the statue of the god" and his associated Akantun. The Akantun represents the World Tree, symbolic of the creation or regeneration of the world. Befitting its importance as a token of new life, the Akantun receives the highest of offerings: human blood (Landa 1941, 141–146).

Landa writes that the Kanal Acantun (K'anal Akantun, meaning "Yellow Seated Stone") received blood offerings from the principal men of the community at the culmination of the Wayeb' days, and that it was linked with the god of that year whose image is temporarily situated in the same household. Blood is the most precious offering and is only mentioned in connection with the Akantun in Landa's description of the Wayeb' rites, indicating that it is an important object of veneration. *Akan* means "to be seated," with the connotation of being "established" or "set in its place." Thus this stone monument is raised or set in place during New Year's observances. It is the "yellow" version of the Akantun because it is erected when the B'akab' is in the south, a direction linked with the color yellow. In successive years a similar stone is set up bearing the title of the other directional colors—Chac Acantun (Chak Akantun, meaning "Red Seated Stone") in the east, Sac Acantun (Sak Akantun, meaning "White Seated Stone") in the north, and Ekel Acantun (Ek'el Akantun, meaning "Black Seated Stone") in the west. In Landa's description of the Chak Akantun he adds that "there were many people who drew their blood, cutting their ears, and anointed with the blood the stone of the god called Chac Acantun, which they had there. Here they took boys and drew blood from their ears by force, making gashes in their ears. . . . And those who were devout had to draw their blood and to anoint the stone of the idol Chac Acantun with it" (Landa 1941, 144–145). In his description of the Sak Akantun Landa mentions that in addition to blood the image was also "perfumed," meaning that it received offerings of incense along with the other major deities of the Wayeb' period (ibid., 147).

In another section of his book Landa mentions the Akantuns in connection with carving sacred images of gods, a dangerous procedure that required offerings of blood, fasting, sexual abstinence, and ritual purity, as it was associated with the creative process of birthing the gods themselves. In fact this ritual was so dangerous that often the sculptors "would make excuses, since they feared that they or someone of their family would die on account of the work, or that fainting sickness would come upon them" (Landa 1941, 160). All four Akantuns, placed at each of the cardinal directions, surrounded the artists as they carried out their work, indicating that the formation of the gods conceptually took place at the very center of creation:

> While they [the carvers] were fasting the man to whom the idols belonged went in person or else sent someone to the forests for the wood for them, and this was always cedar. When the wood had arrived, they built a hut of straw, fenced in, where they put the wood and a great urn in which to place the idols and to keep them there under cover, while they were making them. They put incense to burn to four gods called Acantuns, which they located and placed at the four cardinal points. They put what they need for scarifying themselves or for drawing blood from their ears, and the instruments for sculpturing the black gods, and with these preparations, the priest and the Chacs and the workmen shut themselves up in the hut, and began their work on the gods, often cutting their ears, and anointing those idols with the blood and burning their incense, and thus they continued until the work was ended. (Landa 1941, 160)

As in the New Year's rites, the Akantuns receive human blood offerings as well as incense to give them life and power. The Akantuns, empowered with human blood, thus oversee the birth of the god as it is carved. In the *Chilam Balam of Chumayel* the Maya scribe describes the creation of the world and refers to the newly born earth as the "land of Acantun" (Roys 1967, 114), emphasizing the importance of the image in regenerating life on a universal scale.

Although Landa did not describe the appearance of these Akantuns, they are likely depicted in the lower registers of pages 25–28 of the Dresden Codex, which commemorate the Wayeb' rites as practiced before the Spanish Conquest (Roys 1965, xxiv, 1967, 114, 171; Thompson 1972, 91; MacLeod 1989, 114, 120–124; Newsome 2001, 206–207; Taube et al. 2010, 22–23; Paxton 2011, 40–41; O'Neil 2012, 98). The Dresden New Year's pages immediately follow page 74 of the text, which illustrates the death of the world by flood, implying that the New Year's rituals are meant to rebirth or re-create the world and its gods following their death at the close of the calendar year (Taube 1988, 220; Vail and Hernández 2014, 97, 151).

On each of the New Year's pages of the Dresden Codex, a distinct god linked with one of the four directions bears a headless turkey as a sacrificial offering as he approaches a stone column (fig. 8). The columns on all four pages are similar, consisting of a vertical shaft topped by four leaf-bearing branches and a serpent winding through the boughs. The trunk is marked with both *tun* glyphs, indicating that the monument is made of stone, as well as *te'* glyphs that signify "tree." It is therefore identified as an erect "stone

a b c d

8a–d. *Dresden Codex, pp. 25–28. (Förstemann 1880, pls. 54–57)*

tree" (Grube 2001, 502–503). The accompanying inscriptions on pages 25–28 of the Dresden Codex are identical and refer to each of the monuments as trees, specifically the *yaxte'* (first tree) erected in each of the four cardinal directions during the New Year's rites (Taube 1988, 220–242; Grube 2001, 503; Knowlton and Vail 2010, 720). In Post-Classic Maya codices sacred trees are commonly depicted as stone columns, particularly on the New Year's pages describing the days of the Wayeb', as we have seen (Dresden 25c–28c; Madrid 34–35), but also in numerous other appearances (Madrid 24a; 45–49, 79c, 89c–90c, 91a, 93a, 102b, 102d).

World Trees are frequently depicted in ancient Maya art as a major feature of the creation of the world. In Classic Maya depictions of the *yaxte'*, the trunk is marked with the face of a god whose mouth swirls with blood. Stephen Houston notes that the tree's appetite for blood is so distinctive that, when the glyphic sign for the *yaxte'* is combined with other elements, its most important feature, the blood-gorged mouth, is all that remains (Houston 2014, 15). Blood offerings are thus considered essential to the ancient World Tree just as they are in Landa's account of the analogous Akantun.

This blending of stone and tree attributes is also seen in the colonial Maya text known as *Ritual of the Bacabs* where the *akantun* (seated/established stone) is given the alternative name of *acante'* (*akante'*, seated/established tree) (Roys 1965, 12), or *cante'* (*kante'*, four trees), which Ralph L. Roys translates as "arbor" (ibid., 10, 12, 18). The identification of the *akantun* with trees is thus explicit in indigenous Maya texts. In Maya accounts that reference creation the raising of a sacred tree, often called the World Tree, is a metaphor for the birth (or rebirth) of life itself. In *Ritual of the Bacabs* the four *akantuns*/trees are located at each of the cardinal directions; their establishment or "opening" is when birth and creation occur (Roys 1965, 10; see also Macleod 1989, 119). Just as in Landa's description of the Akantuns in association with the New Year's rites, the *akantuns* in *Ritual of the Bacabs* are venerated with blood offerings:

> Hun Ahau! Unique Can Ahau! Can Ahau would be the creation; Hun Ahau would be the darkness. Four are the doors to his arbor [*cante*—"four trees"]; four are those to his *acantun* [seated/established stone], where his birth occurred. Four splotches of blood, four splotches of clotted blood are behind the *acantun*, the *acante* [seated/established tree]. (Roys 1965, 12)
>
> Four are the doors to his arbor [*cante*], four are the openings to his *acantun*. Four splotches of blood, four splotches of clotted blood were behind the *acantun*, behind the *maxcal*-plant, when his birth occurred. (ibid., 18)

> At one time there was the *acantun*, the *acante*, a great splotch of blood behind the *acantun-acantc*. Onc time there was a great rainstorm, a great whirlwind with rain. (ibid., 31)

The "great rainstorm" apparently refers to the deluge that destroyed the world, because it follows a passage describing the eclipse of the sun and moon and the stinging of the sky, all associated with world devastation in Maya belief. Thus the raising of the World Trees takes place following the death of the world by flood, just as it does in the New Year's pages of the Dresden Codex. In the *Chilam Balam of Chumayel* the destruction of the world is followed by the erection of four World Trees at the points of the compass, each associated with the same directional colors as those described by Landa, with a final green tree raised at the center:

> Then, after the destruction of the world was completed, they placed <a tree> to set up in its order the yellow cock oriole. Then the white tree of abundance was set up. A pillar of the sky was set up, a sign of the destruction of the world; that was the white tree of abundance in the north. Then the black tree of abundance was set up <in the west> for the black-breasted *piɔoy* to sit upon. Then the yellow tree of abundance was set up <in the south>, as a symbol of the destruction of the world, for the yellow-breasted *piɔoy* to sit upon, for the yellow cock oriole to sit upon, the yellow timid *mut*. Then the green tree of abundance was set up in the center <of the world> as a record of the destruction of the world. (Roys 1967, 100)

In this passage the "white tree of abundance" is also called *yocmal caan*, which Roys translates as "pillar of the sky." In the Yukatek Mayan language *yokmal* is a post or supportive column, consistent with the columnar appearance of the World Trees in the Dresden Codex New Year's pages.

Accompanying each of the columnar stone trees in the Dresden Codex is a glyphic text that refers to the monuments as *yaxte'* (first/green tree), identifying them as World Tree effigies. Each of these inscriptions is affixed to the glyph for the principal sky god Itzamna, giving the title of the monument as Itzamna Yaxte' (first/green tree of Itzamna). The link between Itzamna and the World Trees of the creation is seen in other indigenous Maya sources. An incantation for curing asthma in *Ritual of the Bacabs* invokes the creation of the world as well as the Akantun, the stone tree monument described by Landa. As part of the incantation, the name of Itzamna is called upon over a period of four days, each day's incantation linking him to one of the four cardinal direction colors, the same four colors appended to the World Trees (Roys 1965, 23–29).

The establishment of the effigy World Trees identified with the creator god Itzamna on the Dresden New Year's pages implies the reestablishment of divine authority tied to the creation of the world. Pages 75–76 of the Pre-Columbian Madrid Codex (fig. 9) illustrate a stylized World Tree at the center of the four cardinal points of the world with two gods (Itzamna on the right and the goddess Chak Chel on the left) seated beneath it, demonstrating a further linkage of Itzamna, World Trees, and the creation of the world (Paxton 2009, 85; Knowlton and Vail 2010, 712).

In other late Post-Classic Maya texts Itzamna is depicted as a sky deity and an important participant in creation (Thompson 1972, 228; Vail and Hernández 2014, 112, 136). A text from Structure XIX at Palenque, dating to the latter years of the reign of K'inich Ahkal Mo' Naab' III (ca. 721–736), mentions the god Yax Naah Itzamnaaj (First Itzamnaaj or First House Itzamnaaj) in conjunction with a creation narrative, perhaps in reference to the establishment of a sacred temple in the far distant past (Stuart 2005, 66n19; Taube 1992, 31). This suggests that Itzamna was worshipped as a creator deity at least as far back in time as the Classic period. The *Relación de Valladolid*

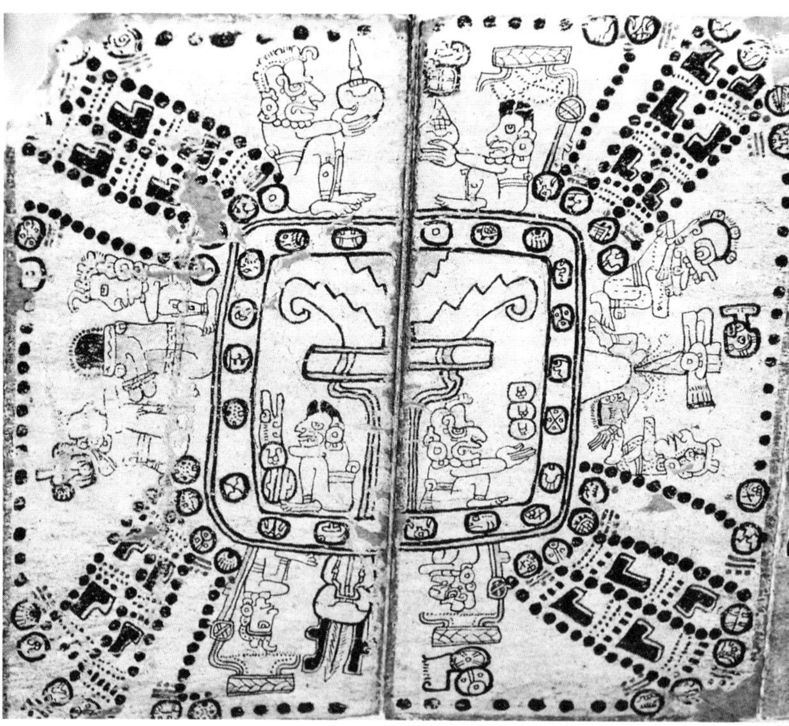

9. *Madrid Codex, pp. 75–76. (Facsimile, Museo de las Américas, Madrid)*

10. *World Trees: west wall, Las Pinturas, San Bartolo. Illustration by Heather Hurst © 2008*

refers to him as the *ah tepal* (supreme ruler) of the sky, while the *Relación de Ekbalam* declares that "[the Maya] worshipped only one god, whose name was Hunab [Junab', meaning "alone, sole, singular"] and Zamna [Itzamna]" (Taube 1992, 35–36).

Each World Tree effigy on the New Year's pages of the Dresden Codex is linked with one of the principal Maya deities. These gods are God G (the sun god, K'inich Ajaw) associated with the east (page 25c); God K (perhaps B'olon Tz'akab', although he appears to be linked as well with the god Chaak, also a rain deity) in the south (page 26c); God A (a death god) in the west (page 27c); and God D (Itzamna, a sky deity) in the north (page 28c). These are the same gods that appear in Landa's account of the Yucatec Maya New Year's observances that are placed in temporary shrines at the four cardinal directions—K'inich Ajaw in the east, Itzamna in the North, Wak Mitun Ajaw, an underworld death god, in the west, and B'olon Tz'akab', a manifestation of God K, in the south. This suggests that both Landa's account of the Wayeb' days and the New Year's pages of the Dresden Codex refer to the same or closely analogous ceremonies linked to New Year's observances as well as the creation of the world (Thompson 1972, 228; Taube 1988, 220).

The raising of four World Trees at the limits of the world at the moment of creation is one of the most ancient Maya themes. William Saturno recently discovered a spectacular series of murals (Pinturas Sub-1A) painted in the first century BC on the interior walls of a temple at San Bartolo (a site in the northern Peten, Guatemala), which focuses on creation imagery. The first scenes depicted in the mural show four World Trees, each accompanied by a god offering copious amounts of his own blood adjacent to an altar bearing a distinct sacrificial offering (fig. 10). All four trees are topped by a bicephalic serpent held in the beak of the Principal Bird Deity. Karl Taube identifies these four trees as the same effigy World Trees illustrated on the Dresden Codex Wayeb' pages and points out that the same four offerings seen in the San Bartolo murals match perfectly those illustrated in the Dresden Codex

(Taube et al. 2010, 12–13, 25–29). This is a remarkable testament to the consistency of Maya ritual practices tied to New Year's observances over a period of at least 1,500 years.

In ancient Maya art and literature the raising of the central World Tree is the culminating act of creation, a symbol for rebirth following death. Numerous examples of such trees are known from the Maya world, extending far back into antiquity. Perhaps the best known is the cross-shaped tree that dominates the sarcophagus lid of the ruler K'inich Janab' Pakal of Palenque, dating to the late seventh century AD (fig. 11). This carved stone lid depicts the king within the jaws of the underworld while a cross-shaped motif emerges from his body (or grows behind it) with tokens of renewed life and royal power. Although highly stylized, the cross-shaped central motif is meant to be a tree, with its trunk and branches repeatedly marked with *te'* (tree) glyphs (Stuart and Stuart 2008, 176, 198). A similar tree appears at the center of the Sanctuary Panel of the Temple of the Cross from the same site, carved a few years later in 692 (fig. 12). The accompanying hieroglyphic text identifies the cross-shaped tree motif as the "Shining Jeweled Tree." Similar cross-shaped sacred trees are also depicted in late Post-Classic codices, such as Dresden pages 3 (fig. 13) and 69a and Madrid pages 75–76 (fig. 9). Like the effigy World Trees in Landa's account, these mythic trees are composed of polished stone that would shine with reflected light (Houston 2014, 97).

The trees on both Pakal's sarcophagus lid and the Panel of the Cross are strikingly similar to the World Trees from the Dresden New Year's pages, each bearing the same *te'* glyphs (marking them as trees), a snake winding through their branches, and deity markers. David Freidel, Linda Schele, and Joy Parker identify this tree as a ceiba, which has branches that extend horizontally away from the trunk (fig. 14), giving it a distinctive cross shape (Freidel et al. 1993, 393–397). In the Yukatek Mayan language the ceiba tree is called *yax che'*, which literally means "first tree" (Barrera Vásquez 1995, 972), the same name given to the World Tree in both the Dresden New Year's pages and the *Chilam Balam* texts cited above.

In the *Chilam Balam of Chumayel* the raising of the *yax che'el kab'* (first tree of the world) is specifically linked to creation:

> During the creation thirteen infinite series' <added> to seven was the count of the creation of the world. Then a new world dawned for them. The two-day throne was declared, the three-day throne. Then began the weeping of Oxlahun-ti-ku. They wept in this reign. The reign became red; the mat became red; the *yax cheel cab* [first tree of the world] was rooted fast. The entire world was proclaimed. (Roys 1967, 101–102)

11. *Sarcophagus lid of K'inich Janab' Pakal. Copyright Merle Greene Robertson, 1976, 2006.*

Because the tree-columns depicted on the New Year's pages of the Dresden Codex are also called *yax che'*, it is probable that this passage refers not only to creation but also to the New Year's Wayeb' rites, in which the World Tree in its effigy form is raised as part of the five days at the end of the calendar year. Although little is known about Oxlahun-ti-ku, he functions in the *Chilam Balam* texts as a sky deity, suggesting that the "weeping" is divine in origin and linked

12. *Sanctuary Panel, Temple of the Cross, Palenque. Drawing by Linda Schele © David Schele*

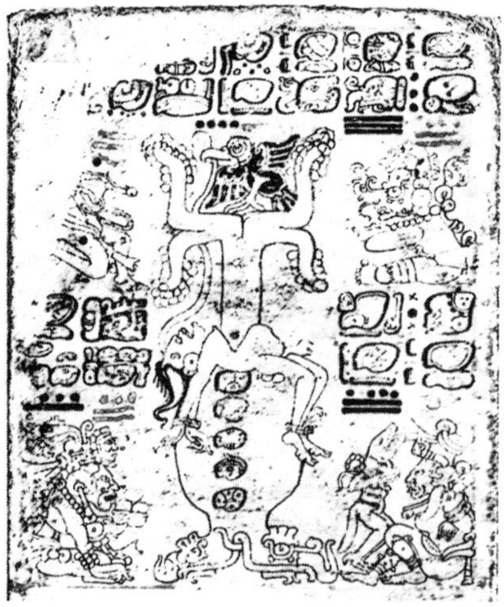

13. *Dresden Codex, p. 3. (Förstemann 1880, pl. 3)*

14. *Ceiba, Yaxchilan*

with rain (Thompson 1970, 180), perhaps a reference to the destructive rains that destroyed the world just before the creation of the present age. The reference to weeping is also appropriate, as these days are marked by fasting, self-mortification, and other penitential observances. The "two-day throne" and "three-day throne" perhaps refer to the brief period in which legitimate sovereignty, both divine and earthly, is suspended and the B'akab' god becomes the temporary ruler of the world. Although Landa does not specify when the B'akab' is set up to receive offerings and tribute, his account of this phase of the ceremony does appear approximately in the middle of his description of the five-day Wayeb' period, thus giving the B'akab' a two–three day reign.

Fray Bartolomé de Las Casas notes in his *Apologética historia* that certain Maya elders, probably in Yucatan, claimed to have worshipped a trinity of gods parallel to the Christian trinity and that the Son was named B'akab', the god of the Wayeb' rites as described by Landa:

> There had been found a principal lord who, upon inquiring concerning his beliefs and ancient religion while he resided in his ancient kingdom, said that that they knew and believed in God and that he was in the sky, and that this God was the Father and Son and Holy Spirit, and that the Father was called Izona, who had created mankind and all things. . . . Bacab was the Son, and they say that he was killed by Eopuco, who whipped him and placed on him a crown of thorns, and hung him from a tree, for they understood that he was bound to it rather than nailed (and this is how they indicated that his arms were outstretched), and there he finally died; he was there dead three days, and on the third day he came to life again and rose up into the sky with his Father. After this came Echuac, who is the Holy Spirit, and he filled the earth with all that it had need for. Upon asking what Bacab or Bacabab meant, he said that he was the Son of the Great Father and that the name Echuac meant merchant. (Las Casas 1967, 1:648–649, translation by author)

It is easy to dismiss this passage as a misunderstanding of Maya belief on the part of Las Casas or alternatively as a misunderstanding of the Christian trinity on the part of his Maya consultants. But despite its obvious problems, it may well represent an early attempt on the part of the Maya to harmonize their beliefs with those of their Christian conquerors and thus provides a somewhat murky window into the Maya concept of the gods associated with the Wayeb' rites. Although Las Casas first refers to a single B'akab', he immediately glosses this with the pluralized form of the name, B'akab'ab', an accurate reference to the multivalent nature of that god linked to each of the four cardinal directions. During the Wayeb' rites preceding the rebirth of the world, one of the four B'akab's is tied to or hung from a pole or effigy tree. It is unclear from Landa's account when this occurred during the five-day period of the Wayeb', but it may well have been three days before the conclusion of the ceremony. At the end of the Wayeb', the image of B'akab' is indeed taken away. He then resumes his role as a sky-bearing god, a reasonable interpretation of "rose up into the sky." In Las Casas's account, Izona (Itzamna) is described as the great Father deity who dwells in the sky and "created all things." Itzamna is the principal sky god in Maya cosmology as well as the most prominent creator deity among the Yucatec Maya at the time of the Spanish Conquest. It is therefore understandable that the unnamed Maya consultant would identify the supreme Christian god with Itzamna. The third member of the Maya Trinity in Las Casas's account is Echuac (Ek' Chuwak in modern orthography). Ek' Chuwak is primarily a god of merchants, as Las Casas notes in the passage cited above. He is also connected with night fire ceremonies, particularly the striking of New Fire, an important symbol for rebirth that Landa describes as occurring at the conclusion of New Year's ceremonies (Landa 1941, 153). Thus Ek' Chuwak appears on Madrid Codex 33b, holding a fiery torch in connection with the depiction of New Year's rites (fig. 15). Paired Ek' Chuwak gods are illustrated on Madrid 51a, striking New Fire with a twist drill (fig. 16), one of several scenes in Maya codices that depict the god creating fire. Landa writes that traveling merchants would set up a hearth of three stones (a small-scale version of the three stone hearth set up by the gods at the time of creation) and burn incense in honor of this god so that he would bring them back home safely (Landa 1941, 107). Because of Ek' Chuwak's association with fire and abundance it is understandable that the Maya lord quoted by Las Casas would associate him with the Holy Spirit, who is described in Christian doctrine as the god who bestows blessings and baptizes "with fire" (Matthew 3:11).

THE WAYEB' RITES AND HUMAN SACRIFICE

Returning to Landa's account of the Wayeb' rites, the ceremonies at the conclusion of the ceremonial cycle included human sacrifices by heart extraction in the presence of the principal god of that year. In the K'an years, when the B'akab' is set up in the south, this was Itzamna Kauil:

> Then he bade them make an idol named Itzamna Kauil, and that they should place it in their temple, and that they should burn in its honor in the court three balls of a sap or resin which they called *kik* [*kik'*, meaning blood, rubber], and that they should sacrifice to it a dog or a man, which they did observing the method which in Chapter 100 I said they observed with those whom they sacrificed except that the manner of sacrificing in this feast was different, since they built in the court of the temple a great pile of stones, and they placed the man or dog whom they were going to sacrifice on something higher than it, and throwing down the bound victim from the height on to the stones, those officials seized him and took out his heart with great quickness, and carried it to the new idol and offered it to him between two platters. (Landa 1941, 142–143)

15. *Madrid Codex, p. 33b. (Brasseur de Bourbourg 1869, pl. 24)*

16. *Madrid Codex, p. 51a. (Brasseur de Bourbourg 1869, pl. 6)*

The published version of Landa's narrative as we have it today has no chapter 100, although there is a description of sacrifice by heart extraction earlier in the text that clarifies how the ceremony was carried out:

> If the heart of the victim was to be taken out, they led him with a great show and company of people into the court of the temple, and having smeared him with blue and put on a *coroza*, they brought him up to the round altar, which was the place of sacrifice, and after the priest and his officials had anointed the stone with a blue color, and by purifying the temple drove out the evil spirit, the Chacs seized the poor victim and placed him very quickly on his back upon that stone, and all four held him by the legs and arms, so that they divided him in the middle. At this came the executioner, the Nacom, with a knife of stone, and struck him with great skill and cruelty a blow between the ribs of his left side under the nipple, and he at once plunged his hand in there and seized the heart like a raging tiger and snatched it out alive and, having placed it upon a plate, he gave it to the priest, who went very quickly and anointed the faces of the idols with that fresh blood. (Landa 1941, 118–119)

It is interesting that Landa uses the word *coroza*, the tall, conical paper hat worn by those condemned by the Spanish Inquisition to die for heresy, to describe the headdress worn by the sacrificial victim in conjunction with Maya Wayeb' rites. The ancient Maya adorned persons intended for sacrifice with bark paper, often drawing strips of it through their earlobes. It is therefore possible that the headdress described above was made of bark paper or had a conical shape. It is also possible that Landa simply used a term familiar to him as an inquisitor for a headdress worn by those condemned to die.

CONCLUSION OF THE WAYEB' RITES

Once the proper rituals had been carried out and the five days of Wayeb' were over, the B'akab' and his standard were dismantled and moved to the periphery of the community, while the legitimate gods were returned to their temples or sanctuaries and people could resume their lives as normal. If the proper rituals were not carried out, however, or if these proved to be done improperly, the deathly influences of the Wayeb' would carry over into the new year:

> They made a heart out of bread and another kind of bread with the seeds of gourds, and they offered these to the image of the god Kan u Uayeyab [the yellow Wayeb' B'akab' of the South]. Thus this statue and the image

> were kept during these unlucky days and they perfumed them with their incense, and with the grains of maize ground with incense. They believed that if they did not observe these ceremonies, they would be sure to have certain sicknesses, which they have in this year. When these unlucky days were passed, they carried the statue of the god Bolon Dzacab to the temple and the image to the eastern side, so that another year they could go and get it there. And they left it there, and returned to their houses, each occupying himself with whatever there was to do for the celebration of the new year. When once the ceremonies were ended and the evil spirit was chased away, according to their mistaken views, they considered the year as a good one. (Landa 1941, 141–142)

THE YUCATEC NEW FIRE CEREMONY

Landa elaborated on the conclusion of the New Year's rites in his description of the ceremonies connected with the beginning of Pop, the first month of the solar calendar year, with an account of a New Fire ceremony:

> All having come together with the presents of food and drinks, which they had brought, and also a great quantity of wine, which they had made, the priest purified the temple, seating himself in the middle of the court, clothed like a pontiff, having near him a brazier and the little boards with incense. The Chacs [four attendant priests dressed in the guise of the rain god] seated themselves at the four corners, and stretched from one to the other a new cord, within which were to enter all those who had fasted, in order to drive out the evil spirit. . . . Once having expelled the evil spirit, all began to pray with great devotion, and the Chacs kindled the new fire, and lighted the brazier for in the feasts in which all joined in common, they burned incense to the idol with new fire and the priest began to throw this (kind of) incense into it, and all came in their turn, beginning with the lords, to receive incense from the hands of the priest, which he gave them with as much gravity and devotion as if he were giving them relics. And they threw it into the brazier little by little, waiting till it had finished burning. (Landa 1941, 152–153)

The striking of new fire is a major element of New Year's rituals throughout Mesoamerica. The Aztecs struck new fire on the chest of a sacrificial victim at midnight before the first day of the New Year as well as at the beginning of the great cycle of fifty-two years (Sahagún 1953, 25–30; Miller and Taube 1993, 87; Aveni 2000, 260–262). The New Fire ceremony described by Landa is undoubtedly a reenactment of the Maya concept of creation in which the gods set three hearthstones and struck new fire at their center in order to initiate life (Freidel et al. 1993, 79, 112).

Having completed the cycle of rituals associated with New Year's Day, the Maya celebrate the regeneration of the world with a period of feasting:

> After this perfuming, they all ate the gifts and presents, and the wine went round till they became very drunk, and this was their new year and a service very acceptable to their idols. Afterward there were some others who in the course of this month Pop celebrated this festival with devotion with their friends, and with the nobles and the priests; for their priests were always the first in their rejoicings and drinkings. (Landa 1941, 153)

MAYA WORLD-RENEWING CEREMONIES IN YUCATAN AFTER THE SPANISH CONQUEST

Wayeb' rituals continued to be practiced in much the same way for centuries after the Spanish Conquest, despite repeated efforts to suppress them. In written accounts of these ceremonies the B'akab's as temporary lords of the Wayeb' days were replaced by a god named Mam. *Mam* means "maternal grandfather" in Yukatek Mayan and by extension someone who is elderly. Like the B'akab's, Mam is conceived as a deity with destructive attributes. The Motul dictionary describes him as a "feared deity of evil among the Maya, who comes out of his dwelling beneath the surface of the earth only during certain days of crisis (Wayeb'), at the conclusion of which they suspend all reverence for him and he is rudely expelled or disinterred" (Barrera Vásquez 1995, 491, translation by author). Diego López de Cogolludo, who lived in Yucatan during the seventeenth century, also describes Mam as a deity who presides over the Wayeb' or New Year's rites:

> They had a wooden idol which they placed on a bench over a mat, and offered him things to eat and other gifts in a festival called Uayeyab. And at the end of the festival, they undressed him and threw the pieces of wood to the ground without giving him any more reverence. And this idol they called Mam. (Cogolludo 1957, book 4, chapter 8, 197, translation by author)

The *Chilam Balam of Mani* describes a similar ceremony at the close of the calendar year, although the temporary god of the Wayeb' is not named:

> During these five days [the Wayeb'] one god is worshipped. On the first day he is feted with great enthusiasm, on the fourth day he is placed at the door of the house at dawn and the worship is less, and on the fifth day he

is exiled so that he will go away. The sixth day begins the new year with the first month, which is named Pop. (Craine and Reindorp 1979, 88–89)

The same ceremonial cycle is described in another version of the indigenous Maya *Chilam Balam* text as recorded by don Juan Pío Pérez:

> There is a god whom they worship or fete, during the first four of these days [of Wayeb']. On the first day many offerings and feasts are made to the god. After the fourth day there is a diminishing of the worship of his image which they have in the middle of the house. After the fourth day they place the god's image at the door of the house, and on the fifth day they banish it and carry it into exile. On the sixth day the New Year begins; it is New Year's Day. (ibid., 170–171)

This description of the temporary elevation of Mam as the god of the Wayeb' matches well the accounts of the short-lived veneration of the B'akab's during the final five days of the calendar year, after which the Mam is taken away with the inauguration of the New Year.

MAYA WORLD TREES AT THE TIME OF THE SPANISH CONQUEST

In the late Post-Classic period (AD 1250–1524), cross-shaped tree stones called *yax che'el kab'* (first tree of the world) were set up as markers for the axis between earth and sky (Farriss 1984, 303; Taube 1988, 245; Freidel et al. 1993, 53, 251). These were linked with abundance and life-giving rain. This echoes Dresden Codex page 25c, where the first columnar stone effigy of the *yax che'* (World Tree) is set up in the east and bears the head of the rain god Chaak (fig. 8a).

The first Spaniard to remark on Pre-Columbian Maya cross-shaped World Trees was Bernal Díaz del Castillo, who participated in the expedition led by Francisco Hernández de Córdoba to explore the coast of the Yucatan Peninsula in 1517. While they were disembarking to replenish their supplies somewhere in Campeche, a group of Maya invited them to enter one of their temples:

> And they led us to some very large houses, which were the temples of their idols. These were very well constructed of limestone and mortar. On some of the walls were painted the figures of serpents and snakes, and on others were paintings of idols. Within one of these temples was something like an altar that was covered with very fresh drops of blood. And in another

> area of the idols there were signs in the form of crosses, painted with other figures of Indians. We were astonished by all of this as things never seen nor heard. It appeared that they had just sacrificed certain Indians to their gods so that they would give them victory over us. (Díaz del Castillo 1984, book 3, chapter 3, translation by author)

In 1518 another expedition set out to explore the coast of the Yucatan Peninsula, led by Juan de Grijalva. Accompanying Grijalva on this voyage were a number of Spaniards who would later figure prominently in the conquest of New Spain. Among these were Francisco de Montejo y Álvarez, who would make the first serious attempts to invade the Yucatan Peninsula; Bernal Díaz del Castillo, who would later accompany Hernán Cortés in his successful conquest of the Aztec Empire; and Pedro de Alvarado, who would go on to conquer the Maya highlands of Guatemala as well as Honduras. Antonio de Herrera y Tordesillas chronicled the Grijalva expedition, including a description of a brief visit to the island of Cozumel off the northeastern coast of the Yucatan Peninsula. There the explorers saw a number of stone crosses:

> They saw some shrines and temples. One in particular had the form of a square tower, wide at the base and narrow at the top, with four large windows and corridors within. And in its interior, which was the chapel, were idols. At the back was a sacristy where they kept the things of service to the temple; and at the foot of this was an enclosure of stone and lime, crenellated and plastered. And at its center was a limestone cross three varas in height [slightly less than three meters], which they held to be the god of rain, being very certain that he would not forget them when they devoutly made their petitions to him. And in other parts of this island, and in much of Yucatan, were seen painted crosses of the same kind. (Herrera y Tordesillas 1726, década 2, book 3, 59, translation by author)

Fray Bartolomé de las Casas also wrote that cross-shaped monuments were particularly venerated on Cozumel Island, where they were associated with rain and water:

> In the kingdom of Yucatan, when our people discovered it, they found crosses. There was one on the island of Cozumel, just off the mainland of Yucatan, that was made of stone and mortar, ten palm spans [nearly seven feet] tall, in the middle of a patio or walled enclosure that was highly polished and crowned with battlements. It was located adjacent to a very imposing temple that was much visited by a great number of devout people. They say that this cross was worshipped as a god of water and rain, and

> that when they lacked water they sacrificed doves to it, according to what they say. (Las Casas 1967, chapter 123, 648, translation by author; see also Román y Zamora 1897, 58–59)

Juan de Torquemada apparently described this same monument as well as other crosses on the island of Cozumel in his book *Monarchia Indiana*, noting that it was "much visited by great numbers of devout people" (Torquemada 1723, book 13, chapter 49, 3:132). Tomás López Medel wrote that the island of Cozumel and its cross-shaped images were the object of sacred pilgrimages throughout the Yucatan and beyond:

> And the priesthood and cult and religion of Yucatan were held in great esteem and honored by all the neighboring regions. And a certain part of Yucatan which is called Cozumel, and a temple which was there, was considered a very religious thing, and all that land made its pilgrimages and repaired to that place, which was like going to Rome here among us, both on account of the religiousness of the place and because the Yucatecan priests were considered to be the most religious, wise, and learned people. (Landa 1941, 223; see also Cogolludo 2006, book 4, chapter 7, 285)

The earliest Spanish explorers and missionaries who saw these cross-shaped monuments confused them with Christian crosses and assumed that the Maya had some knowledge of Christianity. Francisco López de Gómara wrote that the early Spanish conquerors found many crosses on the Yucatan Peninsula and wondered how the Maya could have had knowledge of the "Most Holy Sign of the Cross," as there was no evidence that Christian doctrine had been preached among them before the arrival of the Spaniards in the early sixteenth century (López de Gómara 1554, book 52, 60–61).

Diego de Landa dismissed any suggestion that the Pre-Columbian cross-shaped monuments had anything to do with Christian-inspired crosses, finding no evidence that the Maya had knowledge of Christian symbols before the arrival of the first Spanish missionary priests. In support of this assertion he quoted an aged lord, a man he described as "of very good intelligence and of wide reputation": "Speaking of this subject one day and asking him if they had at any time heard news of Christ, our lord, or of his Holy cross, he told me that he had never heard anything from his ancestors of Christ or the cross" (Landa 1941, 207).

What the Spanish explorers and missionary priests saw were undoubtedly effigy World Trees, whose cruciform shape resembled that of the Christian cross. Such sacred effigy trees continued to be worshipped in independent Maya communities long after the initial Spanish conquests in the early sixteenth century. The Franciscan friar Andrés Avendaño y Loyola saw a stone effigy tree that the local Maya called the *yax che'el kab'* (first tree of the world—the same name that appears in Maya texts to refer to the World Tree as described above) in January 1696 in Nojpeten, the capital of the Itza kingdom and the last major independent Maya state to resist conquest by the Spaniards. Avendaño had learned the Itza language in the hope that he could convert them to Christianity and thus pacify the region without the force of arms. He also made a study of the ancient Maya calendar in order to time his missionary efforts to the close of a major calendric cycle, knowing that this was the period when the world itself would be reborn in Maya belief.

Avendaño set out from Mérida on December 13, 1695 bearing a letter from governor Martín de Ursua on behalf of the king of Spain, offering peace and royal protection from Spanish colonists if its king, Kan Ek', declared fealty to the Spanish Crown and abandoned the practices of human sacrifice and cannibalism. Soon after Avendaño and his companions arrived on the western shores of Lake Peten Itza, they saw Kan Ek' sailing toward them from the island capital city of Tah Itza at the head of a flotilla of eighty canoes holding some five hundred Maya "painted and dressed for war" (Avendaño y Loyola 1987, 30). Fray Avendaño was hastily, and somewhat forcibly, loaded onto the royal canoe and paddled to the island of Nojpeten. When they reached the island a delegation of Maya lords greeted them, including a nephew of Kan Ek', who noticed the crucifix that the friar wore. Twice he asked Avendaño to give him the crucifix, but both times he was refused (ibid.). Finally he took it by force. Nothing else was taken from the friar, indicating a particular interest in the image of the cross. The Maya lord's fascination with the crucifix perhaps stemmed from its resemblance to the cruciform-shaped Maya World Tree. Avendaño was subsequently taken to the capital city of Kan Ek', where he saw a stone monument that the Itza told him was called the *yax che'el kab'*, prominently displayed at the entrance to the palace compound:

> On the shore of the landing place is situated the house of the said petty King at the distance of half a quarter of a league [approximately 42 meters], in the middle of which, open to the street, stands the fragment of a column of round stone, the circumference of each part of which is about three quarters of a yard across and one quarter high. It is made of stones placed on top of each other with mortar of lime and *cah cab* [place/dwelling of bees/honey-honeycomb], which is usually used for that purpose; the middle is filled in with bitumen so it is like a table, with a round pedestal upon which and set together with the stone column, the petty King and the rest of his family and followers worship. The said column is called, in the name by

> which they worship it, *Yax cheel cab*, which in their language means the first tree of the world, and as is understood in their old songs (which few people understand) they wish to have it known they worship it because it was that tree of whose fruit our first father Adam ate, who in their language is called Ixanom. In the small part which is fortunately preserved, and the mask, which stands in the said foundation of the said column, they worship him with the title of the son of the very wise God. In their language they call him Ahcocahmut. (Avendaño y Loyola 1987, 32)

Prudence Rice identifies this stone column as the Akantun/World Tree in Landa's account of the New Year's rites in Yucatan as well as the New Year's Pages of the Dresden Codex (Rice 1985). Fray Avendaño's claim that the *yax che'el kab'* was the same as the Judeo-Christian Tree of Knowledge of Good and Evil in the Garden of Eden is curious if the monument that he saw was a Maya Akantun. It is possible that the Itza had already conflated the ancient Maya World Tree with the Christian tradition of the tree in Genesis. The Itza had had periodic contacts with European Christians for more than a century prior to Avendaño's visit (Knowlton and Vail 2010, 710–711). Hernán Cortés himself passed through Nojpeten in March 1525 on his way to Honduras. During this encounter the Franciscan friars who accompanied Cortés celebrated a solemn Mass and sermon translated into Yukatek Mayan by their interpreter, Doña Marina. Though the subject of this sermon was not recorded, the king of the Itza at the time, also named Kan Ek', requested a cross afterward, suggesting that the topic of the crucifixion of Christ was broached (Cogolludo 2006, 86–87).

In Avendaño's account the *yax che'el kab'* monument was not only linked with the tree in the Garden of Eden but also tied to the "son of the very wise God," a reference to Jesus Christ and undoubtedly the cross as well. The earlier Kan Ek's request that Cortés leave a cross with him, as well as the fascination with the cross displayed by the nephew of the Itza king more than a century later, suggests that this Christian symbol resonated with indigenous ideas linked to the Maya World Tree. Timothy Knowlton and Gabrielle Vail suggest that Cortés's sermon to the Itzas may have reflected a common Christian polemic that merged Christ's cross with the Tree in Eden as a strategy aimed at converting Jews and Muslims in Spain (Knowlton and Vail 2010, 727–729). Subsequent contact with baptized Maya as well as early missionary visits would have reinforced the linkage of the *yax che'el kab'*, the Edenic tree, and the Christian cross.

It is also possible, however, that Avendaño simply misinterpreted what he was told about the image either consciously or unconsciously and that the *yax che'el kab'* was primarily an indigenous Maya symbol, specifically an Akantun or World Tree. Avendaño's command of the Itza language was imperfect despite his claims to the contrary, which may explain his difficulty in making himself understood during the reading of the governor's letter (Avendaño y Loyola 1987, 35; Jones 1998, 201). Any reference that the Maya made to a World Tree associated with the creation or birth of the world would have been linked in Avendaño's mind with the Garden of Eden. His stated purpose in coming to Nojpeten was to tie Christian doctrine with ancient Maya traditions regarding the death and rebirth of the world as an aid to his efforts to convert the Itzas to Roman Catholicism. Certainly the Maya World Tree is also associated with creation, sacrifice, death, and rebirth on a universal scale. This is especially clear on Madrid 75–76 (fig. 9) and Dresden 3 (fig. 13), both of which show human sacrifices in conjunction with the World Tree. I prefer this interpretation, considering the fierce opposition to Christian evangelization efforts in the region and the continued reluctance of the Itza hierarchy to accept baptism. Avendaño himself wrote that he recognized the motif immediately as an authentic Maya symbol that he had seen in indigenous painted codices:

> At the instant we landed and I saw the said column and mask I came to recognize it, since I had already read about it in their old papers and had seen it in their *anahtes*, which they use—which are books of barks of trees, polished and covered with lime, in which by painted figures and characters they have foretold their future events. By which means I knew that there were found in the said Peten Ytza the said idol of Yaxchecab, that of Cocahmut, and that of Ytzimna Kauil. (Avendaño y Loyola 1987, 32–33)

From this passage it is clear that Avendaño saw the *yax che'el kab'* monument as an indigenous Maya object that he had seen previously in "old" painted codices and not as a syncretic Maya/Christian symbol. In addition, Avendaño's account links the *yax che'el kab'* with the gods Cocahmut (Kokaj Mut) and Ytzimna Kauil (Itzamna K'awil), both well-known Maya deities that predate the Spanish Conquest. The Cordemex dictionary lists Itzamna K'awil as a Maya *deidad, dador de alimentos* (god, giver of food/nourishment) (Barrera Vásquez 1995, 387). As seen above, Itzamna is the god whose name is attached to the World Trees in the Dresden Codex New Year's pages, analogous to the *yax che'el kab'* seen by Avendaño.

Kokaj Mut is a Maya deity who is not known to have been conflated with a Christian god in any colonial documents. Landa specifically names Yax Cocah Mut (Yax Kokaj Mut, "First/Green Kokaj Mut") as the god associated with

Wayeb' New Year's rituals when B'akab' was placed in the east, associated with the Chak Akantun (Red/Great Akantun):

> There were many people who drew their blood, cutting their ears, and anointed with the blood the stone of the god called Chac Acantun, which they had there. Here they took boys and drew blood from their ears by force, making gashes in their ears. They kept this statue till the unlucky days were passed and meanwhile they burned their incense to it. . . . But in spite of all this, the devil caused them to make an idol named Yax Cocah Mut to place him in the temple and to take away the old images, and to make in the court in front of the temple a figure of stone, upon which they should burn their incense and a ball of resin or the milk *kik*, making a prayer there to the idol and asking of him a remedy for the calamities which they feared that year. These misfortunes were a scarcity of water, the abundance of sprouts in the maize and things of this kind, for preventing which the devil ordered them to offer him squirrels and a cloth without embroidery, which the old women should weave whose duty it was to dance in the temple, in order to appease Yax Cocah Mut. (Landa 1941, 144–145)

Yax Kokaj Mut is a manifestation of Itzamna in his avian form, *mut* meaning "bird" (Roys 1967, 153n5; Landa 1941, 145n695; Taube 1992, 36; Bassie-Sweet 2008, 130–140; Knowlton and Vail 2010, 717–720). In Avendaño's account, Kokaj Mut is appropriately linked with Itzamna K'awil. One of the definitions for K'awil in the Cordemex dictionary is *el santo pájaro* (the sacred bird) (Barrera Vásquez 1995, 387), further strengthening the notion that the creator god Itzamna appears here in his manifestation as a divine bird. There is an entry in the Yucatec Maya Vienna dictionary that clearly links Itzamna and Kokaj Mut together as a single god. Under the entry "Hun Itzamna, Yaxcocah-mut" we find: "Principal idol (god), which these Indians of this land had, from which they said all things proceeded and who was incorporeal; hence they made no image of" him (Bassie-Sweet 2008, 130).

In this entry the god Kokaj Mut bears the *yax* (green, first) designation, just as he does in Landa's account of the Wayeb' rites as well as in the *Chilam Balam of Tizimin*. In the *Chilam Balam of Chumayel* he is named as Ek-Cocah-Mut (Ek' Kokaj Mut, "Black Kokaj Bird") (Roys 1967, 153). Both green and black are world directional colors, suggesting that the god is to be interpreted as multivalent, with manifestations tied to each of the cardinal directions plus the center. The four Principal Bird Deities atop World Trees in the San Bartolo murals (fig. 10) dated to the first century BC are Itzamna birds, suggesting that the linkage dates back to a Pre-Classic version of Maya New Year's observances (Taube et al. 2010; Bassie-Sweet 2008, 132).

Returning to Fray Avendaño's account of his visit to Nojpeten, the friar gathered the principal lords of the city in order to read the letters that he had brought from the provincial governor. The wording of this letter, however, was difficult for the Itza to understand:

> Then, leaving off reading the [governor's] letter, since it was (although in their language) more corrupted than the ancient idiom in which they speak, which I had studied purposely, and explaining the said message to them in the ancient idiom and inserting a spiritual sermon about the good they would get from the Spaniards' friendship and from receiving their laws, and the good their souls would receive by accepting holy baptism, the first door to the new regeneration, as a necessary thing for seeing the face of their creator and true God—powerful in every part—and without this cleansing their souls would be lost; all this was explained to them with some eagerness, mixing in some words of their prophecies. (Avendaño y Loyola 1987, 35)

Avendaño carefully crafted his argument to link the "new regeneration" of Christian baptism with the end of the *k'atun* calendric cycle and its attendant Maya traditions regarding the death of the old world and its rebirth as a new age. He reinforced this concept by referring to the Christian God specifically as the "creator," "mixing in some words of their prophecies" (Avendaño y Loyola 1987, 35). It is clear that the Itzas understood this connection, because they informed Avendaño that they would not accept baptism until four months from that time when the end of the cycle actually occurred:

> Coming to where they stood, and with embraces and endearing expressions, I drew them to where they had stood at first, telling them I wished to speak to them of the old manner of reckoning which they use, both of days, months and years, and of the ages, and to find out what age the present one was (since for them one age consists only of twenty years). . . . I also made a computation of these accounts (the King and some of the priests aiding with their opinions) so that, confessing that they were convinced, we agreed that four months thereafter was the time wanting to fill out the said period when all the older men would receive baptism. (Avendaño y Loyola 1987, 39–40)

But Avendaño never returned to Nojpeten. A party of soldiers that was sent soon afterward to arrange for the peaceful surrender of the region was massacred, leading to a much larger expeditionary force in March 1697, which resulted in the military occupation of the capital city and the capture of Kan Ek' with at least one of his sons. The last independent king of the Maya was taken to the Spanish capital at Santiago de los Caballeros, where he died under house arrest.

CONFLATION OF THE MAYA WORLD TREES AND THE CHRISTIAN CROSS AFTER THE SPANISH CONQUEST

With the introduction of Roman Catholicism after the Spanish Conquest, the Maya of Yucatan soon conflated the Christian cross with their ancient World Tree and the Wayeb' period with Easter. Gaspar Antonio Chi, a Maya nobleman and one of Landa's principal sources of information, wrote that a few years before the arrival of the Spaniards a Maya prophet named Chilam Balam (reputed to have authored the original *Book of Chilam Balam*) came to the community of Mani. He directed the lord of that town, Mochan Xiu, to erect a stone image of the *yax che'el kab'* in the central plaza as a focus of worship and pilgrimage. Although this was done before the arrival of the Spaniards, the Maya later found the Christian cross so similar to this stone image of the World Tree that the rulers of Mani reportedly adopted Christianity when it was taught to them by the first Spanish missionaries:

> And he [Chilam Balam] commanded that [Mochan Xiu] make this cross symbol of worked stones along with others, and place them in the patios of the temples where they would be seen by all; and he said that this was the green tree of the world, and that many would go to see it as a new thing; and it appears that they worshipped it from then on. Later, when the Spaniards came, they realized that they carried the sign of the Holy Cross that was like the one that the prophet Chilam Balam had depicted. And so they took it as certain what he had told them and they decided to receive the Spaniards in peace and did not war against them, but instead were their friends. (Garza 1983, 69, translation by author)

Chi does not say in this text that the monument erected under the direction of Chilam Balam was a Christian cross, but rather the "first/green tree of the world," a direct translation of the title *yax che'el kab'*, revered by the Maya before the Spanish Conquest. In fact he was careful not to make a direct connection between this monument and a Christian cross. In the passage above, Chi describes the tree stone simply as a *señal de cruz* (cross or cross-shaped sign). Some transcriptions by modern authors have incorrectly cited this passage as *señal de la cruz* (sign of the cross), which would be a more direct connection with the Christian cross than Chi apparently intended (Restall 1998, 149–150; Knowlton and Vail 2010).

The erection of a monument in token of the sacred World Tree is prominent in the various versions of the Chilam Balam texts. The following is the prophecy of Chilam Balam in the *Chilam Balam of Chumayel* as translated by Munro Edmonson:

Yum e	O my fathers,
U chicul hunab ku canal	It was a sign of the sole god on high:
Hulom uaom che	Come is the standing tree.
Etçahan ti bal cah e	It is manifested in the world,
Uchebal u sas-hal y okol cab e	It is to be his radiance over the world,
Yum e	O my fathers.

(LINES 503–508 IN EDMONSON 1986, 73)

The text describes the erected monument as *uaom che* (*wa'om che'*, literally "raised/standing/upright tree"). This "standing tree" is described in the next two lines as holding a preeminent position in "the world," an apparent reference to the *yax che'el kab'* (first tree of the world). The same phraseology appears in the analogous passage of the *Chilam Balam of Tizimin* (lines 3951–3965, in Edmonson 1982, 142–143). There is no doubt that the *wa'om che'* (raised tree) of the world came to be interpreted as a foreshadowing of the Christian cross by both Spanish missionaries and converted Maya soon after the Conquest (Landa 1941, 207nn1153–1154; Cogolludo 2006, book 4, chapter 9, 293; Knowlton and Vail 2010) and that the traditions regarding Chilam Balam were subsequently redacted and reinterpreted by Maya intellectuals to harmonize with Christian teachings promulgated by early missionaries (Hanks 2010, 356–357). But I believe that the original tradition in its Pre-Columbian context is preserved in the Chilam Balam texts. The Chumayel document consistently uses the Spanish word *cruz* when referring to the Christian cross (see lines 3486, 3576, 3585, 3588, 4469, 4567, 4682 in Edmonson 1986) yet does not do so in the context of the Chilam Balam prophecy, which preserves the phrase *wa'om che'* (raised tree). The authors of the Chilam Balam texts thus appear to have chosen to distinguish clearly between the two as separate entities. In addition, *hunab ku* (*junab' k'u*, "sole god") was a title used prior to the Spanish Conquest for the creator god, Itzamna (Landa 1941, 146n707; Bricker and Miram 2002, 47). Like Junab' K'u, Itzamna is described as the sole god of Yucatan in the Post-Classic period in the *Relación de Ekbalam*: "They worshipped only one god who they knew by the names Hunab and Zamna [Itzamna], which is to say one only god" (Garza 1983, 2:139). As we have seen, Itzamna was intimately linked with the World Tree in Maya codices and Post-Conquest literature as a creator god and the principal god of the ancient Maya New Year's rites.

CHRISTIAN CROSSES AS WORLD TREES

As at Mani, most Maya seem to have readily accepted the cross into their traditional worship. Early in the Post-Conquest period this was perhaps because of its resemblance to the ancient cross-shaped World Tree, but in the succeeding centuries it became the most ubiquitous religious symbol throughout the Maya world. Crosses were placed at the four pathways entering into each colonial Maya community with an additional cross at the center, just as the World Trees functioned in the Pre-Columbian world to mark the four cardinal directions as well as the center point of creation (Farriss 1984, 315). Crosses were also placed atop boundary markers, at the doorways and rooftops of private homes, and most especially at the symbolic center of each town in the main plaza. These crosses were considered living entities and were sometimes clothed in Maya dress (fig. 17). The Christian cross and the Maya World Tree eventually blended into a single entity (Farriss 1984, 315; Clendinnen 1987, 182–183; Early 2006, 240). Fernando Cervantes suggests that the adoption of Christian imagery such as the cross involved a "process where the Indians were piecing their cosmos together in the new Christian configuration" (Cervantes 1994, 61).

During the Caste Wars of the nineteenth century, the Yucatec Maya rebelled against the Mexican government as well as the Roman Catholic Church, expelling both from their lands in the Yucatan. Yet the cross continued to be central to their religion. The rebels called themselves the Kruzob' (Crosses) and set up adorned crosses throughout the region as a symbol of their rule. They consulted "Speaking Crosses" that were believed to have the ability to prophesy and advise them in important matters. In 1868 the Kruzob' Maya crucified a man on one of their great crosses, hoping that in sacrificing him they would be empowered to overcome their Ladino oppressors (Nash 1968, 320).

Tree-crosses continue to be venerated among the Maya today as living entities adorned with foliage or pine boughs (fig. 18). Evon Vogt notes that modern crosses in Zinacantan represent a continuance of ancient Maya shrines adorned with foliage:

> One of the major symbols of Catholicism—the Christian cross—probably was adopted by the Zinacantecos early in the Postconquest period. But it was successfully encapsulated into the ceremonial system by the development of a complex set of procedures for decorating the cross shrines with pine boughs, red geraniums, and other plants to the point that one can hardly see the cross when the decorations are completed. I believe it likely

17. *Clothed crosses, Valladolid. Photograph by Marina Hayman, PhD*

18. *Painted and adorned Maya crosses, Chamula. Photograph by Marina Hayman, PhD*

> that aboriginal altars were composed of pine boughs and flowers decorating some type of idol. . . . There is the further evidence that the pine boughs rather than the wooden crosses are the crucial symbols. (Vogt 1969, 586)

In 2000 Miguel Astor Aguilera conducted a survey in Yucatan and Quintana Roo where he described both Latin crosses as well as a cross "more like a tree branch with two up-tilted arms." The Maya referred to both types of crosses as *santo*, which his Maya consultants interpreted as "entity" or "spirit" rather than the Roman Catholic notion of "saint" (Aguilera 2002, 14). He further notes that these crosses are conceived as being *k'uxaan* (alive) rather than as mere symbols. These crosses are often "painted a blue-green hue, which signifies centrality, and are referred to as *ya' as che'* or 'first/green tree'" (ibid.), linking these crosses to the ancient *yax che'el kab'* (first green tree of the world).

Aguilera describes a unique stela-shaped stone "cross" within the shrine of Chuumuk Lu'um that the local Yucatec Maya venerate as "being alive and growing from the earth as a plant does; indeed, it is literally regarded as a living holy tree placed at the center of the earth by the Itzá before the Spanish came to their ancestors' land" (Aguilera 2002 19). Although called a cross, it has no horizontal cross piece, echoing the form of the World Tree stone column seen in the New Year's pages of the Dresden Codex as well as the *yax che'el kab'* monument described by Avendaño at Nojpeten. The modern tree stone at Chuumuk Lu'um is specifically linked by the local Maya with the god Itzamna, the same deity associated with ancient Yucatec World Tree stones (ibid., 18).

Landa's investigations into the continued practice of Pre-Columbian Maya ceremonies in Yucatan uncovered the widespread practice of incorporating Christian elements into ancient Maya rituals, including the sacrifice of humans by means of crucifixion. In some cases the body was tied to the cross with vines and in other cases nailed to it (Farriss 1984, 287, 291). Tozzer cites the testimony of Francisco Camal, taken in 1562, which described one such incident of crucifixion:

> This witness saw how about three months ago, a little more or less, another sacrifice was made within the cemetery of the church at the foot of a cross to some idols and demons which were there, in which they killed a boy who was called Ah Tzu, whom in order to sacrifice and kill him, they crucified and placed on a large cross, and they nailed his hands and raised him on high. And they lowered him again, and thus, on the cross, alive as he was, Luis Nauat went and opened him and took out his heart and gave it to the

> *Ah-Kin*, Francisco Balam, who offered it to the demons and idols which were there. And after (he was) dead, he (Balam) made them a sermon to the effect that that was good and what they should do since they were their gods and those of their ancestors, and that they provided them with the necessary things, and that they were not to believe what the friars told them and these which the friars say are idols are gods and in them we must believe and the friars are deceiving us. And when this sermon was finished they went to throw the said boy in a *cenote* which was out of the way from there which is called *Chemzenote*, and they threw the said boy in nailed to the cross as he was. (Landa 1941, 116n533)

Francisco Balam emphasized that the Spanish friars were liars, which suggests that the cross used in this sacrificial ceremony was not intrinsically Christian. Page 3 of the Dresden Codex illustrates a very similar sacrifice by heart extraction in association with a cruciform sacred tree (fig. 13). Francisco Hernández, writing in 1545, noted that the Christian cross came to be worshipped by the Yucatec Maya as a rain god soon after the Spanish Conquest (Saville 1921, 209), just as the Pre-Columbian crosses on the island of Cozumel were considered rain deities, as seen above. This suggests that many early colonial Maya venerated the form of the Christian cross while maintaining an essentially indigenous view of its underlying power.

THE MAYA WORLD TREE/CROSS AND EASTER

From the testimony of Francisco Kantun, the Maya schoolmaster in the community of Usil, a series of crucifixion sacrifices was held in that province during the Easter season, demonstrating that the Maya associated their ancient sacrifices with the death of the Christian God. The second of these was specifically timed to coincide with Pascua (Easter) and the crucifixion of Jesus Christ:

> And in addition to this sacrifice the witness saw that fifteen days later, which was after *Pascua*, all who have been mentioned assembled and performed another sacrifice in the church itself, and the idols were there. In this sacrifice they crucified two more boys named Euan, whom the said Juan Pech and Melchior Be placed on the crosses. And so placed on the cross they opened them, saying to those who were there, "You see here the figure of Jesus Christ and we offer to our gods the hearts of these who are crucified." And they threw the bodies in the cenote of Tabi in the same way as the others. (Landa 1941, 116n533)

The association of the Christian cross with the ancient Maya World Tree is likely to have been a major reason why the Maya adopted the crucifixion of Christ during Holy Week as the focus of their world-rebirthing ceremonies. Landa aggressively prosecuted those engaged in ceremonial human sacrifice, as is evident from the testimony given by Francisco de Toral at Landa's trial for excessive cruelty in Spain:

> He has instituted certain proceedings against the persons most guilty of the evils which exist in these provinces, who are some caciques and lords who have caused them to be committed and other dogmatizers and preachers of false and abominable doctrines and other blasphemers of the Divine Name and evangelical teaching, and sacrificers of innocents placed on crosses, giving them the name of Christ, our Redeemer, and then taking out their hearts, in derision and scorn of His (Divine) Majesty and offering them to the demons, which they took to the church in order to do what has been said; all of which they have done after being baptized and very well instructed in the matters of our Holy Catholic faith. (Landa 1941, 116–117n533)

Such ceremonies did not always result in the death of the victim. A Maya named Juan Xiu reported the case of a boy that he claimed was born with stigmata (the appearance of nail marks in his hands and/or feet in token of Christ's crucifixion), a miracle that he included in a letter to Fray Pedro de Ciudad Rodrigo, guardian of the Mani monastery. Although far from convinced of this miracle, the friar did not immediately dismiss it. Three years later Landa referred to this case during his trial, saying that it was an obvious case of an actual crucifixion and that Fray Pedro was stupid to think that the marks on the boy's body could have been miraculous (Karttunen 1994, 99).

The boy with the wounds on his hands was probably a participant in a Maya Passion Play, reenacting the crucifixion of Christ as part of indigenous ceremonies. Such Passion Plays continue to be carried out in many communities to the present time and are often brutally realistic. In the late 1970s I saw two such Passion Plays performed over a period of several days in Totonicapán, culminating in the crucifixion of living participants that lasted for three hours on Good Friday. Although the men involved were only tied to their crosses with ropes, viewers noted with admiration that one of the performers was especially devout because he refused to rest on the block of wood provided for him below his feet and was thus in very real pain. I worked with an elderly man in the same community who said that in his youth he had the honor of being crucified during Holy Week several years in succession, with real nails driven through the palms of his hands. Actual crucifixions had been banned years before I met him, but he still kept the holes in his hands open by inserting small sticks through the wounds. He said that at first this was in case the ban on crucifixions was lifted; but he continued to do it because if he were to let his hands heal "God would no longer bless me for my sacrifice and might even punish me and take away the good things in my life."

Chapter 2

NEW YEAR'S CEREMONIES IN THE MAYA HIGHLANDS

New Year's rituals as described by Fray Diego de Landa were not limited to the Yucatan Peninsula. Similar ceremonies were celebrated throughout the Maya world. At present the best source for New Year's ceremonies as practiced by the ancient Maya of the Guatemalan highlands is Fray Bartolomé de las Casas (fig. 19), a Dominican priest who devoted thirteen chapters of his monumental work *Apologética historia sumaria* to the highland Maya. Despite the importance of Las Casas's work on the subject, it is far less well known than the writings of Landa. It did not appear in print until 1909 (Las Casas 1909) and has never been published in any language other than the original Spanish. Consistent with many of Las Casas's writings, the *Apologética historia* was intended to convince Spaniards that the indigenous people of the newly discovered American continents deserved to be treated as fellow human beings, possessing a culture that was worthy of respect and even praise, comparing favorably with other great civilizations of the world such as the ancient Greeks or Romans.

Three chapters of book 3 from the *Apologética historia* deal with New Year's ceremonies in the Guatemalan highlands, including a rather lengthy prayer, a description of clothing worn by participants, the appearance of temples, and other specifics that suggest that the information came from someone who had witnessed the events described (Las Casas 1967, book 3, chapters 177–178, 214–222). Las Casas writes that these ceremonies were carried out by the "kingdoms of Guatemala" without specifying which province. He was Dominican, however, and that order had authority principally among the K'iche's, so it is probable that this area would have been emphasized. Several K'iche' words and deities appear in this section of Las Casas's book as well, suggesting that the K'iche' region of west-central Guatemala was the focus of his writings.

When Las Casas first arrived as a missionary priest in Guatemala in 1536, only twelve years after the Spanish Conquest, many of the ancient royal cities of the highland Maya languished as burned-out ruins. For the first months of

19. *Fray Bartolomé de las Casas*

his ministry he resided in the newly established Spanish capital at Santiago de Guatemala. There he studied highland Maya languages under the tutelage of the first bishop of Guatemala, Francisco Marroquín. According to Fray Antonio de Remesal, Bishop Marroquín spoke K'iche' fluently and wrote the first treatise on Christian doctrine in that language for use by clerics and missionaries (Remesal 1964, book 3, chapter 7, 205–206). Daniel Brinton casts some doubt as to whether this tract was composed in K'iche' or in Kaqchikel, another closely related highland Maya language, but there is no question that both languages were studied by early missionary priests under Marroquín's direction (Brinton 1884, 351–352).

It is doubtful that Las Casas gained any significant fluency in K'iche' or Kaqchikel, as his studies were frequently interrupted. His position demanded that he be absent for months at a time before he left the capital the following year, including a prolonged stay in Oaxaca, Mexico, where he contended with Franciscan missionaries over their practice of mass baptisms without what Las Casas considered to be proper instruction in the Christian faith. When Las Casas did begin his missionary efforts in 1537, they were focused in the Q'eqchi' area of the Alta Verapaz, far from the K'iche' provinces. He therefore had little time to use whatever K'iche' language skills he may have acquired.

Nevertheless there is no reason to doubt that Las Casas would have learned at least the rudiments of the language that may have helped him in gathering information on Pre-Columbian K'iche' ritual practices.

In 1538 Bishop Marroquín sent Las Casas to Mexico, where he spent a year before traveling on to Spain. He did not return to the New World until 1545, when he was appointed the bishop of the newly organized Archdiocese of Chiapas in Mexico. He rarely if ever ventured into Guatemala after his return from Spain, particularly as he had come into conflict with Bishop Marroquín over the institution of the New Laws, intended to correct some of the Spanish abuses perpetrated against the indigenous populations of the Americas. These laws prohibited their enslavement and forced labor, placed them under the direct protection of the kings of Spain, and restored some measure of secular power and jurisdiction to their traditional rulers. Marroquín sided with Spanish settlers who claimed that the New Laws violated their property rights under the *encomienda* system, which parceled out land to former conquistadores and other officials as spoils of war. As part of the *encomienda*, Spanish overlords were responsible for protecting the indigenous peoples occupying their land from other Spaniards as well as from unconquered groups. They were also charged with teaching them the Spanish language and instructing them in the Roman Catholic faith. In practice, however, the *encomienda* system amounted to little more than an excuse to wage new wars in order to gain more land and reduce their inhabitants to slavery. Las Casas was a strong supporter of the reforms, while Bishop Marroquín adamantly opposed them, a conflict that soured their relationship.

Las Casas served as bishop of Chiapas only a brief time before he was recalled to Spain to defend the New Laws against Spanish settlers who had petitioned the court to have them repealed. Las Casas never returned to the New World again. In 1550 he led the defense of the New Laws at the Council of Valladolid. The principal issue was whether it was lawful for the king of Spain to wage war against the people of New Spain in order to seize their lands and subject them to unjust servitude. After a heated debate, it was determined that further wars of conquest were to be outlawed as "evil, unlawful and unjust" (Las Casas 1992, 9). Nevertheless, no judgment was rendered regarding the *encomienda* system due to the unsettled state of affairs in the New World, particularly the potential threat of rebellion should the New Laws be fully implemented.

Las Casas subsequently resigned his bishopric in Chiapas in order to continue work with the imperial court in matters relating to the Indies. He remained an important advocate for the rights of the indigenous population of the New World until his death in 1566. Beginning in 1551 he occupied a cell at the Dominican College of San Gregorio in Valladolid, where he lived with his assistant and friend Fray Rodrigo de Labrada. Much of the remainder of his life was occupied with writing the *Historia general de las Indias* (General History of the Indies), chronicling the history of the New World from the first explorations by Christopher Columbus down to his own day. In his preface to the *Historia general* (written in 1552), Las Casas admits that "although it has been many years since I began to write this history . . . due to my many travels and occupations I have not been able to complete it," and in the interim "there have appeared others who have written" (Las Casas 1957, 16). From this passage it appears that Las Casas began to collect the information contained in his history long before he put pen to paper, probably soon after his arrival in Guatemala in 1536. He specifically mentions that his notes included cultural information on the inhabitants of the New World in addition to a history of the Spanish Conquest and subsequent Christian evangelization of the region:

> [I shall] not only relate the worldly and secular occurrences in my times but also that which touches upon the religious, interposing at times some ethical notes, creating a mixture that includes something of the qualities, nature, and properties of these regions, kingdoms, and lands; as well as what may be found there regarding customs, religion, rituals, ceremonies, and the condition of the indigenous people there. (ibid., 16–17, translation by author)

Las Casas initially planned to include this type of ethnographic material in his *Historia general*. Yet little information of this nature actually made it into the book. Instead Las Casas decided to write a separate work, the *Apologética historia sumaria de las gentes destas Indias* (Apologetic Summary History of the People of these Indies), the book that contains a description of highland Maya ceremonies that are the focus of this chapter.

Nowhere in the *Apologética historia sumaria* does Las Casas give a date for its completion, an important factor in determining his potential sources. Lewis Hanke wrote that Las Casas completed the book as part of his preparation for the Valladolid debate in 1550 (Hanke 1949, 1951, xiv–xv). This is highly unlikely. None of its contents appear in Las Casas's testimony during those debates, the text of which was published soon afterward in 1552 under the direction of Las Casas himself (Las Casas 1992; Hanke 1952, 40–41). Considering his heavy obligations during and after his ministry in the Guatemalan highlands, he would have had little time to devote to such a massive undertaking (the 1966 publication of the text runs to 1,349 pages, not including introductory materials or appendices). It is far more probable that Las Casas did not begin to compile the *Apologética historia* until after 1552, when he revised and expanded his *Historia general* (Las Casas 1967, chapters 23–36). Based on internal evidence from Las Casas's writings, Edmundo O'Gorman suggests that he started to write the *Apologética historia* sometime around 1555 or 1556. Las Casas mentioned the death of Gonzalo Fernández de Oviedo in the *Apologética historia* (which took place in Valladolid in 1557), providing a secure date for at least that portion of the text. The book would have been completed no later than 1559 or so, when Las Casas's poor health prevented him from writing extensively (Las Casas 1967, chapter 35).

Before analyzing Las Casas's description of New Year's observances among the highland Maya it is important to consider where he may have obtained his information. An exploration of these possible sources also provides an opportunity to reach a better understanding of the interaction between early Spanish missionaries and surviving members of the old highland Maya nobility in the years immediately following the Spanish Conquest. At least four major potential sources would have been available to Las Casas in compiling his account. First, he may have obtained the information from indigenous K'iche' nobles at firsthand during his residence in the Spanish administrative capital of Santiago de Guatemala from 1536 to 1537. Second, he may have derived at least some of his knowledge of highland Maya ceremonialism from indigenous painted manuscripts, interpreted for him by K'iche' consultants or Spanish missionaries familiar with their contents. Third, he may have relied on the writings of other priests, principally of the Dominican order (one of these, Domingo de Vico, is known to have written a lengthy treatise on indigenous highland Maya myth and ceremonialism during the years of his residence in the Guatemalan highlands from 1545 to 1555). Finally, Las Casas may have based his writings at least in part on conversations he may have had with a K'iche' lord named don Juan de Cortés who traveled to Spain in 1557 at the very time when Las Casas was composing his *Apologética historia*. The following section briefly considers each of these potential sources in order to determine the nature and validity of the information on Pre-Columbian highland Maya culture that would have been available to him.

LAS CASAS AND DIEGO REYNOSO

Las Casas never claimed that he actually witnessed the New Year's ceremonies that he describes in the *Apologética historia*. These ceremonies involved living Maya rulers who engaged in bloodletting and human sacrifice, practices that were prohibited immediately after the Conquest in the areas that Las Casas worked in the central highlands of Guatemala. Like Landa, Las Casas and other early Christian missionaries in the area would have relied on Maya consultants who witnessed the events they described at firsthand. If Las Casas had obtained this information himself from K'iche' sources, the most likely time would have been soon after he arrived in Guatemala in 1536, when he was engaged in a study of highland Maya languages under Bishop Marroquín.

At least one possible candidate for such an indigenous highland Maya consultant was Diego Reynoso, a K'iche' nobleman who accepted Christianity soon after the Spanish Conquest and subsequently worked closely with the Spanish clergy. Reynoso was the son of Lajuj No'j, who served at the K'iche' royal court in the capital city of Q'umarkaj (Carmack and Mondloch 2007, 94–95). We do not know what his Pre-Conquest Maya name was. Diego Reynoso was the name that he adopted following baptism. Sometime around 1535 Bishop Marroquín brought Reynoso to the Spanish administrative capital of Santiago de Guatemala where he was "taught to read and write" (Ximénez 1929–1931 [1722], book 1, chapter 40, 119; Anonymous 1935 [ca. 1700], book 2, chapter 4, 191; Carmack 1981, 146; van Akkeren 2011, 104). We do not know how old he was at the time. The anonymous Dominican author of the *Isagoge histórica apologética* (1700–1711) writes that he was already an *indio principal* (principal Indian) when he arrived in Santiago, so he must have been a person of sufficient maturity to warrant a position among the K'iche' nobility (Anonymous 1935 [ca. 1700], book 2, chapter 4, 191). Reynoso was undoubtedly born before the Spanish Conquest of 1524 and could recall the major ceremonial practices in his home city of Q'umarkaj that he witnessed growing up. Reynoso at some point prior to the 1550s received the title Popol Winaq, an honorific given to members of the K'iche' Maya governing council (Carmack and Mondloch 1983, 182).

Soon after he arrived at the Spanish capital under the auspices of Bishop Marroquín, Reynoso began to work with Roman Catholic missionaries from Spain, helping them to compose religious tracts in the K'iche' Maya language for use in their evangelization efforts. One of these is a now-lost manuscript on the Passion of Christ that was quoted by both the anonymous author of the *Isagoge* and by Francisco Ximénez more than a century later. In his role as a member of the indigenous K'iche' hierarchy, Reynoso was the principal author of the *Título de Totonicapán* (fig. 20), completed in 1554, a land title claiming sovereignty rights over K'iche' territories based on Pre-Columbian precedent (Carmack and Mondloch 1983, 14–15; van Akkeren 2011, 104). This document is second in importance only to the *Popol Vuh* among early colonial K'iche' texts, containing extensive information on Pre-Columbian history, myth, and ceremonial practices. Reynoso would have been an ideal source for

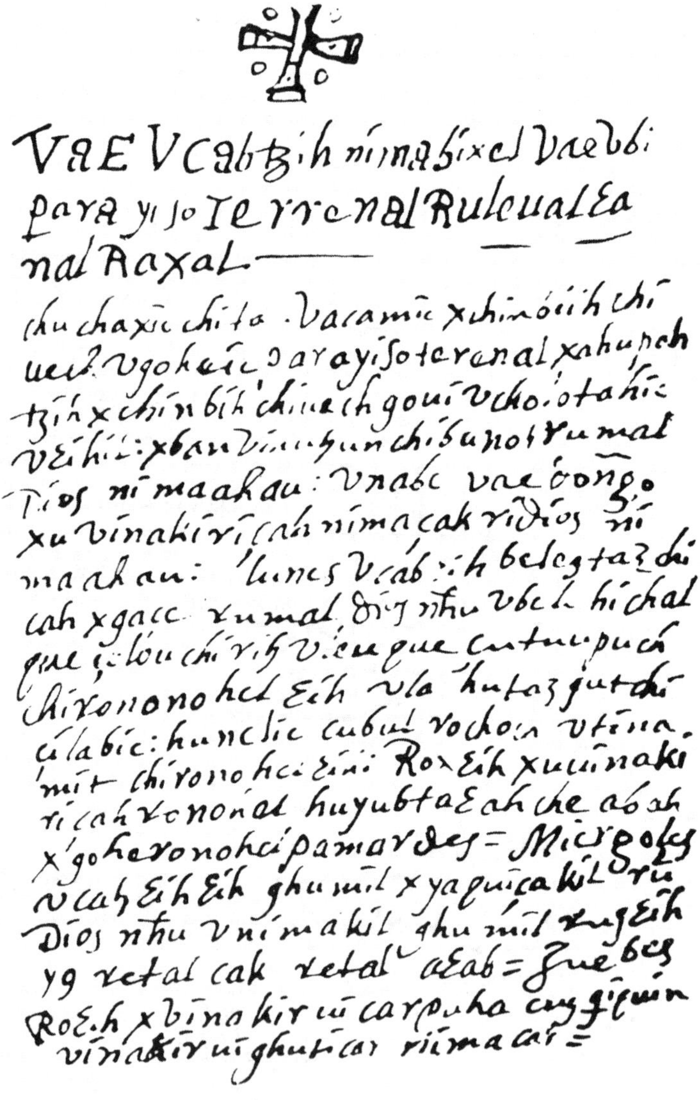

20. Título de Totonicapán. *Courtesy Robert Carmack*

this kind of information, being the son of a K'iche' nobleman and an important member of the K'iche' aristocracy in his own right.

Las Casas arrived in Santiago de Guatemala in 1536, approximately the same time when Reynoso was brought to the city by Bishop Marroquín. The two men studied with the bishop and no doubt knew each other well. It is perhaps significant that Las Casas's account of the origin of the K'iche' kingdom parallels the account written by Diego Reynoso in the *Título de Totonicapán* in specific ways. For example, Las Casas notes that the four principal lords of the K'iche's each had a certain number of canopies:

> The king had four canopies of very fine feathers, one above the other so that the waters from each fell upon the other, for they were not joined but separate—a thing worthy of a great lord and not a little was it seen and praised. The administrator of the king had three canopies, and the other two had two each. (Las Casas 1958, chapter 234, 342–343, translation by author)

Diego Reynoso also emphasized the canopies of the four K'iche' lords in his account of the founding of the K'iche' kingdom in the *Título de Totonicapán*:

> The lord Ajpop has four canopies with green feathers over his throne, a bone flute, and a drum. The Ajpop K'amja has three canopies above him. The Nima Rajpop Achij two canopies, and the Ch'uti Rajpop Achij only one. (Carmack and Mondloch 2007, 98–99, translation by author)

Although the canopies of the K'iche' lords are mentioned in other indigenous texts, only Las Casas and Reynoso agree in assigning four canopies to the principal lord, with fewer canopies belonging to each of the three other lords in descending numbers. The *Popol Vuh* and the *Título K'oyoi* both mention royal canopies but do not number them (Christenson 2003, line 7429; Carmack 1973, 294). Although this is hardly conclusive evidence, it does at least suggest that Reynoso's information was consistent with that included by Las Casas in his book.

LAS CASAS AND INDIGENOUS HIGHLAND MAYA TEXTS

Las Casas may also have had access to the contents of painted manuscripts composed by the Maya themselves, at least to some degree. He claims to have seen examples of these texts and to have known enough about their contents that he could describe them as containing information on history, religion, and calendrics. Las Casas included this description in his account of the traditions in highland Guatemala, specifically the regions of "Ultlatlán [the

K'iche' kingdom], Guatimala [the Kaqchikel kingdom, centered at Iximche'], and Tezulutlán [the Alta Verapaz]":

> I wish to touch upon the opinions that they [the inhabitants of highland Guatemala] had concerning the creation and also the flood. For it should be known that in all the republics of those great lands and kingdoms of New Spain, and others, among the offices and officials, there were those who served as chroniclers and historians. These knew the origins of all things concerning their religion, gods, and rituals, as well as the founding of their towns and cities; how the dynasties of their kings and lords began; the method of their elections and successions; of the number and identities of the lords of the past; their works and deeds and memorable acts, both good and bad; how well or poorly they governed; the great and good men, the valiant captains that governed; the wars that they had waged and how they had distinguished themselves. They knew of the earliest traditions of the first inhabitants and whether their migrations came out well or not, and everything that pertains to history so that there would be understanding and memory of things past. These chroniclers kept a count of the days, months, and years, and although they did not have writing like ours, they nevertheless had figures and characters with which they could signify anything they wished, and these great books were of such ingenuity and subtle artifice that we might say that our own letters in this regard would be of little advantage to them. (Las Casas 1967, chapter 235, 504–505, translation by author)

An intriguing passage in Las Casas's account of the highland Maya New Year's celebrations suggests that he may have based part of his knowledge on the contents of a painted text or *lienzo*. He wrote that the robe worn by the Maya high priest during the climactic sacrifice could not be described, since "none among us have seen it." He then went on to describe the robe with a great deal of detail, adding the phrase *según figuran ellos* (according to what they represent/draw) (Las Casas 1967, chapter 178, 151). This is the same phraseology that Las Casas used in the passage above to describe the contents of indigenous paintings that he saw, which were composed of *figuras y carácteres* (drawings/figures and characters) that were unlike European letters (ibid., chapter 225, 504). This suggests that Las Casas either saw a painted image of the priest's robes himself or was quoting another Spaniard who did and that he based his description on that image.

Painted manuscripts were apparently used widely in the Guatemalan highlands as an aid in prognosticating future events. It is one of the great tragedies of New World history that none of these indigenous highland Maya manuscripts are known to have survived from the early Post-Conquest period. Las Casas witnessed the destruction of a number of Maya texts, some perhaps in the highlands, that were burned in an effort to "protect" the Maya from their traditional beliefs: "Some of our clergy have seen these books, and even I saw a portion of them which have since been burned, for the friars felt that at this time, at the beginning of their conversion, that they would perhaps do them harm" (Las Casas 1967, chapter 235, 504–505, translation by author).

Although no known indigenous painted manuscript from the highlands survived these purges, the K'iche' authors of the *Popol Vuh* (composed using a modified Latin script sometime between 1554 and 1558) asserted that they based their writings on an ancient Pre-Columbian book that bore the same name (Christenson 2007, 33, 64, 259). Ancient K'iche' rulers before the Spanish Conquest consulted the ancient version of the *Popol Vuh* in times of national distress as a means of seeing their world with greater clarity: "They knew if there would be war. It was clear before their faces. They saw if there would be death, if there would be hunger. They surely knew if there would be strife. There was an instrument of sight. There was a book. *Popol Vuh* was their name for it" (Christenson 2007, 287).

The Pre-Columbian version of the *Popol Vuh* has unfortunately been lost, at least so far as non-Maya investigators are concerned. Even the authors of the sixteenth-century version wrote that the more ancient book could no longer be seen in their day and that what they compiled was based on the original (Christenson 2007, 64). But early Spanish missionary priests in highland Guatemala were aware of the existence of indigenous painted manuscripts. One of these was seen by Alonso de Zorita, the *oidor* (principal judge) of Guatemala, who represented the legal interests of the governing tribunal in Mexico. In March 1555 Zorita initiated a six-month tour of inspection in the Guatemalan highlands. He found that in much of the region the Maya continued to worship their ancient gods in secret and gave special attention in his report to the seizure of a large number of idols, having sent warnings ahead in each town that he came to that they must relinquish their gods to him or suffer severe punishment (Zorita 1963, 35). In addition to carrying out his duties as judge, Zorita also interviewed local indigenous rulers regarding economic and political affairs. As part of his travels, he visited the ancient K'iche' capital city at Q'umarkaj (known also by its Tlaxcalan name of Utatlan). There he met with the descendants of the K'iche' ruling dynasty who still held some measure of political authority as indigenous *caciques*. Zorita named these lords as don Juan de Rojas, don Juan Cortés, and Domingo. Zorita included in his report a reference to an indigenous Maya painted source that contained a history of the K'iche's dating back centuries before the Spanish Conquest:

> Through the services of a religious of the Dominican Order, a great servant of Our Lord and a very fine interpreter, a most learned and eloquent preacher who is now bishop, I learned with the aid of paintings that they had which recorded their history for more than eight hundred years back, and which were interpreted for me by very ancient Indians. (Zorita 1963, 272)

The unnamed Dominican priest who served as Zorita's translator could only have been Fray Tomás de Cárdenas. Cárdenas arrived in Guatemala in 1553 and served in the Dominican monastery at Santiago de Guatemala, where he was one of the few early missionary priests who learned K'iche' well. Cárdenas did indeed later become the bishop of Verapaz from 1574 until his death in 1578. The presence of such paintings is also documented for the Tz'utujil Maya of the Lake Atitlán region in Guatemala. The following account was recorded in 1577 with regard to the Tz'utujil community of San Andrés, a community located near Santiago Atitlán:

> They gathered the old men of the town and took out certain ancient paintings that they had, in which they counted the months and years. They cast lots, and by the painting on which the lot fell, they knew and understood the time in which there was to be war, famine, or pestilence which had been declared by their *demonio* [god's image]. And in this way they ascertained when all that which their [god] had indicated would happen. (Acuña 1982, 128, translation by author)

Three of the four Maya hieroglyphic codices from the Maya lowlands known to have survived the Spanish Conquest contain just this type of divinatory information in the form of day counts with their associated auguries. As noted above, Las Casas claimed to have seen Pre-Columbian painted manuscripts in the Guatemalan highlands and would have had the opportunity to discuss their contents with indigenous K'iche' noblemen like Diego Reynoso. It is perhaps more likely that he became aware of their contents secondhand from other Dominican clerics familiar with indigenous sources composed within the sphere of their influence.

LAS CASAS AND FRAY DOMINGO DE VICO

In his introduction to chapter 235 of the *Apologética historia*, which deals with the language and religion of the ancient highland Maya, Las Casas wrote that what was known in his day concerning these things came from the work of unnamed members of the Dominican Order who were then diligently "penetrating the secrets" of highland Maya language and customs (Las Casas 1967, chapter 235, 504). He acknowledged that he relied on their knowledge. Las Casas apparently derived at least part of his account of the New Year's observances from sources written by one or more of these unnamed Dominican missionaries. Dominican accounts must have been compiled and made available to him prior to the completion of the *Apologética historia*, sometime before 1559. Although Las Casas failed to name his sources, there were very few who possessed the linguistic ability and contacts necessary to compile such a detailed account of ancient highland Maya ceremonies. The most likely candidate is Fray Domingo de Vico, who served in Guatemala from January 1545 until his death in 1555 (fig. 21). Remesal wrote in his history of Guatemala that his principal source for the ritual practices of the highland Maya was a "large" book on Maya religion and culture written by Vico:

> Those first padres who worked with the idolatrous Indians took great care to know the histories of their superstitions, the origin of their gods, the beginning of their idolatry, and from whence they derived the abomination of their sacrifices. Father Domingo de Vico wrote in the Cachiquel language and the language of the Verapaz a large book on this subject, so that the padres that came later, while learning the language in order to preach the truth to the Indians, would know of these lies in order to drive them away. (Remesal 1964 [1619], book, 7, 420, translation by author)

The large book mentioned by Remesal was entitled *Todas las historias, fábulas, consejos, patrañas y errores en que vivían* (All the Histories, Fables, Counsels, Tales, and Errors in Which They Lived) (Remesal 1966, book 10, chapter 8, 297). If Las Casas used Vico as a source for at least some of his knowledge concerning the culture of highland Guatemala, which seems probable, this book would have been invaluable to him. Its title suggests that it contained information similar to that found in the *Apologética historia.* Las Casas was a dedicated scholar and collected a large number of treatises, particularly those that he considered to be the most authentic and original sources of information. While engaged in his ministry in Guatemala, Las Casas gathered letters and documents from many parts of America. Lewis Hanke suggests that "no historian writing about the Americas has collected first-hand reports so assiduously" (Hanke 1952, 7, 23–25). Even after permanently settling in Spain in 1547, he continued to solicit documents from the New World, accumulating a vast library of books and manuscripts in Valladolid. These he used in compiling his own histories. Although it is unknown

21. *Domingo de Vico. Photograph by Ruud van Akkeren*

when Vico wrote his book on highland Maya religion and ceremonialism, it would of course have been composed before 1555, when Vico was killed in a Q'eqchi' uprising in the Alta Verapaz region. Thus it was potentially available to Las Casas before he completed the *Apologética historia* around 1559. It is regrettable that Las Casas's personal archives were never catalogued after his death. His collection of documents has since been either lost or destroyed.

Scholars would dearly love to know what was in Vico's book on highland Maya religion. Unfortunately not a single copy is known to have survived after Remesal used it in preparing his history of the Indies, published in 1619. Robert Carmack attempted to locate it without success, despite a concerted search in the archives of Spain, France, and the Americas (Carmack 1973, 100; 2011, 19). In the past few years Garry Sparks has made a similar search in the archives of Guatemala for any manuscripts written by Vico but has also thus far been unable to locate this particular work (personal communication, 2014). It may have been lost over the intervening centuries or may be languishing somewhere waiting to be found in yet another dusty archive. Although it is not unusual for sixteenth-century manuscripts to disappear, writings concerning ancient Maya religion such as the work compiled by Vico have fared particularly poorly. Carmack believes that the loss of works of this type may have been the result of a conscious effort to destroy or hide such information, consistent with the early friars' tendency to "suppress reports about the persisting native religion" (Carmack 1973, 89).

There is no reason to doubt that Las Casas would have known of Vico's work and followed it closely, as Las Casas was the one who first convinced Vico to leave the Dominican college at Salamanca and go to Guatemala in 1544 (Remesal 1966, book 10, chapter 6, 1, 289). They would have known each other well. The focus of Las Casas's notes on the religion and culture of the highland Maya is perhaps significant. He specifically mentions the provinces of "Ultlatlan" (Utatlan, the Tlaxcalan/Spanish name for the K'iche' region centered at Q'umarkaj), "Guatimala" (Guatemala, the Kaqchikel region centered at Iximche'), and "Tezulutlan" (the Q'eqchi' Maya province of the Alta Verapaz) (Las Casas 1967, chapters 234–235, 342–345). These happen to be the same three regions where Domingo de Vico carried out his extensive linguistic and ethnographic work. It is doubtful that this is a coincidence. I believe that Vico is the best candidate for some if not all of Las Casas's description of the New Year's ceremonies in the Guatemalan highlands.

Vico would have been in a unique position to elicit the kind of information found in Las Casas's book. He arrived in Guatemala in 1544, soon enough after the Spanish Conquest to have interacted with any number of indigenous consultants with firsthand memories of ceremonies that took place at the old centers of highland Maya power. He was also among the first of the Dominican missionaries to undertake the peaceful evangelization of the Verapaz region. In other words, he came into contact with highland Maya communities that were still ruled by indigenous lords and practiced ancient Pre-Columbian ceremonies before the population of the region was introduced to Christianity.

Vico's linguistic skills were extraordinary. According to Remesal, he was dedicated to learning the languages of the indigenous groups wherever he went and spoke seven Maya languages:

> When he came to Guatemala, he made himself master of all that pertained to that province. And he hadn't trod more than three or four days in a town before he knew their language so well that he could speak it as if it was his first and mother tongue, even though it was a singular and unusual language. And with this perfection, he came to know seven different languages. (Remesal 1966, book 10, chapter 8, 2–3, 297, translation by author; see also book 10, chapter 6, 1, 289)

Despite Remesal's obvious exaggerations, Vico's language abilities were unquestionably excellent. Fray Francisco Ximénez noted that Vico had written treatises on Christian doctrine in Kaqchikel, K'iche', Tz'utujil, Q'eqchi', Pokomam, and Lakandon that were still used by Roman Catholic priests in various communities in his day at the beginning of the eighteenth century (Ximénez 1929–1931 [1722], book 1, chapter 23, 57–58). Vico was one of the first priests to compile linguistic studies in highland Maya languages, most notably a remarkable dictionary and grammar in the K'iche', Kaqchikel, and Tz'utujil languages, which has survived in manuscript form. Vico's dictionary contained accurate descriptions of the highland Maya calendar, including some of the earliest information on the five nameless days preceding New Year's. Carmack claims that his linguistic work is "unexcelled among Spanish writings in terms of accuracy and familiarity with native culture" (Carmack 1973, 115).

Vico worked closely with highland Maya lords and their families. From 1551 to 1554, he served as the prior of the Dominican Convent in the Spanish capital city of Santiago de Guatemala. In this capacity he was assigned by Bishop Marroquín to instruct the children of Maya lords in Christian doctrine as well as how to read and write using Latin characters. Among those who attended the school were some of the future authors of important indigenous texts such as the *Memorial de Sololá*, the *Popol Vuh*, and the *Título de Totonicapán*. The *Memorial de Sololá*, composed by members of the Kaqchikel nobility, noted the death of Vico in 1555 and asserted that *qitzij chi nima ajtij qatata'* (truly a great teacher [was] our father) (Maxwell and Hill 2006, 301, translation by author), suggesting that some or all of its authors attended Vico's school.

The principal work written by Vico that has survived is the *Theologia Indorum*, a lengthy theological text written in the K'iche'-Maya language. The

Theologia was written in two parts. Part one was completed in February 1553 and consists of a redaction of Old Testament history and doctrine from the creation of the world until the coming of Christ. The second part was completed in 1554 and describes the lives of various saints as well as the final judgment (Ximénez 1929–1931 [1722], book 1, chapter 23, 57–58). Although the original manuscript written by Vico is lost, many of the numerous copies made over the years have survived. The work was so well respected in his day that several indigenous highland Maya texts incorporated passages from it into their own writings. Diego Reynoso included large portions of the *Theologia Indorum* in the introductory section of the *Título de Totonicapán*, compiled about a year after Vico completed his work (Carmack and Mondloch 2007, 10–12). It is a testament to Vico's linguistic skills that the Maya themselves would borrow heavily from his writings. More than this, however, the timing suggests that Reynoso and perhaps others may have assisted Vico in the composition of the *Theologia* (van Akkeren 2011, 104–107; Sparks 2011a, 2011b). Such close collaboration would have given Vico the opportunity to question members of the K'iche' hierarchy of his day regarding matters touching on their religious practices in antiquity that he later included in his "large book" on highland Maya beliefs.

Many of the same gods and mythic locations listed by Las Casas in his *Apologética historia* also appear in Vico's writings, suggesting a familiarity with Vico's works. Chapter 25 of the *Theologia Indorum* concerns the "idolatry" of the highland Maya. In this chapter Vico lists the gods of the underworld realm of Xibalba that were worshipped in antiquity:

> Great in your hearts is Xibalba, great in your hearts are Hunahpu, Xbalanqueh, Taçul Huracan, Ɛeteb Pubaix, Hun Hunahpu, Vucub Hunahpu, Hun Came, Vucub Came, Quic R'e, Quic R'ixcac, Mam, Yɛ Choa, Voc Hunahpu. (Acuña 1985, 291, translation by author)

Several of these gods appear in chapter 235 of Las Casas's *Apologética historia* as well as in contemporary indigenous Maya texts, particularly the *Popol Vuh* and the *Título de Totonicapán*. These include Hunahpu and Xbalanqueh. In K'iche' tradition these twin gods defeated the lords of death in the underworld prior to their apotheosis as the sun and moon, thus establishing the present era of time (Christenson 2007, 158–191; Carmack and Mondloch 2007, 66–67). Xbalanqueh also appears in the creation account found in the *Título de Totonicapán*, likely written by Diego Reynoso, with the same spelling as appears in both the *Theologia Indorum* and Las Casas's *Apologética historia*. In other contemporary Maya texts, such as the *Popol Vuh*, the name of the god is written consistently as "Xbalanque" without the terminal *h*. In addition to Reynoso, Vico undoubtedly interacted with a number of members of the K'iche' nobility in his school or in his ministry for whom this type of information would have been common knowledge.

LAS CASAS AND DON JUAN DE CORTÉS

Las Casas often visited with indigenous lords and *caciques* who came to Spain following the Council of Valladolid in 1550 (Las Casas 1967, chapters 23–36). On occasion he intervened personally by aiding visiting nobles in preparing their cases and even arguing for them at court. The petition of one don Francisco Tenamaztle who came to Spain to ask the royal court for redress concerning mistreatment in Mexico was written by Las Casas himself in or about 1555 (Hanke and Giménez Fernández 1954, 171–172).

Among the indigenous rulers who visited the Spanish court was the K'iche' lord don Juan de Cortés. Although K'iche' lords continued to exercise some authority, such as the right to appoint subsidiary governors, the Spanish Crown had revoked their tribute rights. Don Juan Cortés as Ajpop K'amja, the second highest position in the K'iche' hierarchy, would have been responsible for collecting such tribute, and he repeatedly petitioned the Spaniards to restore these rights (Tedlock 1996, 56). In 1557 he traveled to Spain to press his claims directly to the Spanish Crown. In support of his efforts he was accompanied by a Dominican priest (that order had been particularly sympathetic to the restoration of some indigenous royal privileges). Spanish authorities often recognized land claims and some limited sovereignty for important indigenous noble lineages if these could be documented based on written proof of genealogy and history. Many sixteenth-century highland Maya texts were prepared specifically as "royal titles" and were duly signed by indigenous rulers as legal documents. The *Título de Totonicapán*, for example, was written as a title of territorial possession presented as a claim to the Spanish Crown for *cacique* privileges (Carmack 1973, 28–29). Other K'iche' documents were also composed in order to assert territorial rights elsewhere in the Guatemalan highlands, including the *Título Tamub*, the four *Títulos Nijaib*, the *Título Sacapulas*, the *Título C'oyoi*, the *Título Huitzitzil Tzunun*, the *Título Zapotitlan*, and the *Título Santa Clara*. Where possible, these titles were based on Pre-Columbian sources or the testimony of "old men" who had lived before the Spanish Conquest. Such firsthand information served to bolster the authenticity of the *caciques'* claims in court. Dennis Tedlock suggests that don Juan Cortés may even have carried a copy of the recently compiled *Popol Vuh* with him as proof of his claims to sovereignty (Tedlock 1996, 56). While this is impossible to prove one way or the other, Cortés must have carried with him official documents of some type to confirm his claim.

Unfortunately the luckless K'iche' lord's vessel was attacked at sea by French pirates who seized his possessions, including some if not all of his official documents (Carrasco 1967, 254). Perhaps because of the lack of written evidence to prove his claim for sovereignty rights, Cortés's petition was ultimately declined, and he returned to Guatemala empty-handed.

It is probable that Las Casas would have met with don Juan Cortés during his official visit to Spain, which took place at the time when Las Casas was writing his *Apologética historia*. The K'iche' ruler was accompanied by a Dominican priest who would certainly have contacted Las Casas, still the most influential Dominican cleric at the Spanish court in matters concerning indigenous rights. Considering his intense interest in manuscripts regarding Maya history and religion, Las Casas would no doubt have inquired about the contents of the documents that don Juan carried with him and requested copies of any that might have survived the French pirate attack. Even if don Juan was not the primary source for the information in the *Apologética historia*, he would have been an ideal consultant in correcting or augmenting Las Casas's writings on K'iche' belief and ceremonialism.

THE INFLUENCE OF THE *APOLOGÉTICA HISTORIA SUMARIA* IN OTHER EARLY COLONIAL WRITINGS

Las Casas's *Apologética historia* was well known among Spanish historians and clerics. Large sections of the book were quoted in works composed in the early colonial period. The chapters on New Year's observances that are the focus of the remainder of this chapter were copied with some alterations in two other major sources. The first was in book 1, chapters 10 and 17–18 of the *Repúblicas de Indias*, a history of the "idolatries and government" of ancient Mexico and Peru prior to the Spanish Conquest, published in 1575 by Jerónimo Román y Zamora, an Augustinian monk and historian.

Although it is doubtful that Román y Zamora ever traveled to the Americas himself, he had access to all the sources on Guatemalan religion and history available in Spain, some of which have since been lost. It would be simple enough to assume that Román y Zamora simply copied his material on the highland Maya New Year's ceremonies directly from Las Casas, particularly since entire paragraphs from each are virtually identical. Yet significant information that appears in each does not appear in the other. This strongly implies that at least some of the material in the writings of Las Casas and Román y Zamora was based on an unknown earlier written source, perhaps Domingo de Vico's lost book.

The second major version of Las Casas's description of Pre-Columbian New Year's observances is found in book 1, chapters 29–30, of the *Historia de la Provincia de San Vicente de Chiapa y Guatemala*, published by Fray Francisco Ximénez in 1722. Although he mostly follows Román y Zamora's secondhand version of the story, Ximénez adds significant ethnographic information that clarifies important elements of the account. Ximénez is a uniquely authoritative source because he was an outstanding linguist in his own right and had served as parish priest in K'iche' communities since 1694. Ximénez was intensely interested in the ancient traditions of the K'iche's. Between 1701 and 1704 he served as the parish priest of Chichicastenango, the community where most of the descendants of the K'iche' nobility settled after the mid-sixteenth century. Ximénez's curiosity concerning ancient highland Maya history and religion may have overcome the suspicion of the local Maya elders who allowed him to borrow and make a copy of the *Popol Vuh* manuscript, the first time that text is known to have been seen by non-Maya since it was composed in the sixteenth century. It is beneficial to refer to the commentaries of both Román y Zamora and Ximénez in order to supplement Las Casas's version of the ceremonial cycle associated with highland Maya New Year's observances.

HIGHLAND MAYA NEW YEAR'S OBSERVANCES

In his *Apologética historia* Las Casas wrote that the major ceremonies carried out by the Maya of the Guatemalan highlands took place during a period that he called the *cuaresma* (Lent), which fell on the last days of the indigenous Maya calendar, including the five days of the Wayeb'. The Spanish word *cuaresma* is derived from the Latin *quadragesima* (fortieth), because the Lenten season is approximately forty days in European Christian tradition, beginning on Ash Wednesday and ending on Easter Sunday. Las Casas undoubtedly chose the term *cuaresma* because, like the Wayeb', it is a period of intense prayer, penance, and self-denial preceding a sacred day of rebirth or resurrection (of Christ in the case of Easter and of the world itself in the case of the Maya New Year's Day).

Las Casas describes the highland Maya *cuaresma* as the period just before the close of the 365-day solar calendar year, a "universal sacrifice" in which "all the people and community participated" (Las Casas 1958, chapter 177, 148). Because it was timed according to the ancient Maya calendar, Las Casas began his account of the New Year's observances with a description of how the calendar was organized:

> The great calendar had eighteen [months] of twenty days each, and this was the way they counted and divided time. Each twenty days of this calendar had a name, just as we give a name to each of our months; and each day also had its name, and to each was dedicated an idol that they believed presided over that day. (Las Casas 1958, chapter 177, 148, translation by author)

Román y Zamora expanded on this brief description of the calendar, adding that the final five days at the close of the 365-day period were observed with solemn rituals prior to the celebration of the New Year:

> They had a calendar of the year, with days and months. They had a year of three hundred and sixty-five days; they had eighteen months, each month having twenty days . . . with five days left over. They did not know to include, as we do, the leap year, because they did not realize that there were an additional six hours in our year. . . .
>
> Each day had its fiesta as well as its own idol. There were fiestas and holidays during the year, principally those five days left over at the end of the year that they called *baldíos* [Spanish useless, barren, wasted]. They observed these five days with great solemnity, with great sacrifices performed on each one of them until the new year arrived, which was in March. (Román y Zamora 1897, book 1, chapter 10, 125–126, translation by author)

Ximénez repeated the same information found in Román y Zamora's account but appended additional information concerning the five extra days, recording that those days were not associated with any legitimate god and that the Maya in his day continued to observe them in secret:

> The other five days left over they called closed days, and said that they did not have a *dueño* [lord, master, owner]. . . . All this is full of superstition, and they are still governed by this calendar even until now in many towns; but this they do in great secrecy. (Ximénez 1929–1931 [1722], book 1, chapter 36, 102, translation by author)

As Román y Zamora pointed out, the ancient highland Maya calendar year began in March, the time of the first maize planting (Román y Zamora 1897, 1:125–126; Carmack 1981, 87–88). Apparently because of its proximity to the Lenten season on the Christian calendar, both falling in early spring, Las Casas associated the five days prior to the Maya New Year with the Christian season of Lent, particularly because both focus on fasting and other forms of abstinence. Both Román y Zamora and Ximénez follow Las Casas in linking the final days of the highland Maya calendar with Lent but make the association even stronger by calling the Maya New Year itself *pascua* (Easter):

> Now the people of this Province [Guatemala] knew the time when *la pascua* commenced, and when to carry out the preparations for it; they began their fast called *cuaresma* (for this is what we understand is the major fast that they did, like that which we call Lent), and this they did, all gathering with great devotion, the men as well as the women. (Román y Zamora 1897, 1:xviii, 195, translation by author; see also Ximénez 1929–1931 [1722], book 1, chapter 30, 83)

I believe that Román y Zamora and Ximénez were not alone in associating the Maya New Year with Easter and that the Maya of the Guatemalan highlands conflated the two almost immediately after the Spanish Conquest. As seen in chapter 1, the Wayeb' ceremonies preceding the ancient Maya New Year were linked with Easter soon after the Spanish Conquest in the Yucatan region. Román y Zamora's reference implies that this was true in the highlands as well.

The regular order of highland Maya communities was disrupted during the time prior to New Year's Day. As in Yucatan, the highland Maya marked the final days of the old year by blackening their bodies with soot, abstaining from sexual relations, fasting, and rendering sacrificial offerings—including offering their own blood:

> Once the day is known, they observe the festival with abstinence, and this pertained to all, both small and great. They had to leave the beds of their wives for 68 or 100 days, more or less, according to the solemnity or necessity that was demanded. During all these days, everyone underwent self-sacrifice, shedding blood from the fleshy parts of their arms, from their thighs, from their tongues, and from other parts a certain number of times a day and night. They also burned incense and other things. Men were not to bathe, and they blackened themselves with smoke from torches, so that they appeared as black as the devil, and this was an indication and sign of penitence. All had to sleep, not in their own houses, but in those prepared during the time of this penitence near the temples. Fire was constantly kept burning in the braziers next to the temples.
>
> All kept these ceremonies inviolate, for if it became known that anyone broke [these requirements] they were harshly punished, and they had a terrible fear that they would surely die soon thereafter, for they considered this sin to be very serious. And we know from our clerics that this commonly

> happened either because the devil (God permitting) caused their death . . . or because having imagined that committing such a sin was so serious, that they would die just from sheer sorrow. (Las Casas 1958, chapter 177, 148–149, translation by author)

Las Casas emphasizes that ceremonies carried out in the final days of the Maya calendar year were particularly fraught with danger and that the Maya feared retribution if traditional rituals were not performed properly according to established precedent. Landa also noted that the Maya were especially anxious regarding ceremonies conducted during the Wayeb' days in his description of the Yucatec New Year's observances, writing that "in case misfortunes came, they [the Maya priests] made the people understand and believe that it was owing to some sin or fault in the services or in those who performed them" and "they believed that if they did not observe these ceremonies, they would be sure to have certain sicknesses" (Landa 1941, 136, 142, 152). This may simply be due to the Maya's general fear regarding the failure to perform ritual obligations, but both Landa and Las Casas stress that this was particularly true of New Year's ceremonies, undoubtedly because they are linked with the death of the world.

In Santiago Atitlán today, if a leading planner or participant in a major ceremonial observance falls ill, particularly during Holy Week, it becomes a significant topic of conversation in the community as to what violation of tradition that person may have committed to warrant punishment. If the perceived breach is severe, people often say that they expect that person to die as a result. This is because people believe that during the days of Holy Week the deities and saints that normally watch over and protect them, particularly Jesus Christ, are overcome by death and hence normal activities are suspended. People are therefore particularly susceptible during that time to the punishment of malevolent entities that come out to afflict those who do not act properly with disease and even death.

WORLD RENEWAL AND THE MAYA BALLGAME

The Wayeb' rites that immediately precede the Yucatec New Year involve the temporary death or removal of the principal life-bearing gods from their accustomed places. This is consistent with the overall death of the world at the close of the calendric cycle. The next section of Las Casas's account suggests that the gods of the highland Maya also undergo passage into the underworld during the days of their New Year's ceremonies, symbolized by their placement in the community's ballcourt:

> They decorated and adorned their idols for these fiestas and sacrifices with gold, precious stones, and mantles, the finest materials that they had and could use. They placed [the idols] on litters and carried them in procession with inestimable devotion accompanied by drums and trumpets and other musical instruments. They carried them to plazas that they always had in prominent places in the towns for playing ball, and there the lords and principal persons played ball before them in order to celebrate them. (Las Casas 1958, chapter 177, 149, translation by author)

Ancient Maya rulers are frequently depicted on ceramics as well as carved stone panels playing a sacred ballgame in which they reenact the confrontation of ancestral gods with death lords. Among the Maya the ballgame was not played for simple entertainment, at least not in the kind of ritual context described in Las Casas's account. Rather, it was a means of regenerating the world (Miller 2001, 86; Stone and Zender 2011, 67). In ancient Mesoamerica ballcourts represent a cleft in the earth leading to the underworld realm of gods who have the power to cause death and disease (Miller and Houston 1987; Scarborough and Wilcox 1991; Freidel et al. 1993, 348–370; Miller and Taube 1993, 43; Whittington 2001, 46–48, 115; Mendoza 2008, 414–418; Stone and Zender 2011, 101). Players symbolically fill the roles of gods, thus becoming engaged in a larger conflict between the Lords of Life and the Lords of Death.

The link between ballcourts and the underworld is explicit in monuments from the Maya Classic period. A series of thirteen panels on the upper stairway of Yaxchilan Temple 33 depicts a ritual ballgame played by King Bird Jaguar IV, who reigned from AD 752 to 768 (fig. 22). The hieroglyphic text accompanying the central panel of the series notes that the game took place in the Ek' Way (Black Transformation), the symbolic portal into the underworld. Here the ballplayers *och bih* (enter the road), one of the principal glyphic statements indicating the death of an individual (Freidel et al. 1993, 351). The implication is that human kings metaphorically descend into the underworld ballcourt at significant times of crisis in their community in order to confront death itself, often in the guise of a war captive. Ultimately the opposing player would be defeated and sacrificed as a token of the king's victory over death. His reemergence from the ballcourt in triumph was perceived as the reestablishment of life-giving power in the upper world.

Each of the three ballcourt markers from Copan Ballcourt A-IIb, dating to the reign of Waxaklajuun Ub'aah K'awiil (695–738), depicts supernaturals playing the ballgame within a quatrefoil frame representing an underworld portal. On the central marker of the series (fig. 23), the king, dressed in the

22. *Ritual ballgame, Step 7, Structure 33, Yaxchilan*

guise of the god Jun Ajaw, confronts a Death Lord on the other side of a large ball (Fash 1991, 114; Freidel et al. 1993, 366–368; Houston et al. 2006, 205). Houston et al. write that Jun Ajaw served "as an exemplar for kings" and embodied the themes of "resurgence, recycling and mythic charter" (Houston et al. 2006, 205). As in Las Casas's account cited above, the king himself played the game in the ballcourt, thus replicating the actions of the primordial gods in the underworld. Ancient Maya kings who performed sacred dramas clothed in the garments of deity were not merely engaged in mummery but shared in the divinity of those gods. They were not "theatrical illusion but a tangible, physical manifestation of a deity" (Houston and Stuart 1996, 299).

In Las Casas's account the patron gods of the K'iche's were carried to the ballcourt, an indication that they were taken from their accustomed places of power to a location associated with death and the underworld during the final days of the calendar year (fig. 24). These richly adorned gods oversaw the game played by the ruling lords in their presence. I think it likely that the K'iche' lords in this account, like the ancient Maya kings before them, conceived of themselves as proxies, playing the game on behalf of the attendant gods. Their presumed victory in the game reflected the defeat of death by the gods themselves.

23. *(Left) Central marker, Copan Ballcourt A-IIb. Drawing by Barbara Fash*

24. *(Below) Ballcourt at the K'iche' capital of Q'umarkaj*

A more direct link to Las Casas's description of the procession to the ballcourt is found in the *Popol Vuh*, a highland Maya text composed by descendants of the Pre-Columbian K'iche' nobility who conducted these ceremonies only a few decades earlier. Jun Ajaw, the god who plays the ballgame in the Copan ballcourt markers, is the Classic period equivalent of the highland Maya god Hunahpu, the twin brother of Xbalanque and son of Hun Hunahpu, the founding ancestral god in the narrative of the *Popol Vuh* (Houston et al. 2006, 205; Stone and Zender 2011, 45; Coe 2011, 68). In the *Popol Vuh* the twin sons of Hun Hunahpu were summoned by the Lords of Death to descend into their underworld realm of Xibalba to confront them in a ballcourt. Ultimately the Hero Twins succeeded in defeating death and resurrecting their father, who had also been summoned to play in the underworld ballcourt but had been defeated and sacrificed.

The *Popol Vuh* account serves as a metaphor for the cycle of life itself and is likely the mythic origin of the New Year's ballgame as described by Las Casas. The *Popol Vuh* offers the following description of the Hero Twins' summons to Xibalba:

> Messengers have arrived from Xibalba, the messengers of One Death and Seven Death. "In seven days they will come here to play ball with us. They must bring their gaming things—the rubber ball, yokes, arm protectors, and leathers. They will liven up this place," say the lords. (Christenson 2007, 159)

The final lines of this passage are a play on words, mocking the Hero Twins as "live" beings entering into the place of death. The descent of the Hero Twins into Xibalba is a metaphor for their deaths. Thus before they leave they plant maize in the house of their grandmother Xmucane (a goddess who participated in the creation of the world) as a visible symbol of their passage from death in the underworld to their eventual rebirth:

> "This is the sign of our word that we will leave behind. Each of us shall first plant an ear of unripe maize in the center of the house. If they dry up this is a sign of our death. 'They have died,' you will say when they dry up. If then they sprout again, 'They are alive,' you will say, our grandmother and our mother. This is the sign of our word that is left with you," they said. (Christenson 2007, 160)

In Xibalba the Hero Twins confront the Lords of Death, along with numerous other deities of disease and affliction with such wonderfully descriptive names as Flying Scab, Gathered Blood, Pus Demon, Jaundice Demon, Bone Staff, Skull Staff, Bloody Teeth, and Bloody Claws (Christenson 2007, 161–163). Hunahpu and Xbalanque play with these demons in their underworld ballcourt on several occasions, undergoing horrific trials that by all accounts should have resulted in their deaths. Nevertheless, in each case they are able to trick death and triumph in the end (ibid., 163–176). Ultimately the Hero Twins give themselves up to be sacrificed in a pit oven, arranging their deaths in such a way that they could be reborn, literally from the ashes. In this regenerated state they are able to turn the tables on the demons of Xibalba and sacrifice the Lords of Death (ibid., 180–186). As a result of their rebirth to new life, the maize plants that the Hero Twins had left behind were able to sprout anew:

> Now at the same time, the Grandmother was weeping, crying out before the ears of unripe maize that had been left planted. They had sprouted, but

> then they dried up when they were burned in the pit oven. Then the ears of maize had sprouted once again, and the Grandmother had burned copal incense before them as a memorial. The heart of their grandmother rejoiced when the maize sprouted a second time. (Christenson 2007, 188)

Following their victory the Hero Twins punished the underworld lords, limiting their influence only to frail and ephemeral things:

> "Here then is our word that we declare to you. Hearken all you of Xibalba; for never again will you or your posterity be great. Your offerings also will never again be great. They will henceforth be reduced to croton sap. No longer will clean blood be yours. Unto you will be given only worn-out griddles and pots, only flimsy and brittle things." (Christenson 2007, 187)

Las Casas knew significant elements of the story of the Hero Twins' descent into Xibalba, indicating that he was familiar with some version of the underlying mythology from independent sources. He wrote in the *Apologética historia* that Exbalanquen (the Hero Twin Xbalanque in the *Popol Vuh*) was a deified ruler who originated K'iche' practices as a founder of the royal dynasty. Thus living rulers, like those who played in the ballcourt during New Year's ceremonies, would have considered themselves the successors and heirs of Xbalanque:

> According to what they say, among other fables, [Exbalanquen] went to wage war against hell, and fought with all the people there and defeated them, and took the king of hell captive along with many of his forces. And as he set out to return victorious to this world with his captive, the king of hell pleaded with him not to take him further, for they were then three or four levels from the light; and the conqueror Exbalanquen, with much anger, gave him a kick, saying: "Go back and let there be for you all that is rotten, and decomposed, and foul smelling." (Las Casas 1967, book 3, chapter 124, 650, translation by author)

Later in his account Las Casas wrote that the Maya in the Guatemalan highlands called hell Chixibalba (at Xibalba) and that there were portals in the earth that led to this place underground. One of these was at Cobán in the Alta Verapaz region, which was "closed by that devil called Exbalanquen, who, as we said above in Chapter 124, had introduced human sacrifice" (Las Casas 1967, book 3, chapter 235, 506, translation by author).

In their preamble to the text the K'iche' authors of the *Popol Vuh* wrote that "great is its performance and its account of the completion and germination of all the sky and earth" (Christenson 2007, 65). This suggests that the mythic deeds of the gods and sacred ancestors outlined in the book were performed by living persons as sacred dramas (Tedlock 1996, 63, 219). The ritual ballgame described by Las Casas was an example of this type of ritual performance, staged as a means of defeating death in the underworld ballcourt during the final days of the calendar year, thus bringing new life into the world in preparation for New Year's Day.

Las Casas's account of the highland Maya New Year's rituals demonstrates that this practice continued until the Spanish Conquest in the Guatemalan highlands and that it was tied to major period endings associated with the death and rebirth of the world. The K'iche'an kingdoms in fact built more ballcourts in the centuries immediately preceding the Spanish Conquest than anywhere else in the Maya world. Every major capital city in the Guatemalan highlands had multiple ballcourts, and virtually every subsidiary fortified center had at least one.

RITUAL FASTING AND AUTO-SACRIFICE

During highland Maya New Year's observances, the people prepared a special "green house," adorned with boughs of foliage, where the ruler underwent penitential sacrifices. This is analogous to the house that was prepared especially for the "chief of the town" in Landa's description of the New Year's rites which was similarly "cleaned and adorned with green" (Landa 1941, 140). Sacrificial blood offerings are prominent in both accounts. Landa notes in particular that all "drew blood from themselves, cutting their ears" (ibid., 141). Las Casas's version goes into greater depth regarding these sacrifices on the part of the ruler:

> All the time his penitence lasted, he offered many sacrifices other than men—all kinds of birds, animals, vegetables, meats, incense, and everything else; and every day he shed much of his own blood—sometimes from his ears, other times from his tongue, other times from the fleshy parts of his arms, other times from his thighs, and other times from his genitals. This terrible penitence he paid and offered to the gods on behalf of all the people as a good prelate who bears upon himself the recompense and penalty for all of their collective sins. (Las Casas 1958, chapter 177, 149, translation by author)

In the next passage Las Casas further elaborates on aspects of the New Year's rites that are analogous to those described by Landa in a more cursory manner in the Yucatan. Landa notes that men "began to fast and to abstain from their wives, as well as those who wished to do so on account of their devotion, for such time beforehand as they judged proper," anywhere from a maximum of three months to a minimum of thirteen days, during which time they blackened themselves with soot (Landa 1941, 152). According to Las Casas, the highland Maya also smeared soot on their bodies during the fasts of the *cuaresma* and assembled together in the temple precincts away from their homes so as to abstain from sexual relations with their wives:

> Returning to the subject above, when the day had arrived to begin the feast and its vigil, which was the *cuaresma*, all the married men covered themselves as penitents, which was to smear their entire bodies with black; but the young men about to be married did not take upon themselves so much penance, coloring themselves reddish-brown instead. All these young men had as their master and guide the son of the lord; or if he had no son, then his nephew or the closest relative. He was tasked with gathering those that were the age of seven or eight and above, arranging to separate them from their families and assigning to each his guide and captain. These all brought firewood, for in these days the great braziers consumed a great amount. Once the *cuaresma* had begun, everyone, both women and men, withdrew into seclusion and mortification—the women in their houses, understanding what their obligations were, and the men to the temples to pray. When they returned to their houses to eat, they treated their wives as if they did not know them, nor did they speak to them even a word, but when they were finished eating they returned without delay. (Las Casas 1958, chapter 172, 149–150, translation by author)

Landa wrote that the Maya in the Yucatan sacrificed birds and offered incense during the days of the Wayeb'. They also bled themselves by cutting their ears, noting that in the case of young boys the adults "drew blood from their ears by force, making gashes in their ears" (Landa 1941, 141, 144). Las Casas describes much the same practice in the highland Guatemalan New Year's rituals:

> Late at night they called for their wives and children, those who had use of their faculties, and they all went to a hilltop, if there was one close by, or to a crossroads, and there they carried out their sacrifices with the knives that they brought with them. They taught their children to do the same, calling on their gods for health, good years, and other worldly needs. And if the children refused because they were not as yet accustomed to it, the parents did their sacrifices by force until the children lost their fear of the knives. After they had sacrificed themselves, they made their petitions, all according to what they felt were the needs of the people.

> All offered what gifts they could, killing birds, burning incense, resinous wood, or fragrant resins and other things that they were able to give; in this they spent the greater part of the night, and walked their stations each according to what he most esteemed—some to the heights of the mountains and hills, others to caves, others to springs, and others to diverse places. Having made these processions and devotions, they dismissed their wives to return to their houses along with the children, or they themselves went with them if there were no others to accompany them, and subsequently returned to the temples. And thus in this manner and with these works, they spent all their time during the *cuaresma*. (Las Casas 1958, chapter 178, 150, translation by author)

THE GREAT SACRIFICE

In the next section of his account Las Casas writes that the men who were to be sacrificed in the New Year's rites were given liberty to enter into any household they wished, including the palace of the king, to demand food and drink:

> On the first day of *cuaresma* they released those slaves that were to be sacrificed in the fiestas or ceremonies. To these they gave liberty in this way, as it should be known: to each they affixed a collar of gold, or silver, or copper, around their necks and passed a shaft through it to fasten it well. And they assigned three or four men to guard them. These went anywhere in the town, entering any house they wished; and they ate with whomever they wished, even the high lord. Only they had to have their guardians and the collars and they could not leave the town. In everything else they need only say the word and it was given to them in any house they entered, even, as was said, the house of the king. And thus, wherever they went, they were given food and drink in whatever house they came to, even if they were very poor. And the ones who guarded them also enjoyed these liberties. Seven days before the fiesta, they gathered all those who were to be sacrificed in a house prepared for them near the temple, and there they were given to eat and drink until they were drunk. (Las Casas 1958, chapter 177, 150–151, translation by author)

Although Landa attests that human sacrifices were carried out at the culmination of the days leading up to New Year's in the Yucatan (Landa 1941, 143), he does not discuss the treatment of the victims before their deaths. He does, however, describe the treatment of captives destined for sacrifices in general, and it is probable that the same held true during the days of the Wayeb':

> Besides the festivals in which they sacrificed persons in accordance with their solemnity, the priest or *Chilan*, on account of some misfortune or necessity, ordered them to sacrifice human beings, and everyone contributed to this, that slaves should be bought, or some in their devotion gave their little children, who were made much of, and feasted up to the day (of the festival), and they were well guarded, so that they should not run away or pollute themselves with any carnal sin. (Landa 1941, 115–117)

The temporary release of captives intended for sacrifice and their special treatment with feasting and other honors indicates a reversal of societal norms. As Landa describes in his account of the Yucatec Wayeb', the presiding gods are also temporarily removed from their customary shrines during the five days at the close of the ancient Maya solar calendar and replaced by the B'akab's, who are given the temporary right to rule (Landa 1941, 139–142).

Three days before the conclusion of the New Year's festival, the highland Maya swept their community and adorned the temples with pine boughs, flowers, and decorated arches. Similar lustrations and adornments took place during the days of the Wayeb' in the Yucatan (Landa 1941, 140, 151–152), although Las Casas's account is more detailed:

> For two or three days before the day of the fiesta, they swept the streets and the plazas; and they cleaned and decorated the temples, filling them with a great multitude of roses and flowers of diverse colors. Some young men were sent by their captains to bring green boughs, others brought pine needles to scatter on the floors, just as we scatter sedge in Spain.
>
> On the eve of the fiesta, they swept out all of the places for fire in the temple as well as in the subsidiary houses that were built around it, and all the ashes were taken to a certain place reserved for this. They then washed themselves of all the blackness that they had smeared on themselves for so many days, and dressed themselves in clean garments and mantles, the finest that they had, all according to their status and abilities. With great joy they adorned their houses with boughs, as well as the places of their idols and everything that belonged to them. (Las Casas 1958, chapter 177, 151, translation by author)

Las Casas continues his account of the New Year's festival with an extended description of the elaborate processions and sacrifices conducted on the final day. Landa also notes that at the close of the Wayeb' the Maya bathed themselves and offered blood sacrifices. Although these mostly consisted of birds, they also culminated in human sacrifices (Landa 1941, 142–143). Las Casas's account adds greatly to our knowledge concerning these practices:

On the night immediately preceding the fiesta and sacrifice, the sons of the supreme lord and other lords went to retrieve the idols. They carried these idols with great reverence, stopping periodically to offer birds and macaws, doves, and other birds of various species and colors; and they periodically sent young men to tell the high lord and the other lords with him that the gods had arrived at such and such a place, and this was done many times.

At length the great priest went out to receive them, accompanied by the other priests and ministers of the *culto divino* [divine cult] a good distance outside the town. Once they arrived they offered sacrifices, and when they entered the town they came in silence, giving a certain signal by which the town understood that the idol was in the temple. All that night was spent walking stations and observing their religious duties, coming and going to the temple and sleeping little. Now that the idol, or idols, were in the temple, they began to play their musical instruments, singing and dancing, performing plays, pantomimes, and other types of diversions and celebrations, as many as they could invent and as could be carried out. And thus they did until dawn.

And at dawn all bathed themselves and brought their incense and birds, presenting them to the priest to offer on their behalf, and thus all came to worship and make their petitions with great humility and sorrowful devotion for what they felt were the needs of the lords and vassals. When the hour of the sacrifice had arrived, the high priest clothed himself in sacred garments, the finest that could be obtained. This was a certain type of robe, according to what they draw in figures, for there are none among us who have seen it. They wore crowns of gold or silver, or another metal, the most precious that they could have, adorned with precious stones and other things by which they made it very beautiful. They had some litters, richly prepared with many jewels of gold, silver, and stones, arranged with roses and flowers upon which they placed the idols, dressed in a careful and curious manner. With these they walked in procession around the patio of the temple with great songs, music, diversions, dances, and eminent persons, all arranged in order without a hint of confusion. In some parts they walk in procession with those that were to be sacrificed; in others they did not, but rather they were in place at the end of the procession.

After they had been processed in their litters, the gods were seated in an eminent place that must have been like an altar, and there the sacrifice was carried out before them. Close by were the flautists and musicians and singers and dancers, who never ceased their performances. What they sang and performed in their pantomimes and plays were their ancient things, and the musicians did not interfere with those who sang, nor those who

> performed the pantomimes, nor those who performed in the plays; in this matter they were all in accord. In everything there was a great order, acting together in concert. (Las Casas 1958, chapter 177, 151–152, translation by author)

Both Román y Zamora and Ximénez add that the unidentified "musicians" that accompanied the flautists in this account were drummers (Román y Zamora 1897, 200; Ximénez 1929–1931 [1722], 85). This account is one of the most detailed descriptions that we have of the pageantry that surrounded Pre-Columbian Maya public ceremonies—including processions, music centered on the flute and drum, ritual songs, dances, pantomimes, and dramatic performances. Although Landa does not describe such entertainments, Song 12 of the *Cantares de Dzitbalche*, composed in early colonial period Yucatan, does mention that the close of Wayeb' observances included "musician singers, buffoons, dancers, contortions, jumpers, and hunchbacks" that performed in the "center of the plaza" of the community (Taube 1988, 293).

Las Casas continues his account with a description of the human sacrifices that mark the climax of these rites:

> The hour of the sacrifice having arrived, the highest lord and the other lords with him went to the room where the slaves were who were to be sacrificed and he seized the slave by his hair; and if there were more than one, the other lords took his own and brought them out; and the supreme lord cried out with a loud voice as he went, and the other lords helped him, saying:
>
> "Lord God, remember us, that we are yours; give us health, give us children and prosperity so that your people increase and serve you; give us water and good seasons so that we are sustained and that we live; hear our petitions; receive our prayers; help us against our enemies; give us rest and repose."
>
> All these words and petitions were repeated as well by the people who heard them as they followed behind. (Las Casas 1958, chapter 177, 152, translation by author)

The prayer was apparently standardized, as all repeated the words in unison. It is similar to an intercessory prayer recorded in the *Popol Vuh* that was recited by the ancestors of the K'iche' people just prior to the first dawn. Its similarity to the prayer in Las Casas's account suggests that its core elements were a standard element of regenerative ceremonies:

> They would lift up their faces to the sky as they pleaded for their daughters and their sons:

> "Alas, you, Framer, and you, Shaper: Behold us! Hear us! Do not abandon us. Do not allow us to be overthrown. You are the god in the sky and on the earth, you, Heart of Sky, Heart of Earth. May our sign, our word, be given for as long as there is sun and light. Then may it be sown, may it dawn. May there be true life-giving roads and pathways. Give us steadfast light that our nation be made steadfast. May the light be favorable that our nation may be favored. May our lives be favored so that all creation may be favored as well." (Christenson 2007, 206)

"Dawn" is a metaphor in highland Maya literature and belief for the inauguration of a new age, particularly connected with the foundation of political power and legitimacy. It is thus akin to the New Year's rites, which are also meant as a rebirth of the world as well as a reaffirmation of the king's right to rule. Like the prayer cited in Las Casas's account on the final day of the *cuaresma* rites, this prayer focuses on similar themes: the daughters and sons of the lords, protection against enemies who would overthrow them, life-giving sustenance, and the continued cycle of the seasons. Another prayer given by the K'iche' kings recorded in the *Popol Vuh* follows the same basic pattern, paralleling the wording in Las Casas's account even more closely:

> "Yea, pleasing is the day, you, Huracan, and you, Heart of Sky and Earth, you who give abundance and new life, and you who give daughters and sons. Be at peace, scatter your abundance and new life. May life and creation be given. May my daughters and my sons be multiplied and created, that they may provide for you sustain you, and call upon you on the roads, on the cleared pathways, along the courses of the rivers, in the canyons, beneath the trees and the bushes. Give, then, their daughters and their sons.
>
> "May there be no fault, confinement, shame, or misfortune. May no deceiver come behind them or before them. May they not fall or be wounded. May they not be dishonored or condemned. May they not fall below the road or above the road. May they not be stricken or have impediments placed behind them or before them. May you place them on green roads and on green pathways. May they not be blamed or confined. Do not hide yourselves from them nor curse them. May their existence be favored, so that they may be providers and sustainers to you, to your mouths and to your faces, you, Heart of Sky and you, Heart of Earth." (Christenson 2007, 289–290)

In the Yucatan human sacrifice was carried out by heart extraction on a stone altar, after which the priest "went very quickly and anointed the faces of the idols with that fresh blood" (Landa 1941, 119, 143). The same procedure was followed with the sacrificial victims offered in the Guatemalan highlands:

> Upon reaching the altar of sacrifice the lord placed the victim in the hands of the butcher priest, who was there ready for them. He with his ministers removed his heart with a knife and offered it to the idol, and the priest with three fingers took some of the blood and sprinkled it on the idol and then toward the Sun, carrying out many ceremonies that we will leave out so as not to dwell upon it further; and from there he walked to each of the altars, doing the same to each idol, because each had an altar dedicated to him; and the Sun had his, and the Moon, and the East, and the West, and the North, and the South. (Las Casas 1958, chapter 177, 152, translation by author)

Such sacrifices were relatively rare in both Yucatan and the Guatemalan highlands, reserved for periods of extreme crisis such as droughts or famine or for major festivals such as the Wayeb'/New Year's observances, representing the death and rebirth of the world on a universal scale. Taube suggests that Maya sacrificial offerings represented a type of substitution (*k'ex*), in which the life of the victim renews or replaces the life lost during times of crisis (Taube 1994, 669–675). Period-ending ceremonies such as the Wayeb' are particularly fraught with danger because they represent the temporary death of the world. Stephen Houston, David Stuart, and Karl Taube (2006, 131) add that sacrifices must involve bloodletting or the death of the sacrificial victim because only the most powerful of offerings can fully compensate for life-debt.

Blood is offered to the most important deity images in order to give them life and the power of speech. Thus in the *Popol Vuh* the ancestors of the K'iche' kings rubbed the blood of birds and deer, as well as their own blood, into the mouths of the carved stone images of their patron gods, Tohil and Auilix, in order to animate them:

> Thus they began to seek out the offspring of birds and deer which were taken and offered by the bloodletters and the sacrificers. They would find the birds and the young deer, and go to place their blood in the mouths of the stones. Tohil and Auilix drank this therefore. It was the bloody drink of the gods. Straightaway, then, the stones spoke when the bloodletters and sacrificers came to give their burnt offerings. . . .
>
> Then they pierced their ears and their elbows before the faces of their gods. They scooped up their blood and rubbed it inside the mouths of the stones. (Christenson 2007, 235–236)

Similar blood offerings are made among the modern Maya of highland Guatemala. On a hilltop outside the K'iche' community of Chichicastenango

25. *Sacrifice of a hen to Paxkwal Ab'aj, Chichicastenango, 2006*

is a roughly carved stone venerated as a god called Paxkwal Ab'aj (Paschal or Easter Stone). In addition to offerings of candles, flower petals, and incense, traditionalists sacrifice turkeys and chickens before it, rubbing or sprinkling the blood on the god's mouth and eyes to give him strength (fig. 25). A similar image once existed in a shrine above Santiago Atitlán, which also received blood offerings in its mouth (Mendelson 1956, 43). It is probable that this was the image of the patron deity of the Tz'utujils, Saqibuk, mentioned in the *Relación de los caciques y principales del Pueblo de Atitlán* as receiving blood offerings in its mouth (Acuña 1982, 87). When the existence of this image came to the attention of the local Roman Catholic priest, he had it destroyed in the mid-twentieth century.

THE REBIRTH OF THE WORLD THROUGH SACRIFICE

Las Casas continues his account with a description of how the heads of the sacrificial victims were displayed:

> They placed the heads of the sacrificed victims on wooden poles above a certain altar that was dedicated solely for this purpose, and there they kept them a certain time, after which they buried them. They say this was for certain reasons: first, primarily and principally, so that the idol or the god that it represents will remember the sacrifice that they had made in order to serve him, so that he will do them good and drive out all that is bad; also so that those who see it will consider that they were sacrificed for their good; also so that the king or lord who succeeds him, will see it and magnify that worship rather than take away from it; and also so that their ene-

mies who heard of it would fear to offend them, because if they did it was certain that they also would be sacrificed. (Las Casas 1958, chapter 177, 152, translation by author)

The "wooden poles above a certain altar" described by Las Casas were likely a scaffold or skull rack, a monument used throughout the Maya world in the Post-Classic period. The *Título de Totonicapán* illustrates such a structure at the center of a stylized map of the ceremonial district of Q'umarkaj, the ancient K'iche' capital (Carmack 1981, 189; Carmack and Mondloch 1983, 38). In the drawing the altar is labeled *tzumpan*, a Maya spelling of the Aztec word *tzompantli* or skull rack (fig. 26). The *tzumpan* is shown in profile, with four vertical posts supporting eight horizontal poles on which the skulls were hung. Chichen Itza has a monumental stone version of such a platform adjacent to the Great Ballcourt, covered on all four sides with regular rows of carved skulls (fig. 27). Other stone versions have been found at the highland Maya sites of Chalchitan near the headwaters of the Chixoy River (Sharer 1994, 427), and the Plaza A platforms at Iximche'. Most skull racks would have been constructed of wooden poles, as described by Las Casas, and were meant to be temporary structures (fig. 28).

The display of decapitated heads on a wooden monument may be a reference to the *Popol Vuh* account of the sacrifice of Hun Hunahpu by the death lords of Xibalba, in which the god's head was placed in the dry branches of a dead tree (Christenson 2007, 126; Mendoza 2008, 416–417). Immediately upon receiving the head of the god, the tree was regenerated to new life:

> Now when they went to place his head in the midst of the tree, the tree bore fruit. The tree had never borne fruit until the head of Hun Hunahpu was placed in it. This was the tree that we now call the calabash. It is said to be the head of Hun Hunahpu.
>
> One Death and Seven Death marveled at the fruit of the tree, for the round fruit was everywhere. Neither could the head of Hun Hunahpu be seen clearly, for his face had become identical in appearance with the calabashes.
>
> This was seen by all Xibalba when they came to look at it. In their hearts they perceived the greatness of the essence of that tree, for it was accomplished immediately when the head of Hun Hunahpu entered into its midst. (Christenson 2007, 126–127)

In this myth the god Hun Hunahpu became fused with the reborn tree, giving it the power to bestow life. Ultimately the head of Hun Hunahpu, secreted among the fruits borne by the tree, miraculously impregnated the

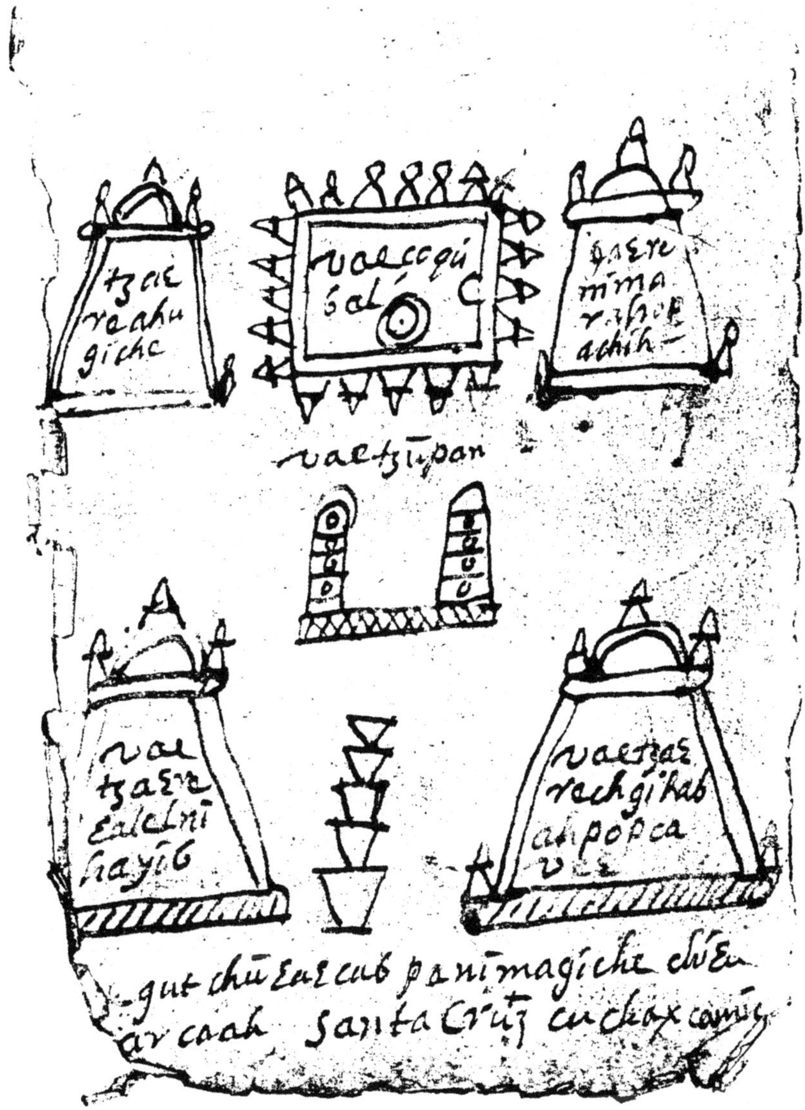

26. *Central complex of Q'umarkaj,* Título de Totonicapán. *Courtesy Robert Carmack*

27. *Platform of the Tzompantli, Chichen Itza*

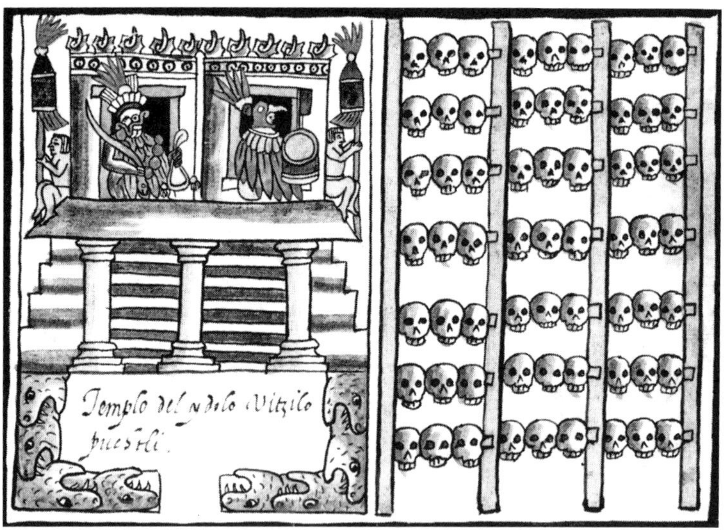

28. *Great Temple at Tenochtitlan with adjacent Tzompantli, Codex Tovar, ca. 1585*

29. *Decapitation sacrifice with flowering vines emerging from the victim's neck, east-central panel, Great Ballcourt, Chichen Itza. Drawing by Linda Schele © David Schele*

daughter of a Xibalba lord who subsequently gave birth to the Hero Twins, Hunahpu and Xbalanque. As noted above, these Twins eventually defeated the Lords of Death and raised their father from his burial place, thus completing the cycle of life, death, and rebirth. The tree is specifically described as having been "planted at *Puk'b'al Cha'j*" (Crushing Ballcourt), the same underworld ballcourt where the lords of Xibalba confronted their opponents from the upper world (Christenson 2007, 125, 187, 190–191). When Hun Hunahpu's son, Hunahpu, was later beheaded in Xibalba, his head was "placed atop the ballcourt" (ibid., 172). The ballcourt in Las Casas's account would have been a symbolic proxy for the ballcourt in Xibalba, where living lords, believed to be the descendants of Hun Hunahpu and his twin sons, confront the Lords of Death in order to bring new life into the world.

The ancient Maya did not perceive human sacrifices as acts of death-dealing but rather as the means to sustain life. Thus at Chichen Itza the six decapitated bodies depicted in the panels that line the walls of the Great Ballcourt sprout flowering squash vines laden with mature fruit (fig. 29). In both the *Popol Vuh* and the Chichen Itza ballcourt panels, the metaphor for this renewal of life is the miraculous growth of a fruit- and flower-bearing plant that immediately follows the death of the sacrificial victim.

On the first page of the *Chilam Balam of Chumayel* the creation of the world results in the placement of four "ceibas of abundance" or World Trees at each of the cardinal directions (Roys 1967, 64). Each of these trees is said to be the *dzulbal* of the gods. Roys translates *dzulbal* as "arbor," suggesting that it represents an arch of leaves and branches that the Maya set up in connection with New Year's ceremonies. Colonial dictionaries define *dzulbal* or *dzulub* as a structure made of bound poles or tree branches (Barrera Vásquez 1995, 892). Taube suggests that it may refer to a scaffold on which the Maya sacrificed their victims with lances or arrows (Taube 1988, 336–337, 341). Alternatively, it is also possible that it represents a skull rack for the display of sacrificial heads as described by Las Casas. The reference in the *Chilam Balam* text links the *dzulbal* specifically with creation and World Trees. The *Ritual of the Bacabs* mentions four *dzulbal*s and associates them with both sacrificial blood and the Akantun, the stone World Tree column of the Yucatec Wayeb' rites (Roys 1965, 12). The highland Guatemalan skull rack may therefore function like the Yucatec Akantun as an effigy World Tree (MacLeod 1989, 124). Both are animated by the blood of sacrificial victims near the close of Wayeb' observances as a symbol of regenerated life.

Las Casas writes that after the sacrifice the flesh of the victims was consumed by the ruling lords:

> The remainder of the flesh of those sacrificed was cooked, and dressed, and they ate it as a very sacred thing, consecrated by the gods, and he that was able to eat a bite was happy. The hands and feet and other delicate parts were presented to the great priest and the king as that which was most delicious and esteemed. All the rest was distributed to the other priests and ministers of the altar, for none of it remained for the people of the town. (Las Casas 1958, chapter 177, 152, translation by author)

Landa describes much the same procedure in his writings:

> The custom was usually to bury in the court of the temple those whom they had sacrificed, or else they ate them, dividing him up among those who had arrived (first) and the lords, and the hands, feet and head were reserved for the priest and his officials, and they considered those who were sacrificed as holy. (Landa 1941, 120)

THE GREAT FEAST OF THE GODS

Las Casas concludes his account of the highland Guatemalan New Year's rites by writing that after the sacrifices the highland Maya participated in great feasts as a sign that the days of fasting were over and the gods had been returned to their accustomed shrines:

> Returning to the subject at hand, on that day there were great feasts in which they ate many birds, and much game, and they drank diverse wines, mostly the highest lord and the high priest, who celebrated from one house

> to the other in town. They danced and leapt before the altars and gave the gods to drink of the most precious wines, soaking their mouths and faces. . . .
>
> These fiestas lasted three, five, or seven days according to what their prognostications declared. Each afternoon they walked in procession with great songs and music, bearing this principal idol, or as many as there were, placing them in eminent places; and there the lords played ball before him and the rest. From that night on, all went to sleep in their houses, other than those who, because of their administrative responsibilities and occupations, had to serve in the temple night and day; and they carried the idol or idols to their places and the fiesta came to a close. (Las Casas 1958, chapter 177, 152, translation by author)

Before the Spanish Conquest ritual feasting was a major part of the ceremonial life of the highland Maya. The *Popol Vuh* notes that feasting and drinking were a major (if not *the* major) function of the Great Houses that each lineage constructed at Q'umarkaj (Christenson 2007, 265–267; see also Carmack 1981, 160, 294). Ximénez wrote that the images of the gods were brought from their temples to join in these feasts, receiving the same food and drink that the mortal celebrants consumed (Ximénez 1929–1931 [1722], book 1, chapter 30, 85–86; see also Carmack and Mondloch 1983, 196).

Such shared meals between gods and humans continue in the Maya highlands today. As Evon Vogt wrote concerning the Maya of Zinacantan, "men eat what the gods eat," and the interaction between humans and gods in such ceremonies is considered essential to good life and the regeneration of the universe. Food and drink thus become the medium of contact with the gods:

> Although Zinacantecos of low status may sit around the foot of the ritual table, no one sits at the head. There the ancestral gods preside and partake of the liquor and food served. Their living descendants are arranged in such a way that the elder ones are seated at the sides of the head of the table, next to the gods. . . . With the gods invited to join and partake of the meal, liquor is served from the same glass to all in the house, an action expressing communality and continuity from the deceased ancestors down to the youngest Zinacanteco. (Vogt 1993, 41)

The seating order at the table reinforces the social system, both uniting the participants with their gods and ancestors as mediators and solidifying the hierarchy within that system. As Houston et al. suggest, feasting socially unifies participants, constructing intimacy, a "sense of social bond and community," and even kinship (Houston et al. 2006, 102). Because the ancient

Maya nobility ate the same food and drink as their ancestral gods, they ritually shared a common divine essence, a corporeal bond.

Las Casas wrote that this feasting took place in conjunction with the sacred ballgame. As we have seen, ancient Maya rulers played the ballgame in the guise of deities who defeated the Lords of Death in order to restore life to the world. This was not seen by the Maya simply as imitative theater but as a recapitulation of the actions of deities, with the rulers serving as the physical embodiments of the gods. Their ceremonies were thus believed to have real regenerative power. Ritual feasting with the gods reinforced this identification and was not merely celebratory. It served to solidify the perception within the community that, with the close of the five dangerous days at the end of the calendar year, their rulers had successfully vanquished death as proxies for the gods and the world had been restored with the capacity to nourish and sustain life.

EASTER AND THE SPANISH CONQUEST

Chapter 3

Hernán Cortés, the future conqueror of the Aztec Empire, first landed on Mexican soil on Easter Sunday in 1519. He planted a cross on the beach and renamed the place Vera Cruz (True Cross) to commemorate the crucifixion of Christ. The campaign against the highland Maya began five years later, also waged during the Easter season. I do not believe that the timing was coincidental in either case but was rather a conscious effort to link Spanish military campaigns with the victory of God over death itself on the *día de la Pascua* (day of Easter). As indigenous documents from the period demonstrate, the Maya themselves recognized this linkage and perceived the destruction of their world at the hands of the Spaniards in much the same way that period endings functioned on their ancient calendar—as a period of universal death followed by rebirth. As a result Easter came to replace the ancient Maya Wayeb' observances as the focus for ceremonies meant to regenerate the world (Thompson 1970, 297–300; Bunzel 1952, 412; Cook 2000, 165; Carlson 2011, 170). This practice continues to the present day in many traditional Maya communities, preserving core elements of ancient Maya ceremonialism within a new Christian-influenced context. The same process took place following the Spanish Conquest in the Maya lowlands, where the Yucatec Maya equated the crucifixion and subsequent resurrection of Christ with the raising of the ancient World Tree at the culmination of the Wayeb' period before the beginning of the new year.

CONQUEST OF THE MAYA HIGHLANDS

Unlike the experience of Alexander the Great, there were always new worlds to conquer for the early Spanish *conquistadores*. Cortés sent his principal captain, Pedro de Alvarado, to invade the Maya lands to the southeast of the Aztec Empire in early 1524 (fig. 30). The initial focus of the invasion was the powerful K'iche'-Maya kingdom in the highlands of what is today Guatemala. Alvarado was mindful of the need for divine aid in his endeavors. In a letter to Cortés written immediately after the fall of the K'iche' capital,

30. *Pedro de Alvarado. Museo Colonial, Antigua, Guatemala*

Alvarado requested that Cortés "ordain that a procession be held in your city of all the priests and friars so that our Lord may help us. We are so far from help that if He does not help us, nobody can" (Alvarado 1924, 66–67). Alvarado took with him 120 horsemen, 300 infantry, and several hundred Cholulan and Tlaxcalan allies. Following a brief battle at El Pinal in the Quetzaltenango valley, Alvarado marched on the K'iche' capital of Q'umarkaj in late March 1524. Easter Sunday fell on March 27 on the Spanish calendar in 1524, the approximate time when the principal battles were waged against the highland Maya.

Following his initial victories against K'iche' forces, Alvarado and his Spanish soldiers were invited to enter Q'umarkaj as honored guests, so long as they left their indigenous allies outside the boundaries of the capital. Fearing a trap, Alvarado chose to remain encamped outside the city, where his cavalry could better maneuver if attacked. After establishing his own defensive measures, Alvarado invited the two rulers of the city, Oxib' Kej and B'elejeb' Tz'i', to visit him at his camp. Suspecting them of treachery, he held them as captives. A force of K'iche' warriors attempted to liberate their kings, killing one of the Spanish soldiers and a number of their indigenous allies. In response Alvarado executed the K'iche' rulers and burned the city to the ground:

> And seeing that by fire and sword I might bring these people to the service of His Majesty, I determined to burn the chiefs who, at the time that I wanted to burn them, told me, as it will appear in their confessions, that they were the ones who had ordered the war against me and were the ones also who made it. They told me about the way they were to do so, to burn me in the city, and that with this thought (in their minds) they had brought me there, and that they had ordered their vassals not to come and give obedience to our Lord the Emperor, nor help us, nor do anything else that was right. And as I knew them to have such a bad disposition towards the service of His Majesty, and to insure the good and peace of this land, I burnt them, and sent to burn the town and to destroy it, for it is a very strong and dangerous place. (Alvarado 1924, 62–63)

In his report to Cortés Alvarado mentioned that after defeating the K'iche's he had left the burned-out ruins of Q'umarkaj on Monday, April 11, arriving two days later at Iximche', the principal city of his Kaqchikel allies (Alvarado 1924, 65). Allowing for the consolidation of his victory at Q'umarkaj and preparations to transfer his headquarters to Iximche', this letter confirms that Alvarado's conquest of the city and subsequent punishment of its kings fell on or near Easter.

Diego Reynoso, the earliest K'iche'-Maya chronicler of this destruction, confirmed that the fall of Q'umarkaj took place at Easter and linked the defeat of the K'iche' kingdom to the death of Jesus Christ. As outlined in chapter 2, Reynoso was the son of a K'iche' lord named Lajuj No'j and bore the title Popol Winaq, an honorific given to members of the indigenous governing council. Although most of his writings have been lost, both Francisco Ximénez and the anonymous author of the *Isagoge histórico* drew upon Reynoso's history when writing their accounts of the Spanish Conquest. The *Isagoge* is a fascinating document, composed by an anonymous Dominican sometime between 1700 and 1711. It chronicles the history of Guatemala and surrounding areas from Pre-Columbian times until the end of the seventeenth century. Describing the arrival of Alvarado at Utatlan, the name given to the K'iche' capital of Q'umarkaj by Alvarado's Tlaxcalan allies, the *Isagoge* records:

> This was at the end of Lent and the beginning of Eastertide of the year 1524, according to the ancient account of Diego Reinoso [Reynoso], principal Indian of said village of Utatlan, who, at the time of the destruction of the city of Guatemala [1541], was learning to read and to write by order of Sr. D. Francisco Marroquín. In a very devout book on the Passion of Our Lord, Jesus Christ, he [Reynoso] makes some very curious marginal notes worthy of attention about their antiquities, which the authors do not include, and in one of them he says in his language: "*Chu pan Quaresma xul Donadi capitan ahlabal varal pa Quiché, lax porox tinamit taxcoh ahuarem tox tané patan, rumal ronoxel amac xpatavih Chiquivach camama cacahau pa Quiché.*" (Anonymous 1935 [ca. 1700], book 2, chapter 4, 191, translation by author)

The final lines quote Diego Reynoso directly in the original K'iche': "During Lent arrived Donadi [Pedro de Alvarado], warrior captain, here in Quiché, when the town was burned, when the Lordship was destroyed, when tribute was established. For all the nations paid tribute before him, our grandfathers and lords in Quiché." I find it significant that while writing a treatise on the Passion of Christ (the final days before the crucifixion and resurrection) Reynoso linked the crucifixion of Christ at Easter to the seemingly unrelated conquest of Guatemala by Pedro de Alvarado. The death of Christ apparently reminded him of the "death" of his world at the hands of the Spanish conquerors, to be followed by rebirth to a new Christian age.

The same association was made by Alvarado himself. The *Isagoge* notes that because the destruction of Q'umarkaj took place at Easter Alvarado renamed the conquered K'iche' city Santa Cruz (Holy Cross), similar to Cortés's naming of the first Aztec lands that he claimed as Vera Cruz (True Cross):

> And in another place he [Diego Reynoso] notes that it was in the month of April, in the final days of Lent and the beginning of Easter, that this took place [the conquest of the K'iche's]. And it appears that because this took place in those days of Holy Week, they gave the new city of Quiché the name of Santa Cruz ["Holy Cross"], and with this Santa Cruz they extinguished the rage of that nation. As a result, this place has been, and continues to be, among the most peaceful, most faithful, and obedient of this entire kingdom. (Anonymous 1935 [ca. 1700], book 2, chapter 4, 191, translation by author)

As is evident from the writings of Diego Reynoso, both the Spanish conquerors and the Maya themselves linked the defeat of the K'iche' kingdom with the crucifixion of Christ from the very beginning of the Post-Conquest period. Alvarado was a transitional figure who oversaw the death of the old Pre-Columbian world and its rebirth as a new, and in many ways more powerful world. Though certainly not beloved, Alvarado was respected as a powerful instrument of world renewal, even if it involved an unthinkable measure of cruelty and death as a precursor.

THE SPANISH CONQUEST AND THE INAUGURATION OF A "NEW SUN"

In Reynoso's account quoted above Pedro de Alvarado is called Donadi, the K'iche'-Maya pronunciation of Tonatiuh, the Aztec sun god. The author of the *Isagoge* wrote that this was a common title that the Maya of Guatemala used to refer to Alvarado: "During Lent arrived Donadí, who is don Pedro de Alvarado, whom the Mexicans called Tonatio, the Indians of these provinces corrupting the word in various ways, some calling him Donatio, others Donativo, and here Donadi" (Anonymous 1935 [ca. 1700], book 2, chapter 4, 191, translation by author).

Pedro de Alvarado was widely known by this name among the highland Maya, as seen in the numerous references to him as "Donadiu" in indigenous texts composed in the sixteenth century, including the *Popol Vuh* (Christenson 2007, 295), the *Títulos de la Casa Ixquin-Nehaib, señora del territorio de Otzoya* (Recinos 1957, 84), and the *Título Real de Don Francisco Izquin Nehaib* (Recinos 1957, 97). The Tlaxcalan chronicler Diego Muñoz Camargo wrote: "They called don Pedro de Alvarado 'the sun,' because they said he was the son of the sun for being blond and ruddy, of very beautiful face, charming and of good appearance" (Acuña 1984, 238, translation by author). Fair hair was a physical trait unknown in the Pre-Columbian New World, except for albinos, who are still called *ralk'ualab' q'ij* (children of the sun) in many K'iche'-Maya communities.

There may be a larger cosmological reason why the Maya associated Pedro de Alvarado with the sun beyond his fair skin and hair. Oswaldo Chinchilla Mazariegos notes that throughout Mesoamerica "the Spanish conquest and the introduction of Christianity were repeatedly represented in terms of an overarching model of the past that conceived a series of successive eras that came to an end and were eventually superseded by new creations, often marked by the advent of a new sun" (Chinchilla Mazariegos 2013, 694). Thus in the *Popol Vuh* the age before this one was dominated by a false "sun" in the guise of Wuqub' Kaqix (Seven Macaw), whose light and glory depended on his glittering gold, silver, and jewels. Wuqub' Kaqix thus declares:

> "I am great. I dwell above the heads of the people who have been framed and shaped. I am their sun. I am also their light. And I am also their moon.
>
> "Then be it so. Great is my brightness. By the brilliance of my silver and gold I light the walkways and pathways of the people." (Christenson 2007, 92)

The text makes it clear, however, that Wuqub' Kaqix was "not truly the sun" but "desired only greatness and transcendence before the light of the sun and moon were revealed in their clarity" (Christenson 2007, 93). The gods therefore determined that he had to be defeated for the dawn of the true sun to take place, ushering in the present age of humankind. It was only after the creation of the first four men that the dawn of the true sun of the present era arose, linked with the establishment of legitimate political power (ibid., 202–204). The first men were said to be miraculous. The gods themselves, rather than human mothers, created their bodies (ibid., 197). Thus they were literally seen as the first human beings of the present creation and belonged to no other age of existence. The creator gods specifically linked their appearance with the creation of light as a precursor to the first dawn of the sun:

> "The dawn approaches, and our work is not successfully completed. A provider and a sustainer have yet to appear—a child of light, a son of light. Humanity has yet to appear to populate the face of the earth," they said.
>
> Thus they gathered together and joined their thoughts in the darkness, in the night. They searched and they sifted. Here they thought and they pondered. Their thoughts came forth bright and clear. They discovered and established that which would become the flesh of humanity. This took place just a little before the appearance of the sun, moon, and stars above the heads of the Framer and the Shaper. (Christenson 2007, 192)

Among the titles of the first four men was K'enech Ajaw (Sun-Faced Lord) (Christenson 2007, 203n505). This was also the lowland Maya title given to the principal sun deity (Thompson 1970, 207, 228–229; Morley, Brainerd and Sharer 1983, 470; Taube 1992, 50–56). K'enech Ajaw represented the sun's daily journey across the sky and had been closely associated with the various Maya royal dynasties for more than a thousand years (Miller and Taube 1993, 106; Stuart 1996, 167). In Yucatan a deified ruler named K'inich K'ak'mo' (Sun-Faced Fire Macaw) was remembered as the founding ancestor of Izamal (Roys 1967, 82, 160n2; Craine and Reindorp 1979, 83–84n78). Apparently the K'iche' lords also saw themselves as earthly manifestations of the sun deity. The *Popol Vuh* describes the four founding ancestors of the K'iche' kings as "the root of the sun and light of the people" (Christenson 2007, 301). They were repeatedly described as coming from the East, which in the K'iche' language is *releb'al q'ij* (the place of emergence of the sun) (ibid., 203–207). This association with the East and dawn is metaphoric. The text emphasizes that prior to their migration to the Guatemalan highlands the four K'iche' progenitors lived in darkness, as the true sun had not yet appeared:

> Many people arrived in darkness in the days of their increase, for the sun was yet to be born. There was no light in the days of their increase. They were all as one, crowded together as they walked there in East. There was no one to provide for their sustenance. They would merely lift up their faces to the sky, for they did not know where to go. . . . They fixed their eyes firmly on their dawn, looking there to the East. They watched closely for the Morning Star, the Great Star that gives its light at the birth of the sun. (Christenson 2007, 205–207)

The birth of the sun here is not meant to be the rise of the physical sun but rather the establishment of political authority. Thus in their prayer to the gods who created the world the four founding dynasts link the hoped-for dawn with protection from their enemies and the establishment of a powerful nation:

> "Alas, you, Framer, and you, Shaper: Behold us! Hear us! Do not abandon us. Do not allow us to be overthrown. You are the god in the sky and on the earth, you, Heart of Sky, Heart of Earth. May our sign, our word, be given for as long as there is sun and light. Then may it be sown, may it dawn. May there be true life-giving roads and pathways. Give us steadfast light that our nation be made steadfast. May the light be favorable that our nation may be favored. May our lives be favored so that all creation may be favored as well. Give this to us, you, Huracan, Youngest Thunderbolt, and

> Sudden Thunderbolt, Youngest Nanavac and Sudden Nanavac, Falcon and Hunahpu, Sovereign and Quetzal Serpent, She Who Has Borne Children and He Who Has Begotten Sons, Xpiyacoc and Xmucane, Grandmother of Day and Grandmother of Light. Then may it be sown. Then may it dawn," they said. (Christenson 2007, 206–207)

The pairing of "sowing and dawning" in this prayer is used throughout the *Popol Vuh* to describe the creation of the world itself and of the first human beings (Christenson 2007, 60, 71, 78, 80, 82, 200). It is therefore a metaphor for the opening of the present age, established by the gods themselves.

The *Popol Vuh* stresses that the progenitors received their authority as legitimate rulers from Nacxit, the ruling lord of an older kingdom centered at a place called Tulan Suywa that the text locates "in the East," linking it with the place of dawn (Christenson 2007, 213, 218–219, 255–256). Tulan is the K'iche' version of the Nahua language place-name Tullan or Tollan (Place of Cattail Reeds), a toponym used throughout Mesoamerica as a center for political and spiritual power. In the Aztec version of the myth Tollan was inhabited by the Toltecs, great sages who invented the sciences of astronomy, calendrics, agriculture, and medicine as well as the arts of writing, painting, sculpture, metalwork, jade carving, and weaving (León-Portilla 1980, 207). The K'iche's also recognized the primacy of Toltec knowledge as a precursor to their own power and creative skills. In the *Popol Vuh* one of the titles for the creator deities was Aj Toltecat (He/She of the Toltecs) (Christenson 2003, 80n102). The ancient Toltec kingdom was located in the Nahua-speaking area of central Mexico. Throughout Mesoamerica in the late Post-Classic era the legendary Toltecs were the founders and principal bearers of political legitimacy. Nacxit itself is a Nahua-derived name or title, meaning "four foot" (Campbell 1983, 84), perhaps referring to the reach of his power, extending to the four cardinal directions of the earth.

The *Popol Vuh* locates Tulan *chaq'a palo* (on the other side of the sea) (Christenson 2007, 221, 255–259). The *Título de Totonicapán* also asserts that the progenitors of the K'iche's left the court of Nacxit at Tulan, "passing over here from the other side of the sea" (Carmack and Mondloch 2007, 71, translation by author). This myth was widespread throughout the Guatemalan highlands. In the Kaqchikel version of the myth contained in the *Xajil Chronicle* their ancestors accompanied the K'iche's from their place of creation at Tulan in the East: "'From across the ocean we came. Pa Tulan is the name of the hill where we were born, where we were begotten by our mothers [and] our fathers, you, our sons,' said the ancient fathers [and] grandfathers" (Maxwell and Hill 2006, 1–2).

Frauke Sachse suggests that Tulan's location on "the other side of the sea" is not to be taken literally, serving as a metaphor for an otherworldly place of creation rather than a specific geographic location (Sachse 2008). She cites numerous examples from Maya literature and oral tradition to demonstrate that the notion "sea" is a rather common element of Maya thought, even in modern times, as a conceptual boundary between this world and a supernatural otherworld with links to creation and the primordial actions of gods. Thus the religious beliefs of the K'iche's "shape the perception and recollection of history" in order to conflate mythic and historic time (Sachse 2008, 155).

The mythic nature of Tulan is evident in highland Maya literature of the early colonial period, where the Maya clearly blended their traditions concerning Tulan with biblical stories introduced to them by Christian missionaries soon after the Conquest. Thus in the *Título de Totonicapán* Tulan is situated by the K'iche's in Sineyetón (Sinai), which they associate with the place of their creation in the East (Carmack and Mondloch 2007, 65, 171n68). The K'iche's undoubtedly associated Tulan with Sinai because it was where authority was given to the Israelites by their God (similar to the authority and religious paraphernalia given by Nacxit to the highland Maya) and because it was the first major stop in the forty-year migration of the Israelites toward their eventual homeland in Palestine (as Tulan was the beginning of the migration toward the Guatemalan highlands). Thus the account of the K'iche' migrations from Tulan in the Totonicapán text specifically links their ancestors with the Israelites in the time of Moses:

> We are the descendants of the Israelites, of Saint Moses. From the regions of the Israelites came our grandfathers and fathers. They came from where the sun emerges, there in Babylonia [where] they observed ceremonies with the lord Nacxit; [and this was] the origin of our lineage. (Carmack and Mondloch 2007, 65, translation by author)

In the *Historia Quiché de don Juan de Torres*, the legendary place of origin of the K'iche's is in "the East, the other side of the lake, the other side of the sea" that was called "Babilonia" (Recinos 1957, 24–25). The reference to Babylonia in this and other early highland Maya texts undoubtedly reflects an early attempt by K'iche' intellectuals to conflate the K'iche' migration from Tulan with the migration of the Jews under Zerubbabel from Babylon after their liberation by Cyrus I (Ezra 1–2; 2 Chronicles 36:22–23).

At Tulan the K'iche' progenitors received their titular gods and the right to rule but recognized that their own dawn would not be established there, which the *Popol Vuh* text specifically links with "glory" and "lordship":

> When they were there at the place called Tulan Zuyva, their gods came to them. But it was surely not then that they received their ultimate glory or their lordship. . . .
>
> "Alas, it is not here that we shall see the dawn, when the sun will be born to illuminate the face of the earth," they said as they came.
>
> They merely stayed on the road. The people of each of the nations remained sleeping and resting together on the road. Yet always they looked for the star, the sign of the sun, the sign of the dawn in their hearts when they came from the East. (Christenson 2007, 218–219)

The dawn ultimately took place for the founders of the K'iche' royal dynasty at the mountain of Jakawitz, which they established as their first capital in the Guatemalan highlands:

> This therefore is the dawn, the appearance of the sun, moon, and stars. . . . Great was the joy in the hearts of Balam Quitze, Balam Acab, Mahucutah, and Iqui Balam. There they multiplied on the top of the mountain that was to become their citadel. There it was that the sun, moon, and stars truly appeared. Everything on the face of the earth and beneath the sky had its dawn and became clear. (Christenson 2007, 230)

In at least one K'iche' text composed in the sixteenth century the power and tokens of authority from Tulan were associated with both the Spanish Conquest and ceremonies carried out at the close of the ancient highland Maya calendar. The *Título C'oyoi* is an important K'iche' text compiled by noblemen of the K'oyoi lineage of Quetzaltenango aided by the descendants of K'iche' rulers from the capital city of Utatlan. The principal author was Juan de Penonias de Putanza, a close kinsman to one of the K'oyoi military lords killed in the Spanish Conquest (Carmack 1973, 39). It dates somewhere between 1550 and 1570. In order to establish the authority of the K'iche's, the *Título C'oyoi* recounts the origin of their tokens of authority, which were originally brought by the various K'iche' lineages "from the other side of the sea," a reference to Tulan:

> [The] Lords that come from the East, who started (it all); (the) nine days; the Waliom people came from the East, together they came with the Cawek, Nijaib (from) across the water and the sea; they had their parasols, their lion throne, their jaguar throne, the claws of the lion, jaguar, and eagle, the feathers of the macaw, the feathers of the heron, the mantles; then the messengers leave, when the twenty (day) period ends, the 360 (day period). . . . The thirteen invaders, the lancers; (so) was the changing (of

the lordship) by the symbols of the spearing and sling which came from the East, from the other side of the sea. (Carmack 1973, 295)

Unfortunately the text is in rather poor condition, resulting in a number of breaks in the narrative. But the general sense of the story is clear in this passage. The founding members of the K'iche' lineages brought their symbols of authority from the East, specifically from "across the sea." A similar list of powerful objects is listed in the *Popol Vuh* as the tokens of K'iche' royal authority brought from Tulan (Christenson 2007, 257–258). Curiously, the *Título C'oyoi* then adds a passage dealing with period endings, specifically the close of the 360-day period of the solar calendar year when the New Year's rites are observed. This is further linked with the "changing of the lordship." This portion of the text immediately precedes the account of the K'iche's defeat at the hands of Pedro de Alvarado in 1524, suggesting that the K'iche' author of the text associated not only the "changing of the lordship" with the Spanish Conquest but period endings and New Year's rites as well.

Following an extensive description of the K'iche' preparations for battle with the Spaniards, the author then turns to the actual battle in the Quetzaltenango Valley. The commander of the K'iche' forces is named as Lord Tecum (fig. 31): "The Lord Tecum came from the sky, when this captain gave himself (to the fray) among the Spaniards . . . Tecum was pierced by the great . . . . Earth" (Carmack 1973, 303).

This description of the battle describes the K'iche' Lord Tecum in mythic terms, descending out of the sky to confront the Spaniards. Reinforcing the flight metaphor, the text goes on to emphasize that he had *q'uq' rismal elenaq uloq chupam utio'jil* (quetzal feathers coming out from within his body), rather than that he was simply dressed in clothing adorned with quetzal feathers (Carmack 1973, 283, my transcription and translation). The manuscript is severely damaged at this point, so it is unclear if the text means that he was pierced by Spanish weapons or more poetically by the supernatural forces associated with the earth. Tecum's death, however, is portrayed in overtly cosmological terms in folio 39:

Keje ri' xqaj uloq	Then he descended/set hither
jun q'ij ch . . . kaj	a sun from the sky
kitzij nima q'aq'tepe chi ri'	truly great *q'aq'tepe* there.

(Carmack 1973, 283, my transcription and translation)

The death of Tecum uses the same verbal phrase, *xqaj uloq*, that is used by K'iche's to describe the setting of the sun in the west, a concept reinforced in the next line, which specifically refers to the sun. The metaphor is continued

31. *Tecum Uman Monument, Quetzaltenango*

in the next lines, which assert that "the sun in the sky turned red because of the blood" of Tecum's companions in the battle (Carmack 1973, 303).

The third line of the passage is difficult to translate: it includes a compound word, *q'aq'tepe*, that combines a K'iche' word with a term borrowed from the Nahua language of central Mexico. *Q'aq'* is K'iche' for "fire," but it is also used frequently in early colonial texts as a metaphor for glory or political power. Thus the principal symbol of authority left behind by the first K'iche' progenitors was called Pisom Q'aq'al (Bundled Fire/Glory) and consisted of tokens of royal power wrapped in a deerskin bundle (Christenson 2007, 254–255). Following the deaths of the first K'iche' lords the Pisom Q'aq'al was venerated by their successors with offerings of incense and prayers (ibid., 255, 290). The *Título de Totonicapán* asserts that the Pisom Q'aq'al bundle was given to the progenitors of the K'iche' people by Nacxit, the lord of Tulan, as an emblem of their authority to rule (Carmack and Mondloch 1983, 175, 181–182; see also Tedlock 1996, 179–180). According to the Totonicapán document, the bundle was left wrapped for years, until the K'iche's established their first royal capital on the mountain of Jakawitz. Only then were they worthy of opening and displaying its contents, thus exercising the royal authority promised to them at Tulan. It was the presence of this bundle that proved the K'iche's "power and glory" before the other lineages (Carmack and Mondloch 1983, 177).

The second part of the compound phrase, *tepe*, is a Nahua loan word. Carmack believed that this should read *tepetl* (mountain), making the compound word read "fire mountain" or "volcano," suggesting that Tecum died "before the great fire mountain" (perhaps the nearby volcano Santa María, which is active). Based on the grammatical construction of the K'iche' text, however, it is more likely that *tepe* should instead be read as *tepeu* (Nahua for "sovereignty, glory, power, authority"), paralleling the first element of the compound word, *q'aq'*, the K'iche' word for the same concept.

Thus the *Título C'oyoi* equates the death of Lord Tecum with the setting sun and by extension the end of the era of K'iche' power and authority. This inference is reinforced in the following section of the text in which Pedro de Alvarado "sat down at the great throne and stool which had come from the East" as the K'iche's played the drum and bowed down before him as a lord (Carmack 1973, 304). Alvarado thus sealed his role as the founder of a new dynasty by occupying the same royal throne that was originally brought from Tulan by the founding K'iche' lords. Considering the location of Tulan "in the East" and "the other side of the sea," it could not have escaped the K'iche's that this is precisely where the Spanish conquerors came from. The Spaniards, however unknowingly at the time, could therefore be seen as claiming legitimacy by the same mythic conventions that the founding lords of the highland Maya dynasties asserted in their traditions. As we have seen, the principal title that the K'iche's gave to Alvarado was Donadi, a sun god, thus reinforcing the idea that a "new sun" or age of power had dawned on their world. The authors of the *Título C'oyoi* describe the Spanish Conquest in theological terms as the work of God: "We saw the coming of the word of God with don Pedro de Alvarado the great Captain, *Adelantado* [Provincial Governor], Conqueror, [who] came from Castilla with our great Lord God and king" (Carmack 1973, 276, translation by author).

The parallel with K'iche' traditions of lordship would have been apparent to the surviving highland Maya nobility: Pedro de Alvarado acts as a founding dynast (like the K'iche' progenitors) who came from across the sea in the East (Spain/Tulan) bearing the new titular God (Jesus Christ, analogous to their patron god Tohil) under the auspices of a distant king and overlord (Charles V/Nacxit). As Chinchilla Mazariegos writes, the Maya modeled the past "after cosmogonic myths that described several eras, termed suns," each succeeding its predecessor as the legitimate heir of authority established in mythic traditions (Chinchilla Mazariegos 2013, 699). From the writings of Diego Reynoso as well as Juan de Penonias de Putanza, the author of the *Título C'oyoi*, it is apparent that at least some members of the old K'iche' nobility saw the Spanish Conquest as the dawn of a new age with a new sun in the guise of Pedro de Alvarado.

Modern K'iche's remember the Spanish Conquest as a traumatic blow to their sovereignty and self-determination but accept its aftermath as an unalterable part of their history. Even today K'iche's acknowledge Alvarado's role as the founder of the present age, whether for good or ill. This is explicit in the *Baile de la Conquista* (Dance of the Conquest), composed in 1542 by a Dominican priest with significant collaboration by highland Maya nobles (Carmack 1973, 168–170). Although the dance was intended as a justification for the Spanish Conquest and the institution of Christianity, a modified version continues to be performed throughout Guatemala today as a wholly indigenous Maya dance drama that interprets historical events from a Maya perspective. The *Dance of the Conquest* reenacts the battle between the forces of Pedro de Alvarado, identified with the sun god, and the K'iche' lord Tecum Uman (or Lord Tecum). In the dance Alvarado wears a mask with pinkish skin and golden hair (fig. 32). He is the principal actor in the drama, delivering the most lines. The mask of Tecum, the war captain of the K'iche's, is dark-complected and adorned with one or more distinctive quetzal birds in his headdress (fig. 33). History is reinterpreted in the dance to make Tecum

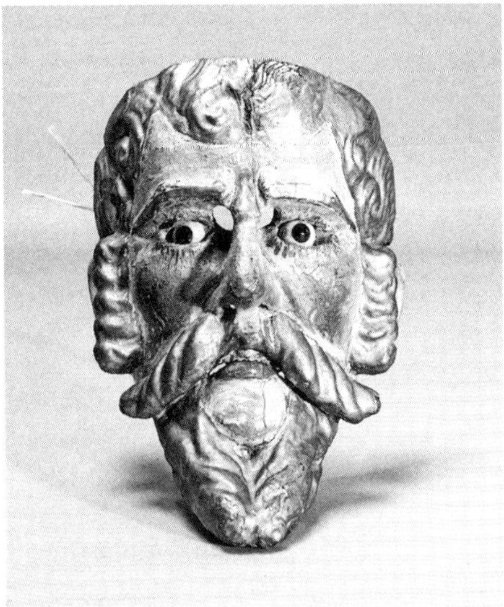

32. *(Left) Mask of Pedro de Alvarado,* Baile de la Conquista

33. *(Below) Tecum Uman at the center surrounded by his lords,* Baile de la Conquista. *Grupo Folklórico, San Cristóbal, Totonicapán*

the aggressor. Alvarado is played as trying to avoid war and offers repeated pleas for peace. Tecum personifies predawn liminality, much like the *Popol Vuh* description of Wuqub' Kaqix as a "sun" of the previous age who needed to die in order for the dawn of the new age to occur (Cook 2000, 119; Chinchilla Mazariegos 2013). The dance is performed frequently in the traditional K'iche'-Maya community of Momostenango. According to Miguel Castillo, a K'iche' who has played the role of Pedro de Alvarado numerous times, Alvarado was the legitimate ruler of the new age:

> So if Tecum had accepted the peace he wouldn't have died, and neither would so many people. This still happens today when there is a government that doesn't want to make peace or avoid war. Then another [presidential aspirant] declares. As when Castillo Armas entered through Esquipulas and took Chiquimula and Zacapa, and President Arbenz didn't do anything. It was the same as what Alvarado did. It happens that if a president doesn't want to leave his office that another wants to enter, he rules badly and won't leave. This has been explained to me by my father and other elders who know of old times. Maybe he won't give up his office, so a war begins. This is like what happened with Alvarado. (Cook 2000, 136)

In this view of history don Miguel sees Alvarado as the legitimate heir of the K'iche' kingdom who is unjustly resisted by the doomed representatives of a previous age. The use of the sun as a metaphor for political and spiritual power was apparently widespread in the Guatemalan highlands at the time of the Spanish Conquest and in the ensuing colonial period. Although surviving members of the old Maya nobility recognized that the arrival of the Spaniards represented the dawn of a new age, many undoubtedly cherished the hope that eventually their own "sun" would dawn again. Luis Carrillo wrote that a concerted effort was made by Bishop Marroquín in about 1554 to seek out and destroy pagan images in the Guatemalan highlands because it was rumored that many still worshipped them behind the backs of the Christian friars. In the community of Motocintla alone over seventy such images were found and taken away by force, suggesting that traditional Maya worship was still widely practiced in secret. This adherence to older indigenous traditions was specifically linked to the reestablishment of political and cultural autonomy as symbolized by the dawning of the sun:

> In many towns of that bishopric, a large number of idols were taken away that were made of stone, clay, wood, lesser gold, and copper, adorned with rattles, feathers, woven coverings, scallop shells, and other large shells. And the natives gave to these images offerings because they asserted that in the time of their paganism, each type of idol gave evidence of its power; and they believed and understood, and thus affirmed that when their aged ancestors were about to die they entrusted their idols to other old men to watch over them, honor them, and venerate them. For they believed that they and those who followed their laws and customs would prevail and that the Spaniards, who were foreign newcomers, would soon come to an end; and when they were dead, these gods would send another new sun that would illuminate those that would follow them, and they would recover what was lost in

their generation and that they would possess their land in tranquillity and peace. (Scholes and Adams 1938, 2:53, translation by author)

After the Spanish Conquest in 1524 it was common for the K'iche's to identify Jesus Christ with either their ancient patron god, Tohil, or Hun Hunahpu, one of the principal heroes of the *Popol Vuh* (Ximénez 1929–1931 [1722], 1:108). This process of religious syncretism almost triggered a religious war in Guatemala among many of the highland Maya survivors who saw nothing new in Christianity and wished to continue to worship their own gods:

> It happened in this kingdom shortly after being conquered that, upon hearing of the life of Christ which the friars taught them, there arose a Mexican Indian, a pseudo-prophet. He taught them that Huhapu [Hunahpu, the elder of the Hero Twins in the *Popol Vuh*] was God and that Hununapu [Hun Hunahpu, father of the Hero Twins] was the son of God. . . . For this reason there was such a commotion among the Indians that the work was nearly lost, for they came to imagine that our Holy Gospel told them nothing new. (Ximénez 1929–1931 [1722], 1:57, translation by author)

The K'iche's undoubtedly equated Jesus Christ with Hun Hunahpu because both were sacrificed by their enemies and hung on a "tree" before rising from death (Christenson 2007, 125–127). This association did not end with the defeat of the Mexican pseudo-prophet. Spanish conquerors and missionaries habitually set up crosses in places of indigenous worship to symbolize the victory of Christianity over paganism. In most instances the Maya probably adopted the Christian symbol of the cross willingly as a symbol of regeneration that fit well with their own indigenous beliefs. Fray Gerónimo de Mendieta notes that recent converts used Christian crosses to hide the continued veneration of their own gods:

> And because the friars commanded them to make many crosses and place them at crossroads and the entrances to towns, and on the tops of high mountains, they did so, placing their idols beneath or behind the cross. And giving the appearance of worshipping the cross, they instead worshipped the figures of the demons that they had hidden there. (Mendieta 1993, book 3, chapter 23, 234, translation by author)

It is possible that Mendieta is correct in interpreting the actions of early Christian converts as merely feigned devotion to the Christian cross. It is also possible, however, that the association of certain deity images with the cross was purposeful and represents an early attempt to harmonize the two faiths while preserving a fundamentally indigenous worldview. Thus Carmack writes that while the Maya adopted the external forms of Christianity willingly, "their basic values and beliefs continued to be those of their ancestors" (Carmack 1981, 337). As we have seen, the Maya apparently attributed the virtues of their defeated gods to the cross itself and gave offerings to it as a symbol of the ancient World Tree, both having a similar form. This may explain why modern Maya often paint major crosses green or decorate them with foliage.

THE CONQUEST OF THE TZ'UTUJIL MAYA

The conquest of the Tz'utujils, the people who are the focus of the remaining chapters of this book, took place soon after the fall of the K'iche' kingdom. It is important to take the history of the Tz'utujil conquest into account in order to understand why much of the community of Santiago Atitlán has maintained its essentially Maya worldview despite nearly five centuries of pressure to adopt orthodox Roman Catholicism and European norms of language, dress, and societal behavior.

The territory now occupied by Santiago Atitlán was once the capital of the ancient Tz'utujil kingdom, which extended from the southern shores of Lake Atitlán to the rich cacao-producing lands of the Pacific coastal plain. Following the destruction of the K'iche' capital and the execution of its kings, Pedro de Alvarado inquired if there were any other hostile forces that might hinder the establishment of Spanish power in the Guatemalan highlands. Alvarado's Kaqchikel allies informed him that the Tz'utujils on the southern and western shores of Lake Atitlán had been their traditional enemies for centuries and could pose a powerful threat, particularly considering their reputation as fierce warriors:

> I knew from the chiefs of [the Kaqchikels] that seven leagues from here was another city on a very large lake, and that it made war against this city, and against Utlatan and against all others in their neighborhood, and that they were very strong on account of the lake and their canoes, and that from there they came out to make night raids on this land; and as the people of this city [Iximche'] saw the damage that they received from them, they told me they were good people and in the service of His Majesty and that they did not wish to make war or go against them without my permission, praying me that I should help them. And I told them that I would send to call them on the part of our lord the Emperor and that if they should come I would command them not to make war nor do anything wrong in

> this land, as they had heretofore done, and if they did not come, I would go with them to make war and punish them. I therefore sent them two messengers, natives of this city, whom they killed without any fear. (Alvarado 1924, 69–70)

The death of the messengers prompted Alvarado to invade the Tz'utujil region in force with 60 cavalry, 150 Spanish infantry, and several thousand Kaqchikel and Tlaxcalan allies. The Tz'utujils formed a defensive line against the attack northeast of present-day Santiago Atitlán, which was quickly broken up by Spanish crossbowmen. The battle is commemorated in the *Lienzo de Tlaxcala*, painted soon after the Conquest (fig. 34). Some of the Tz'utujil defenders were able to escape by jumping into Lake Atitlán and swimming to a nearby island, while others were slaughtered by the late arrival of 300 Kaqchikel war canoes (Alvarado 1924, 71). After nearly five hundred years there is still lingering animosity between the Tz'utujils on the southern and western shores of Lake Atitlán and the Kaqchikels who occupy the northern and eastern shores because of their alliance with the Spanish invaders during the Conquest.

34. *Conquest of the Tz'utujils at the Battle of Tecpan Atitlán.* Lienzo de Tlaxcala *(1581–1585). Painting by Alfredo Chavero, 1892*

That evening Alvarado and his troops spent the night in a maize field and prepared for a siege of the capital city, Chiya', the following morning. The ancient city of Chiya' is located at the base of San Pedro volcano, across the bay from present-day Santiago Atitlán. It is protected on three sides by the waters of Lake Atitlán, while the remaining approach to the west abuts the steep slopes of the volcano, making it easily defensible from hostile attack. The Tz'utujil lords, however, had apparently seen enough to know that defeat was inevitable and abandoned their capital without a fight (Anonymous 1935 [ca. 1700], 364). Alvarado sent several captured Tz'utujils into the mountains to demand that the fleeing inhabitants return to their homes under the promise that they would not be harmed. If they did not return, however, he threatened to continue hostilities, burn their towns, and destroy their maize and cacao fields. Within three days the ruler of Chiya', Joo No'j K'iq'ab', declared fealty to the Spanish king, commending Alvarado for his skill in war and noting that until that day "their land had never been broken into nor entered by force of arms" (Alvarado 1924, 72). The Tz'utujil king presented the victor with abundant gifts of tribute and promised that he would never again resume hostilities. Alvarado reported the Tz'utujils' submission in a letter to Cortés:

> I gave them to understand the greatness and power of our lord the Emperor, and that they should appreciate that for all that had passed, I, in his Royal name, would pardon them, and that from now on they should behave themselves and not make war against anybody in the neighborhood, as all were now vassals of His Majesty; so I dismissed them, leaving them safe and peaceful, and returned to this city. At the end of three days after my arrival there, all the chiefs, principal people and captains of the said lake came to me with presents and told me that now they were our friends and considered themselves fortunate to be vassals of His Majesty and relieved of hardships, wars and differences that they had amongst themselves. And I received them very well and gave them some of my jewels and sent them back to their country with much affection, and they are the most pacific that are in this land. (ibid., 72–73)

Despite the Tz'utujils' reputation as aggressive warriors with a penchant for shifting alliances, the rulers of Chiya' never rebelled openly against the Spaniards. The Lake Atitlán region remained one of the most peaceful in the country. This lack of aggression is unusual, considering the succeeding decades of forced labor and exorbitant tribute demands that drove other Spanish "allies" to take up arms (Anonymous 1952, 436). The Kaqchikels chafed under this oppression and eventually rebelled openly against their former Spanish allies. As a result, Alvarado hanged the last Kaqchikel king, Kaji' Imox, on

May 26, 1540. Soon afterward, in the same year, the last of the K'iche' kings, Tepepul, was also hanged following a long period of imprisonment (Recinos and Goetz 1953, 132–133; Maxwell and Hill 2006, 287–289). The Tz'utujils proved to be loyal allies during the Kaqchikel rebellion, contributing warriors to assist the Spaniards in quelling the revolt (Recinos and Goetz 1953, 125).

In gratitude for his peaceful submission to Spanish authority, Alvarado allowed King Joo No'j K'iq'ab' to remain as the *cacique* of the Tz'utujils at Chiya'. *Caciques*, the Spanish title for indigenous rulers, were exempt from tribute and labor obligations. Spanish law considered them to be the direct vassals of the Crown, not subject to the orders of local governors or military administrators. *Caciques* who proved their loyalty to the king were allowed to use the Spanish title *don*, own and ride horses, display a coat of arms, and possess weapons.

At some point soon after the Conquest, the Tz'utujil king adopted the name don Pedro, perhaps in honor of Pedro de Alvarado, who had defeated him in battle (Carlsen 1997, 84). Rather than viewing him as a hated enemy, the Tz'utujil king apparently saw Alvarado as a warrior lord whose power he wished to emulate. The Tz'utujils chose Santiago for their city's titular saint (fig. 35), the patron of the Spanish army and the founding saint of Alvarado's first capital at Ciudad del Señor Santiago de los Caballeros (City of Lord Santiago of the Knights). In doing so the Tz'utujils hoped to assimilate the warlike characteristics of Santiago, the saint whose divine favor was widely believed by the Spaniards to have brought them success in their long and ultimately successful war against the Moors in Spain in the fifteenth century and, more importantly for the Maya, the recent Spanish victories in the Guatemalan highlands.

I doubt that the adoption of Pedro and Santiago into the Tz'utujil pantheon was arbitrary. The Maya were quite selective about which saints they chose to adopt as their patrons, based on their attributes and the timing of their festivals. In adopting the names of these two saints, the Tz'utujil king applied to himself and his capital city the protective power of the two most prominent divinities whose patronage had given the Spaniards their astonishing success. He undoubtedly meant to usurp their supernatural power and place them at the service of the Tz'utujils.

Due to the ruthlessness of the Spanish Conquest under Pedro de Alvarado, few highland Maya rulers survived to administer their lands as *caciques*. By the time Alonso López de Cerrato came to power as the governor of Guatemala in 1548 and instituted reforms aimed at imposing legitimate Spanish law, he noted that "when the Spaniards entered this land, they killed some *caciques* and removed others from their thrones to such an extent that in all this prov-

35. *Santiago as patron saint of Santiago Atitlán, Cofradía Santa Cruz, 2010*

36. *Sixteenth-century highland Maya* cacique. *(Fuentes y Guzmán 1972 [1690], 3:267)*

ince there is almost no natural nor legitimate *cacique*" (*Relación Cerrato*, in Carmack 1973, 379). The continuation of an unbroken sequence of Tz'utujil lords in orderly succession after the Spanish Conquest is thus exceptional among the highland Maya.

The first Tz'utujil *cacique*, don Pedro, remained in power at Chiya' until his death. He was succeeded by his son, don Juan, who reigned from 1540 to 1547. A descendant of don Pedro, don Bernabé, reigned in Santiago Atitlán well into the seventeenth century. In 1630 he was visited by Father Bernabé Cobo, a Jesuit missionary and naturalist. Father Cobo noted in a letter to a friend in Peru that the *cacique* of Santiago Atitlán had in his possession a painted *lienzo* (a sheet of cloth painted with indigenous pictorial writing) showing Joo No'j K'iq'ab' greeting the first Spaniards: "Adjacent to the Guest House was the house of the *cacique*, where I saw a painted *lienzo* showing the arrival of the Spaniards in this land, and the *cacique* who received him in peace offering gifts. And the *cacique* who showed me this history was the grandson of he who was depicted in the painting" (Vázquez de Espinosa 1944, 195–196, translation by author).

The office of *cacique* thus remained within the royal family in Santiago Atitlán for at least a hundred years, preserving much of the old power structure without serious disruption (fig. 36). As a result, immediate authority in the secular and religious affairs of the community would have remained in the hands of local Maya lords. Maya rulers represented the embodiment of divine power to act in earthly affairs, a belief noted by Spanish authorities. López de

Cerrato wrote a warning in 1552 that indigenous *caciques* like don Pedro of the Tz'utujils wielded tremendous religious as well as political power over their subjects and could prove dangerous if they were to rebel, "because anciently they revered [the *caciques*] as gods, and if this persists, the lords could raise the land easily" (Carmack 1973, 379, translation by author). The survival of the Tz'utujil king and his continued dominance at Chiya', where the old temples still stood, must have seemed a confirmation to the local populace that the old order continued to hold relevance in Post-Conquest society.

In contrast to the fatalistic acceptance of defeat found in K'iche' and Kaqchikel accounts of the Conquest as well as contemporary myths, most Atiteco legends about the arrival of the Spaniards emphasize the supernatural power of their ancient kings and gods in escaping the destruction that befell other highland Maya kingdoms. This version is from Nicolás Chávez Sojuel:

> In a great battle near Chukumuk [a small settlement near the lake, northeast of town], Rey Tz'utujil threw down a great stone before the invaders which broke into 2,000 pieces, each becoming a crab that pinched the Spaniards and halted their advance. He then blew in their direction, causing a wind that killed many of the invaders and drove them into the lake. Rey Tepepul then hurled a long staff at them that became a serpent that killed many more. In those days the lake was lower and you could walk on dry land to the old capital city across the bay. But when the Spaniards came the daughter of Rey Tepepul, a girl named María, stood on the peninsula and wept, making the water rise and drowning the Spaniards who wished to cross. That is why the Virgin María owns the lake and has her home there. (translation of his account by author)

From this account and many other similar legends about the Conquest we would hardly know that the Tz'utujils had lost the war. The Virgin Mary is already assimilated into the Tz'utujil pantheon as the daughter of the deified king of Chiya' as well as the patron goddess of Lake Atitlán. In this view Christian divinities were not imposed on the Tz'utujils by the Spanish Conquest but actually sided with their ancestors to protect them from the destruction that visited neighboring highland Maya kingdoms.

Nicolás Chávez Sojuel told me that when the Spaniards came the earth died along with the ancient gods and kings. The finality of this view must be understood in the context of the Maya belief in the repetition of all past events. He went on to point out that the earth has died many times already. Each time the world and its gods are reborn to new life they regain their former power and new gods are added. Chávez explained that "the saints today have Spanish names because the old earth died in the days of the Spanish conquerors. When the spirit keepers of the world appeared again they were the saints, but they do the same work that the old gods did anciently."

A few years ago an *ajq'ij* asked me why North Americans were so fascinated by what the Maya had to say about the end of the ancient Maya calendar in 2012. I told him that they mistakenly believed that the Maya claimed that the world would end then. He replied that of course the world would die when the calendar came to a close. When I looked surprised by his answer he laughed and said the world dies all the time—every evening when the sun sets, at Easter, at harvest time, and on and on. He told me not to worry because he and the other *ajq'ij*s were always able to get it going again with their prayers and ceremonies.

Chapter 4

POST-CONQUEST CEREMONIES OF WORLD RENEWAL

In most highland Maya communities the Spanish Conquest resulted in the abrupt curtailment of the more public aspects of the ancient Wayeb' rituals such as human sacrifice and bloodletting, both intended to help rebirth the world. Without these ceremonies the Maya undoubtedly feared that the earth would never recover from the devastation wrought by the conquistadors. Easter observances soon became the substitute for the ancient Wayeb' rites as a means of restoring life to the world in a form that was acceptable to Spanish authorities. The Maya adopted Jesus Christ as the supreme God of the conquering Spaniards soon after the Conquest and equated him with one or another of their ancient life-bearing gods. This syncretic blending of ancient Maya and Christian traditions continues to the present day in some highland Guatemalan communities that practice elements of traditional Maya worship. For these traditionalists, the days preceding Easter, called Holy Week, not only commemorate the passion and death of Christ but the death of the world itself, requiring an intensive period of ceremonial renewal.

HOLY WEEK AND THE REBIRTH OF THE WORLD

In the Guatemalan highlands Holy Week marks the end of the dry season, followed by the first rains and the planting of maize. These seasonal changes reflect the belief that the death and resurrection of Christ parallels the dissolution and sterility of the world during the dry season and its rebirth with the coming of the rainy season and the regeneration of life-sustaining crops, particularly maize. Traditional Maya believe that the world is under constant threat of disaster. If the proper rituals are not carried out at the proper time, all creation would sink back into the primordial world of darkness and endless death. Martín Prechtel quotes a Tz'utujil from Santiago Atitlán as saying: "A forgotten God was an angry God, or a dead God. In either case, the life sap [cosmic force] would stop flowing, and all this life would be as if it had never existed. We would cease" (Prechtel 1998, 107).

To prevent this horror, the traditionalists of Santiago Atitlán observe a complex and exhausting cycle of prayers, processions, and ceremonies throughout the year in order to maintain the power of the world to sustain life. Many of the ceremonies conducted during the days of Holy Week retain important elements of ancient New Year's ceremonies practiced during the five days of the Wayeb' at the close of the Pre-Columbian solar calendar. As outlined in chapter 3, the Tz'utujil Maya of Santiago Atitlán are unique among highland Maya groups in that their royal family and members of the old nobility survived the Spanish Conquest intact, thus allowing an unbroken continuation of their political and social structure. Santiago Atitlán's geographic location, far from the Spanish centers of power, undoubtedly contributed to their ability to practice many of their ancestral ceremonies and ritual performances relatively unhindered during much of the colonial period.

EARLY EVANGELIZATION EFFORTS IN HIGHLAND GUATEMALA

Fray Antonio de Remesal wrote at the beginning of the seventeenth century that Pedro de Alvarado and his followers initiated the conquest of Guatemala to accomplish four purposes: to enlarge the domain of Spain, to extend the Roman Catholic faith, to achieve immortal fame, and to enrich themselves (Remesal 1964 [1619], book 1, chapter 1, 81). There is nothing to indicate, however, that any serious attempts were made to convert the highland Maya to Christianity in the first years after the Spanish Conquest. Political and economic dominion were the focus of the early colonial era. In his letters to Hernán Cortés, Alvarado mentioned that he planned to attack the Tz'utujils "to bring the Infidels into the service of his Majesty," the king of Spain (Alvarado 1946, 460). After the fall of Chiya', the capital city of the Tz'utujils, Alvarado wrote that he received the lords from the Lake Atitlán region and "made them know the greatness and power of the Emperor" (ibid.). In these letters, Alvarado addresses only the political subjugation of the Maya. His writings do not mention religious indoctrination; nor did missionary priests accompany his troops. Although the Tz'utujil king was eventually baptized and given the new name of don Pedro, Fray Francisco Ximénez doubted that this took place when Alvarado invaded Tz'utujil territory in 1524. He suggested that the baptism was performed many years later, well after the first Christian missionaries arrived in Guatemala in 1534 (Ximénez 1929–1931 [1722], book 1, chapter 41, 128).

There does not seem to have been a regular Spanish presence in Chiya' of any kind for years following the Spanish Conquest. Pedro de Alvarado assigned half of the Tz'utujils' tribute payments to himself and the other half to one of his soldiers, Sancho de Barahona el Viejo. Barahona's share of the spoils took the form of an *encomienda*, an institution whereby the Crown authorized Spaniards who participated in the Conquest to collect tribute and demand labor from the Maya in return for services such as providing protection from traditional enemies and arranging for the spiritual welfare of indigenous people under their control. Following the deaths of both Pedro de Alvarado and his wife, Beatriz de la Cueva, in 1541, the king of Spain seized their half of the Tz'utujil payments. The Barahona family continued to receive tribute into the seventeenth century (Carlsen 1997, 89). But Sancho de Barahona and his descendants never resided in Tz'utujil lands. The *cacique*, don Pedro, was free to administer his former kingdom as he saw fit, so long as the tribute payments were delivered without incident. Although these financial pressures were often exorbitant, Robert Carlsen suggests that the Tz'utujils may have considered them a tolerable payoff to deter Spanish meddling in their affairs while the land and means of production remained in their hands (Carlsen 1996, 147).

During the first decades after the Conquest Spanish clerics had little influence over religious affairs in the Tz'utujil region. In this early period it was left to the conquistadors who held *encomiendas* to indoctrinate the Maya in the Catholic faith. Despite the legal obligation to do so, however, the Barahona family made no serious attempts to convert the Tz'utujils in its charge to Christianity. According to the *Relación de los caciques y principales del pueblo de Atitlán*, composed in 1571, the Barahonas even refused to contribute funds to build a church in Santiago Atitlán (Anonymous 1952, 437–438). Fray Bartolomé de Las Casas decried this policy as a failure everywhere in the New World, asserting that most *encomenderos* failed to keep their religious obligations, being themselves vicious and woefully ignorant of even the most basic tenets of the Catholic faith. He cited the case of one Juan Colmenero, who held a large town in *encomienda* in exchange for his promise to be the pastor for the people there: "He who, when he was examined by one of our friars once, did not know how to make the sign of the cross, and when asked what he was teaching the Indians of his town, answered that he gave them to the devil" (Las Casas 1971, 176–177). In another instance Las Casas reported that in a certain province the Indians voluntarily surrendered their idols to the Christian friars, only to have the local *encomendero* cart in loads of idols from other regions to sell in the market in exchange for slaves (Las Casas 1971, 177).

Christianity was not formally established in Guatemala until 1534, when the first bishop, Francisco Marroquín, arrived in the capital city of Santiago de los Caballeros, recently founded by Pedro de Alvarado. In the next few years Marroquín sent out a small number of missionary friars with portable

37. *Baptism of native* caciques, Lienzo de Tlaxcala *(1581–1585). Drawing by Alfred Chavero, 1892*

altars to the various Maya towns and villages to baptize the inhabitants and destroy any remnants of ancient "idolatry" that might have survived. These evangelization efforts focused on the *caciques* and other indigenous leaders in the hope that they would set an example for the rest (fig. 37). It is probable that the Tz'utujil king was baptized in conjunction with one of these early missionary forays.

The earliest missionaries to the Tz'utujil area were sent out with little or no language training. Because these itinerant priests did not speak Tz'utujil, their ability to communicate Christian doctrine effectively would have been highly problematic. The missionaries did not remain in one place for long periods, and there were too few to do more than baptize some of the local leaders before moving on to the next community. In 1556 a judge of the Audiencia in Guatemala sent a report to the king of Spain, lamenting the lack of progress in converting the Maya to Christianity:

> [The friars], although they do all they can, cannot reach all the pueblos which are in their charge because there are so many and because of their size. There is a lack of doctrine in the pueblos because the religious cannot

> get around to all of them. They might be eight or fifteen days or a month in a pueblo and in this time they say Mass, baptize and preach and then they go to another. Then four months pass or eight or sometimes a year before the Indians hear Mass or preaching and there is no one to baptize them. There are many pueblos of five hundred houses and more which are most of the year without Mass and without anyone to watch over their spiritual state, and being young in the faith, they forget what has been taught them. (O'Flaherty 1979, 185)

Sandra Orellana suggests that few Tz'utujils were baptized by the first priests, and the bulk of the population continued to practice their indigenous religion as before when the priests moved on (Orellana 1984, 195). Early efforts to evangelize the Tz'utujils in many ways resembled the military conquest of the region—a brief show of force to establish predominance and secure the fealty of the ruler, followed by long periods of relative noninterference.

Baptism was a necessary step for any Maya of noble birth who aspired to a place in the new political order. Without it the Spanish authorities would not recognize his legitimacy or territorial claims. In addition, baptism afforded some protection from the excesses of Spanish rule in that unconverted pagans were subject to enslavement until the reforms of judge Alonso López de Cerrato, president of the Royal Audiencia of Guatemala, abolished the practice in 1548. Few if any of these early converts likely understood the implications of baptism beyond a vague acknowledgment of the power of the new Christian divinities and a promise to incorporate them into their worship. It is doubtful that they understood baptism as a sweeping renunciation of Maya deities and traditional ceremonial observances. As Fernando Cervantes writes, "[T]he initial enthusiasm of the Indians to accept Christianity had more to do with the Mesoamerican tradition of incorporating alien elements into their religion than with any conviction about the exclusivist claims of the Christian faith" (Cervantes 1994, 42). Fray Gerónimo de Mendieta complained at the end of the sixteenth century that paganism continued unabated in New Spain despite the Indians' acceptance of Christian deities:

> And among the idols of the devils were found as well images of Christ our Redeemer and of Our Lady that the Spaniards had given them, thinking that with them they would be content. In addition if they had 100 gods, they would want 105, and more if they were given more. (Mendieta 1993, 233–234, translation by author)

THE BLENDING OF TRADITIONAL MAYA PRACTICES AND ROMAN CATHOLICISM

Ximénez wrote that most priests in his day (at the close of the seventeenth century) were more concerned with administrative duties and building churches than with preaching. The sermons that they did give in highland Maya areas were mostly delivered in Spanish and were of little benefit to the indigenous population (Ximénez 1967 [1722], 7–8). As a result the K'iche's of Chichicastenango continued to practice their traditional faith in secret, including the preservation of Maya texts like the *Popol Vuh*:

> It was with great reserve that these manuscripts were kept among them, with such secrecy, that the ancient ministers knew nothing of it; and upon investigating this point, while I was in the parish of Santo Tomás Chichicastenango, I found that it was the doctrine which they first imbibed with their mother's milk, and that all of them knew it almost by heart; and I found that they had many of these books among them. (Ximénez 1929–1931 [1722], book 1, chapter 1, 5, translation by author)

Seventy years later Fray Pedro Cortés y Larraz wrote that the people of Chichicastenango were still steeped in "superstition and idolatry," ignorant of even the most basic Christian doctrines. He laid the blame for this situation squarely at the feet of the priests who labored there, writing that "in all the Christian world there are no lazier priests than those in the Americas" (Cortés y Larraz 1958 [1770], 1:61). Thomas Gage, an English Catholic priest working in the same region of Guatemala in the seventeenth century (who later converted to Protestantism), wrote that the priests and friars in his day were "deluding the poor people for their ends, enriching themselves with their gifts, placing religion in mere policy. Thus the Indians' religion consists more in sights, shows, and formalities than in any true substance" (Gage 1958, 240). John Lloyd Stephens traveled through the K'iche' region in 1840 and visited the ruins of the ancient capital of Q'umarkaj. He noted that the people of the region still clung to their ancient traditions:

> For here they still exist, in many respects, an unchanged people, cherishing the usages and customs of their ancestors; and though the grandeur and magnificence of the churches, the pomp and show of religious ceremonies, affect their rude imaginations, the padre told us that in their hearts they were full of superstitions, and still idolaters; had their idols in the mountains and ravines, and in silence and secrecy practiced the rites received from their fathers. He was compelled to wink at them. (Stephens 1969, 2:191–192)

As noted in chapter 2, an ancient stone deity in the hills above Chichicastenango named Paxkwal Ab'aj continues to be the object of pilgrimage by devout Maya traditionalists from all over the region, attesting to the perseverance of indigenous ceremonial practices down through the centuries.

Large numbers of carved idols were discovered in the Atitlán area in the mid-sixteenth century. Although many of these were destroyed by Roman Catholic authorities, others continued to be venerated (Vázquez 1937–1944 [1714], 1:110, 2:20). In the 1560s the priests assigned to Santiago Atitlán, Fray Juan Alonso and Fray Diego Martín, discovered that the Tz'utujils still practiced human sacrifices. One custom was to throw young people into the Atitlán volcano when it erupted in order to placate it (ibid., 1:70, 178). Although the priests attempted to stop the practice, they were unsuccessful. A decade later Fray Gonzalo Méndez climbed the trail up to the top of the volcano at night just in time to discover a group of Tz'utujils about to sacrifice a young girl:

> When the volcano near the town of Atitlán roared or thundered, flaring up and casting forth fire (as was its custom with horrific suddenness), the devil persuaded them that it was hungry and was asking for something to eat; and its preferred feast was Indian maidens, which they had always sacrificed in their time of heathenism, casting them into the fiery mouth of that conflagration; for only with this bloody offering could its fury be assuaged. (Vázquez 1938–1944 [1714], 2:28, translation by author)

After the initial evangelization efforts in the colonial period, Santiago Atitlán had no resident priests between 1821 and 1964. This allowed many indigenous religious beliefs and practices to continue relatively unabated, while others became mixed with the Tz'utujils' interpretation of Roman Catholic doctrine. In 1964 the Archdiocese of Oklahoma adopted the community and sent a team of priests, nuns, and laypeople, many of them Americans, who administered "various development efforts that included agricultural, credit, and weaving cooperatives; a medical program with a large clinic and later a small hospital; a literacy program that included a small radio station; a Montessori school; and a pastoral program that attempted to develop a liturgy that would convey the basic concepts of Christianity" (Early 2006, xiv). Before this Roman Catholic priests rarely visited the town, and then only to celebrate Mass and perform baptisms (Mendelson 1958b, 4–5).

Mendelson noted in the 1950s that the Tz'utujils were prone to merge deities, substituting one for another and declaring that one was the same as the other (Mendelson 1957, 140). The question is whether this blending of faiths was imposed and arbitrary or consciously selective by the Tz'utujils themselves. John Watanabe suggests that the Maya tend to alter new experiences and ideas to fit already established indigenous cultural patterns, modifying rather than adopting them whole-cloth (Watanabe 1992, 15–17). In this view the Maya do not resist innovations and foreign influences outright but structure them in such a way that they resonate with older indigenous patterns. For the most part this syncretic blending of Maya and Christian ideology appears to have been directed by the Maya themselves (Watanabe 1990; Carlsen 1997, 50–58). From my experience the Tz'utujils are often eager to adopt non-Maya ideas and symbols if they fit their ancestral view of the world, but either ignore or openly reject those that do not. I suspect that most of the syncretism in Atiteco society over the centuries has been the result of this kind of selective appropriation of Christian forms while maintaining their fundamentally indigenous view of the world.

THE CONGREGATION OF SANTIAGO ATITLÁN

To aid in the process of conversion Spanish missionaries initiated the consolidation of formerly scattered highland Maya settlements into large nucleated centers in a process called *congregación* (congregation). In a letter to the Spanish Crown, Bishop Marroquín insisted that this was essential to facilitate the Maya's indoctrination in the Christian faith because "in the Province of Guatemala, the greater part is mountainous with houses being very far apart," making it impossible to reach everyone (Estrada Monroy 1979, 116, translation by author). Congregation also solved administrative problems related to the collection of tribute and tithes. Spanish settlers supported the policy because it assigned restricted territorial limits to Indian lands, making room for the expansion of their own estates. Tragically, the crowded conditions of the newly congregated cities also created an ideal environment for the rapid spread of disease, while the constriction in available land for cultivation fostered famine and malnutrition.

Because the older fortified Tz'utujil center at Chiya' was difficult to reach and too small to accommodate a large, concentrated population, a new Tz'utujil capital city was laid out across the bay in 1541 where the city of Santiago Atitlán now lies. At first the settlement bore the same name as the older abandoned center, Santiago Chiya'. As in the case of most other Guatemalan towns, however, Spanish authorities ultimately adopted the Tlaxcalan translation of Maya toponyms in their records. By at least 1585 the town was called Santiago Atitlán, the Tlaxcalan translation of Chiya' (both meaning "by the lake"). If the newly congregated city of Santiago Atitlán paralleled other communities in Guatemala, there would have been a subsequent devastating population collapse from malnutrition and disease. It is estimated that approximately 2 million Maya lived in Guatemala at the time of the Spanish Conquest in 1524. By 1595, less than a century later, the population had fallen to 133,280, a decline of more than 93 percent (Early 2006, 148–150).

The congregation of Santiago Atitlán was carried out by two Franciscan missionaries, Fray Francisco de la Parra and Fray Pedro de Betanzos, who gathered Tz'utujil speakers from the old capital at Chiya' as well as numerous settlements along the southern shores of Lake Atitlán and the surrounding mountains. In a letter to King Philip II, Fray Betanzos described the indigenous people that he brought to the new city as "elusive and frightened," suggesting a degree of reluctance on the part of the Tz'utujils to abandon their traditional homelands (Orellana 1984, 122). The Franciscans founded a monastery next to the church for the use of future missionaries, although the community apparently had no resident priests until the arrival of Fray Juan Alonso and Fray Diego Martín in 1566.

The process of congregation followed a uniform pattern in the principal communities such as Santiago Atitlán (García Peláez 1943, 161–166; Betancor and Arboleda 1964). First, a church was erected at the center of the proposed site fronted by an *atrio* (open plaza) for large assemblies to gather for Roman Catholic ritual observances and indoctrination. The rest of the town was organized into squares divided by streets laid out oriented to the cardinal directions. While the new settlement was under construction, families planted their maize on plots assigned to them in the nearby countryside. When the crops were ready to harvest, the older Pre-Columbian structures at Chiya' were destroyed to prevent reoccupation and the people moved into their new homes across the bay. Christian missionaries staged elaborate festivals to celebrate the event "so that they would forget their ancient dwellings" (García Peláez 1943, 163).

Santiago Atitlán follows the general plan of most major congregated Maya communities in the sixteenth century, although the Spanish arrangement of streets set at right angles to form squares extends for only a few blocks around the central district because of the irregularity of the terrain. The town is situated on a lava terrace that rises from a narrow arm of Lake Atitlán toward the slopes of two great volcanoes to the east, now known as Volcán San Lucas and Volcán Atitlán. A third volcano dominates the western horizon above the ruins of Chiya' to the west, Volcán San Pedro. The location of Santiago Atitlán at the center point in the midst of three volcanoes mirrors sacred Maya geography, which describes the place of first creation as centered among three stones or mountains (Freidel et al. 1993). Partly because of its setting, the

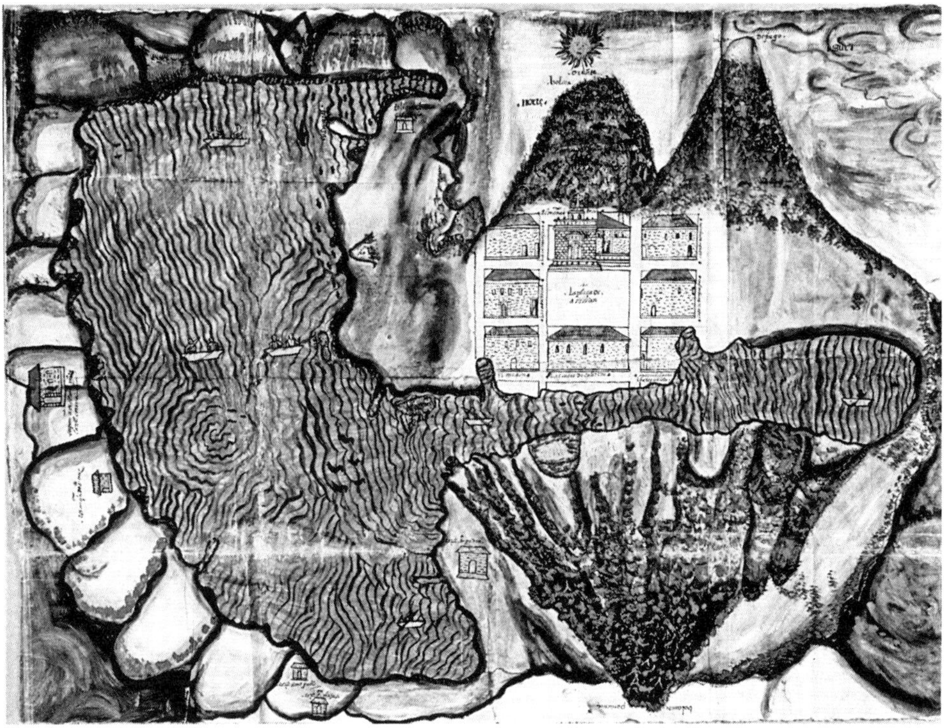

38. *Map of Santiago Atitlán, 1585. Nettie Lee Benson Latin American Collection, University of Texas Libraries, The University of Texas at Austin*

Tz'utujils today refer to their community as *rumuxux kaj, rumuxux ruwachuliw* (the navel of the sky, the navel of the face of the earth). A map of Santiago Atitlán painted in 1585 emphasizes these volcanoes and shows the town as it existed a few decades after congregation, with a church occupying the central position adjacent to the monastery complex (fig. 38).

The foundations of the present church at Santiago Atitlán were laid in 1570, and the building was completed in 1582. Within three years five resident priests were living in the monastery under the leadership of Fray Pedro de Arboleda. The church is one of the oldest in Guatemala and is unusually well-constructed of stone masonry with a plastered floor (fig. 39). The original roof consisted of a wooden framework covered with tiles (Anonymous 1952, 437). The plan of the church is consistent with the most common early colonial designs, with a single continuous nave and no side aisles or transepts (fig. 40), although the roof was supported by wooden posts until the 1970s. Such single-nave churches were part of the sixteenth-century Spanish re-

39. *Colonial-era church, Santiago Atitlán, 2006*

40. *Interior of the church, Santiago Atitlán, 2008*

form movement to return to the simplicity of the apostolic age (Kubler 1948, 2:239–242; Peterson 1993, 153).

Because the Barahona family refused to assist in the construction of the church, the entire cost in labor and materials appears to have been supplied by the Tz'utujils themselves (Anonymous 1952, 437–438). Although financially burdensome, this allowed a certain degree of autonomy for the Maya to incorporate traditional Maya dedicatory offerings into the fabric of the new building. During renovation efforts in the church complex carried out under Father Stanley Francis Rother in the 1970s, workers discovered remnants of a Pre-Columbian platform beneath the foundations of the church, indicating that its original builders followed the common New World precedent of constructing Roman Catholic churches over indigenous shrines in order to attract Christian converts (Farriss 1984, 309; Wagner 1997, 3). Stones from the older temple were incorporated into the steps leading up to the principal western entrance as well as the walls of the new church. By so doing, missionaries hoped to demonstrate the victory of Christianity over paganism while preventing the Maya from using the space to perform their ancient rites.

It is unlikely, however, that the Maya would perceive the construction of a new church over the remnants of one of their temples as the permanent death of the old gods once worshiped there. It was a rather common practice among the ancient Maya to demolish their pyramid temples and build over them periodically, maintaining the sanctity of the space while reinforcing its power with ever-grander constructions. The demolition of the older Pre-Columbian temple would represent the death of the building, followed by its rebirth in the form of a Roman Catholic sanctuary. Because the Maya believe that inanimate objects such as stones have living souls, their use in the new church would ensure the continued sanctity of the building as an ancestral shrine with an essentially Maya nature.

There are numerous stories current in Santiago Atitlán of elaborate burials and Pre-Columbian stone carvings found beneath the church floor and the adjacent *convento* complex to the north. Many, if not most, of the stories are apocryphal, describing underground tombs of perfectly preserved Tz'utujil kings wearing elaborate feather costumes trimmed with gold and jade and guarded by snarling jaguars or hissing serpents. As in other Guatemalan churches, important persons were certainly buried beneath the floor for centuries, a practice that continued until the 1950s in Santiago Atitlán before local officials prohibited it (Mendelson 1957, 542). As a result, the space beneath the floor of the church today is considered a major access point to the realm of the dead.

The intensive building efforts in Santiago Atitlán in the years following congregation ended soon after the close of the sixteenth century. Carlsen suggests that one of the major reasons for the Spanish presence there was to exploit Tz'utujil cacao orchards in the coastal piedmont (Carlsen 1996, 144). When the cacao industry collapsed a few decades later there was no longer an incentive to remain. Most of the Spanish clerics in Santiago Atitlán eventually moved on to more economically stable communities.

Roman Catholic policy for missionary orders in the sixteenth century was to evangelize newly conquered regions of the New World, build up local churches, and then turn over the newly organized parishes to bishops and secular clergy (Early 2006, 179). But this never happened in Santiago Atitlán. The church and monastery complex slowly fell into disrepair without the necessary funds to maintain them properly. By 1683 the Tz'utujils submitted requests to withhold a portion of their tribute to help pay for repairs, although their application was denied (Orellana 1984, 200).

After the independence of Guatemala from Spain in 1821, anticlerical legislation resulted in the abrupt end of the Franciscan presence in Santiago Atitlán and the community had no resident clergy thereafter until 1964. Colonial-era churches are normally owned by a Catholic diocese, a legal corporation under the jurisdiction of a bishop. The situation in Santiago Atitlán is unusual in that for most of its history after the Spanish Conquest it was either under the jurisdiction of Franciscan missionary priests or, after 1821, had no resident priest at all. As a result, the church in Santiago Atitlán does not technically belong to the Roman Catholic Church. It is considered the property of the community, in which "Catholic priests are invited guests" (Early 2006, 13). The Tz'utujil *cabecera* (the head of the indigenous *cofradía* system) holds copies of all of the keys. For most important actions the Roman Catholic priest must obtain the consent of the Comité de la Iglesia (Church Committee), which is wholly indigenous in its membership and often includes traditionalists who defend their ancestral practices from interference by the orthodox clergy.

TRADITIONAL MAYA CEREMONIALISM AFTER THE SPANISH CONQUEST

The *Título Pedro Velasco* records that prior to the Spanish Conquest the highland Maya of Guatemala conducted ritual dances in special "houses" in which their rulers danced in honor of the gods: "Each of the lineages had a house to hear the word and to administer judgment. There the lords danced the Junajpu C'oy and the Wukub Cak'ix, the Awata Tun, and the Jolom Tun. Each lineage had divisions, each with a housc" (Carmack and Mondloch 1989, 178, translation by author). This was a widespread practice in Mesoamerica. Fray Gerónimo de Mendieta wrote:

> One of the principal things that existed in this land were the songs and dances to solemnize the festivals of their demons, whom they honored as gods, as well as to rejoice and find solace. The house of each principal lord thus had a chapel for singers and a place for dances. The great dances were held in the plazas or in the house patios of the great lords, for all had large plazas. (Mendieta 1993, 140, translation by author)

Sometime before 1530 Fray Pedro de Gante wrote a number of songs that were intended to accompany a dance reenacting the Nativity of Christ performed by the Aztecs of central Mexico. He hoped that these newer Christian-inspired performances would eventually replace indigenous dance rituals and thus speed the process of conversion:

> And because I saw that all of their songs were dedicated to their gods, I composed a very solemn song concerning the law of God and of Faith, . . . and also I gave them liberty to paint on their robes in which they danced, for thus they were accustomed to do; thus in keeping with the dances and the songs that they once sang, they now clothed themselves with joy. (García Icazbalceta 1889–1892, 2:231–232, translation by author)

In the Cofradía San Juan in Santiago Atitlán a number of painted tunics are kept within a sacred bundle, locked away in a wooden chest for most of the year. On November 11 a Maya shaman known as a *nab'eysil* opens this bundle and wears one or more of the tunics in succession as part of a sacred dance that is intended to rebirth the world. The tunics appear to be very old and may be early colonial or even Pre-Columbian in origin (Christenson 2003, 154–166). Although the dance clearly has indigenous Tz'utujil elements that have nothing to do with Orthodox Catholicism, the bundle is called "Martín." November 11 is the day on the Roman Catholic liturgical calendar dedicated to St. Martin of Tours, indicating that at some point the dance became a syncretic blend of traditions in a process much like that described by Fray Pedro de Gante. Fray Domingo de Vico did much the same thing in the highlands of Guatemala, composing Christian hymns in K'iche'an languages to be used in ceremonial Maya dance performances:

> He [Vico] wrote poetic songs for each town, many stanzas and verses in which he wrote all the life of Christ our Lord, of the apostles, and of many

saints of the Church. These were principally intended for those charged with the festivals dedicated to the saints of the Church, so that the Indians would sing them in their fiestas and dances and others would hear them and learn. (Bossúz, 1990, 201, translation by author)

The Maya dedicated private houses called Guachibales (*wachib'al* in modern orthography, a term used to refer to both the place where sacred images were kept and the images themselves) for the veneration of particular saints where such songs and dances were performed, much as they had done in the houses of their lords prior to the Spanish Conquest. These became widely popular as places where the Maya could worship relatively independent of the Roman Catholic authorities. Thus Fray Francisco Antonio de Fuentes y Guzmán wrote that in the seventeenth century few communities in the Guatemalan highlands lacked Guachibales, within which the Maya placed images of saints that they owned themselves, surrounding them with flowers and continually offering incense and other precious things (Fuentes y Guzmán 1932–1933 [1600], 1:331–332). Over time the myths and attributes associated with the ancient Maya gods came to be conflated with those of the saints. Fuentes y Guzmán lamented that the Maya acknowledged the Christian saints during their ceremonies but nevertheless continued to honor their Pre-Columbian gods as well:

> They celebrate today the festivities of the saints called Guachibales, dancing around with the tenacity that we shall see, adorned with the same regalia that they used in that deluded time [before the Conquest]: but their songs have been reduced to the praise of the saints, relating and representing their miraculous histories composed by their ministers . . . . They dance singing the praises of the saint that they celebrate, but in the prohibited dances they sing the histories and deeds of their ancestors and false gods. (Fuentes y Guzmán 1932–1933 [1600], 1:77, 216–217, translation by author)

Fray Francisco Ximénez wrote that the Maya preferred their own ancient songs and dances to those composed for them by the early Catholic missionaries and continued to perform them in secret:

> Although the ancient Fathers gave to them certain histories of the Saints in their language that they may sing them to the accompaniment of the drum in place of those they sang in the days of their heathenism, nevertheless I understand that they sing these in public where their priest may hear them, yet in secret they carry out very pretty memories of their heathenism. (Ximénez 1926, 93, translation by author)

Fray Diego Durán complained that most priests were ignorant of the language of recently converted Indians in the New World and thus were easily deceived by them. In their dances and festivals they continued to honor their "heathen gods" while hiding the practice beneath a thin veil of Christian faith by occasionally shouting out the name of God or some saint (Durán 1867–1880, 2:71–80). Fray Bernardino de Sahagún agreed, writing that indigenous songs and dances were "like a cave or forest" where Satan had taken his last refuge (Sahagún 1956, 1:255).

The most common ritual performances instituted by early Spanish missionaries were Passion Plays during Easter season that reenacted the crucifixion and resurrection of Jesus Christ. As June Nash writes:

> The Spanish missionaries employed dramatic techniques in introducing Catholicism into the New World. The most significant of these dramas was the Passion Play, which contained the central core of Catholic ideology. Because the priests did not control the ideological or social context in which the ceremonial events they scheduled took place, a transformation of significance attached to rituals and roles has taken place. The play has become a vehicle for expressing indigenous themes. In the cultural interpretation of roles, both the Indians and their spiritual conquerors have identified protagonists of the original drama with pre-Columbian mythological antecedents. This has given them a link to the past. (Nash 1968, 318)

Ruth Bunzel suggested that the process of conflating Pre-Columbian deities with Christian saints may have been related to the way in which Maya rulers understood the ritual of baptism soon after the Spanish Conquest (Bunzel 1952, 264–268). As part of the baptismal ceremony Maya lords were christened with the names of saints as a token of their acceptance of Christianity. Those who remained loyal to the Spanish Crown and paid their regular tribute obligations were generally allowed to remain in office as *caciques*, administering the affairs of their communities in much the same way as they had done before the Conquest. The lords themselves had not changed, but they now received an additional name with powerful religious associations adopted from the Christian conquerors. In the same way, the Maya christened their ancient gods with the names of saints without altering their essential natures in a significant way.

Early missionaries often used Pre-Columbian terms for deities in order to express the Christian doctrines that they taught. For example, Tz'aqol, B'itol (Framer, Shaper) were the paired titles of the principal Maya deities who carried out the creation in K'iche' tradition (Christenson 2007, 68–90). In his

Theologia Indorum, Vico used *tz'aqol b'itol* to refer to the creator deity in his translation of the Old Testament book of Genesis (Carmack and Mondloch 1983, 13, 168). Practices such as this made the new Christian doctrines more readily understandable to the Maya, but they also fostered syncretism with the old indigenous gods. As a result, the practice was soon abandoned by the Spanish authorities. Nevertheless, as Bunzel noted, the precedent was set and continued to foster comparisons and identifications between the two theologies to the point where they came to "live together in unlegitimized union" until the present time (Bunzel 1952, 269).

Rather than destroy the practice of traditional Maya worship, the early colonial policy of comparing Christian saints and deities with ancient Maya gods actually facilitated the continued survival of Pre-Columbian ritual practices. Thomas Gage wrote in the seventeenth century that the saints' images were still worshipped by the Maya in the same way as their ancient "idols":

> They yield unto the popish religion [Roman Catholicism], especially to the worshiping of saints' images, because they look upon them as much like unto their forefathers' idols. . . . The churches are full of them. . . . Upon such saints' days, the owner of the saint maketh a great feast in the town. (Gage 1958, 234–235)

Gage noted that certain ritual dances were performed only by the ruling elite of the community in honor of their patron deity, an indication of the importance of ritual dance long after the Conquest:

> Thus they dance in compass and circle round about that instrument [a split-log drum], one following another sometimes straight, sometimes turning about, sometimes turning half way, sometimes bending their bodies and with the feathers in their hands almost touching the ground, and singing the life of their saint, or of some other. All this dancing is but a kind of walking round, which they will continue two or three whole hours together in one place, and thence go and perform the same at another house. The chief and principals only of the town dance this *toncontin*. It was the old dance which they used before they knew Christianity, except that then instead of singing the saints' lives, they sang the praises of their heathen gods. (Gage 1958, 244–245)

Gage described a traditional dance in which wild beasts were sacrificed in honor of one of the saints. The dancers involved were all important lords who clothed themselves in painted animal skins and headpieces, particularly those of pumas and jaguars. He also noted that at times humans were the object of the hunt, pursued by dancers who leapt at them and struck their bodies as they shrieked like wild animals. He noted that the Maya particularly favored such dances in connection with a ritual reenactment of the beheading of St. John the Baptist (Gage 1958, 245–246). A similar deer and jaguar dance is performed in the Cofradía of St. John the Baptist today in Santiago Atitlán, complete with shrieks and whistles as the dancers wearing deer costumes are symbolically hunted down and "killed" (Christenson 2003, 160–162). These were not merely symbolic Passion Plays in the eyes of the Maya but repetitions of the events themselves:

> Most of the Indians who take part in this dance are superstitious about what they have done, and they seem almost to believe that they have actually done what they only performed for the dance. When I lived amongst them, it was an ordinary thing for the one who in the dance was to act St. Peter or John the Baptist to come first to confession, saying they must be holy and pure like that saint, whom they represent, and must prepare themselves to die. So likewise he that acted Herod or Herodias, and some of the soldiers that in the dance were to speak and to accuse the saints, would afterwards come to confess of that sin, and desire absolution as from bloodguiltiness. (Gage 1958, 247)

From Gage's description, it is clear that the Maya did not see their sacred dances as entertainment or dramatic interpretations of mythic events but as the acts of gods and other sacred beings made corporeal by the performers. Modern Maya continue to believe that participants in ceremonies performed to commemorate ancient events are transformed into the saints and deities themselves and thus carry out their rituals in mythic time (Christenson 2001, 24, 158–166).

ESTABLISHMENT OF THE *COFRADÍA* SYSTEM

Perhaps to counter the popularity of the private Guachibales, Spanish authorities encouraged the establishment of *cofradías* (confraternities), voluntary associations charged with supervising the veneration of saints and organizing festivals in their honor (fig. 41). Each *cofradía* was organized with a hierarchy of ranked offices (*cargos*), held for one year as a voluntary service. Service generally began at the bottom of the system, with obligations that required little more than running errands and procuring materials for the saints' festivals. Having given successful service in these menial positions, individuals could rise through the ranks over their lifetime, accruing increased authority and influence in the community. The highest position within each *cofradía* was the *alcalde* (mayor, leader), who owned the *cofradía* house and directed its activities (fig. 42).

It was hoped that these *cofradías* would facilitate Maya integration into the Church and provide a more efficient mechanism for collecting tithes and offerings (Carlsen 1997, 93). They quickly became popular in Maya communities, however, as a means of asserting a measure of indigenous control over public religious ceremonies. Sandra Orellana writes that the *cofradías* allowed the Maya to maintain indigenous ritual practices free from clerical interference by Roman Catholic authorities:

> The cofradía became a focus of ritual activity which followed the Roman Catholic ceremonial calendar but preserved ancient religious customs. The saints were carefully dressed for processions and ceremonies just as pre-Columbian idols were. Fasting, ritual purification, abstinence from sexual relations, burning incense, drinking, and dancing characterized aboriginal general celebrations as well as those of Colonial cofradías. (Orellana 1981, 173)

In the centuries after the Spanish Conquest the opportunities for Maya lords to advance within the Spanish hierarchy lessened. Real positions of ecclesiastical authority became unavailable to them. As contacts with the Spaniards decreased, the Maya developed the *cofradía* system as an alternative religious organization independent of the Roman Catholic Church (Farriss 1984, 336–338; Hanks 2010, 78–79). The lavish care and adornment of the saints' images became an expression of the importance of the indigenous officials in whose houses they resided. As Matthew Restall writes, "the more extravagant the image and its celebration . . . , the better the projection of *cah* [indigenous community] pride and importance" (Restall 1997, 153). Possession of these images represented a measure of social currency and prestige that enhanced the owner's position, because the saints represented divine authority. The more important the perceived power of the saint within the community, the greater the status afforded to its guardian.

Whatever its original intention, the *cofradía* system developed into a means of preserving core elements of traditional worship that the Maya considered vital (Jones 1994, 76; Carmack 1995, 134, 227). In a letter composed by Spanish authorities in the eighteenth century, the Guachibales and *cofradías* were equated as identical indigenous institutions practiced in the private houses of prominent highland Maya leaders (Orellana 1984, 209). Soon after they were first organized *cofradías* became refuges for the private practice of traditional Maya worship, much as the Guachibales had been. Spanish au-

41. *(Above) Cofradía San Juan, Santiago Atitlán, 2004*

42. *(Left)* Alcalde, *Cofradía San Juan, Santiago Atitlán, 2007*

thorities became alarmed at the situation, as evident from a letter composed in the seventeenth century on the state of affairs in the Lake Atitlán region:

> In leaving the church they gather in the house of the *mayordomo*, where there is food and drink . . . which they eat and drink until they are drunk. They have music and dancing . . . in which they spend the whole day and night in heavy excess. To this, and nothing else, are the fiestas of the Indians reduced . . . . Although they appear so poor and miserable, for their own ideas, orgies and caprices, they spend money generously and abundantly. I do not know where they get it . . . . Being so ancient and sought after, although without any idea of Christianity, [the *cofradías*] cannot be suppressed, reformed, or changed in any manner because this would stir up the Indians who would abandon their towns . . . . Having removed them in the *alcaldía* of Sololá (according to an account of the *cura* of that *parroquia*), the Indians did not even want their children baptized until they were reinstituted. (Orellana 1984, 213)

An order issued by the Audiencia of Guatemala dated March 20, 1637, attempted to suppress nonsanctioned *cofradías*, which were quickly becoming a serious threat to ecclesiastical authority in the region:

> In view of the growing number of *cofradías* in the Indian towns and of the excesses committed during dances and feasts celebrated during the day of the patron saint, it is ordered in the confines of the *Audiencia* . . . that all *cofradías* not authorized by the bishops be suppressed . . . for the offenses which are made against God our Lord with drunkenness and feasts which are celebrated the day and night of the fiesta when it is customary for many drunken Indians to gather together in the house of the Indian *mayordomo* of the *cofradía*, . . . where with dances and fiestas they recall their antiquity and idolatry in scandalous form which devalues their devotion before the images, . . . and without more authority than their own [the principals] found and institute . . . *cofradías* and . . . make the poor Indians pay, taking their hens away from them . . . so that they are unable to pay tribute to their *encomenderos* . . . . It is an excess so great that in most of the towns where there are no more than one hundred Indians there are ten or twelve *cofradías* so that all year long they are occupied and impeded from working in their fields. (Orellana 1984, 213–214)

Cofradías, in addition to being religious sodalities, also provided financial support both to their local economies and to the Church. By at least the eighteenth century they provided nearly one-third of the total funds received by the Church in Guatemala, funds that were essential to its survival (Jones

1994, 76). Efforts to curtail the activities of the *cofradías* ultimately failed in most traditional Maya communities, partly due to the threat of financial retaliation if *cofradía* privileges were not conceded. Pedro Cortés y Larraz wrote that by 1770 the system of *cofradías* in Santiago Atitlán was so powerful that the Roman Catholic authorities in the area feared to restrict their activities lest Tz'utujils withhold financial support for the clergy or even renounce Christianity altogether (Cortés y Larraz 1958, 2:162–163).

COFRADÍA CEREMONIALISM IN SANTIAGO ATITLÁN

Much of the traditional ceremonial life in Santiago Atitlán still takes place in the *cofradías*. Although these are ostensibly Christian organizations, generally named for one of the Roman Catholic saints, their administration is wholly indigenous and independent of the Church's control. Indeed many of the ceremonies conducted in the *cofradía* houses retain significant elements of ancient Maya tradition that run counter to European notions of Christian orthodoxy. Roman Catholic and Protestant authorities alike frequently counsel their congregations to stay away from the *cofradías* because of their continued adherence to "pagan" Maya gods and traditions. Linda O'Brien-Rothe, an ethnomusicologist who served with the Maryknoll Sisters in Santiago Atitlán in the 1960s, recalled that the parish priest, Father Ramón Carlin, regretted that he could not reach out to the traditionalists in the *cofradías* in order to foster mutual understanding:

> I had seen their public rituals and wanted to know more about traditional beliefs, but we were prohibited by church policy (a policy that Carlin lamented) from visiting the prayer-houses lest we give the impression of approval of a religion that was not Catholic. (O'Brien-Rothe 2015, 7)

With some exceptions, the town's Roman Catholic clergy and *cofradía* leaders have maintained a peaceful if uneasy accommodation in which neither interferes directly with the other. Traditional Maya public ceremonies are mostly allowed to take place unhindered, although occasional disputes arise over what can and cannot be done on church grounds, as the next chapters of this book show.

In 1997 I was told by the parish priest of Santiago Atitlán, an American from Missouri, that he had wanted to establish better relations with the *cofradías*. He asked a number of his parishioners if they would accompany him on an impromptu visit to the Cofradía Santiago. They were horrified by the idea and told him that he should never set foot in any of the *cofradías* because they were pagan Maya houses where "witchcraft" was practiced. If people saw him going there many would believe that he had turned to devil worship and refuse to take Communion from him. In any case, they said, the *cofradía* officials would not welcome him in their houses and would resent his "invasion" of their domain. He finally abandoned the idea but said that he often regretted the lack of trust between traditionalists and orthodox Catholics in the community.

Today Santiago Atitlán has ten public *cofradías*: Santiago, Santa Cruz, San Juan, San Nicolás, Rosario, San Francisco/Ánimas, San Gregorio, Concepción, San Antonio, and San Felipe. Some have been combined in the same *cofradía* house due to the desire on the part of the owner to attract more visitors (and thus accrue greater influence in the community) or because of insufficient funds or interest to maintain a separate house. Each *cofradía* consists of a single room in the house complex of its highest-ranking member, the *alcalde*. Traditionally, the *alcalde* administers the *cofradía* for one year, after which it transfers to another location. In recent years, however, many *cofradías* have been retained by the same individuals for long periods.

Each *cofradía* has a number of subsidiary officers who often devote an enormous amount of time and personal resources as a voluntary service. Lower positions are generally taken by younger individuals who may rise through the ranks over the years by volunteering for positions of increasing responsibility and prestige. Generally the positions within the *cofradía* are the *alcalde* (leader, mayor); followed by the *juez* (judge); five to seven *cofrades* ranked by ordinal number beginning with the *nab'e* (first) *rukab'* (second), *rox* (third), and so forth; and five or more *tixeles*, female members who may or may not be married to the *cofrades*. The senior female *cofradía* official is the *xo'*, who participates in the administration of the *cofradía* and presides over the activities of the *tixeles*. She is most often the wife or mother of the *alcalde*. The *xo'* and the *tixeles* take the lead in all processions of *cofradía* saints' images, bearing large candles wrapped with banana leaves to prevent them from being extinguished by wind or rain (fig. 43). In these processions the women are followed by the men in order of rank. On important ritual occasions and during processions, senior *cofradía* officials wear a special dark woolen overgarment called the *manq'ax*. In addition, *alcaldes* wear a headscarf called the *xk'ejk'oj* and bear in their right hands a long staff of office topped by a silver carved wooden religious symbol that is distinctive for each *cofradía*. For the most important ceremonial occasions this staff is adorned with fresh flowers or sprigs of evergreen (fig. 44).

At the top of the hierarchy is the *cabecera*, who coordinates the activities of all the *cofradías*, particularly during community-wide ceremonies such as Holy Week (fig. 45). In recent years, however, there has been something

43. *(Above) Procession, Santiago Atitlán, 2010*

44. *(Left)* Cofradía alcalde *holding his staff of office, 1988*

45. Cabecera, *Santiago Atitlán, 1997*

of a revolt within the system. Two competing *cabeceras* have been trying to assert control, each supported by a faction of *alcaldes* who do not recognize the authority of the other. This situation results in occasional open disputes, even during public ceremonies. As of this writing, the conflict has not been resolved.

Although the principal responsibility of the *cofradía* centers on the feast day of its titular saint, the members meet often throughout the year to pray, eat ceremonial meals, conduct business, clean and renew the decorations of the *cofradía* house, and care for the saints. This includes changing their clothing periodically and providing them with offerings of candles and incense smoke. The most important celebrations of each *cofradía* theoretically require participation by all the officers of the nine other *cofradías* (although in practice this does not always work out due to illness, disputes, or other factors). Thus there is nearly constant activity in the form of planning meetings, the procurement of supplies, and participation in major ceremonies throughout the year.

In the more popular *cofradías* visitors come to pray and give offerings to the saints in a near-constant stream every day of the year. These visitors must be provided with mats to kneel on, access to sacred objects used in their prayers, and sometimes gifts of tobacco or alcohol as a token of gratitude for their devotion. In return visitors are expected to give offerings to the saints to help with the expenses of the *cofradía*. They often bring their own drinks and cigarettes to share with *cofradía* members and other supplicants. As Mendelson writes, "the cofradía is a small universe with exquisite rules of courtesy which prevail from the moment a man enters the cofradía house until he emerges" (Mendelson 1957, 133).

Upon arrival, each male visitor removes his hat and places it on a series of pegs on the wall. For as long as the individual's hat is on its peg, the visitor is conceptually under the protection and authority of the saints on the altar and is subject to the rules of the *cofradía*. The visitor then bows slightly and shakes the hand of everyone present in the *cofradía* house, preferably in order of rank beginning with the *alcalde*, addressing them by their titles rather than by their given names. On important occasions visitors may take the *alcalde*'s right hand in both hands and kiss it, touch it to their forehead, or take in a short breath from the *alcalde*'s palm. This token of respect is relatively rare today in Santiago Atitlán other than on the highest ceremonial occasions. In less densely populated areas in the Maya highlands it is common for young people to kiss or breathe from the hands of elderly men and women they meet, addressing them as "grandmother" or "grandfather" whether they are of the same family lineage or not. In return, the youth is given a brief blessing while placing a hand, palm-down, on the younger person's head. I've been told that breathing from another's palm is a means of sharing spirit essence, binding the one to the other in a unity of heart and mind.

Once everyone in the room has been greeted, the visitor is invited to sit on a long bench. Customarily this is in order of rank, although on most occasions the practice is only loosely observed, other than the tradition of the *alcalde*'s position nearest the altar. On occasion the *alcalde* may choose to honor a visitor by offering the seat next to him. If a ceremony is carried out, the participants purify themselves in turn with incense smoke from a brazier, usually a small metal container with a wire handle. This is passed under one armpit, then across the chest to the other armpit, and then briefly waved in front of the face while breathing in so that the interior of the body may be ritually cleansed as well. On some occasions this is supplemented by a *cofrade* spraying a bit of aerosolized cologne onto the center of each visitor's chest. In 2002 the most popular brand of cologne was Bravura by Kent, but Brut for Men was preferred when it could be purchased in bulk to lower the cost.

Visitors often are offered a drink of alcohol or a soft drink (Coca-Cola is the most common), which must be accepted as a token of fellowship and out of respect for the saints of the *cofradía*. It is also customary to purchase a gift of drinks to share with those who may be in the *cofradía* house. When this occurs, everyone present in the room participates in the gift by drinking as a shared experience. Alcohol is a prominent feature of *cofradía* ceremonies, providing a means by which participants may share in the offering with one another as well as with the saints and images housed there. The bottles are first presented to the saints on the altar while acknowledging their generosity in providing for those who honor them. Before drinking, the glass is first raised toward the altar, then to the *alcalde*, addressing him by his title, and waved in the direction of each person present with a brief word of thanks or blessing. The glass is generally emptied quickly in one series of uninterrupted gulps and then passed back to the person pouring the drinks to be refilled. Rarely, individuals may choose to pass on the gift for health reasons, but the ceremony must still be carried out by lifting the glass and giving thanks before passing it along to the next person. Some *tixeles* (and occasionally *cofrades*) pour their drink into a plastic bottle secreted about their persons especially for that purpose in order to drink it later. Whether the visitor's stay is brief or lengthy, everyone in the room must be individually acknowledged before leaving with a handshake and a word or two of good wishes. In all their activities, *cofradía* members strive to maintain an atmosphere of goodwill toward one another. Seldom is anyone evicted from a public ceremony. Even a drunken individual who causes a bit of disruption is generally tolerated unless he or she becomes belligerent.

COFRADÍA WORSHIP AND FRANCISCO SOJUEL

Many traditionalists in Santiago Atitlán claim that the *cofradía* system was founded by Francisco Sojuel, a legendary Tz'utujil Maya culture hero who lived in the second half of the nineteenth century (an old sacristan told me that his father had known Sojuel as a boy and was present when he was buried in 1912). It is unlikely that Sojuel was the founder of the first *cofradías* in Santiago Atitlán, as there are references to them in the Lake Atitlán region in colonial Spanish documents centuries before his time. The Cofradía San Juan possesses papers listing officials, expenses, debts, and goods owned by the *cofradía* that run from 1712 to 1885 (Orellana 1984, 211). It is possible, however, that Francisco Sojuel modified the system and set the pattern for important elements of *cofradía* worship as they are practiced today (fig. 46). According to Mendelson, "very few names were mentioned as frequently during my stay in Atitlán as that of Francisco Soxuel [Sojuel]. . . . Let it be said that scarcely a ritual could be watched, let alone discussed, without some mention of this prophet cropping up" (Mendelson 1957, 488).

The highland Maya frequently tell stories about visitations from ancestors like Francisco Sojuel who continue to work on behalf of their community whenever necessary. Alfred P. Maudslay, an English photographer and explorer, passed through Santiago Atitlán in the late 1880s and photographed a

46. *Ritual chest with a carved image of Francisco Sojuel holding the Martín Bundle, Cofradía Francisco Sojuel, 2010*

47. *Men on the steps of the municipal building, Santiago Atitlán (1881–1882). Photograph by Alfred P. Maudslay, © Royal Geographical Society, London (with* IBG*)*

group of men arranged in front of the municipal office (fig. 47). My colleague Andrew Weeks and I recently gave a copy of the photograph to the son of the *alcalde* of the Cofradía San Francisco/Ánimas. He immediately identified the man standing in the doorway as Francisco Sojuel and named a number of the other individuals as powerful ancestors from Sojuel's circle. When I asked how he knew them, considering that they had died long before he was born, he replied:

> We all know them. They still visit us in dreams and in person. We know their faces. They are still very powerful—the very soul of the town. Their minds and their souls are *saq* [white, light, pure, clear, clean]. This is our heritage. These people are still alive because I live. I carry their blood. I *remember*. They are not forgotten. As long as I live, they live in me and will never die.

Atitecos, like the *alcalde*'s son, believe that some essential part of the ancestors continues to live within the blood of their descendants. As David Stuart notes, the Maya believe that ancestral gods reside within the blood and define political and social power (Stuart 1988, 193). The Maya are in a sense embodiments of their ancestors, who retain the ability to manifest themselves in the present through "memory." Powerful ancestors like Francisco Sojuel are a living part of the community because their descendants bear their blood, which is where Tz'utujils say that memory resides. It is this ancestral memory that empowers the Tz'utujils to perpetuate life-renewing ceremonies in the proper way. The remaining chapters of this book are devoted to the way in which this is done during Holy Week in Santiago Atitlán.

Chapter 5 HOLY MONDAY

As seen in the foregoing chapters, major elements of the ancient Maya Wayeb' observances as well as related period-ending ceremonies were transferred to Holy Week in much of the Maya world soon after the Spanish Conquest. Core elements of these earlier Pre-Columbian ceremonies have survived the intervening centuries in some of the more traditionalist Maya communities. The remainder of this book focuses on the Tz'utujil-Maya town of Santiago Atitlán in the Guatemalan highlands. Modern Atiteco ceremonialism is the product of centuries of interaction between the Tz'utujils and Roman Catholic missionaries and secular priests that can never be completely traced through time. Nor is it particularly important to do so. There are no pristine survivals of Pre-Columbian rituals in Santiago Atitlán that are unaffected by Spanish Christian and other foreign influences. This study seeks only to identify certain fundamental aspects of modern Tz'utujil traditions in the context of their unique history and culture. Many elements of these ceremonies may be common to both the Maya and Europeans, but their perceived meaning may be radically different.

Soon after the Spanish Conquest the Tz'utujils adopted Jesus Christ as one of their principal deities associated with life-renewing ceremonies. Modern traditionalist Atitecos believe that the death of Christ as observed during Holy Week echoes the symbolic death of the world, requiring an exhausting series of rituals, both public and private, to regenerate life. As seen in chapter 2, the Pre-Columbian Maya of the Guatemalan highlands believed in an annual cycle of universal decline and dissolution, culminating in ceremonies to renew the ability of the earth to sustain life, particularly during the five days that fall at the end of the calendar year. Modern Tz'utujil Holy Week ceremonialism echoes important aspects of these ancient rituals, blended with elements of Roman Catholic Easter observances. The Maya do not generally reject innovations and foreign influences outright but structure them in such a way that they resonate with older indigenous patterns. The process of Atiteco mythmaking and ceremonial practices is therefore one of accumulation, adding new elements to older traditions rather than replacing them.

Orthodox Christianity assigns the death of Christ to Good Friday and his entombment to a three-day period ending on the morning of Easter Sunday. Traditionalist Tz'utujils, however, solemnize the death and passage of Christ into the underworld over a five-day period beginning on the Monday preceding Easter. On the fifth day, Good Friday, Atitecos raise a towering cross bearing a life-sized image of Christ in the center of the nave within the town's Roman Catholic church. In the view of traditionalist Tz'utujils this represents the elevation of a World Tree, similar to those erected by their ancient ancestors during Maya New Year's rites. The crucifixion thus does not represent the death of Christ but rather his triumphant rebirth in the boughs of a life-giving tree. Easter Sunday is somewhat anticlimactic in Santiago Atitlán, with comparatively few major public ceremonies, the "real" rebirth of the world having already taken place two days before.

THE MALEVOLENT NATURE OF THE FIVE DAYS OF THE TZ'UTUJIL HOLY WEEK

> *The five days that fall at the close of the three hundred and sixty-five days [of the calendar] are called days without name (* ixma kaba kin*). They held these to be ill-omened and on those days occurred miserable and sudden deaths: stings and bites from vipers and wild and venomous animals, as well as quarrels and dissensions, particularly on the first day. On these days they took care not to leave the house, arranging for necessary things beforehand so that they would not need to go into the fields or any other place. During these days they attend most to their pagan rites, praying to their idols to save them from the evil of those dangerous days so that they would give them a good new year, fertile and abundant. [Cogolludo 2006, book 4, chapter 5, 274 (translation by author)]*

Like the five days of the ancient Maya Wayeb' period, the traditionalist Tz'utujils of Santiago Atitlán consider the week preceding Easter, known as Semana Santa (Holy Week), to be fraught with danger. This is particularly true of the five-day period from Monday to Friday. On these days the principal image of Jesus Christ in the town's colonial-era Roman Catholic church is covered with a large cloth, symbolizing his death and journey through the underworld. During the week Western-style dirge music is a near constant accompaniment to Atiteco activities, amplified by loudspeakers at the municipal offices and televisions and radios scattered throughout the community, casting a funereal pall over what is usually a vibrant and bustling town. Because of Christ's absence, malevolent forces are free to come into this world, bringing with them the threat of disease, misfortune, and even death. If the proper rituals are not carried out during this period in order to revive Christ, the world would remain in a state of perpetual darkness and chaos. As one of the members of Cofradía San Juan told me in 1997, "if we neglect to do our work during Semana Santa, the world will die and everything in it."

This is a widespread belief in the Guatemalan highlands. In the seventeenth century the Maya adopted a deity known as Rey Pascual, a syncretic being who combines the attributes of the Spanish saint San Pascual Baylón with a Pre-Columbian death god (Navarrete 1982, 13–23). He is generally depicted with a skeletal body holding a sickle with which he harvests his victims. The skeletal form of Rey Pascual was undoubtedly borrowed from European traditions of a similar figure borne in a cart during Good Friday processions, a personification of death that was ultimately overcome by the resurrected Christ on Easter Sunday. In the colonial period the Maya venerated Rey Pascual as a powerful god during Holy Week, praying to him and giving him lavish offerings, which led Spanish authorities to try to suppress the practice (Hill 1992, 107). Nevertheless, Rey Pascual is especially venerated during Holy Week in many Maya communities today due to the coincidental similarity of his name to "Pascua" (Spanish for Easter). In Tz'utujil tradition he embodies death itself. A large image of Rey Pascual wearing a triumphant crown as a token of his inevitable victory over the living occupies a prominent place to the left of the principal altar in the Cofradía San Gregorio. There he receives petitioners bearing offerings, particularly during Holy Week, when death rules the world (fig. 48). This practice should not be misinterpreted as a fondness for death or its tangible image in the form of Rey Pascual but rather as an acknowledgment of the terrible power that he wields. That power must be appeased in times of crisis, like Holy Week, when the usual life-generating gods are absent.

UNCOVERING THE WORLD'S NAVEL

> *When the days and months that make up a year pass, the five nameless days are counted. These are the bad days of the year, the ill-fated days in which there is every kind of danger or misfortune; sudden deaths, bites by wild beasts or snakes, wooden splinters in the feet, and other things. For this reason they are called the painful or ill-fated days.*
>
> *CHILAM BALAM OF MANI*, IN CRAINE AND REINDORP 1979, 170

During Holy Week the most feared demons and monsters are released from their customary boundaries to walk among the living. As with most early colonial churches, the space beneath the church at Santiago Atitlán contains

48. *Rey Pascual, Cofradía San Gregorio, 2010*

49. *Cleaning the world navel hole, Holy Monday, 2000*

a number of burials. The floor of the nave thus constitutes a thin barrier separating the living from the underworld, where all the creative and destructive elements inherent in nature gather.

The most sacred opening into the world of the dead within the church is a small hole called *pa ruchi' jay xib'alb'a* (at the doorway of the underworld) or *rumuxux ruchuliw* (navel of the face of the earth), located about three meters west of the raised altar in the center of the nave. It is approximately a meter deep, 35 cm across, and is normally covered with a removable tile (fig. 49). This "navel" hole is believed to be a portal leading to the realm of the dead and the symbolic center point of creation. Atitecos often place candles on the tile that covers the hole, "feeding" the benevolent dead with its light. Evon Vogt describes a similar concept among the Tzotzils of Zinacantan, who make offerings at a low rounded mound of earth at the center of the town that they also call "the navel." They believe that this mound is the center spot from which the four corners of the world extend (Vogt 1969, 3). The navel hole at Santiago Atitlán is only uncovered during Holy Week, early in the morning of Holy Monday, in order to clean it of debris. It is reopened on Good Friday, when the great cross bearing the sculpted wooden image of Christ is planted within it.

While the navel hole is open, Atitecos believe that the spirits of the dead, both good and bad, are liberated to come out into the world. While most ghosts are benign, those who die violently or who are taken before their time can be angry. If given the opportunity they may take their revenge on the living. A woman who dies in childbirth, for example, may cause harm to pregnant women or newborn children. It is considered very dangerous to give birth during Holy Week for fear that the spirit of such a woman might try to drag the mother or the child into the underworld.

Atitecos also fear demons, underworld deities who cause disease and other misfortunes. During the five days of Holy Week they are believed to congregate in dangerous areas of the city such as crossroads, the cemetery, the roads leading into town, and the plaza cross in front of the church. They may also hide in shadows, particularly at night. Atitecos thus avoid walking through the shadows cast by buildings when walking through town after sunset.

In Atiteco myth, among the things that go bump in the night are the *xorokotel*s (also called *q'isom*s). These are humans who have the ability to transform into animals. They are sometimes described as malevolent beings that hunt for victims in the night. But others see them merely as poor, afflicted people who cannot help what they are and rarely cause harm. Still others say that they are evil shamans who practice dark arts to transform themselves into ferocious beasts in order to attack their enemies. *Xorokotel*s may be heard making noise outside doors and windows or running across rooftops late at night after people have gone to bed. In their human form they tend to be reclusive and do not make eye contact. People say that they are particularly active on Thursday night of Holy Week, coming out in groups. Although they do not usually mean to cause harm, they are frightening and may disturb a person's soul or even cause it to leave the body if the terror is great enough, resulting in death if the soul cannot be retrieved. People say that this is particularly dangerous for children, whose souls are not yet firmly attached to their bodies.

The tile covering the navel hole is generally replaced after it is cleared of debris on Monday and is not opened again until early Friday morning. Nevertheless, demons and the spirits of the malevolent dead that escape from the underworld on Monday are free to move about town and cause their damage for the next five days. Many also continue to linger around the underworld hole in the church. The lowering of Christ's cross into the navel hole on the fifth day of Holy Week signifies that he has returned to seal the portal and prevent evil spirits from causing trouble in the world during the following year. A sacristan who participated in the raising of Christ's cross in 1998 told me that the cross is "planted" in the hole in the church's nave just like planting a seed and that is why it must be watered with Christ's blood. Christ is reborn on the cross just like new maize plants. Once this is done, "we don't have to fear death or the evil things in the underworld."

The five days of Holy Week are considered particularly appropriate for carrying out "black" ceremonies intended to appease malevolent spirits in order to prevent them from causing harm or to persuade such spirits to curse specific individuals. Those who practice such rituals regularly are called *ajitzii'* (they of evil or malevolence). Although less common than traditional Maya ceremonies meant to bless people in positive ways, black ceremonies are a part of Atiteco life. They are usually carried out in secret, away from the public eye, as these practices invite potentially violent retaliation by the friends and family of the intended victim if they were to become known. But some of the most powerful sources of dark power are in plain view, particularly in the church. Therefore an *ajitz* may on rare occasions be seen leaving "black offerings" accompanied by whispered prayers intended to cause harm. This is particularly true during Holy Week, when the forces of death and illness are at the height of their power and approachability. On such occasions the *ajitzii'* will go about their business as if nothing untoward is happening and if challenged deny that they are doing the very thing that they are quite obviously doing.

In 2002 I arrived soon after dawn at the church on Holy Monday to help prepare for the day's ceremonies. An *ajitz* was arranging the last of a series of offerings that he had placed at various locations within the church. These mostly consisted of black candles—two at the entrance to the baptistery; three in front of an image called Cristo Niño (Christ Child) or Niño de Muerte (Child of Death) on the northwest side of the church, which depicts Christ as a youth with one foot on a skull and the other on a black sphere; one in front of the third saint from the right in the same group of images; and one in front of each of the four saints in the far southwest corner of the church, the direction associated with death. Finally he placed a black candle in front of the fifth lower panel of the central altarpiece, which depicts the funeral of an infant, the Day of the Dead, and the Pietà (the Virgin Mary cradling the dead body of Christ on her lap). Next to the black candle at this last location he placed a crumpled newspaper opened enough to show that it contained moldy bread dough, two rotten bananas with black peels split open along the sides, and a moldy orange cut open to reveal the spoiled fruit within. Tiny flies covered this black offering. I watched the *ajitz* out of the corner of my eye reciting a long prayer in muffled tones in front of the altar. He noticed that I was curious, so he beckoned me over and we chatted about ordinary things as he laid out the rotten fruit. Before he resumed his prayers I asked him why he was burning black candles. As he lit the last one, he said that he most certainly was not lighting black candles and that he had no idea what I was talking about—all the time smiling mischievously and giving every appearance of enjoying his work immensely. Soon after the *ajitz* left, another traditionalist bearing yellow and white candles (symbolizing abundance and purity) entered the church to pray on behalf of a female client who was ill. Traditionalist Maya in Santiago Atitlán who carry out ceremonies on behalf of the sick or otherwise afflicted are called *ajkunaa'* (they of medicine or healing). The *ajkun* also placed his candles in front of several of the saints but purposely avoided those that had black candles in front of them.

FASTING, SELF-MORTIFICATION, AND SEXUAL ABSTENTION

> *For this festival, the lords and the priest, and the principal people began to fast and to abstain from their wives, as well as those who wished to do so on account of their devotion, for such time beforehand as they judged proper. . . . Those who once began these fastings did not dare to break them, because they believed some calamity to themselves or to their houses would befall them.*
>
> LANDA 1941, 152

During the five days of Holy Week the normal life of Santiago Atitlán is disrupted. It is considered unlucky to travel or to initiate business negotiations. Farmers abandon their fields for fear that work done during this period will curse their crops with bad harvests. One commonly held belief is that seeds sown during Holy Week will not germinate properly and will wither away. *Ajq'ijaa'* (shamans who use the ancient Maya calendar for divination) generally use the red seeds of the *tz'ajte'l* (coral tree) in their ceremonies during the year, but during Holy Week the use of *tz'ajte'l* seeds for any purpose is avoided, instead substituting grains of dried maize (fig. 50). One *ajq'ij* told me that *tz'ajte'l* seeds used during the five days of Holy Week might be tainted by the bad influences of those days and "lie" when used again.

Cofradía members and other traditionalists often go for long periods without sleep, regular meals, or bathing during Holy Week. Some of this is a natural result of their heavy commitments, requiring long hours in the *cofradía* houses and in public ceremonial activity around town. As in the week preceding New Year's observances in Pre-Columbian times, this ritual activity is more or less continuous, with all-night vigils planned for each day of Holy Week.

The fasting described by Landa did not involve a complete lack of food and drink. He wrote that some people engaged in fasts that lasted two to three months, although a minimum of thirteen days was mandatory for Wayeb' preparations, in which men were expected to stay in the temples and other ceremonial houses performing their ritual services (Landa 1941, 152). Among

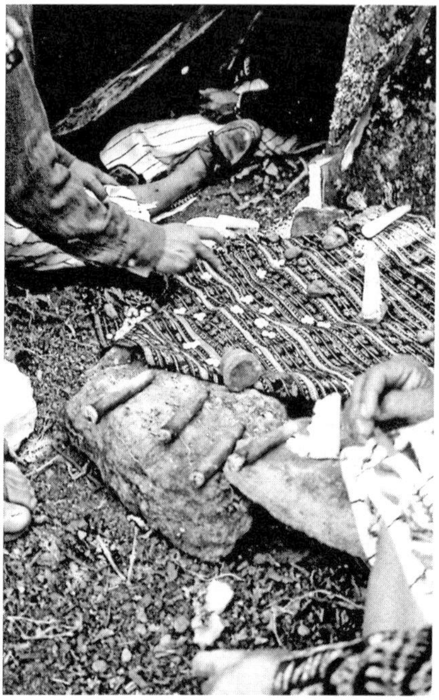

50. Ajq'ij *using maize seeds in a ceremony during Holy Week, 2006*

the ancient Tz'utujils before the Spanish Conquest, lords would fast for two hundred and sixty days before consulting their god directly. This fast entailed eating only one meal a day, consisting of cacao, toasted *pataxte* (*Theobroma bicolor*, a lesser grade of cacao), or turkey. During the fast the lords stayed away from their homes and avoided sexual relations with their wives as well (Acuña 1982, 105–106).

This type of limited fasting is also characteristic of traditionalist Tz'utujils during modern Holy Week activities in Santiago Atitlán. It is not uncommon for participants (particularly men) to be away from their homes for days at a time, with only sporadic opportunities to eat anything, much less a regular meal. Fasting is considered a form of sacrifice, often mentioned in conjunction with other burdensome obligations such as lack of sleep, long pilgrimages on foot to obtain ritual offerings, taking long periods away from work as an economic sacrifice, donations to support the *cofradías* and their activities, and the purchase of essential ritual paraphernalia for personal use, such as flowers, candles, incense, and alcohol.

Bathing is avoided throughout the week but is especially prohibited on Thursday and Friday, when malignant forces in the world are considered to be particularly strong. Mendelson was told that one woman who tried to bathe during Holy Week emerged from the water half-fish, half-human. His informant even claimed that a photograph of the woman could be seen hanging on the wall of a pharmacy in Chicacao (Mendelson 1957, 256, 277c n42).

During Holy Week in 1998 I was asked to accompany various members of the Cofradías of San Juan, Santa Cruz, and Santiago as they carried out their work. The endurance of the *cofradía* members was at times unbelievable. From early Wednesday morning to dawn the following Saturday I did not sleep more than an hour or two, and that was from sheer exhaustion while sitting on a bench in a *cofradía* house or leaning against a wall on the street during a late-night procession. This marathon of ritual obligations followed four days of nearly continuous meetings, processions, ceremonies, and prayers that often continued throughout the night. I did my best to participate in as many of the activities of the week as possible but found that I was simply unable to keep up with the physical and mental demands. I knew of several Atitecos who never went home the entire week, going without regular food and sleep for well over seven days. After eight hours of fitful sleep in bed on Saturday night I dragged myself to yet another ceremony at the Cofradía Santiago early Sunday morning. Many of the *cofrades* there had been up all night again and were obviously drained, yet they managed to smile when greeted and were more or less awake. When I asked a friend who was serving as a *cofrade* that year how he could possibly endure the stress of his responsibilities during the week and still muster the strength to keep working, he replied:

> It is a heavy weight that we carry, a sacrifice of the heart, but we must do this. No one else will. The Catholics and the Evangelicals don't have the strength or the desire to do it. Our hearts are pure and this gives us strength. The rains will come now and the crops will grow because we sacrificed. We can always eat and sleep later when the world doesn't need us as much.

Both Landa and Las Casas emphasize that Wayeb' observances require sexual abstinence as well as fasting (Landa 1941, 152; Las Casas 1958, chapter 177, 148–149). Traditionalist Tz'utujils consider it particularly dangerous for men to sleep with their wives for a period of ten days or so before Easter for fear that any pregnancy that might result would end in miscarriage, stillbirth, or children born with severe malformations, blindness, mental deficiencies, or character defects. Mendelson wrote that in the 1950s members of the *cofradías* had to remain apart from their wives for fifteen days, while the most important officers abstained for thirty days (Mendelson 1957, 240). Recently married young men and women are particularly cautioned not to engage in sexual relations during Holy Week. The more powerful a couple's ability to produce children, the more dangerous the malevolent influences of that period are against the creation of new life. This is the only time during the year that sex is specifically proscribed for non-ritual specialists in the community. I have heard young men joke about the prohibition, boasting that they were not afraid, but the consensus seems to be that people in town generally honor the tradition out of fear of the consequences if the curses turned out to be true.

Although sexual abstinence during Holy Week is a well-known injunction in the community, it is particularly expected of those charged with carrying out important ceremonies and prayers. There was a rumor one year that a recently installed *nab'eysil*, the traditional priest tasked with maintaining the Martín Bundle in the Cofradía San Juan, had engaged in sex during Holy Week. Maize crops were very slow in ripening that year, and the harvest was one of the poorest in recent memory. Some blamed it on the *nab'eysil*'s indiscretion. He was replaced soon afterward by a much older man. No explanation was given, but rumor was that the new *nab'eysil* was less of a danger because of his advanced years and declining libido.

BLOODLETTING AND SELF-MORTIFICATION

> *Late at night they called for their wives and children, those who had use of their faculties, and they all went to a hilltop if there was one close by, or to a crossroads, and there they carried out their sacrifices with the knives that they brought with them. They taught their children to do the same, calling on their gods for health, good years, and other worldly needs. And if the children refused because they were not as yet accustomed to it, the parents did their sacrifices by force until the children lost their fear of the knives. After they had sacrificed themselves, they made their petitions, all according to what they felt were the needs of the people.*
>
> LAS CASAS 1958, CHAPTER 178, 150 (TRANSLATION BY AUTHOR)

In addition to fasting, ancient Yucatec and highland Maya Wayeb' rites required participants to undergo acts of self-mortification, including cutting themselves with sharp blades until they were covered with blood (Landa 1941, 141–145, 152; Las Casas 1958, chapter 177, 148–149). Father Thomas Gage wrote in the seventeenth century that the Maya of Guatemala engaged in similar bloody rituals, specifically during the week before Easter. This suggests that the Maya had transferred the practice of ritual bloodletting from the earlier Wayeb' ceremonies to Holy Week. No such bloody rites are mentioned at any other season of the year:

> The Indians' religion consists more in sights, shows, and formalities than in any true substance. But as sweet meat must have sour sauce, so this sweetness and pleasing delight of shows in the church hath its sour sauce once a year (besides the sourness of poverty which followeth to them by giving so many gifts unto the priest). For, to shew that in their religion there is some bitterness and sourness, they make the Indians whip themselves the week before Easter, like the Spaniards, which those simples, both men and women, perform with such cruelty to their own flesh that they butcher it, and mangle and tear their backs, till some swoon. Nay, some, to my own knowledge, have died under their own whipping, and have self-murdered themselves. (Gage 1958, 240–241)

Of course penitential rites of self-flagellation are also a part of European Christian tradition, particularly in the early colonial period. But Gage's description appears to go well beyond customary practice and likely represents a syncretic blending with Maya rites of self-mortification once practiced during ancient period-ending observances such as Wayeb'. This tradition is no longer practiced in the Guatemalan highlands, having been banned early in the twentieth century. Nevertheless, a less violent survival of the practice continued to be performed in Santiago Atitlán until recent years. Mendelson noted that in the early 1950s the *fiscal*, the highest ranking Tz'utujil official within the Roman Catholic Church hierarchy, gently whipped the backs and buttocks of young women one by one as they left Mass on the Monday before Easter. The belief at the time was that this made them more fertile in their marriages. Although the "whipping" was benign and the women accepted the lashes with giggles and good humor, it was nevertheless stopped a few decades ago as an outdated reminder of bloodier beatings during the colonial period. Further beatings were delivered at the culmination of Holy Week on Saturday morning:

> In compounds along the street leading to the cofradía people were whipping the corners of their huts with leather thongs or belts and took turns to whip each other too in a playful mood. When the bells ring, heads of families in the houses, anyone who happens to be about in the street, should castigate and be castigated. This is either considered to be a punishment for the year's sins (Catequista opinion) or a payment for the year's evil doings and a security that children should grow up and adults remain, in good health (a more traditional opinion). Fruit trees are also beaten so that they should give more fruit and not catch the illness "argenio" (*shuna'ul*). In cofradía Santiago the cofrades were beaten by the Alcalde who was beaten in turn by [the] Juez and the corners of the cofradía were also hit. . . .

> In church, after the mass, all the people who had attended filed into the Sacristía. The Ladinos were allowed to go first as a concession for the slowness of the proceedings, some Ladino women wanted to escape but were not allowed to. Everyone received two lashes from the first fiscal's whip; the fiscal turned the victim round and applied the strokes at the base of the spine. Men were hit harder than women whose zutes were lifted from their backs. They held them in front of their faces, giggling: the atmosphere was far from serious. The Cabezera replaces the Fiscal at one point, but must at the end be beaten by the Fiscal. Most people kissed the beater's hand before and after being beaten. (Mendelson 1957, 267)

One elderly church official told me that the *fiscal* once held a great deal of authority before foreign priests came to live in town on a permanent basis. He traditionally carried a whip during Holy Week and would administer blows so severe that they caused people to bleed. The official said that when he was young people used to say that it was necessary for blood to be shed during Holy Week to help women to have healthy babies, for the earth to produce maize, and for Christ to be reborn out of the underworld. Without this the first rains would not come and everything would dry up and die. After the practice of shedding human blood ceased, people sacrificed animals instead, mostly turkeys and chickens. This is still a common practice in other traditional highland Maya communities, particularly during Holy Week. Although it is less common in Santiago Atitlán, it is still performed in secret both in town and in the surrounding hills (Orellana 1981, 171). The beatings are no longer allowed within the church, although people still do it in their houses, striking each other, trees, animals, household implements, tools—everything that is to serve the household during the coming year (Tarn and Prechtel 1997, 269).

WASHINGS, SWEEPINGS, AND OTHER LUSTRATIONS

> *For two or three days before the day of the fiesta, they swept the streets and the plazas, and they cleaned and decorated the temples, filling them with a great multitude of roses and flowers of diverse colors. . . . [O]thers brought pine needles to scatter on the floors.*
>
> LAS CASAS 1958, CHAPTER 177, 151 (TRANSLATION BY AUTHOR)

Early in the morning on the Monday of Holy Week a large group of men gathers at the church to thoroughly clean it. The streets, businesses, and homes throughout town are also thoroughly swept and dusted. Traditionalists believe that dust and other debris are laden with demons that carry all manner of malevolent influences. These must be taken away for the world to be renewed properly. Consistent with Las Casas's description, doorways, household shrines, and interiors are often decorated with pine needles and cypress boughs during the week. Evergreens are considered tokens of indestructible life because they do not lose their leaves or turn brown during the dry season.

Santiago Atitlán is not a village. It is a busy town that is never really quiet. Even at dawn when the first men arrive to clean the church on Holy Monday, there is the thumping sound of gas-powered maize-grinding mills, boats coming and going in the harbor, buses, trucks, and most recently the near-constant lawnmower engine noise of three-wheeled Tuk Tuks (small taxis that nearly everyone now rides regularly) darting up and down the uneven streets at high speed. But there are comforting sounds as well—women slapping tortillas, gentle conversations, wind in the trees, dogs barking in the distance, roosters crowing, and hens making contented chicken sounds. The constant smell of wood smoke is accented with a hint of copal incense. Even the interior of the church is never silent due to the sounds of loudly chirping birds that live in the rafters. Holy Week falls during nest-building time so periodically a bird swoops in and out of the church bringing straw and twigs to line its nest.

The first task to inaugurate Holy Week is to remove all of the long, heavy wooden-slat pews. These are quickly carried out by teams of men and stacked up in the back of the priest's quarters to the right of the church. For the duration of Holy Week the church is left devoid of benches. Until recently the only object that occupied the floor of the nave during this time was a large basalt font filled with holy water and surrounded by evergreen boughs and flowers. This occupied the very center of the church (fig. 51). In orthodox Roman Catholic tradition the font should be placed in the baptistery, located just to the left of the west portal as one enters the church. In 1998 the newly arrived American parish priest tried to move the font out of the nave to its proper place but was told that this would have to be approved by the church committee, a council of Tz'utujil officials that oversees the care and upkeep of the building. After several formal meetings it became clear that the priest was being stonewalled. Each meeting accomplished little more than an agreement to meet again to discuss the issue further. Finally the priest took matters into his own hands, enlisting two young men to carry the font over to the baptistery. The following morning the priest entered the church to find that the font was back in the center of the nave with fresh boughs of pine needles and flowers surrounding it. He was also angry that someone had dropped pine needles in the holy water itself. A test of wills ensued in which the priest peri-

51. *Baptismal font in the center of the church nave, 1997*

odically had the font moved, only to find it returned overnight to the nave. Because the committee, not the priest, kept the keys to the church, he could do nothing to assert his will.

The priest and I had become friends by this time, sharing care packages of goodies from home. While we were enjoying the delights of a box of homemade cookies that he had recently received in the mail, he asked me if I knew why the church committee was so adamant about keeping the font in the nave when it clearly did not belong there. I was aware of the backstory because I had a number of friends on the church committee. The Tz'utujils believed that the font had to occupy the middle of the nave because that was the symbolic center of the world and the holy water was the place where life was born and renewed. The evergreen boughs and flowers gave the water its life-regenerating power. The committee was upset that the priest removed the pine needles from the bowl of the font, rendering the water "dead." The priest decided that this was a permissible interpretation of Christian doctrine and included in his homily the following Sunday a brief sermon on the evergreens in the font as a token of the eternal life offered by Christ as the fountain of living waters. Although it continued to bother him to see pine needles in the holy water, he tolerated it as an acceptable compromise with local traditions. A few years later a less tolerant priest ended the practice and succeeded in moving the font permanently to the baptistery, threatening ecclesiastical punishment for anyone who attempted to place it in the nave again or decorate it with evergreens. It now stands lonely and unadorned behind a locked metal gate.

Once the nave is cleared of benches, the leaders of each *cofradía* arrive to remove the saints that line the interior walls. Most of these saints do not belong to the church but are the property of the major *cofradías*. This is also true of the great altarpieces that occupy the space behind the sacramental altar at the east end of the church. The one to the left is the responsibility of the Cofradía Santa Cruz, the largest one in the center pertains to Cofradía Santiago, and the one to the right is cared for by Cofradía Rosario. The *cofradías* therefore bear primary responsibility for the cleaning and maintenance of the altarpieces. Members of the *cofradía* lay the heavy wooden saints on the floor of the nave atop long mats made of plaited reeds. After they have all been laid on the mats, the saints are covered with colorful plastic sheets to protect them from the dust raised as the church is swept. Other lengths of plastic are hung across the altar, the pulpit, the fonts, the priest's chair, and the central and right altarpieces.

The dominant figure on the left altarpiece is a life-sized image of the crucified Christ as well as another life-sized Christ with articulated arms wrapped in blankets that lies in a glass chest. This latter image will be crucified on a tall wooden cross on Good Friday. While the church is cleaned, members of the Cofradía Santa Cruz drape a large white cloth across this altarpiece, concealing the crucified Christ figure from view (fig. 52). The cloth remains in place for the next five days. One of the *cofrades* told me that that this is because from Monday until his crucifixion on Friday afternoon "Christ is in hiding. He goes to the place of the dead and people can't come to pray to him as they do during the rest of the year because he is not here and cannot help them." He added that the veil is removed on Friday because that is when Christ returns and "has power to help people again, after the five days of Holy Week are over."

Among traditionalist Tz'utujils, the absence of Christ as a god with life-giving power lasts from Monday to Friday. During this time the world is in crisis, requiring a complex cycle of private and public rituals to initiate the coming of the first rains of the season and to strengthen Christ to return from the underworld. This echoes the ancient Maya Wayeb' or New Year's observances, in which the legitimate gods are removed from their temples and descend into the underworld during a five-day period marked by misfortune and death. The raising of Christ's cross on Friday represents the renewal of his power to sustain the community and bring life back into the world. At that time the shroud is removed from the left altarpiece as a sign that God is again with his people and may be approached for favors and blessings. This

52. *Covering the image of Christ on the left altarpiece, Holy Monday, 1998*

53. *Sweeping the church, Holy Monday, 1998*

of course deviates from the orthodox Roman Catholic view that Christ died on the cross on Good Friday and lay in the tomb until the following Sunday morning. Traditionalist Tz'utujils pay far less attention to Easter Sunday observances because for them the climax of Christ's triumph over death already took place on the previous Friday with the elevation of the cross.

The raising of the cloth to cover the left altarpiece is preceded by a lengthy discussion over even the smallest points. The *alcalde* of Cofradía Santa Cruz directs where each man is to stand, where to put the ladders, who will pull on one side of the cord and who will pull the other, which end of the cloth will be on top, which side will face outward, and so forth. No one approaches the altarpiece until a consensus is reached. Everything is decided down to the last detail before anything is started, the various voices softly blending, with little evidence that anyone is in a hurry to move things along. Once a unity of ideas is reached, the actual raising of the cloth takes far less time than the discussion and seems somewhat anticlimactic.

After the saints have been safely removed from their pedestals and covered with plastic, a small army of men sets to work sweeping the church from floor to ceiling (fig. 53). Others scrape the area around each of the altarpieces and saints' images to remove old candle wax and debris. Until the walls were refinished a few years ago one team of men would use the blunt side of machetes, gently tapping away loose plaster and white paint that had come loose from the thick stone and adobe walls. I was told that this had to be removed each year even though it exposed the underlying masonry because the plaster and paint "no longer wished to serve God" and were therefore unfit to carry out their responsibilities. In many cases this left patches of bare stone and mortar during the proceedings of the week.

In order to reach the upper portions of the nave's high walls, straw brooms are bound to long, heavy bamboo poles that are swept back and forth repeatedly until the plaster and white lime-based paint is thoroughly revealed beneath the accumulated dust and debris. Others climb very old, rickety wooden ladders to access high places that are hard to reach. These ladders are extremely dangerous, with obvious rot and holes bored by wood beetle larvae over the years, so each step is cautiously tested by tapping it with a foot before placing full weight on it. In recent years these ladders for the most part have been replaced with newer, sturdier aluminum ones. Other young men climb up into the rafters by means of an iron ladder in the baptistery that leads up into the bell tower. This gives access to a narrow gap around the top of the walls beneath the corrugated metal roof. This crawl space is choked with accumulated dust, which, when swept out into the nave, fills the air so completely that it soon becomes difficult to breathe. It is also dangerous to stand too close to the walls of the church while this is going on due to the falling plaster and debris.

None of this process is particularly well-coordinated. In 2003 I sat for a time with the *cabecera* as he oversaw the cleaning. The *cabecera* that year was a kind, gentle man who often carried out his duties during Holy Week while holding the hand of his young grandson. He found it endlessly amusing when a section of the church's floor was thoroughly swept clean only to have a great mountain of dust swept down from the rafters onto the same spot, necessitating starting all over again. One year a young sweeper cleaning the back of the loudspeakers near the top of the south wall disturbed a nest of twenty-two newborn bats. He was so shocked when they started crawling out toward him that he almost fell. He was still shaking a half hour later when he climbed down the ladder. Bats are considered messengers from the realm of the dead and are very bad luck. The poor creatures were unceremoniously swept off the wall onto the floor of the nave below. Whatever life remained after the fall was immediately beaten out of them with broom handles. Everyone at some point or another went to look at them, many commenting that this was proof of what an evil year they had just passed through and that they needed to be especially careful to clean the church thoroughly.

Despite the frustrations, the men carry out their work in high spirits and a great deal of good-natured laughter and joking. I have been told that angry words are especially to be avoided during Holy Week as it invites misfortune. One young man who braved the dangers of the upper rafters told me

54. Cabecera Administering Justice, *panel by Diego Chávez Petzey*

that if you don't have a good heart when cleaning the church, you can't get the dust off of your hands or clothes. This may cause illness or even death, because the dust in the church carries the worst of the sins and evils of the past year. In Atiteco society sweeping is a rite of purification that cleanses not only physical surfaces but the body of the sweeper as well. Diego Chávez Petzey, a traditionalist Atiteco artist who reconstructed the central altarpiece of the church in the 1970s, carved a large high-relief panel to decorate his own home. It depicts a *cabecera* in former times administering justice (fig. 54). Diego is particularly proud of this piece and told me that he would never sell it:

> It reminds me of the old days when people respected the Maya *cofradía* officials and we had no need for jails. Now all people know is killing and thievery. In this panel I show a woman accused of not respecting her family. At that time if she were found guilty, the *cabecera* would send her to sweep all of the dust around the church. In this way she would remember to sweep the uncleanness from her own life as she swept the church for the benefit of the town. If her offense had been less severe, she would only have had to sweep the floors of her own home or property, but the idea is the same. Sweeping cleanses the soul.

While the church is being cleaned, others thoroughly sweep the surrounding area, particularly the *convento* complex to the north, the large church plaza to the west along with its great cross, and the small chapel on the northeast corner of the plaza, an ancient domed structure that was built at the same time as the church itself in the sixteenth century. Similar cleansings take place throughout the city: each street, home, and business is thoroughly swept and washed to remove any trace of dust.

Once the men have finished dusting and sweeping the church, they return the saints to their customary places. It is then the women's turn to wash everything clean. I'm told that once the women had to be unmarried virgins and that the water was brought from the center of the lake to ensure its purity. Although most of the women who wash the church on Holy Monday are young nowadays, elderly matrons also participate in the ritual using ordinary tap water. I was told by one of the women that the water is blessed by an *ajkun* to give it power. Certainly hers was, though other women said that they knew nothing of this.

Women carrying plastic jugs filled with water on their shoulders and heads begin to arrive about an hour before the men complete their tasks (fig. 55). One year a little girl about five years old came to help, carrying a small jug full of water that she emptied and refilled at the same pace as the older women. Her mother told me that children must be taught early to respect the traditions of the community or they will forget their importance when they grow older. Working in relays, the women soon fill the stone-walled fountain in the *convento* patio. Once the men have finished their work, the women refill their vessels from the fountain and pour them out onto the floor of the church again and again until a shallow lake of water is produced (fig. 56). They then sprinkle powdered soap over the surface and scrub the floor thoroughly with mops and wide commercial brooms. Other women use towels dipped in water to wipe down the altarpieces and all of the saints on their shelves along the sides of the church. Once the women are satisfied that everything is clean, the water is quickly and efficiently swept in waves through the nave and out the great entry doors on the west, producing a cascade of foaming water that streams down the ancient stone stairway leading to the plaza below. Compared to the uncoordinated labors of the men in dusting the church, the women work methodically and with admirable unison. Men often comment on this as they stand by watching the women's efficiency, yet they never seem to learn from it by improving their own efforts the following year. One of the women told me that men cannot wash the church with water because women are the daughters of the Virgin Mary and she is the patron of Lake Atitlán. Therefore "water belongs only to women."

While the floor of the church dries, the *cabecera* and other *cofradía* officials lock the doors to the church and *convento* in order to clean and inventory the contents of the *caja real* (royal box) in private. This is a large chest kept in-

55. *Bringing water to the church, 2003*

56. *Washing the church, 2010*

side the baptistery containing old vestments, some silver religious paraphernalia, a bell, several crosses, old books including missals, and a printed copy of the *Popol Vuh* published in 1973. These objects are removed only once a year and "fed" with offerings of copal incense and prayers. Each item is carefully checked against an inventory and then laid out on a cloth so as not to touch the ground directly. Sometimes they are placed on the floor of the baptistery and sometimes in the open air of the *convento* so that they can "see the sun." Traditionalists believe that such objects have a living *k'ux* (heart, soul) and need to be cleaned and revived. Taking them out of the chest allows them to "breathe" the copal smoke and be purified.

CONSTRUCTION OF THE MONUMENTO

Once the church has been thoroughly cleaned, *cofrades* and other volunteers assemble to construct a great framework of ancient wooden columns, planks, and ropes called the Monumento immediately in front of the central altarpiece at the back of the church (fig. 57). The columns are of the baroque or Solomonic style, with spiraling shafts adorned with vegetal motifs. The men loop ropes around the Monumento's framework to create a knotted grid of cords that holds everything together. A green cross is affixed on top and two green, chain-like elements are tied to the upper tier of ropes to complete the structure. I was told by one of the workers that the cross is painted green because it represents a maize plant or tree, growing from the top of the mountain-like Monumento.

The Monumento remains bare until Holy Wednesday, when it is adorned with fruit from the coast along with cypress boughs and corozo flowers. The construction of the Monumento is accompanied by a musician who keeps up a steady beat on a great drum, punctuated by a few brief notes from a flute. The rumbling sound of the great drum fills the church, resonating nearly as loudly at the opposite end of the nave as in the place where he plays near the Monumento. In 2002 both the drum and flute were played by the same elderly gentleman, who was then seventy-six years old. He had served as a sacristan for forty years and had played the drum for major ceremonies since his youth. The drummer said that the columns used in the Monumento are the remnants of twelve great altarpieces (one for each of the *cofradías*) that once lined the walls of the nave. These had collapsed over the years due to age and earthquake damage. The surviving fragments are now stacked in a room adjacent to the church plaza. I asked him what the people did when these altarpieces fell. "Nothing. What can one do? When things fall they fall. All we can do is

57. *Constructing the Monumento, Holy Monday, 2010*

hope that everything doesn't fall in our time. That's why we need the Monumento. It's our responsibility to keep the traditions."

DIVINE RULE TRANSFERRED TO A TEMPORARY GOD

> *Among the multitudes of gods which this nation worshipped they worshipped four, each of them called Bacab. . . . And in these days [the five days of Wayeb'] they held many services for the Bacabs.*
>
> LANDA 1941, 135–136, 139

> *They had a wooden idol which they placed on a bench over a mat, and offered him things to eat and other gifts in a festival called Uayeyab [Wayeb']. . . . And this idol they called Mam.*
>
> COGOLLUDO 1957, BOOK 4, CHAPTER 8, 197

An anthropomorphic figure made of carved wood and other pieces bound together with an elegant web of knotted cords oversees the transition from death to new life during Holy Week in Santiago Atitlán. He wears an eclectic combination of both traditional Tz'utujil and Ladino clothes, dozens of silk scarves, two Stetson hats (or rarely an elegant Borsalino imported from Italy, the gift of a generous donor), and a roughly hewn wooden mask with a cigar

58. *Rilaj Mam in Cofradía Santa Cruz, 2010*

fitted snugly into its mouth (fig. 58). Although he has many names and titles, the figure is primarily known as Rilaj Mam (Ancient Grandfather) or simply Mam (Grandfather), the same name given to the temporary god of the ancient Wayeb' rites described by Cogolludo (1957, book 4, chapter 8, 197). The trunk of the figure is approximately 2.5 feet in height and 6–8 inches thick, with separate pieces attached to form the head and legs. He is believed to be a very ancient being, much older than the Christian saints. Many Atitecos consider him to be a survivor from their Pre-Columbian past, more ancient than Christ himself, having been created "in the beginning of the world." When Mendelson asked one of his Tz'utujil associates how old the Mam was, he was told: "Who is to know? How can we know how many thousands of years old the world is? But he was born at the very beginning" (Mendelson 1957, 338, 1959, 57). His mask is deeply creased with wrinkles, reflective of his extreme age.

Mendelson was the first to associate Rilaj Mam with the B'akab's of the Wayeb' period as well as the Yucatec Mam, the god who was venerated during the five final days of the year after the Spanish Conquest (Mendelson 1957, 472, 480, 1959, 58–60). Sir J. Eric Thompson also made the association, writing that the Yucatec god of the Wayeb' rites was "alive and well" in Santiago Atitlán in the guise of Rilaj Mam (Thompson 1970, 298–300; see also Taube 1992, 97). I agree that core elements of the attributes and function of the B'akab's and the deity known as Mam in ancient Yucatan are consistent with those of Rilaj Mam in Santiago Atitlán, although of course they have been modified by Spanish Christian and other influences over the centuries. Rilaj Mam is not identical to any Pre-Columbian Maya deity, but he does serve a similar function in overseeing the death and rebirth of the world at a critical point in the ceremonial year, and many of his attributes seem to derive from ancient Maya precedent.

Like the B'akab's who preside over the destruction of the world by flood but also hold up the sky so that life can exist, Rilaj Mam fulfills a necessary role in overseeing the transition of the world from death to new life, although in Santiago Atitlán this process takes place during the week preceding Easter rather than at the close of the calendar year. In doing so the Mam has a dangerous, malignant side. He is the lord of wild beasts, particularly jaguars, as well as venomous creatures such as scorpions, serpents, poisonous toads, and tarantulas. Rilaj Mam is the principal lord of both dark magic and the malevolent spirits who often accompany him during his movements around town during Holy Week (Douglas 1969, 104–105, 162). He is the patron of the *ajitzii'* (they of evil), who practice black arts to curse people with disease and even death. He stands in opposition to the established order of the community, disrupting the safe and predictable order of things. He is chaos and unpredictability itself and is therefore associated with forgetfulness, hunger, and sexual depravity. He presides over the sterility of the dry season and the cold of the winter months. As maize ripens, he causes the plants to weaken, turn brown, and decay.

Like the B'akab's, Rilaj Mam is associated with destructive floods and storms, aberrant manifestations of normally life-giving waters that become violent and threatening. In his description of the Yucatec Wayeb' rites, Landa wrote that the five days of misfortune and death preceding New Year's day were dominated by the four B'akab's, gods that belonged to a previous age of the world who had "escaped when the world was destroyed by the deluge" (Landa 1941, 136). Garrett Cook suggests that the Mam's opposition to Christ also represents a kind of "underground survival of powers from earlier, superseded epochs" (2000, 139–140). Many Atitecos believe that Rilaj Mam belongs to a phase of the world that existed prior to this one, having been born at the very dawn of creation.

The Mam's body and mask are made from the wood of the *tz'ajte'l* tree (coral tree; *tz'ite'* in the K'iche'-Maya language). His history and character are reminiscent of the wood people as described in the *Popol Vuh*, who were also made from the same type of tree, and who were creations of the gods prior to a great flood that destroyed the world:

> And when they [the creator gods] had spoken, straightaway the effigies of carved wood were made. They had the appearance of people and spoke like people as well. They populated the whole face of the earth. . . . At first they spoke but their faces were all dried up. Their legs and arms were not filled out. They had no blood or blood flow within them. They had no sweat or oil. Their cheeks were dry, and their faces were masks. Their legs and arms were stiff. Their bodies were rigid. . . . The body of man had been carved of tz'ite' wood by the Framer and the Shaper. (Christenson 2007, 83–85)

Because they had no blood in their wooden bodies, the source of memory in highland Maya belief, they did not remember their creators or their responsibilities, walking without purpose and doing as they pleased:

> Nevertheless, they still did not possess their hearts nor their minds. They did not remember their Framer or their Shaper. They walked without purpose. They crawled on their hands and knees and did not remember Heart of Sky. Thus they were weighed in the balance. (Christenson 2007, 83)

These wooden people of the older population were destroyed by a devastating flood as punishment for their failure to carry out their roles as nourishers and sustainers of the gods (Christenson 2007, 85). It is probable that Rilaj Mam represents a survivor of that previous age of wood people that rebelled against the established order. As such he symbolizes (like the B'akab's) the chaotic world of darkness and world devastation that precedes the dawn of a new age in endless cycles.

The B'akab's and Rilaj Mam are complicated figures. The B'akab's are sky bearers with the power to prevent calamity by holding up the heavens, as well as the power to devastate the world when they fail to carry out their role. Nevertheless, according to Landa the Maya were required to honor the B'akab's that reigned over each Wayeb' season by rendering "worships and offerings, which they were to make to him in order to escape the calamities" of the year (Landa 1941, 136). Rilaj Mam is also an ambivalent god with an equal capacity for malevolence and benevolence. Despite his tendency to do harm, he also enforces justice when societal rules are violated, heals the sick, and prophesies for the benefit of the community. He is the patron deity of the *ajq'ijaa'*, the most powerful of the indigenous ritual specialists in Santiago Atitlán, who use divination ceremonies tied to the ancient Maya calendar to reveal the will of gods and sacred ancestors on behalf of their clients. Throughout the highland Maya world these divination ceremonies utilize the bright red seeds of the *tz'ite'*, the same tree whose wood was used to create Rilaj Mam. In highland Maya traditions, this tree has the ability to speak and foretell the future (Orellana 1984, 98). In the *Popol Vuh* the creator gods themselves determined their actions through a divination ceremony using the seeds of the *tz'ite'* (Christenson 2007, 80–81). Because his body and mask are made from the wood of the *tz'ite'* tree, Rilaj Mam has the ability to reveal the will of ancestral spirits and work other miracles.

Although Rilaj Mam is very old, belonging to another age of the world, his present form is often ascribed to the handiwork of Francisco Sojuel in the nineteenth century. An elderly Tz'utujil *ajkun* told me in 2002 that Francisco Sojuel and a group of powerful ancestors who were his contemporaries carved the Mam's present body 182 years ago, an unusually specific time that would place its creation in 1820. Other Atitecos suggest that Sojuel lived later and was known by their parents or grandparents around the turn of the nineteenth century. In some variants of the tradition Sojuel himself, along with other ancestral figures, participated in the formation of Rilaj Mam's image (Mendelson 1957, 490; Christenson 2001, 179–180). In others he merely carved one of his principal masks, while the body was made much earlier (Mendelson 1957, 490, 1959, 57). In nearly all of the myths associated with the figure, however, Sojuel was instrumental in establishing the role that Rilaj Mam plays in Santiago Atitlán.

Tz'utujil traditions claim that Rilaj Mam was originally formed to safeguard the morals of the community. He may therefore appear as a handsome young man or as a beautiful young woman, tempting adulterous spouses before killing them or driving them insane for their infidelity. Although elderly and sterile himself, he is also characterized by hypersexuality, seducing young men and women about town for his own gratification. Mendelson notes cases in which young Atiteco males took advantage of the myth by disguising themselves as Rilaj Mam to seduce or rape girls (Mendelson 1957, 377). Young men whose proposals of marriage have been rejected may petition the Mam to force women to marry them or be punished with illness or madness. Stories are common of young women who, having spurned sexual advances, are found soon afterward in the dead of night babbling incoherently at a crossroads or at the edge of town with no explanation for how they got there.

Rilaj Mam has a wife, María Batz'b'al (María Spindle). She is also sometimes called Yamch'or (Virgin-Whore) or María Castellana (Spanish María). Her appearance is similar to her husband's, including a wooden mask fitted with a cigar, although she wears female clothing (fig. 59). The image of María Batz'b'al is normally kept lying in a glass case at the home of the Mam's guardian. Her sexual escapades and gender transformations match those of the Mam. Yet their extreme sexual appetites cannot produce healthy children. Stillborn babies or infants with severe congenital malformations are some-

59. *María Castellana, 2010*

times thought to be the result of the Mam's dalliances. Other Atitecos insist that a woman could never become pregnant by him because his touch would either kill her outright or cause her to die soon afterward of insanity.

Although Rilaj Mam was originally formed by the ancestors to guard their community and protect its moral standards and institutions, he soon rebelled against these strictures and reveled in breaking the very rules that he was charged with enforcing. He thus came to personify the instability inherent in nature, which inevitably destroys what it seeks to build. This version of Rilaj Mam's origin comes from Nicolás Chávez Sojuel:

> The great *nuwal*s [sacred ancestors] Francisco Sojuel, Marco Rohuch, and others were once merchants and periodically left town to go to Antigua. They had great power. Fishermen would catch little fish to sell. One, two, three paces and they were there at the market even though it might be over sixty kilometers away, and the fish would still be jumping in their baskets. In those days our ancestors had power, not like today. One of their companions, named Juan No'j, had a wife. One day when he returned from business in Antigua a neighbor told him that his wife had been seeing another man while he was away. Other merchants and farmers had the same problem.
>
> So Francisco Sojuel went into the mountains accompanied by the ancestors who created the world to find a tree that would be willing to watch over the town while they were away. They first asked Tioxche' (Cedar Tree), but

it refused, saying that it could only work a few miracles. Next they asked Q'anxul (Mahogany), but it was too hard and stiff to walk. Next they asked Iximche' (Breadnut Tree), but it was too heavy to work. Finally, they consulted Tz'ajte'l (Coral Tree; Spanish *palo de pito*) who agreed to work for the ancestors, saying: "I want what you want." The *tz'ajte'l* tree was ideal because it does not perish when wounded; it may still sprout even after it is chopped down. So they cut down the tree, which laughed as it fell. They then carved the body of Rilaj Mam from the trunk of the tree. But they did not have to hold the tools as they worked. Francisco Sojuel and the others would strike the tree with a machete and with chisels and the blades would carve the wood all by themselves. Three women accompanied them named María Castellana, María Salome, and María Tak'ir. The women played the split log drum and danced in front of the tree. María Castellana would give the wood a drink of liquor and sing while Rilaj Mam was carved out of the tree. When they began to form the body, heavy rain fell on them and clouds surrounded the place where they worked, hiding them from view. They were completely surrounded by black clouds so no one could see them as they worked.

Once Rilaj Mam was finished, Francisco Sojuel told him to find out if it was true that the wife of Juan No'j was unfaithful. Now Juan No'j had a maize field near Chukumuk and had a boy that worked for him there tending the crops. At noon the wife of Juan No'j used to go to the maize field to deliver lunch for the boy, and there they made love. So Rilaj Mam disguised himself as the wife of Juan No'j and went to the field to deliver lunch. But instead of meat he took cow excrement. When the boy saw Rilaj Mam coming, he thought that it was the wife of Juan No'j and called: "My love, come with my food." While he ate, Rilaj Mam cried out and said: "Ha, I caught you and you will now be punished." Soon afterward the boy became insane and died.

But Rilaj Mam soon got tired of keeping watch over the people of the town and began to wander far away over all the mountains and all the countries without permission. He was supposed to protect the town from theft and adultery, but he started to cause problems, doing whatever he wanted to do. He started to look for beautiful young girls and seduce them. But he could also appear as a beautiful woman himself and drive men crazy who followed "her." So Francisco Sojuel cut away his head, arms, and legs to stop him from wandering everywhere and to make him more obedient. He then tied the pieces back together again with cords after the Mam promised to be obedient. That is why he is often called Maximon [He Who Is Bound], but his real name is Rilaj Mam [Ancient Grandfather, An-

> cient One]. Francisco Sojuel told him: "You are the child of a tree, you were made of a tree, a formed thing only. You were formed to have some power, but you must honor us as your creators. So people know that you are present, you will be accompanied by the scent of a skunk. You will only help the people."
>
> Rilaj Mam can appear in many forms, but when you see him in town at night he is always at a crossroads smoking a cigar. He has a high-pitched voice and pronounces Tz'utujil like a foreigner. Because his legs have been cut and are only tied on, he walks with a limp. When you shake his hand it feels cold like wood, and he only has four fingers because he does not have a thumb. The air feels colder around him. He also has the smell of a skunk. So when you smell this you know he is near and should make offerings to him or he may harm you or drive you mad.
>
> When I was about eleven years old I was out late at night. At a corner I saw an old man wearing a sombrero and smoking a cigar. I couldn't see his face for the shadows. I greeted him but he just grunted. I smelled the scent of a skunk and became frightened. My father had told me that if I was to come across Rilaj Mam at night I was to hurry along and not look back, so I ran toward home. A few blocks later I saw the same old man and again smelled skunk. This time I was curious, so I looked back and saw that he had vanished. When I got home, my father hit me for being out late and warned me that the Mam might punish me with illness for my disobedience, but I didn't get sick.
>
> When he was first created, Francisco Sojuel kept Rilaj Mam in his house. But after Sojuel went away to live in the mountains, the people decided that they did not like what Rilaj Mam did and left him on the south side of the church, where he killed Jesus Christ at Easter. But Rilaj Mam did not like being near the church because he was not a Christian. One night he appeared to an *ajkun* where the town road branches off to go up to the cemetery. He said that if the people didn't treat him with more respect he would find a pretty girl as a wife and really cause trouble. So they took him to the Cofradía Santa Cruz where he lives during the year and watches over the dead body of Jesus Christ that they keep there in a glass coffin. People come to him because he can heal them. But he still sometimes wants payment more than justice. He helps those who give him more so he must be reminded that all offerings are equal and must be accepted.

Although Rilaj Mam has a wooden body that is housed in the Cofradía Santa Cruz, he is not confined to it. He is said to be a great traveler, often spending his nights roaming throughout the world, even to the United States,

France, and Italy. When people come to ask Rilaj Mam to bless them in their endeavors or to curse those who have caused them harm they will often invite him to look into their situation as he goes about his travels to see that they are in the right and deserving of justice. Atitecos often tell stories of encounters that they or someone in their family have had with the Mam in the streets. Here is an example told by a member of the Cofradía Santa Cruz:

> One night I was out late working in the *cofradía*, helping to change the ceiling decorations. It was very dark when we finished and I could hardly see anything because it was a cloudy night with no moon or stars. When I got to the crossroads just north of the church plaza I saw a man leaning against a building in the shadows. It was so dark I could barely see him, and his head was bowed so low that his face was hidden beneath his hat. All I could see was that he was smoking a cigar. As I passed him I said: "Good evening, father." The man greeted me back but with a high-pitched voice and an odd accent that I had never heard before. I don't know how to describe it, it was just strange. The closer I got to him, the more I smelled the strong odor of a skunk. I became very frightened because my grandfather had always told me that if I should see a man at night with a high-pitched voice and smell a skunk I should be very careful because it could be Rilaj Mam out wandering in the night. He told me that to know for sure I should offer to shake his hand. If it was the Mam he probably would refuse to shake hands, but if he did I would see that he had only four fingers and no thumb. I was too frightened to ask him to shake hands so I just hurried on, but I could feel his eyes looking at me as I went by. When I looked back a few feet later, he wasn't there anymore. That night I had a hard time falling asleep because I was still shaking with fear. But when I did fall asleep Rilaj Mam appeared to me in a dream and told me that I shouldn't be afraid of him. He was only out helping a man who had been robbed, looking for the thief so that he could be punished. He said that he knew my heart was good because I had been working late in the *cofradía* decorating the place where he lived, so his heart was content with me. From then on I wasn't afraid because I knew that the Mam was happy with me and that I was doing the right thing working in the *cofradía*. As long as my heart is pure I don't have to be afraid.

The place where the *tz'ajte'l* tree from which the body of the Rilaj Mam figure was carved is today called Xe' Qox Aq'om (Beneath Medicine Power) because people sometimes go there to petition the Mam to heal them from illness. It is in the mountains east of town to the side of a very steep and rocky trail. There is a shrine at the site of Rilaj Mam's birth that consists of three shallow openings in the ground lined with stones. It is usually surrounded by offerings (fig. 60). The stump of the tree from which the wood for the figure was carved is no longer there, having been taken away many years ago by the Protestant owner of the land. It is said that because he did this he died soon after, and the Mam appeared to his daughter in a dream and drove her mad. But another *tz'ajte'l* tree nearby is venerated as a substitute for the original stump. It has a small hole in its base that is called its mouth, through which drink offerings are poured (fig. 61). The hole often has a cigar inserted into it in token of the Mam's cigar, giving the odd appearance that the tree is smoking. Traditionalists continue to go there to pray and leave offerings for Rilaj Mam, although not nearly as often as in the past. One *ajkun* told me that he knows that the birthplace of the Mam is sacred because the opening in the ground there sometimes breathes in and out, just as large caves do. He believed it to be one of the most important entrances into the place where the ancestors live. It is particularly appropriate for ceremonies involving Francisco Sojuel, who is said to appear there if the petitioner's heart is pure.

Before the 1980s Rilaj Mam was kept dismantled for most of the year in the rafters of Cofradía Santa Cruz with his head turned backward, leaving him "without power of speech" so that he could no longer cause harm (Mendelson 1965, 123). Today the sculpted image of the Mam is kept fully assembled during the year but is restricted to the *cofradía* house except for the final three days of Holy Week from Wednesday to Friday. He is brought down from the rafters each day at about 6 A.M. and placed in front of the ceremonial table at the center of the room with flowers and a receptacle for offerings in front of him. There he receives a steady stream of visitors who come to ask for his help with their problems—to be cured of illness, to help with business matters, protection from enemies, money problems, or sex. People often say that they can smell tobacco smoke or the scent of a skunk in their home after the Mam helps them, a sure sign that he was there.

Rilaj Mam is generally flanked by attendants seated in chairs on either side who regularly supply him with tobacco and alcohol. They also ensure that the petitioners who come to pray do so in proper order. Most of those who come to the Cofradía Santa Cruz to approach the Mam do so in the company of an *ajkun* who prays for them. One of the Mam's attendants may also assist petitioners who wish to give an offering or carry out a ceremony, but rarely do nonspecialists pray on their own behalf, any more than defendants represent themselves in court without the assistance of a lawyer. About 6 P.M. the Mam is returned to his place above the ceiling trellis of the *cofradía* to spend the night. There he has a mattress for a bed, surrounded by bundles of his clothing and possessions.

60. *(Above) Offering at Rilaj Mam's birthplace, 2006*

61. *(Left)* Tz'ajte'l *tree with cigar inserted into the trunk at Rilaj Mam's birthplace, 1997*

Rilaj Mam continues to fulfill the role laid out for him by Francisco Sojuel and other sacred ancestors—to safeguard the moral standards of the community and punish those who violate them. Yet he is also a capricious figure, sometimes willfully abandoning his responsibilities. He punishes sexually unfaithful wives or husbands, but he often does so by appearing to them in the guise of their lovers, has sex with them himself, then curses them for their infidelity with madness, disease, or death. Rilaj Mam is said to sit next to the town's mayors and officials when they are in meetings. If they take bribes or act unjustly, he curses them with illness or misfortune. Yet he is not above taking the ill-gotten money for himself to spend on cigars and drinks. On occasion he may accept gifts from people on both sides of a dispute that he is called upon to resolve, favoring the one who gave him the greater offering rather than the one who was in the right. When this happens, the wronged party may return to the *cofradía* house to complain. It is not uncommon for Rilaj Mam to be shamed by his keepers into doing the right thing. The overall feeling among Atitecos is that the Mam has the power to enforce justice and generally does so when the proper offerings are given, but that he is also strong-willed, unpredictable, and occasionally forgets or ignores his responsibilities when they are not in his own self-interest.

A special shaman-priest called the *telinel* (shoulderer) is charged with overseeing the care and maintenance of the Mam. Only he is allowed to carry the god in public, bearing him on his shoulder. Elderly Tz'utujils say that powerful *telinel*s in the past held this position for life but that today few can hold the office for more than a year at a time. This is because constant interaction with the Mam causes them to suffer from overwhelming stress, making even the kindest of men impatient, short-tempered, and belligerent. For the most part *telinel*s serve for one year and then are replaced when the *cofradía* is transferred to its new location. Nevertheless, ex-*telinel*s find it difficult to give up their old relationship with Rilaj Mam. They can be seen on processional routes keeping an eye on the god and how he's being handled by the current *telinel*. Often they try to regain their old position, lobbying prospective *alcaldes* when the Cofradía Santa Cruz moves to a new house.

*Telinel*s often describe their relationship with the Mam as similar to a marriage. As in marriage a certain degree of easy familiarity is mixed with occasional outbursts of frustration and criticism. The Mam is said to love music, dance, and festivals in his honor, so these are arranged frequently during the year. The *telinel* makes sure that the Mam is constantly supplied with tobacco and alcohol, both of which he craves insatiably. Rilaj Mam always has a cigar (generally unlit) or a lit cigarette inserted into a small opening in the mouth of his carved wooden mask. His attendants periodically tap the ashes from the cigarette into a cup or bowl. These ashes are considered particularly efficacious for healing certain illnesses and are thus preserved for later distribution to the Mam's petitioners. Periodically his attendants give him a drink. While one caretaker removes his cigar or cigarette and tilts him backward, the other pours a bit of alcohol into his mouth, wiping his chin afterward with a cloth. One *telinel* told me that it takes 60–80 octavos (an octavo is an eighth of a liter) of Quetzalteca Especial, a popular brand of distilled *aguardiente*, to get the Mam drunk. He related a story about some recent difficulties that he had with the Mam:

> Sometimes the Mam does not wish to do his work and leaves his body. You can often tell when he's not really there because his shoes are askew, which tells me that his feet are gone. Whenever I call upon the Mam I always look at his shoes to make sure that he is there. He loves to travel although he's not supposed to do it during the day when people wish to pray to him. A while ago he went to the coast for two days and drank 120 octavos. When he returned to his body he was very drunk. When he is like this he often lies and says that he will do something for people that come to see him but then doesn't. Or perhaps he just forgets what he promised because he is drunk. Finally I had to kick him to remind him of his responsibilities. I told him: "We are here for the people, not to do what you want to do all the time." After that he was fine and did what he was asked, but when he's angry sometimes he doesn't do what he promises or he'll do the opposite of what he should do just out of spite and he needs to be scolded.

The *telinel*'s description is consistent with the ambiguous nature of the Mam after his creation, sometimes violating the rules that he was created to enforce, resulting in his being dismembered ages ago. The *alcalde* of Cofradía Santa Cruz pointed out that from the beginning the *cofradía* has always had a life-sized statue of Christ within a glass-lined coffin (fig. 62). In part this is because one of the Mam's primary roles is to oversee the death and rebirth of Christ during Holy Week. But the image of Christ is also there to make sure that the Mam does not get into too much trouble the other days of the year, because Christ has enough power to keep him under control. Mendelson was told that many years ago, before he was transferred to the Cofradía Santa Cruz, Rilaj Mam was kept in the sacristy of the church just to the left of the altarpiece containing the town's principal image of Christ in a similar glass coffin (Mendelson 1965, 189). He would therefore have been close to the image of Christ even then, perhaps for the same reason. Occasionally the Mam tires of this situation and complains about constantly being under the watchful eye of Christ. The *alcalde* told me that once the Mam appeared to

62. *Illuminated glass coffin of Christ, Cofradía Santa Cruz, 2010*

him in a dream in which he angrily said that he wanted to get away from Christ for a while:

> He told me in my dream: "I'm tired of being around this goody-goody. I want to drink. I want to sleep with women. I want to travel." That is why it is hard to be his *alcalde* or *telinel*, because he needs constant supervision or he will cause trouble in town. But I told him that he had to stay and work for the people that come to visit him because that is his job and he needed to stay out of trouble.

In 2006 I accompanied a friend and colleague, Simon Martin, to the site of the Mam's birthplace in the hills above town. Afterward we went to visit Rilaj Mam in the Cofradía Santa Cruz, where he was attended by the *telinel* and another *cofradía* member. We gave a small offering and informed the *telinel* that we had just come from the Mam's birth shrine in the mountains. The *telinel* presented our offering to the Mam and soon afterward gave him a drink, most of which dribbled down the chin of his mask. The *telinel* became angry at this:

> Old man, you're an alcoholic and now you won't drink? You're embarrassing me and the *alcalde*. I order you to drink and be courteous to our visitors. Why don't you accept this drink from your children who have come to honor you? Why don't you receive what I give you? I am your bearer, I am

> your *mujer* [wife]. If you're drunk show me a sign. If you're tired, tell me and I will put you up in your bed by yourself. Are you angry? Are you tired? Tell me. These men have been to the place where you were born. They've come from far away and want you to bless them in their travels and to have good health. You are an old brute, why don't you answer me? Accept your offering and don't embarrass me. Give them strength and protection when they leave because there may be thieves and bad people in the streets and they need you to watch over them. You are supposed to help people.

The *telinel* gave the Mam another drink, which successfully went into his mouth without spilling. The *telinel*'s demeanor then abruptly changed. He patted Rilaj Mam on the shoulder affectionately and told him that everything was alright and that he wouldn't get angry if the Mam did what he knew was the right thing for the people in town. Soon after the *telinel* pointed out that the tip of the Mam's cigarette glowed twice as if he were puffing on it, a sure sign that he was content and would bless us. Although there were quite a few people waiting their turn to give their offerings to the Mam and petition him for favors, little notice was paid to this brief altercation, any more than one would pay attention to a few curt words between an old married couple.

Rilaj Mam presides over the annual "death" of the world during Holy Week, but he is not hated because he is essential to the natural order of things. In Maya belief there can be no life without death. Tz'utujils believe that Jesus Christ must undergo sacrificial death to be reborn at Easter time. Rilaj Mam can hardly be blamed for fulfilling a necessary role that ultimately benefits everyone. As Fernando Cervantes writes, "European notions of good and evil, personified in the concepts of god and devil, implied a degree of benevolence and malevolence that was totally alien to Mesoamerican deities" (Cervantes 1994, 42).

Maya gods are not all powerful or immortal. A god cannot be reborn without passing through old age, weakness, and ultimately death. Both life and death must dance together on the great stage of the world or the cycles of the seasons could not continue on their endless spiraling rotations. Rilaj Mam is not a god of death, if death means the finality of nothingness. He is a necessary, if somewhat capricious, means to a desired end: the transition from lifelessness to rebirth. Day follows night. The Maya do not blame the night for being dark, because darkness is neither good nor evil. It is an inevitable precursor to the coming of the new day. The same is true of death in the worldview of the traditionalist Maya. It is neither benevolent nor malevolent. It simply is what it is.

Despite his sometimes unpredictable nature and his role in overseeing the death of Christ during Holy Week, the Mam is revered and even beloved. He is certainly not evil. Traditionalist Tz'utujils seek him out eagerly to help them in their troubles, and he mostly serves the community in positive ways when needed. Seldom have I been in the Cofradía Santa Cruz without seeing at least one or two petitioners waiting to approach him in prayer. If a person wishes to be cured of a severe illness, witchcraft, or madness, it is eminently reasonable to seek out the deity who has the power to cause such things, because he also has the power to heal them. Nevertheless, Rilaj Mam is invoked with more caution than with other saints or deities, and his power has a negative ring to it. Rather than ask for a good harvest, as they would when praying to one of the Christian saints, Atitecos plead with Rilaj Mam that their crops not be destroyed by some blight or other disaster. Petitioners are also perhaps a bit more careful in the wording of their prayers for fear that the Mam may be offended in some way and retaliate against them.

The highland Maya world is made up of an infinite variety of complementary opposites, each flowing naturally into the other. It is one of the principal philosophical differences that the Maya had with their European conquerors, who believed that the opposites of the world—life and death, light and darkness, good and evil—were in constant violent struggle against one another. In the world of the Spanish conquistadors, like Hernán Cortés and Pedro de Alvarado, the conflicts of this world are merely an extension of the greater war between God and the devil. Humans are caught in the middle, surrounded by the forces of good and evil that battle over their eternal souls. Although Roman Catholic missionaries and prelates have tried for centuries to inculcate this worldview into traditional Maya communities, they have failed to alter the fundamental Maya belief that the opposites of the world not only do not struggle with one another, they are each necessary for the continued existence of all things. Spaniards of the Post-Conquest period viewed Maya complementarity through the lens of their own theology and recoiled at their tendency to venerate deities from both sides of the coin. The result was centuries of false assumptions and bigotry that to some degree continues today.

I once sat with an *ajkun* in the Mam's *cofradía* house as he complained that orthodox Catholics and Protestants simply did not understand that Rilaj Mam is necessary: "The Mam does not hate Christ. They are brothers. Each helps the other in their time of strength. How could the rains come if there wasn't a dry season? How could Christ be resurrected if he did not die? The Mam is his brother and friend. Why can't the Protestants see this?" From the *ajkun*'s viewpoint Rilaj Mam and Christ simply play their parts in the endless cycle of the Maya ritual year. Both are essential to the continuance of the world within their respective spheres of power.

WASHING THE CLOTHES OF RILAJ MAM

Until a few decades ago Rilaj Mam was kept in a disarticulated state throughout the year except during the five days of Holy Week. Those who wished to give him offerings or petition his help did so by climbing into the rafters above the Cofradía Santa Cruz. In recent decades the popularity of the image among the Tz'utujils as well as curious non-Maya visitors has prompted the Mam's keepers to leave him with his limbs bound to his body throughout most of the year. At some point before dusk on the Sunday before Holy Week the *telinel* takes the body of Rilaj Mam apart by untying the cords that bind his limbs to the trunk of his body. In so doing the *telinel* replicates the actions of Francisco Sojuel in restricting the power of the god, rendering him impotent for a brief time before the beginning of Holy Week.

On Holy Monday the clothes that Rilaj Mam wore during the preceding year are gathered and bound up into cloth bundles to be washed that evening. The clothes are washed on three large, flat stones that are safeguarded by the *rox* (third) *cofrade* of Santa Cruz during the year. These stones are considered sacred in their own right and are believed to be as old as the Mam himself (Pieper 2002, 91). On Monday morning these are brought to the Cofradía Santa Cruz and placed on the principal table along with candles to "feed" them with light. Attendants periodically cense them with copal smoke in order to purify and strengthen them. About 3 in the afternoon the heavy stones are attached with ropes to leather forehead straps and borne on the backs of three *cofrades* to the place where the washing is to take place (fig. 63). In recent years this has been in the bay south of the city, just below the Posada de Santiago. Here the stones are laid out just offshore on mounds of smaller stones beneath the surface so that they barely rise above the water.

At approximately 9 in the evening, the bundles containing the Mam's clothes are placed in a large net and carried by the *telinel* to the spot where the three stones had been placed earlier in the day. He is accompanied by a formal procession led by *cofradía* women holding candles wrapped with banana leaves, followed by the *alcalde* and other principal male *cofrades* of Santa Cruz. In 2010 the *telinel* chose to affix one of the Mam's Stetson hats and pendant scarf to the top of one of the bundles, a creative touch that received a great deal of approving commentary among those that attended the ceremony (fig. 64).

Once the procession reaches the shore of the bay, a small shrine is prepared by digging a shallow excavation in the side of the nearby hillock or in the grass below. Here the *telinel* places a number of white candles (for purity) and yellow candles (for abundance) before praying over the bundles

63. *Rilaj Mam's three stones, set in the waters of the bay south of Santiago Atitlán, 2003*

containing the Mam's clothes. When people come to ask Rilaj Mam during the year to alleviate their problems, whether disease, ill-fortune, or the curses of black shamans, it is believed that the Mam's clothing soaks up these maladies, tainting them with dark power and rendering the worshipper cleansed. In some cases petitioners wear one or more articles of the Mam's clothing as part of a curing ceremony (fig. 65). Usually this is the Mam's hat or one of his scarves (this is why the Mam wears two hats: so that he will still have one to wear while the top one is used in a curing ceremony), although more severe cases may call for the afflicted person to wear a complete change of clothing from one of the Mam's bundles of old garments kept in a chest within the *cofradía* house. During the course of the year the Mam's clothes become saturated with malevolent forces and must be washed clean prior to the renewal of the year during Holy Week. In the *telinel*'s prayers he asks that the waters of the lake purify the clothes from the heavy burdens that they have borne during the year and that those who wash them may be strengthened in their efforts and not be harmed.

After the bundles of the Mam's clothing have been passed through copal smoke, they are opened and the contents are arranged on the shore according to type (generally three of each: pants, shirts, woven belts, and the cloths used to clean his mask). Three *cofrades*, usually including the *telinel*, wash each type of garment on the three stones simultaneously (fig. 66). The washing takes place in darkness, lit only by candlelight. Unless it happens to be an over-

64. *Bundle containing Rilaj Mam's clothes accompanied by the* telinel, *2010*

cast day, however, the ceremony is illuminated well by the sky. In 325 CE the Council of Nicaea established that Easter would be held on the first Sunday after the first full moon on or after the vernal equinox. As a result the washing of the Mam's clothes always occurs about the time of a full moon. Other than the soft exchange of voices, the singing of the frogs (nearly constant at this time of year), the rhythmic slap of the wet clothes on stone, and the occasional rattle of a *matraca* (a large wooden noisemaker or rattle that makes a grating

65. *Petitioner wearing Rilaj Mam's hat and scarf during a curing ceremony, 2010*

66. *Washing Rilaj Mam's clothes, 2000*

sound when spun as a token of the presence of the Mam), it is one of the more peaceful and beautiful ceremonies of Holy Week. When the wind shifts just so, the heavy copal smoke pouring out of the braziers on shore glides over the dark waters of the bay like mist, glowing faintly with the reflected light of the moon and stars.

Once all the clothing has been washed, it is rebundled and replaced in the net to be carried back to the Cofradía Santa Cruz. The damp garments are laid out to dry the following morning, usually at the home of the *telinel*. Ultimately they will be stored in the rafters of the *cofradía* house along with other large bundles of clothing that have accumulated over the years. When the Mam is reassembled and dressed on Tuesday night, he will wear all new clothes.

GATHERING CYPRESS

> *Some young men were sent by their captains to bring green boughs; others brought pine needles to scatter on the floors, just as we scatter sedge in Spain.*
>
> LAS CASAS 1958, CHAPTER 177, 151 (TRANSLATION BY AUTHOR)

At the same time that the Mam's clothes are being washed in the bay on the evening of Holy Monday, a group of men walks two or three miles south of town to gather cypress boughs that will be used to adorn the Monumento in the church the following Wednesday. In 2010 the procession was accompanied by the principal traditionalist musician in the community, the same elderly man who had played at the construction of the Monumento earlier in the day (fig. 67). He is respected for his knowledge of ancient songs and drum cadences and performs frequently at the more important ceremonies. He claims that his family has kept the drum for more than three generations, passing the knowledge of the beats from father to son. The drum is called the *nima q'ojom* (great instrument) or *nima tun* (great drum). Its keeper claims that it was made by Francisco Sojuel himself and that it is alive, unlike instruments bought in a store, which he says lack souls. The drum occupies the first position in processions, carried on the back of an attendant with a tumpline, with the musician walking immediately behind him.

Those who participate in both the washing of the Mam's clothes and the gathering of the cypress meet together soon after sunset at the Cofradía Santa Cruz, where they drink a special *atole* made from toasted maize called *maatz'*. This drink is reserved for the most sacred occasions. During most of the year *atole* and other maize dishes such as tortillas and tamalitos are prepared from soaked kernels that are ground on a stone to form a moist dough. The prepa-

67. *Atiteco musician with flute and drum, 2003*

ration of *maatz'* is the only time that Tz'utujils grind maize kernels into dry flour or allow maize to come into direct contact with fire. This drink is served as a kind of sacrificial offering. It is traditional to serve it in gourd cups rather than in modern vessels (fig. 68). The preparation of *maatz'* is believed to be fraught with danger and must be carried out under the direction of the wife of a high ranking *cofradía* member, who blesses her beforehand so that she will not be burned in the process. Nicolás Chávez Sojuel suggested that drinking *maatz'* symbolizes victory over death and the fires of the underworld. The resulting mixture is sometimes addressed as mother's milk or sperm, both associated with rebirth and regeneration (Freidel et al. 1993, 180). Although *cofradía* members frequently share food and drink in an atmosphere of informality, they drink *maatz'* with greater solemnity. It is distributed by the highest-ranking *cofradía* leader present, who gives it to those assembled in order of their rank. As he does so he addresses each by name and title, calling on the patron saint of the *cofradía*, in this case, Santa Cruz (Holy Cross), to bless them all so that their feet, knees, heart, arms, head, and thoughts will have power and that nothing untoward will happen to them during the year. Francisco Sojuel is said to have called *maatz'* the true *ruk'u'x way* (heart of food) and refused to eat anything else when carrying out important ceremonies (Mendelson 1957, 139).

While those gathered in the room drink *maatz'*, the drummer beats out a soft rhythmic sequence of three beats on the old, discolored resonant head

68. Cofradía *member with a gourd cup of* maatz' *(maize* atole*), 2010*

of the drum, followed by a brief tap on the wooden rim. After the cups had been cleared in 2010, the musician adjusted the tension on the head by re-tying some of the strings. He said that drums are like pants—they need to be cinched up frequently to keep them in place. The skin of the head is opaque except for a remarkably translucent area in the center where it is struck. He told me that the head of the drum was made from deerskin, which works better than the skin of any other animal. There is a hole about 4 mm wide in the wooden side of the drum, with four smaller holes arranged symmetrically around it. The musician said that this is the drum's mouth: "Like people, the drum gets thirsty after singing for long periods of time and it must be given drink to moisten its throat." This he did by pouring alcohol into the central hole periodically. He once asked me to look inside to see how much light could be seen there. It was unusually bright, which I assumed was due to the translucency of the head, but he insisted that the light inside was the drum's spirit and that it often shines from within at night, giving it a faint glow.

The procession to cut the cypress boughs leaves the Cofradía Santa Cruz about 9 P.M. In 2010 it consisted of the elderly musician who played the drum and flute along the way, a young man who bore the drum on his back, another who periodically twirled a *matraca*, three *cofrades* from the Cofradía Santa Cruz, and eight young men called *alguaciles* (constables), who did most of the harvesting of the cypress. Beyond the last house only the moon and stars illuminate the way. Away from the city there is also little sound: the rhythmic

69. *Harvesting cypress, Holy Monday, 2010*

beat of the drum and the lyrical notes of the flute fill the crisp night air. The remarkable nuances of sound that these two instruments produce when there is little to compete with them are difficult to appreciate in the more populated areas of the city.

As our eyes adjusted, the glow of the moon and stars intensified, making it easy to make out the path. After walking for about forty-five minutes, we saw the horizon begin to glow brightly ahead of us as if there were a town in the distance. Only when we got close did it become apparent that the light came from thousands of fireflies that had congregated around a single tree just off the road to the right. We had seen few fireflies along the road until then. The drummer told me that the fireflies mark the place where the cypress boughs are to be cut. Otherwise it would be difficult to find the small trail that led off to the left a hundred or so feet beyond the tree. I hadn't seen this phenomenon in the lake region before and wonder what attracted the insects to that tree and no other.

The small trail branching away from the road led to a stand of cypresses growing along a rough fence. The drummer made a small tent of leaves within which he placed four white candles as an offering. While one of the *alguaciles* censed the cypresses with copal smoke, the others climbed up into the trees with machetes to cut some of the branches (fig. 69). One of the *alguaciles* brought a ladder. Despite numerous attempts to angle it in such a way that he could reach the upper branches while standing on its rungs, it became clear that it was much easier just to climb the trees without it. The *algua ciles* ignored the boughs closer to the ground, saying that these were old and didn't have as much life in them, preferring to reach as high as possible into the upper branches. From the vantage point of the drummer's shrine, the three stars of Orion's belt hung just above the trees as the *alguaciles* worked. One of the *cofrades* noted the appearance of that grouping of stars as an important marker for the Easter season but did not know any traditional stories about them.

Each of the *alguaciles* binds five to six large cypress boughs together with cords and carries them on his back for the return trip. The procession follows the same road back into town, which passes by the place where the Mam's clothes are washed. The cypress is deposited in a room adjacent to the mayor's office, where it remains until Wednesday morning.

Chapter 6 HOLY TUESDAY

Holy Monday was devoted to ritual acts of cleansing, sweeping away the accumulated dust and debris of the preceding year from the church, public buildings, streets, and private homes, followed by a thorough washing of everything with water to ensure purity. These acts of cleansing are meant not only to render the Atitecos' world clean physically but spiritually as well, expunging as much as possible all traces of soul-taint that might render themselves or their community subject to the dangerous influences of the five days preceding the crucifixion of Christ on Good Friday. The culminating act of Monday's observances is the washing of Rilaj Mam's clothes in the waters of the bay, removing the last and most powerful vestiges of disease, moral corruption, malice, and black arts that had clung to his garments from his many petitioners during the course of the year. On Holy Tuesday Atitecos prepare the offerings and adornments that will be used during the remainder of the week.

OPENING OF THE FRUIT

> *On the first day of* cuaresma *they released those slaves that were to be sacrificed in the fiestas or ceremonies—to these they gave liberty in this way, as it should be known: to each they affixed a collar of gold, or silver, or copper, around their necks, and passed a shaft through it to fasten it well, and they assigned three or four men to guard them.*
>
> LAS CASAS 1958, CHAPTER 177, 150–151 (TRANSLATION BY AUTHOR)

Early in the morning on Wednesday of the week preceding Holy Week a group of young men embarks on a journey by foot to the coastal plain to obtain large quantities of tropical fruit to be used in several important ceremonies during the course of the following week (fig. 70). The fruit is unpacked around noon on Holy Tuesday. The young men who bear the fruit are called *alguaciles* (constables, officers). Traditionally they are recently married, preferably within a year, and are strictly enjoined not to sleep with their wives for

70. *Departure of the* alguaciles *to obtain coastal fruit, 2010*

at least three days prior to the trip. Not long ago it was fifteen days, but the custom changed when it became too difficult to enforce. The belief is that sexual relations during this time will prevent the fruit from ripening properly and by extension cause the crops to fail in the coming year. Older men recall that in their youth those who tried to avoid leaving their wives were kidnapped from their beds and forced to join the procession.

The *alguaciles* consider themselves warriors. The long journey to the coast to obtain the fruit is likened to a raid for the purpose of obtaining captives (Tarn and Prechtel 1990, 74, 79–80, 1997, 284). The *alcalde* of the Cofradía San Juan said that the *alguaciles* are like jaguars who watch over and protect the town and its traditions. In 2003 two of the young men wore US flags as bandanas around their heads. One of them told me that he was a Tz'utujil soldier, just like the US soldiers who had just invaded Iraq on March 19 of that year. During the pilgrimage the *alguaciles* are to have "good hearts" and not fight with one another lest the fruit become infested with worms or become bruised. One of them told me that if any of them were to "lie in their hearts," carrying out the tradition only to get drinks and food without truly believing, they would become ill or even die. An *alguacil* told me the following story:

> A few years ago one of the *alguaciles* didn't take his responsibilities seriously, saying that it was all foolishness and that he'd lay with his wife the day before and nothing would happen to him. But as he walked he became tired and ill. At the top of the mountain we all knelt to pray, as is the custom, to Francisco Sojuel and the other sacred ancestors to give us strength and a good heart. While we were offering incense and praying, the disrespectful *alguacil* became even more ill and nearly passed out. He said that he smelled a skunk, which means that Rilaj Mam was present, and he heard a voice say: "Now you'll believe in me." He got up and ran away, weeping with fright. He came back after we had finished praying and told the *primer mayor* [the elder charged with overseeing the pilgrimage and other activities involving the *alguaciles*] that he was sorry for speaking against the old traditions and was afraid that he would die. The *primer mayor* told him that he needed to show respect and that if he did not he would become even sicker; or worse, he or someone in his family might die because of his actions. As soon as he returned to town he went to the Cofradía Santa Cruz and asked the *telinel* to pray to Rilaj Mam on his behalf so that he would forgive him. The *telinel* put the Mam's hat on his head and one of his scarves around his neck as he prayed. Then he had him share half of the Mam's drink, smoke half of his cigarette, and leave a large offering. All went well, and now he has great respect [for the Mam] because he realized that the traditions were true and that the Mam has power. Even so, when his pack frame of fruit was opened the following Tuesday the fruit was green and had worms on it. His was the only fruit that had problems even though all the fruit was cut from the same trees and packed in the same way.

Atitecos have different opinions regarding the purpose of the fruit. Some say that it is a gift or tribute to the people of Santiago Atitlán, because they are the ones that bear the burden of carrying out the old traditions. The coastal region south of Santiago Atitlán was once a part of the old Tz'utujil kingdom and was required to pay regular tribute. Cacao, one of the four principal fruits brought back by the *alguaciles*, was the main tribute item from the coast. The pilgrimage may therefore be a dim recollection of ancient tribute payments. According to long-standing custom, the fruit must be given to the *alguaciles* without payment. In recent years this has become more difficult to arrange, so the fruit must sometimes be purchased. When this happens, people criticize the fruit growers on the coast for their greed and also scorn those in charge of making the arrangements for not finding a way to follow proper tradition.

Others say that the fruit are "women" captured by the young men of the town as wives for Rilaj Mam. At the opening of the fruit in 1998, I asked one of the leaders of the Cofradía Santa Cruz, the organization that oversees the ceremonies of Holy Week, why it is only young men who bring back the fruit from the coast. He said that the *alguaciles* are warriors and have to be young and strong. He went on to say that the men must cut the fruit from the trees themselves, just as they cut young women away from their families when they marry them, or as their ancestors before the Spaniards "captured their enemies and sacrificed them with machetes." The capture and subsequent presentation at court of both women and men was a prominent feature of highland Maya state policy prior to the Spanish Conquest, as attested in the *Popol Vuh* and other early colonial documents:

> They began to bring back female captives and male captives, who were presented before Quicab, Cauizimah, the Magistrate, and the Herald. They made war with the notch of the arrow and the center of the bowstring, taking female captives and male captives. These envoys came to be warlike then. Thus they were given gifts. They were increased. The lords provided for them when they came to deliver all of their female captives and male captives. (Christenson 2007, 282–283)

I asked a group of *alguaciles* who had made the trip if the walk to the coast was difficult. It was late at night, and they were required to guard the fruit in groups of four or five throughout the day and night, never leaving them unattended. One of them said that it was hard but that they were the town's soldiers. He said that he had prayed for strength and to have a good heart to bring back the fruit, which made the long walk much easier. Another pulled out his machete and said that they had conquered the fruit and taken it by force. He was a bit drunk at the time, but nevertheless the rest grinned and nodded in agreement. This may explain the otherwise odd emphasis on the fruit during Holy Week in Santiago Atitlán. The fruit is the modern substitute for captives taken in battle in ancient times to be sacrificed during New Year's observances. Thus the fruit must be taken by young warriors in a trek with militaristic overtones, which is why the fruit must be guarded constantly as if it might escape. Ultimately, the fruit will be adorned with bits of metallic wrapping paper, similar to the gold, silver, and copper jewelry that adorned those destined for sacrifice, as described by Las Casas. On Wednesday afternoon the fruit is hung on the Monumento in the church, much as the ancient Maya once hung the severed heads of their victims on a skull rack. Before the Spanish Conquest human sacrifice was performed during New Year rites in order to renew the world and sustain life. This is also the purpose of the captured fruit brought to Santiago Atitlán for Holy Week observances. Without the fruit, traditionalist Atitecos say, the rains would not fall at the proper time and crops would fail to mature.

In 2002 a major scandal occurred when the *alcalde* of the Cofradía Santa Cruz, charged with organizing the ceremonies of Holy Week, brought the fruit in a truck with no procession of *alguaciles* to the coast. This act earned him the permanent animosity of most of the traditionalists in the community who firmly believed that this breach of custom would surely be punished severely by the ancestors. Harvests were particularly poor the following year, and many traditionalists blamed it on the *alcalde* for not following tradition properly. For his part the *alcalde* claimed that he had been promised large amounts of money by the town's mayor and others but that they did not follow through at the last minute, leaving him little choice but to cancel the full ceremony.

Yet even in 2002, when important elements of established traditions during Holy Week were not observed properly, there was little outward show of animosity among participants during public ceremonies. It is considered very dangerous to engage in open conflict during Holy Week, as it further empowers the malignant influences that are already present. Community leaders accompanied the fruit to the Cofradía Santa Cruz, as they were obligated to do by tradition, and made every effort to participate as if nothing untoward had taken place. I noticed, however, that they stayed only as long as necessary and that their hearts did not seem to be in it fully. *Cofradía* members and others carry out their complex roles with little or no direction as they know their parts well, the process having been played out in much the same way from generation to generation. It is thus familiar to all of them since their youth.

Deviations from the norm are noted, such as the scandal with the fruit, and endlessly debated in private. The frustration inevitably breeds a bit of harshness with the stress of the endless round of complex ceremonies, but it seldom lasts long and is soon dropped, at least outwardly. Most difficulties that arise are accepted calmly. People all know that they need to adapt to what they can do in financially difficult times and with fewer active participants than in the past, all of which demands the occasional compromise. Tz'utujils tend to become reconciled quickly to painful choices thrust upon them and move on. They do not give up traditions easily but accept their loss when there is no other option with a kind of resigned pride. This does not mean, however, that purposeful breaches of custom are ignored or condoned once the formal ceremonies are concluded and it is no longer required to put on a stoic face. Holy Week observances are endlessly discussed and critiqued for weeks afterward. Those who hold leadership roles during this period know that they will be scrutinized about everything they do and that they will bear the blame if things don't go well.

In 2003 the journey to obtain the fruit was properly carried out with twenty-two *alguaciles* making the trip, stopping frequently to pray and perform the customary ceremonies along the way. The *alcalde* of Cofradía Santa Cruz that year told me that it had been a terrible thing bringing the fruit into town by truck the year before and that his predecessor was a thief:

> The *alcalde* of Santa Cruz last year only cared about money. He said that he couldn't raise enough in offerings to do it the traditional way, but I know this was just a lie. I myself contributed 1,000 quetzals and others did the same. All the fruit is donated. The fruit tree owners there want the blessings and don't charge for the fruit. They're happy to let the *alguaciles* go into their orchards and cut the fruit. I once owned a place near Chicacao and I always donated fruit without cost. The old *alcalde* said that he couldn't get the young men to go, but I know for a fact that many offered to go but he didn't want to bother. This year we have twenty-two that volunteered to go and we could have had more. This is a terrible thing that last year's *alcalde* did. He will suffer for it.

The new *alcalde* mentioned that the fruit is always donated because the growers desire blessings for having contributed to the ceremony. While that may be true on the part of the orchard owners, I have been told by a number of Atitecos that from their perspective the fruit is donated because they are obligated to do so. In fact the tradition is that the *alguaciles* go into the orchards to cut the fruit from the trees unannounced and take the fruit "by force." Although this has all been arranged previously and everything is carried out amicably, the appearance must be that the fruit is "taken," in keeping with the concept of a warlike raid or the collection of tribute.

The *alguaciles* arrive back in Santiago Atitlán on the morning of the Saturday before Holy Week. The fruit is carried in large wooden pack frames called *cacaxtes*, which are secured by a leather strap across the top of the forehead and borne on their backs. Each *cacaxte* is elaborately adorned with palm fronds, red bromeliads, and other tropical flowers and fruits also gathered on the coastal plain (fig. 71). The men arrive in two columns, led by the *primer mayor* and a musician who periodically strikes the great ancestral drum borne on the back of an apprentice or plays a few notes on a flute. Another young man periodically twirls a *matraca*, a noisemaker consisting of a flat, rectangular piece of wood set in a frame that is spun around a long handle with a grooved cylinder on top that produces a loud rasping sound (fig. 72). The *matraca* appears in processions where Rilaj Mam is carried in person or, as in

71. *Arrival of the fruit, borne in decorated* cacaxtes, *2010*

72. *Procession of the fruit bearers led by a* matraca *player, 2010*

this case, where his presence is implied. The sound is sometimes linked to the sound of crows, which are said to have been present at the birth of the Mam in the mountains, or alternatively to thunder, as his reign during Holy Week precedes the coming of the seasonal rains. Often one or two men with guitars sing traditional songs to Rilaj Mam as well as other deities and culture heroes such as Francisco Sojuel. The *alguaciles* and the fruit are constantly censed with clouds of copal smoke pouring out of several braziers swung by other young men as they make their way along the path leading to the southern approach to town.

The procession of fruit is greeted on the outskirts of Santiago Atitlán at about 9 or 10 A.M. They arrive on an unpaved road just above a hotel called the Posada de Santiago south of the main part of town. There they are met by a delegation that includes the *cabecera*, the town's mayor, a small brass band, the *alcaldes* and officials of each of the *cofradías*, *tixeles* (female representatives of the *cofradías*) with copal incense braziers, several boys spinning *matracas*, and a crowd of men and women from town. The spot where the two groups meet is next to a coffee plantation that at this time of year is processing the beans, adding another pungent smell. Every year that I have attended this ceremony a large number of black-headed vultures circle overhead. Local tradition sees this as a sign not of death but of the coming of the rainy season.

The *alguaciles* are greeted as victorious heroes and are complimented for their strength and endurance in a series of lengthy speeches by the town's mayor and the leading officials of the Cofradía Santa Cruz. During the greeting ceremony the *alguaciles* mostly rest beside their pack frames, paying little attention to the speeches, while two *tixeles* walk up and down the path bathing the fruit with thick clouds of copal smoke from their braziers (fig. 73). While sitting on raised hillocks on the side of the road, the *alguaciles* smoke cigarettes given to them by *cofrades* of Santa Cruz that came from Rilaj Mam's own offerings in order to revive them after their long journey and to give them a good heart. I was told by the *primer mayor* in 2003 that it rained hard on the way back from the coast for an hour or two but that the *alguaciles* hardly got wet because they were protected by Francisco Sojuel along the way. He said that traditionally there should be twenty-four *alguaciles*, but two had dropped out at the last minute due to illness so only twenty-two made the journey.

After a half hour or so the town's mayor and *cofradía* heads lead the procession back to the municipal offices, picking up more people as the fruit progresses through the streets of the community. From a distance the movement of the fruit into town appears as a slow-moving cloud of smoke punctuated by occasional glimpses of color from the fruit and flowers on the *cacaxtes*, borne along by great waves of people struggling to keep up on either side. By the

73. Tixel *censing the fruit at the greeting ceremony, 2003*

time the fruit reaches the town center, the press of people makes it nearly impossible to move in any direction other than with the current established by the procession. Partly from the jubilant atmosphere of the moment and partly to display their strength after the long ordeal, many of the *alguaciles* dance the entire way through town in short, swaying hops to the sound of the music, periodically spinning around and around with the heavy pack frames on their backs. One of them called out to his wife in the crowd nearby that his heart was so full of joy at his return that he didn't even feel the weight of the fruit on his back. With a large grin on his face he called back to her as she was swallowed up in the crowd: "I could dance for many more *leguas* [the distance that someone can walk in an hour, approximately four to seven kilometers] with the fruit if they would let me."

While the *alguaciles* keep guard, the pack frames full of fruit are lined up below the raised porch of the municipal offices, where three or four women cense them continually with copal smoke. Using a portable microphone, the *alcalde* of the Cofradía Santa Cruz addresses the crowd, explaining that the fruit has arrived from the coast and that the proper traditions of the ancestors have been observed. He compliments the sacrifices made by the *alguaciles* on behalf of the town and describes at great length their strength and willingness to carry out the customary rituals along the way despite the many hardships that they had to endure. One year the *alcalde* concluded his speech saying: "No one will remain behind in the coming year because the traditions of our ancient grandmothers and grandfathers have been carried out this day. They are pleased with us and bless us with their presence. We will go forward with no misfortune in our path. All will be well."

Following the *alcalde*'s speech, as many *cofradía* and municipal leaders as possible squeeze themselves into the tiny office of the mayor for another round of speeches, mostly formal expressions of gratitude for the continuation of traditions that date back "unknown centuries of time." The prestige of the town's mayor is partly based on his largesse in distributing hospitality in the form of drinks on important occasions and in receiving delegations such as this. Some mayors revel in the attention. Others seek opportunities to excuse themselves because of "urgent business" to avoid dealing with traditionalists and walking with processions. In recent years smartphones provide a good distraction and a means of being called away at the last minute. The *alcalde* of the Cofradía Santa Cruz, holding his staff of office, sits on a large overstuffed couch covered with red velvet in the center of the mayor's office—the place of honor—along with two or three of his fellow *cofrades*. Officials from the other *cofradías* and invited guests stand closely packed together, filling the room to the limits of its capacity and literally leaving no room to move. One year I was caught in the wave of people entering the mayor's office for the ceremony and was so firmly held in place by the crush of people that it took several minutes to lift my hand to scratch my nose. Those that can't wedge themselves inside try to find a place just beyond the door or window, leaning forward as closely as possible to hear what goes on within.

Despite the closeness of the crowd inside, the stifling heat from the densely packed bodies, and the heaviness of the copal-laced air and lack of oxygen, there is little sense of urgency to conclude the formal proceedings. The frequent loud grating noise of the *matracas* outside sometimes makes it difficult to hear the discussion, particularly when it is the turn of the *cofrades* to speak, some of whom are rather soft-spoken and intimidated in large groups. In 2003 when the old traditions enjoyed a significant revival, the mayor seemed to take particular delight in being the focus of attention behind his large desk. He suggested that it was his "benevolent administration" that fostered the continuation of Tz'utujil customs in the town. Many traditionalists who had attended the meeting later laughed at the mayor for taking credit for the ceremonies, when in reality he had done little or nothing to help them. His role was simply to be present in his capacity as the political authority for the town when he greeted the arrival of the fruit. None of this skepticism was apparent in the meeting itself, when the *cofrades* sat or stood stoically with their staffs of office and nodded periodically at the mayor's words.

Outside the mayor's office the crowds grow even larger, although they mostly remain silent with little conversation. It is difficult for a non-Tz'utujil to understand the seemingly boundless fascination that the fruit holds for traditionalists in Santiago Atitlán. Well over a thousand people crowd about shoulder to shoulder in the street between the town plaza and municipal buildings for more than an hour with little to do but stare at the fruit and wait to see what will happen next, which inevitably will be the same thing that happens every year. For most, participation in the public ceremonies of Holy Week involves patient observation over long periods, often with frozen expressions and folded arms for hours at a time. It is not because Tz'utujils are particularly passive or given to wasting time. For the most part, they are quick to smile and engage in lively conversation when the time is appropriate and seem to have boundless energy for hard work. Santiago Atitlán is a wealthy and industrious community founded on commerce that dates back into Pre-Columbian times, when it was a major trade center for cacao and other commodities. Yet during Holy Week, one has the sense that ordinary life is suspended. People are strangely content to watch events play themselves out with little immediate concern for time or circumstances. It seems like the most natural thing in the world to attend the movement of ornately decorated crates of exotic coastal fruit from one area of the city to the next. This is what they have done since early childhood. Its regularity and predictability is comforting in a rapidly changing world of cell phones and Internet cafes.

While waiting for the officials to conclude their meeting in the mayor's office, the *alguaciles* guard the fruit and keep the crowd from coming too close. Throughout Holy Week the *alguaciles* are charged with keeping watch over the fruit as it moves from place to place for various ceremonies (fig. 74). During this time they are given a degree of freedom to act outside the normal social boundaries for young men of their age and social status. Each one carries a small bamboo baton a little over a foot in length wrapped with metallic-colored ribbon with which they "punish" those who violate the customs of the community by giving them a sharp whack on the back, arms, or legs. They often take subversive delight in this role, exaggerating or inventing transgressions in order to use their weapons on the offenders. A few years ago one of the *alguaciles* lightly struck a young Ladina tourist on the legs for wearing a skirt that he deemed immodest and for not showing proper respect. He was harshly punished for this, as the authorities feared that such incidents might keep tourists and their much-needed currency away. Since

74. Alguaciles *guarding the fruit, 2010*

then the *alguaciles* have generally overlooked perceived slights by visiting non-Atitecos, limiting their displeasure mostly to local Tz'utujils who overstep the boundaries of customary conduct. As a result *alguaciles* are forced to compromise their traditional role during Holy Week due to imposed economic and political realities. Some of the freedom to swagger a bit, even for a brief time, has been lost. Modern Tz'utujil life demands many such compromises among traditionalists, which are mostly taken in stride. But it undoubtedly adds one more slice of resentment to the centuries' worth that have accumulated already.

After the fruit has rested for an hour or so in front of the mayor's office, the *cofrades* give a signal and the *alguaciles* wrestle the heavy pack frames filled with fruit onto their backs and again dance in procession through town in two great columns toward the Cofradía Santa Cruz. Traditionally the fruit should go to the house of the *primer mayor*, but in recent years this has proven to be difficult because of lack of space. As before, the fruit is censed along the way by women who walk up and down the line swinging their copal incense braziers. The route changes each year because the *cofradía* shifts locations annually. Upon arrival at the *cofradía* complex, the pack frames are placed one by one in a small room dedicated to this purpose. This room is either windowless or has its windows boarded up, making it very dark inside even during daylight hours. Multiple braziers of incense are placed around the fruit so that the small room is soon so filled with smoke that it is impossible to see from one end to the other. Because of the lack of ventilation, the room also becomes uncomfortably hot, undoubtedly hastening the ripening of the fruit.

Copal smoke is pale in color and has a strong spicy-sweet smell that carries over great distances. During major ceremonies such as Holy Week it is a constant presence in the air throughout the community and is one of the first things that visitors notice when approaching town during times of the year when great festivals are celebrated. Although the smoke is almost tangibly thick, strangely enough it does not sting eyes or throat or make it particularly difficult to breathe. Tz'utujils believe that copal sanctifies the air, purifying those who breathe it. It also permeates everything. The scent attaches itself to clothes for months yet never seems to sour over time. When I worked with the early eighteenth century manuscript of the *Popol Vuh*, now housed in the Newberry Library in Chicago, I could swear that I smelled the faint scent of copal on its pages.

The fruit remains in its special room from Saturday afternoon to Tuesday afternoon, ripening under the vigilant observation of the *alguaciles*, who take turns standing watch and replenishing the incense braziers. Care is taken to keep the room filled with copal smoke, which the *alguaciles* say "feeds" the fruit and keeps it warm. I once asked half-jokingly why the fruit needed to be guarded. Who would dare to steal it? Two of the *alguaciles* raised their baton weapons and in complete seriousness said that they were the captors of the fruit: "We are not here to keep people out but to prevent the captives from escaping." I expected that this would elicit smiles or laughter from the other *alguaciles*. The notion that the fruit would get up and run out the door seemed ludicrous, but they remained stone-faced, nodding their heads in agreement. None seemed to find the statement odd at all. One cannot help but remember Las Casas's description of ancient highland Guatemalan New Year's rites in which captives were watched over closely by young warriors, housed in a special room where they were feasted prior to their sacrifice at the culmination of the week (Las Casas 1958, chapter 177, 150–151).

At approximately noon a large contingent of dignitaries arrives at the Cofradía Santa Cruz, including the *cabecera* and his wife, the town's mayor and his deputies, the *alcalde* of each of the *cofradías* along with subsidiary *cofrades* and their wives, the usual musician with his great drum and flute, and other invited officials and guests. In 2003 they were greeted by the *alcalde* of Santa Cruz and arranged in the single room of the *cofradía* house in order of rank, with the highest officials seated on benches and others standing around the periphery. Once everyone was gathered, drinks were distributed to those present—mostly beer and cola. The most important invited guests received their own bottles, while the rest shared a single glass that was quickly drained, refilled from liter-sized bottles, and passed on to the next person.

After everyone had been given an opportunity to drink, the *alcalde* gave a brief speech in which he thanked those present for coming to honor the *alguaciles* for their success in bringing the fruit, pointing out their strength, sacrifice, and purity of heart. He also acknowledged the power of the saints (whose images stood on the altar of the *cofradía*) for blessing them with the ability to carry on their traditions. He particularly noted the power of Rilaj Mam, who was present in the rafters above (though out of view). A large plaited mat was then spread out on the floor of the *cofradía* house. One by one each *alguacil* brought his *cacaxte* into the room to be opened and inspected (fig. 75). With the *alguacil* standing by nervously, the *alcalde* of Santa Cruz and one or two of his *cofrades* unpacked the fruit, noting its condition, while the other *alguaciles* waited their turn in the patio outside or looked in through the doorway or window.

The fruit is supposed to appear fully ripened and healthy, with no blemishes, parasites, or physical damage. Unripe fruit is widely considered to be the result of the *alguacil* sleeping with his wife or, worse, committing adultery during the period of his imposed chastity over the past two weeks. Sexual abstinence is believed to produce heat that ripens the fruit properly. If this is expended prematurely, the fruit would fail to mature, rendering it useless for its intended purpose in renewing life. Blemished or damaged fruit is an indication that the *alguacil*'s heart is not pure. For example, he may have become angry with the other *alguaciles* over some dispute or doubted the power of Rilaj Mam and the other traditions of the community. Similar explanations for the unripe fruit were recorded by Mendelson:

> If the fruit of any alguacil is green at that time [when the pack frames are opened], it is said by some that he has committed adultery, by others that he has been indulging in family quarrels and by others still that he has performed the fruit tasks unwillingly or has quarreled with another alguacil along the way. The former interpretation seems to be the traditional one but has been modified by some informants to cover the sin of breaking abstinence from sexual contact with their wives which is enjoined upon alguacils before their departure. The two latter interpretations appear to represent more recent rationalisations of the belief on the part of informants who do not wish to talk of sexual matters at all. (Mendelson 1957, 252)

75. *Unpacking the fruit, Cofradía Santa Cruz, 2000*

For the most part the fruit seemed to have been in good condition, having been packed carefully with abundant soft banana leaves or moss as a cushion. A few unripe fruits were laid to one side or put back into the *cacaxte* without comment by the *alcalde*. The other *alguaciles* watching outside the door reacted to this with muffled laughter and crude jokes about the sex life of the young man who had carried that *cacaxte*. This was a source of great embarrassment for the young man in question. Though I have never heard an *alguacil* criticized vocally by the *alcalde* of the *cofradía* while unpacking the fruit, the young man did receive disapproving stares and whispered asides from the officials and their wives arrayed about him in the room. In 2010 the ears of one *alguacil* became visibly red when the *alcalde* took out a nearly green banana from his *cacaxte*. This was taken as a sure sign that he was guilty of some sexual dalliance. He was mercilessly harassed with jokes and innuendos by the other *alguaciles* for the rest of the week to the point that he became ill. On another occasion one of the bananas was overripe, the peel having turned half-brown. In this case the *alcalde* instructed its bearer to take the banana outside and eat it in front of the other *alguaciles*. This did not seem to embarrass him at all. He took it as a sure sign that his sexual potency was the strongest of the group and reveled in taking the entire banana into his mouth while the others encouraged him with hoots and laughter.

Each *cacaxte* contained two or three cacao pods (*Theobroma cacao*, a yellowish brown fruit from which chocolate is made, with a ripe husk shaped like a ribbed rugby ball or US football), two or three *pataxtes* (*Theobroma bicolor*, a lesser grade of cacao that is larger, more rounded, and colored a vivid green), three *melocotones* (*Sicana odorifera*, a large, elongated, fragrant fruit with a hard maroon to dark purple shell and juicy orange-yellow flesh), and twenty-three to twenty-five bananas. When unpacked, each type of fruit is placed in separate piles on the large mat at the center of the floor. In 2003 the total from the 22 *alguaciles* came to 58 cacao pods, 57 *pataxtes*, 65 *melocotones*, and 550 bananas.

After all the fruit had been unpacked and stacked on the mat, the dignitaries soon got up to leave, shaking the hands of everyone present and thanking the *alcalde* for his efforts. As they approached the door to leave, the *alcalde* gave each person some of the fruit. It was received with prolonged expressions of gratitude, more than the usual courtesy given during gift exchanges. The most important officials received a cacao pod or *melocotón* along with a banana or *pataxte*. Lesser invited guests received a smaller gift, usually a single banana. Most stood by waiting for the dignitaries to leave and for the *alcalde* to occupy himself with other duties before leaving empty-handed. In a few cases the *alcalde* went out of his way to give some of the fruit to those standing to the side as a gesture of unexpected honor.

Once everyone has gone, a few of the *alguaciles* and members of the *cofradía* decorate the fruit with small bits of shiny, metallic paper of the type used to wrap presents. The preferred colors are gold, silver, and red, though occasionally other colors are used. Although the Tz'utujil language is otherwise rich in vocabulary, it has only one word for precious metals: *pwaq*. Gold is yellow *pwaq*, silver is white *pwaq*, and copper is red *pwaq*, which perhaps explains the preference for those colors in decorating the fruit. These are the same three types of metal that Las Casas notes were used to adorn sacrificial victims during ancient New Year's rites (Las Casas 1958, chapter 177, 150–151). The paper comes on rolls that is cut into long, thin strips with hand scissors. These are then cut into small squares and rectangles that are pasted onto the fruit with commercial white glue. Once the fruit has been decorated, it is placed into open baskets that will be borne in procession the following day into town on the shoulders of the *alguaciles*. The decoration of the fruit isn't complicated, but it is tedious and often occupies the rest of the day, particularly since nearly every year the glue and paper run out and someone has to go and buy more. As usual the fruit is constantly bathed in clouds of incense smoke from braziers that are periodically waved over and around it.

THE DRESSING OF RILAJ MAM

> *During these five days [the Wayeb'] one god is worshipped. On the first day he is feted with great enthusiasm.*
>
> *CHILAM BALAM OF MANI*, IN CRAINE AND REINDORP 1979, 88–89

While his clothes are washed and dried, Rilaj Mam lies in the loft of Cofradía Santa Cruz in a disarticulated state, with his head and limbs removed from the trunk of his body. In recent decades this is the only time throughout the year when he does not make an appearance during the day to receive petitioners. This unusual state of affairs reflects the legend of the Mam's creation (outlined in chapter 5), when Francisco Sojuel cut the limbs from the Mam's body to prevent him from causing harm in the community. Sojuel subsequently retied the limbs onto the Mam's body with cords after he promised to be obedient. On Tuesday night the rearticulation of Rilaj Mam is repeated, inaugurating his reign as the most powerful deity in the world for the next three days, replacing Christ as the principal deity while Christ is absent in the realm of the dead.

At some point between 9:00 and 10:30 in the evening, a delegation consisting of the *cabecera* and the leadership of each of the *cofradías* goes to the town mayor's office to announce formally that the Mam will soon be reassembled and that the mayor's presence is required at the Cofradía Santa Cruz. It does not matter whether the mayor is a traditionalist, an orthodox Roman Catholic, or a Protestant. He must accompany this delegation to the ceremony (fig. 76), often flanked by one or two armed officers from the local police department. It is unclear whether this is to provide protection for the mayor or to ensure that he fulfills his traditional role. On more than one occasion it seemed that the police were friendlier with the traditionalists than with the mayor. On rare occasions the mayor has tried to avoid this obligation by staying away from his offices on Tuesday night, particularly if he is an Evangelical Protestant. When this happens runners are sent all over town to find him. He is then taken, respectfully but firmly, by the *cofradía* officials to fulfill his duties. The reluctance of some mayors to attend is understandable. The belief among traditionalists is that the reassembling of the Mam represents his ascension to political as well as spiritual authority. From this night until the rebirth of Christ on Friday afternoon the Mam is the ruler of the community and displaces all human authorities.

Upon arrival at the Cofradía Santa Cruz, the delegation receives a formal greeting, including a round of drinks. Dignitaries are seated in order of office on the main bench. *Tixeles*, the female members of the *cofradía* system, generally prefer to sit on mats placed near the opposite wall, each holding a candle. Other invited guests find places to sit or stand against the wall across the room from the altar where the saints preside. At a signal from the *telinel*, a large mat of woven palm leaves is laid out on the floor. All those who are not invited to witness the ceremony are dismissed from the room. The *telinel* and one or two attendants then climb a ladder into the rafters to retrieve the disarticulated body of Rilaj Mam, which is wrapped tightly in a plaited reed mat. The god's bundle follows the general outline of the trunk of his body, including two stumps for the legs. The *telinel* also brings down several bundles containing the Mam's new clothing and perhaps the cords used to bind his limbs. Once these are laid out on the floor, the edges of the mat are drawn up to shield the work of the *telinel* from view. The doors and windows are then barred shut and all lights are extinguished, leaving the room in complete darkness.

The length of the procedure varies widely from year to year, but it usually takes approximately an hour and a half to two hours, ending sometime before midnight. During this time those in attendance are expected to sit or stand quietly in the dark. The prolonged lack of light and the inability to move or communicate eventually produces an odd sense of disorientation, which at

76. *Town mayor (right) accompanied by* cofradía *officials, 2003*

times makes one feel the sensation of floating. One year a policeman checked his watch half-way through the ceremony, which had a faint illuminated dial. Although the light was very dim and only lasted a moment, the *telinel* noticed it immediately on the other side of the mat and in low, harsh tones told whoever had been responsible for the light to put it away or he would be thrown out. The head of the *cofradía* quietly confiscated the watch to make sure. The insistence on complete darkness recalls the tradition of the Mam's creation, which was said to be at the darkest hour of the night, a blackness intensified by a thick cloud or mist that enveloped his creators as they worked.

While the *telinel* reassembles the Mam inside the *cofradía* house, traditional songs are performed in the courtyard outside that refer to the first creation of the god. In the myths surrounding Rilaj Mam's birth, powerful men and women sang to the accompaniment of musical instruments while others carved the god's body from the trunk of a *tz'ajte'l* tree. In some versions the Mam taught them the words and notes of the songs. In others it was the songs themselves that animated him as he was carved. Once formed the Mam rose up and danced to the songs. Ever since that time, the Mam has loved to hear music. For this reason major ceremonies in Santiago Atitlán frequently include musicians: a single guitarist, a marimba with two to four players, or a folkloric band with multiple instruments. The most common song in these contexts is the *B'ix rxin Mam* (Song of Mam). Although the words vary to some degree according to the improvisational talents of the singer, the core verses are essentially the same for each performance. This song is not just a retelling of the Mam's birth but is meant to ensoul and animate the Mam as the words are sung. Linda O'Brien-Rothe recorded and transcribed a version of the *B'ix rxin Mam* in the 1960s as performed by Gaspar Yataz Ramirez. It differs little from the way the song is sung today:

Li lali lali lali lali la
Li lali lali lali la
Oh smart boy, smart man,
Oh boots man, oh jacket man,
Oh fringed silk scarf man, oh towel man.
He makes scary noise at night, he makes things shake in the day,
With his ancient hands, with his ancient feet.

Lila lila lila li
He makes scary noise at night, he makes things move in the day,
A thousand leagues away, a hundred leagues away,
The man he can see in the shadows, the criminal and the sinner.

Li lali lali lali lali
Li lali lali lali lali
Oh smart boy, smart man,
Oh royal boy, oh royal man.
Metal rings are his hands, metal rings are his feet,
Oh son of the tree, oh son of string.

Li lali lali lali lali
He was engendered, he sprouted,
The boy, the man,
In "The Medicine Place" [where they found the tree from which
they made] the boy.

Oh man of the mountain, man of the plain,
Oh son of the drizzle, oh son of the hail,
No-one has hands like his, no one has feet like his,
The boy, the man, the dear.

Li lali lali lali lali
Li lali lali lali lali
Oh boy, man, mama, mama, mama,
Oh son of a skirt, oh son of a blouse,
Oh son of silk, oh son of purple stripes.

He makes scary noise at night, he makes things shake in the day,
With his hands, with his feet,
Oh son of the night, oh son of darkness,
Oh he enjoys himself, oh he has fun,
Oh he is the guardian, oh he is the watchman,
Oh the commissary, oh the foreman, oh the steward.

He blesses the house, he crosses to the ancient four corners,
The ancient Resting Place, the ancient Alighting Place
Of our fathers, of our mothers,
Of Diego, of Juan Martín, of Diego Martín, Canon Martín,
Coban Martín, Chajul Martín,
Oh silk Martín, oh silk girl,
Oh son of María Thread-Beater,
Oh son of María Warp-Beam,
Oh son of María Small Thread-Beater,
Oh son of María Small Heddles,
Oh son of María Large Heddles,

Oh son of María Canon, Juana Canon,
Oh boy, oh man,
Oh son of Diego, oh son of Juan,
Oh image, oh figure made by Francisco Sojuel,
Oh image, oh figure made by Salvador Pablo,
Oh image, oh figure made by Andres Pacay, Salvador Pacay, Juan Polin,
Diego Polin,
Oh image, oh figure made by Marcos Rujuch', Diego Rujuch',
Oh image, oh figure made by Tomás Cop Coo',

Oh smart boy, oh smart man,
Royal boy, royal man.
Oh he makes noise, he makes things shake,
Oh with his hands, oh in the darkness,
He is out of breath, he is panting,
In the north wind, in the winds from the mountains.

He makes himself a corn-husk, he makes himself garbage,
He makes himself a dog, he makes himself an animal,
He makes himself a fly, he makes himself an ant
One hundred percent of the shapes.

He enjoys himself, he has fun in Honduras, Nicaragua, Mexico,
Costa Rica.
He enjoys himself, he has fun, he enjoys himself in France.
He enjoys himself, he has fun in the United States, Guatemala.
He greets them, he talks to them,
Oh ancient boy, ancient man,
Oh smart man, short man.
(O'Brien-Rothe 2015, 90–92)

For the most part the *telinel* makes little sound as he works, rendering the rhythmic cadence of the music all the more hypnotic and powerful. The few words of instruction that he communicates to his assistants are given in very low whispers. Occasionally I could hear the rustle of mats, probably when the Mam's body was unwrapped, the sound of scissors cutting a rope or cord, the tightening of a knot with great force, the hiss of an aerosol spray can of cologne or perfume (the smell of which quickly fills the room), and, toward the end, the sound of arranging clothing on the hard wood of the Mam's body. Curiously, this is one of the few major ceremonies where copal incense is not burned. I once asked the *telinel* why this was the case. He did not know of any reason for it other than that it had never been done as far as he knew and that it was important to do things as they have been done in the past.

An hour into the process the *telinel* distinctly said *xrilo ri Mam*, in a slightly louder voice than at any other time during the ceremony. This can mean either "she/he/it saw the Mam," or "the Mam saw her/him/it." I asked the *telinel* afterward why he had said this. He seemed surprised and said that he didn't recall saying any such thing but that if he did it was the ancestors speaking through him, not him. The next day he asked me if I had really heard him say those words. When I told him that I was sure of it he smiled and nodded before telling me that this was a very good sign that the Mam was truly with us again and had power.

Once Rilaj Mam is fully assembled and dressed, the sides of the mat that were raised to hide the process are lowered and the lights abruptly turned on to reveal him at the center of the *cofradía* house floor flanked by the *telinel* and his attendants. Sometimes the Mam appears standing and at other times he lies on the mat with his feet toward the door. In such cases the *telinel* and another attendant lie on either side of him in the same position (fig. 77). The Mam's clothing is all new: boots, traditional purple and white striped Tz'utujil pants with embroidered bird designs above the lower border, a shirt (which is mostly obscured by other layers of clothing), a traditional Atiteco woven belt, twenty-five to thirty colorful silk scarves of various patterns knotted in front, a Western-style tie centered over his chest, a dark suit coat, a Tz'utujil shawl (or sometimes a brightly colored commercial towel) draped across his shoulders with the ends hanging down the front, a scarf covering the back of his head behind his mask, and two Stetson hats laid one atop the other, with another silk scarf attached to the outer hat so that it falls loosely behind his back.

These are the articles of clothing mentioned in the "Song of the Mam," and he always appears in public dressed in the same way, although the color scheme of the scarves, tie, and embroidered Atiteco garments varies widely. What the Mam wears when he is revealed on Tuesday evening is a popular topic of conversation. This odd blending of traditional Tz'utujil and foreign clothing is unique to the Mam. Some explain that this means that Rilaj Mam is a god of the entire world, not just Santiago Atitlán. He can therefore speak all languages and does not need a translator to understand foreigners. He is a great traveler, going to far-off places each night and collecting clothes from the places that he visits. His guardians sometimes ask me to bring him scarves or other gifts from the United States or Europe because the Mam is a great traveler himself and appreciates things from far away. Diego Molina asked about the clothing in the early 1980s and was told that the Mam wore

77. Rilaj Mam reassembled on the evening of Holy Tuesday, ca. 1968. Photograph by John D. Early

so many expensive clothes because "he is strong. He is wealthy. For this reason he wears good things" (Molina 1983, 15). Others say that his eclectic taste in clothes shows that he is inconsistent and unpredictable—he does not always follow the traditions and rules of the community and sometimes behaves like Ladinos who do not know the proper way to act or dress.

For the remainder of the night petitioners approach the Mam, complimenting him on his beautiful appearance and giving him offerings as they ask for favors. The first to approach him is the *xo'*, the senior female official of the *cofradía*, who lights the first candle in front of him. She is followed by the other *tixeles*, who all light their candles from the first one. After each of the women has greeted the Mam, the *telinel* reminds the newly assembled god to receive all the gifts of "his children" because they have come to honor him. At first most are content to stare at Rilaj Mam or comment in whispers to their neighbor on his appearance. Eventually they all approach him one by one to give an offering of alcohol, tobacco, money, flowers, and so forth. Atitecos believe that the Mam is especially powerful during the next three days and people are content to patiently wait their turn to approach him with their troubles. The *telinel* never leaves his side until dawn and frequently speaks to him, patting him on the back or shoulders, punctuating his words with a litany of respectful titles—*nawal acha* (magical or enchanted man), *nim winaq* (great person), *nab'e acha* (first man), *rilaj acha* (ancient man), and his principal title, *rilaj mam* (ancient/revered grandfather). But the *telinel* also uses more deprecating names like "old goat," "pretty boy," "disobedient child," or "little rascal." Few other than the *telinel* would feel comfortable using such language in the Mam's presence. It is a token of the *telinel*'s intimate relationship with the Mam that he feels free to speak to him in this way. The *telinel* fills the role of Francisco Sojuel, who disarticulated the Mam after the god's misbehavior many years ago, agreeing to reassemble him only after receiving assurances that he would not continue his rebellious activities. The tone of the *telinel*'s voice on this night, however, is indulgently affectionate rather than angry or disapproving.

HOLY WEDNESDAY *Chapter 7*

Rilaj Mam passes the first days of Holy Week in a pitiable state. While the city is being swept clean, his clothes washed, and the coastal fruit opened and adorned, the Mam lies alone in the dark rafters of Cofradía Santa Cruz, his head and limbs severed from his body. In contrast to the Mam's customary presence in the *cofradía* house during the year as watchman over the community, he languishes helpless and virtually abandoned while preparations are being made for his reappearance late in the evening on Tuesday when the *telinel* reassembles his body. By midnight he is revealed fully formed, resplendent in new clothes with freshly attached head, arms, and legs. Often the most powerful Maya ceremonies take place either at midnight or at noon because it is believed that at those times the spirit world lies closer to our own and can be accessed with greater efficacy.

Midnight is reserved for rituals that represent new life, as that is the point where the sun is at nadir, its lowest position in the underworld just before its rebirth and slow rise toward dawn on the eastern horizon. Noon represents the climax of maturity and power, reflective of the sun at its highest point in the sky. Midnight is appropriate for the reemergence of the Mam from his weakened state. At noon the following day he will be borne triumphantly at the height of his powers through the streets of Santiago Atitlán to occupy the mayor's office as lord of the city. For the next three days he is treated as the single most powerful being in the community, honored in the presence of the town's mayor (representing secular dominion), police officials and the *alguaciles* (the modern equivalent of an armed military class), and the *cabecera* and leadership of each of the ten *cofradías*, the principal bearers of spiritual authority and power in Santiago Atitlán.

Soon after dawn the exhausted *telinel* and his male assistants turn over their duties as the Mam's guardians to the most senior *tixeles*, the female representatives of the *cofradía*. This is the only time during the year when women take primary responsibility for the Mam's care (fig. 78). In these first daylight hours nothing is allowed to touch the Mam that might render him impure for the ceremonies of the day. Even a fly or mosquito that comes near his body

78. *Women guard Rilaj Mam on Holy Wednesday morning, 2010*

is scrupulously shooed away with a flick of their shawls before it can come into contact with the Mam's clothes or mask. Normally there is a high tolerance for drunken worshippers or curious tourists in the *cofradía*. But when the *tixeles* are in charge they have little patience for anyone who violates what they deem to be proper conduct in the Mam's presence.

THE PROCESSION OF THE FRUIT AND RILAJ MAM TO THE MAYOR'S OFFICE

> *Then a new world dawned for them. The two-day throne was declared, the three-day throne.*
>
> *CHILAM BALAM OF CHUMAYEL*, ROYS 1967, 102

At approximately 10:30 A.M. the *cabecera* and a delegation of *cofradía* officials arrive to accompany the fruit from the Cofradía Santa Cruz to the town's municipal offices. The fruit is now adorned with shiny metallic paper and arranged in large, bowl-shaped baskets that will be carried in procession by the *alguaciles* on their shoulders (fig. 79). Each piece of fruit is tied up with a length of brightly colored plastic cord so that it can be hung later in the day on the great Monumento structure in the church.

The fruit's journey to the mayor's office is a slow-moving formal procession (fig. 80). It is led by the great drum, which is periodically struck once

79. *Procession of the fruit, 2010*

80. *Procession of Rilaj Mam with the fruit, 2010*

between passages of a flute melody played by the same musician. The drum is followed by the *tixeles*, each carrying a large white candle wrapped with a banana leaf to prevent wind from extinguishing the flame. They are led by the *xo*'s, the female heads of the *cofradías*, who wear a special long blouse or *huipil* with purple stripes called a *nim po't* (great *huipil*) that hangs down to about the level of the knees and is not tucked into the skirt as most Tz'utujil blouses are. The male *cofradía* officials follow next. The *alcaldes* carry their staffs of office—long wooden staves, often adorned with fresh flowers and evergreens, each bearing a carved image on top that is unique to the *cofradía*. The highest *cofradía* officials wear the black or dark brown woolen *manq'ax* over their regular clothes. If there are sufficient funds, the Cofradía Santa Cruz often hires a brass and percussion band to follow next in line. The band easily drowns out the sound of the drum and flute at the head of the procession and can be heard from nearly anywhere in town. Next comes a double line of approximately forty to fifty *alguaciles* and *cofrades* carrying the fruit baskets on their shoulders. Two or three women walk up and down these lines censing the men and fruit with copal smoke that billows thickly from their braziers.

Bringing up the rear of the procession is another double column of young men, each carrying a single large pod from the corozo palm tree (*Orbignya cohune*). Each pod is four to five feet in length, with a thick, striated, woody husk that tapers to a narrow point at both ends (fig. 81). When split open the pods reveal a heavy yellowish to cream-colored flower with fleshy stems and petals. The flowers have a rich, aromatic scent that quickly fills a room. A group of *alguaciles* obtained the corozos from the coast in a formal procession that began on Sunday morning, following much the same route taken by the fruit from the coastal piedmont, although the corozo bearers receive less attention from municipal and *cofradía* officials when they return on Tuesday morning. The pods will be opened later in the day and the flowers used to adorn the Monumento along with the fruit. Atitecos also use corozo flowers to decorate *cofradía* houses, businesses, and private homes during Holy Week, hanging them from ceilings like massive sprigs of otherworldly mistletoe.

I have never heard a consistent myth associated with the corozo flower. Most just say that it bears the scent of Holy Week as a sign of renewed life. The *alcalde* of Cofradía Santa Cruz told me that when Christ died his body was placed inside a corozo pod and that he hides from his enemies within the flower. It is his presence that gives the corozo flower such a beautiful scent. The unopened corozo pod thus represents the sacrificed Christ in his fragrant coffin.

Once the procession arrives at the municipal complex, the fruit and co-

81. *Procession of the corozo pods, 2010*

rozo bearers enter either the mayor's office or one of the larger adjacent halls to deposit their burdens. First a large palm-leaf mat is placed on the floor in the center of the room. The baskets of fruit and corozo pods are then arranged around the edges of the mat, leaving an empty space where Rilaj Mam will eventually be placed. Until recently the room was strewn with pine needles to create a green carpet on which the mat was laid (McDougall 1955, 63). Similar beds of pine needles were laid in other sacred places where Holy Week rituals took place, including *cofradía* houses, the Mam's chapel, and the church itself (Mendelson 1957, 255). This recalls Las Casas's description of New Year's observances in which "some young men were sent by their captains to bring green boughs; others brought pine needles to scatter on the floors" (Las Casas 1958, chapter 177, 151, translation by author).

While the *alguaciles* watch over the fruit, the remainder of the procession returns to the Cofradía Santa Cruz to retrieve Rilaj Mam and accompany him to the mayoral offices. Some years the Mam accompanies the fruit, in which case the *telinel* carries him between the two columns of fruit-bearers. The older tradition, however, is for the Mam to be borne in a separate procession after the fruit has safely arrived at the municipal complex. The *telinel* in

1998 told me that this is preferable, because when the Mam arrives everything should be ready for him to occupy the space as the king of Santiago Atitlán: "The Mam doesn't like to be bothered by the *alguaciles* fussing with the arrangement of the fruit and the corozo pods and other small things that need to be done before he can take his place in the center of the room."

Rilaj Mam appears in public outside the confines of the Cofradía Santa Cruz only once a year, from Wednesday to Friday during Holy Week. When transported from place to place, he is borne on the shoulders of the *telinel*, the Mam's caretaker. Two other *cofrades* attend him on either side, one carrying a length of rope looped around his shoulder and the other the ladder that is normally used by the *telinel* to bring the Mam down from the rafters each morning and return him again to his bed in the evening. The rope and ladder will be employed later in the day to secure the Mam to his post/effigy tree in the chapel on the church plaza.

In contrast to the slow and stately progress of the fruit, the movement of the Mam through the streets is quicker and less structured. It is also attended by far more spectators, throngs of whom line the streets to catch a glimpse of him. Most *telinel*s enjoy dancing the Mam, turning him this way and that to the rhythm of the music played by the band and even spinning him in a full circle once in a while so that everyone can see him from all sides. Because he is lifted above the crowd, the Mam appears to float through the air. It is easy to forget that he is actually being carried as the *telinel* is surrounded by *cofrades* that are more or less the same height, shielding him from sight (fig. 82).

Once Rilaj Mam arrives at the mayor's office around noon he is laid on the mat at the center of the room with his feet oriented toward the doorway, surrounded by the fruit baskets and corozo pods (fig. 83). The Mam's occupation of the municipal offices initiates a period from Wednesday through Friday in which the mayor's normal political business is suspended. Beneath Rilaj Mam's head the *telinel* places a black or dark purple velvet pillow decorated with a gold embroidered cross (fig. 84). This pillow is called the Ruk'ux Muxux (Heart of the Navel—in essence the Center of the Center, expressed in anthropomorphic terms). The pillow represents the navel of the world, with the arms of the cross extending outward toward the four cardinal directions. One of the *cofrades* arranging the pillow in preparation for the Mam's arrival in the mayor's office told me that the vertical line of the cross represents the "heart of the sky" and the horizontal line the "heart of the earth." Where the two come together is the *mero, mero ruk'ux muxux* (the very heart of the navel). The pillow is considered one of the most powerful objects in Santiago Atitlán and is kept under the guardianship of the Cofradía Santa Cruz during the year. Except during the Mam's brief reign during Holy Week, the Ruk'ux

82. *Procession of Rilaj Mam to the mayor's office, 2010*

83. *Rilaj Mam in the mayor's office, 2010*

84. Tixel *carrying the Ruk'ux Muxux, 2010*

Muxux is in the possession of Jesus Christ as the principal life deity in Santiago Atitlán. It is customarily housed within the Cofradía Santa Cruz in or near the glass-enclosed chest containing the image of Jesus Christ that resides there. Some years the Ruk'ux Muxux is used as the pillow for the life-sized image of Christ that lies in a similar glass case at the base of the left altarpiece in the church (fig. 126). This is the principal image of Christ in Santiago Atitlán and is the focus for prayers at the altarpiece during the year. On Holy Monday the left altarpiece housing Christ's image was covered with a large cloth as an indication that he is absent during Holy Week on his journey through the underworld. By using the Ruk'ux Muxux pillow at the inauguration of his public reign, the Mam in essence declares himself to be the temporary substitute for Christ as the principal deity at the center of the world.

For the next two hours Rilaj Mam will occupy the mayor's domain, symbolic of worldly power. Most years the town mayor himself is in attendance, acknowledging the Mam's authority by laying his staff of office on the floor next to the god. At least two senior *tixeles* sit on the floor beside Rilaj Mam at all times, one at his head and one at his feet. The custom, however, is for several *tixeles* to sit with him within the enclosure framed by the fruit. The common belief is that the fruit and women are linked together symbolically and that the Mam lies with them as if they were his wives. Alternatively, the fruit and corozo pods represent captive slaves presented to the Mam as tribute before being placed on display in the church.

HANGING THE FRUIT ON THE MONUMENTO IN THE CHURCH

> *They placed the heads of the sacrificed victims on wooden poles over a certain altar that was dedicated solely for this purpose, and there they kept them a certain time, after which they buried them.*
>
> LAS CASAS 1958, CHAPTER 177, 152 (TRANSLATION BY AUTHOR)

At about 2 P.M., the officials of Cofradía Santa Cruz direct the *alguaciles* to gather up the baskets of fruit as well as the corozo pods for the final leg of their long journey that began at the coast the week before. A formal procession similar to the one that brought the fruit to the mayor's office is quickly formed, although this time Rilaj Mam always accompanies them (fig. 85). The *tixeles* take the lead, one of them cradling the Ruk'ux Muxux pillow in front of her with both hands. An additional group of men brings up the rear, bearing two long wooden trellises already covered with the cypress that had been gathered the previous Monday evening. The trellises were prepared and adorned on the porch of the municipal complex while the Mam occupied the mayor's office. The fruit, corozos, and cypress boughs are used to adorn the Monumento inside the Roman Catholic church located to the east of the mayoral offices. To reach the church the procession must climb a series of steps leading to a large plaza with an elevated stone cross at its center. The church dominates the eastern side of the plaza. The Mam's domed chapel, where he will hold court during the remaining days of Holy Week, is located on the northeast corner of the plaza (fig. 86). It is as old as the church, having been constructed as a processional *posa* shrine. Originally there would have been four of these, built at each of the corners of the plaza. In colonial times religious processions of the faithful circled the plaza on important occasions in a counterclockwise direction, pausing at each of the *posa* chapels for prayer or religious instruction. The chapel used by the Mam during Holy Week is the only one of the original four that has survived.

The Mam accompanies the fruit as far as the base of the stone stairway leading up to the church's entrance. Once this point has been reached, the *telinel* bearing the Mam, along with a number of *cofrades*, veers quickly left to cut across the eastern edge of the plaza to occupy the *posa* chapel. An ex-*telinel* told me that carrying the Mam from the mayor's office on Holy Wednesday was one of the most difficult things that he had ever done in his life:

> I've never weighed the Mam, but usually he is about 30–35 kilograms (approximately 65–77 pounds). After he leaves the mayor's office, however, he

85. *Procession of Rilaj Mam, Ruk'ux Muxux, and fruit to the Roman Catholic church, 1998*

86. *Domed chapel, used as Rilaj Mam's sanctuary, 1988*

> is three or four times heavier because of the weight of his power. If you are not strong, or if you do not have a good heart, he would crush you. I dance between the two columns of fruit with the Mam and it's as if I'm carrying all the fruit as well. When we pass by the cross in the middle of the church plaza, the Mam becomes lighter and sometimes his hat may move, or he'll lean forward or backward without my causing it. This is because beneath the cross is the place of the skulls. The spirits come out when the Mam goes by to support him and bear him along. As soon as we get past the cross, however, the Mam becomes heavy again.

The fruit and corozo bearers continue into the church to decorate the Monumento that was constructed the previous Monday afternoon in front of the central altarpiece. The Monumento consists of a framework of horizontal wooden planks and vertical columns tied together with ropes. In the empty spaces between the columns a spiderweb of cords forms a lattice from which the fruit with its metallic paper decorations is hung. After the fruit is in place, the corozo pods are split open and a dozen or so of the great flowers are hung at intervals across the face of the Monumento. The fruit and corozo flowers are tied so closely together that it becomes impossible to see the lower half of the great altarpiece behind it, other than a space directly in front of the patron saint, Santiago, so that he can continue to receive those who come to pray to him (fig. 87). Finally, the two wooden trellises covered with cypress

87. *Monumento guarded by two* alguaciles, *2010*

boughs are attached to the sides of the Monumento, oriented so that they slope downward diagonally to mimic the mountain-shape of the altarpiece behind it. I once sat with Nicolás Chávez Sojuel at the adornment ceremony. He said that the open portal at the center of the Monumento represents the cave of Paq'alib'al, the place where the most powerful gods and ancestors live in the mountains southwest of town:

> All the great saints and *nuwal* ancestors live in Paq'alib'al (Place of Revelation/Appearance). Their spirits live there in the center of the mountain. This is also where the south wind is born. Strong rains come from this cave because that is where the clouds are formed. There is always the sound of wind coming out of the cave because this is where the ancients live. The entrance is guarded by two pumas and two jaguars and is adorned with abundant fruits such as corozos, bananas, *melocotones*, plantains, *zapotes*, cacao, and *pataxtes* to show that the heart of the *nuwal*s are present inside and that they have power to give good things in abundance. These are the same fruits hanging from the Monumento to show that Francisco Sojuel is present and has power. Inside Paq'alib'al is a gigantic snake one meter thick and fifty meters long that watches over the saints.
>
> Many times there is a woman named María Castelyan standing at the entrance who gives food, or perhaps she is the Virgin Mary. At other times only jaguars and deer circle around the entrance. At New Year's a light appears in the cave. Near the cave, in a small ravine, is a giant tree where angels rest when it rains, and inside the branches are clouds. The branches are covered with squirrels and birds. A peccary circles the trunk when it is about to rain because clouds and the first rays of dawn begin at this tree. Tremors shake the earth every five minutes there because this is where the *nuwal*s live when they leave Paq'alib'al.

On another occasion I accompanied an *ajkun* who laid out a series of offerings to the saints in the church. In his prayers he mentioned the Holy Week Monumento together with the cave of Paq'alib'al. He told me afterward that the two are linked. Entering into one would lead to the same underworld location as entering the other. He added that prayers offered at either place had the power to bring rain and that if the Monumento were not constructed during Holy Week there would be a terrible drought:

> Before the nuwals Francisco Sojuel and Marco Rohuch disappeared, for they did not die, they said that they would leave a sign in front of their home at the cave of Paq'alib'al to show that they still live. This sign was the presence of great piles of fruit, just like those on the Monumento during

> Holy Week—bananas, melocotones, *pataxtes*, and cacao. The last time that I was there I saw beautiful maize fields and bean plants all around it that grew to a miraculous degree. Peach trees and apple trees also grew nearby, which were full of parakeets.
>
> *Ajkun*s go to Paq'alib'al to ask for rain and to speak to the old ones that live there. When you go inside you may be gone for three days, but it only feels like a few minutes. The entrance to the cave is half a meter high, but when an *ajkun* goes there he knows how to ask the mountain to make the hole large enough to walk in without stooping over. Inside are five pumas that guard the cave. The largest puma is named Francisco, the second Diego, the third Juan, the fourth María, and the fifth Marco. These are the animal substitutes for the ancient ones. When the cave opens they roar, but if the person is pure of heart and holds up his hand, they allow him to enter without biting him. For the first few meters the cave is dark and cramped, but then it opens into a large chamber that is brightly lit as if in daylight and it is never cold or hot. Inside is a room with a throne guarded by two giant snakes with limitless length because there is no end to their tails. Sometimes a man is there wearing Atiteco clothes and an old straw hat like Atitecos used to wear a long time ago and asks what the person wants. This is Francisco Sojuel. There is always incense and smoke coming out of the cave and candles burning at the entrance even when there is no one there. Clouds are born from the cave and light rain falls constantly at the entrance because rain comes from the deepest part of the mountain. Did you notice that it rained all last week even though it is the dry season? That is because two *ajkun*s went to Paq'alib'al to ask for rain.

While the corozo pods are being opened during the decoration of the Monumento, children gather to take possession of the empty pods when the *alguaciles* are finished with them. Once split open, these look very much like small canoes or kayaks, the perfect size for a child to sit inside and ride them like toboggans down the nineteen tiers of stone steps that flow down from the church's porch to the plaza below (fig. 88). Steering is of course impossible, so no two rides ever take precisely the same route down the steps. Like toboggans on a rough hillside, they sometimes spill their contents prematurely before reaching the flagstones of the plaza. The pods are remarkably durable, allowing the kids to repeat this hazardous ride all afternoon before the last shredded bits are no longer serviceable. I've always wanted to try it. I've never worked up the courage.

The Monumento in the church is analogous to the ancient *tzompantli* as described by Las Casas, a wooden framework on which the heads of sac-

88. *Children riding corozo pod shells, 2002*

rificial victims were displayed, particularly during New Year's observances. The *alguaciles* who gather the fruit are often likened to warriors invading foreign territory on the coast in order to take captives. As we have seen, the *alguaciles*, as well as the *alcalde* of Cofradía Santa Cruz in 2003, described the cutting of the fruit from the coastal orchards with machetes as a violent act similar to the sacrifices made by the ancient Maya. Nathaniel Tarn and Martín Prechtel were told that the fruit and corozo pods represent Jesus Christ and, like Christ, are taken as captives and prepared for sacrifice (Tarn and Prechtel 1990, 79–81).

The link between ritual sacrifice and fruit is common in ancient Maya literature and art. In the *Popol Vuh* the god Hun Hunahpu descended into the underworld, where he was beheaded by the Lords of Death. The severed head was placed in the dead branches of a tree, which immediately sprang to new life, bearing fruit that was identical to the head of Hun Hunahpu:

> Now when they went to place his head in the midst of the tree, the tree bore fruit. The tree had never born fruit until the head of One Hunahpu was placed in it. This was the tree that we now call the calabash. It is said to be the head of One Hunahpu.
>
> One Death and Seven Death marveled at the fruit of the tree, for its round fruit was everywhere. Neither could the head of One Hunahpu be seen clearly, for his face had become identical in appearance with the calabashes. (Christenson 2007, 126)

Eventually a maiden in the Underworld named Xkik' (Lady Blood) heard of the miraculous fruit and developed a strong desire to taste it, saying that it "is truly delicious" (Christenson 2007, 128). Eating fruit is commonly linked with sexual relations in Maya thought. Tz'utujils, like most highland Maya, are unusually reticent when it comes to talking directly about sex, at least in polite conversation. Most often they refer to it obliquely through metaphors. The most common of these is "to eat fruit." It is impossible to talk about eating fruit without the double entendre coming to mind, so the phrase is avoided even when the topic of conversation is about actual fruit. The symbolism of the young maiden reaching up to taste the fruit of the tree suggests human procreation, which was precisely the result. When she reached for the "fruit," the skull of Hun Hunahpu miraculously impregnated Xkik'. In time she bore twin sons who eventually defeated the death lords and brought new life to the world. Thus the sacrifice of Hun Hunahpu ultimately resulted not only in the rebirth of life in the form of the tree and its fruit but ultimately of human life as well.

The Great Ballcourt at Chichen Itza is bounded on both sides of the playing field by a long panel of carved stone depicting a series of ritual sacrifices. The same scene of a defeated captive being beheaded is repeated six times with little variation (fig. 29). But these sacrifices were not meant to end life but to renew it. Thus vines heavy with fruit and flowers sprout from the headless necks of the sacrificial victims. Adjacent to the ballcourt is a stone Tzompantli, covered with rows of skulls (fig. 27). Originally there would have been a framework of wood atop this platform to hold the skulls of real victims, undoubtedly those sacrificed in the ballcourt. This blending of fruit, sex, sacrifice, and regeneration is also intrinsic to Atiteco thought regarding the fruit brought by the *alguaciles* from the coast. It is linked to both military and sexual prowess. The adornment of the Monumento is believed to bring the first heavy rains of the year and the resultant renewal of life.

The hanging of the fruit is one of most spirited activities during the week. The more important ceremonies during Holy Week are conducted by mature men, the leaders of the various *cofradías*. Although they are supervised by *cofrades*, most of the work of decorating the Monumento with fruit is carried out by the young *alguaciles*. The tradition is that the fruit ripens as a result of the sexual power of the *alguaciles*, augmented by the hypersexual influence of Rilaj Mam. As a result the hanging of the fruit not only is a proud display of the "captives" by victorious warriors but is also linked to the sexual prowess of the captors. Often the *alguaciles* liven up the decoration of the Monumento with good-natured comparisons of one person's fully ripe fruit with the fruit gathered by others. This is greeted with muffled hoots and snickers. Usually this would be quickly squelched with a few harsh words from older officials, but it seems to be tolerated well beyond the usual bounds of propriety in this case. In fact the few older men present seem to enjoy the young men's banter and laugh along with them, adding a few friendly jabs of their own at the target of the moment. Perhaps the hanging of the fruit affords the older men, who undoubtedly did much the same as *alguaciles* in their youth, an opportunity to relive their past. For the most part the *alguaciles* are allowed to swagger a bit, just this once.

In 2003 the parish priest came in while the fruit was being hung and angrily criticized the *alguaciles* and *cofrades* for not showing proper respect in church with their "pagan and abominable practices." The *alguaciles* stopped their work and, speaking in Tz'utujil, claimed not to understand the priest because he was speaking Spanish. This particular priest was a Tz'utujil himself but at that time refused to speak his native tongue. He insisted that his parishioners should abandon indigenous languages and customs in favor of more "civilized" European Christian traditions. The *alguaciles* knew that the priest spoke their language, and the priest knew that the young men spoke Spanish quite well. A few moments of angry stares followed before the priest turned and left. I often think of that brief confrontation, and the memory always saddens me. The priest felt that the sanctity of his beloved church was being violated and was frustrated at not being able to do anything about it. For their part, the traditionalists believed that the priest hated his own people and their most cherished customs. How could he turn away from what the ancestors had left to them? That angry little moment encapsulates for me the unresolved antagonism that underlies nearly all relationships among traditionalists, orthodox Catholics and Protestants in town, the vast majority of whom are full-blooded Tz'utujils. In general it only bubbles up in the form of relatively benign mistrust, pettiness, and religious bigotry. Occasionally the constant tension boils over into open violence. It is heartbreaking.

The hanging of the fruit is primarily the territory of the young men. Often there is only a single woman present, a postmenopausal lady addressed as "grandmother" who censes the proceedings with copal (fig. 89). In 1998 she was a direct descendent of Francisco Sojuel. The *alcalde* of Cofradía Santa Cruz that year told me that the clouds of copal smoke from her brazier had power to bring the first rains soon after Holy Week. Despite being very old and unable to stand erect, she moved with surprising quickness from one side of the Monumento to the other and never seemed to stop smiling. I wondered at first if she might be embarrassed by the sexually suggestive banter of the young men, but she seemed to enjoy it more than anyone, laughing freely

89. *Woman censing the Monumento, 1998*

and even contributing a few sexually suggestive innuendos herself. I asked the *primer mayor* why there was only one woman. He said that she represented María Batz'b'al (sometimes called María Castelyan or María Castellana), a powerful creator goddess who participated in the formation of the Mam. In a bit of Oedipal synergy, she is also the wife of Rilaj Mam. The two of them often act in concert:

> María Batz'b'al is our Grandmother. She is the grandmother of the world, she is the moon. Midwives go to her house to pray for new babies. She weaves everything into existence on her loom. The cords on the Monumento are like the threads of her loom. She's here to make sure that everything goes well.
>
> During the ceremony, the woman wore a simplified version of the traditional Atiteco headdress, a long woven strap that is wound around and around the head to form a halo. Generally, the outer band has a pattern of birds or other figures, but on this occasion it consisted only of a series of solid blocks of color. The primer mayor said that this was the older style of headdress, often called a "rainbow serpent." Diego Chávez Petzey said that this type of headdress was "first worn by the Grandmother Goddess and represents the umbilical cord that ties holy women to the sky." He suggested that the elderly woman, like the ancient Grandmother, presides over the decoration of the Monumento because "only women have the power to create new life, and they must be present at the rebirth of the world." (Christenson 2001, 95–97)

Both the Monumento and the larger altarpiece behind it follow the same basic organization. They are constructed in the shape of a great mountain, with the saints' niches functioning as caves from which sacred beings emerge. The twisted columns are the serpents that guard the mountain. Diego Chávez Petzey's brother Nicolás sat with me one year when the Monumento was being decorated. He placed special emphasis on the fact that the ropes used to hang the fruit are twisted like the columns, because they also represent winding snakes. The Grandmother weaves them together on her loom to provide the framework on which the world itself is formed and decorated with fruit trees, flowers, and cypress.

A cross is affixed to the top of both the altarpiece and the Monumento. The Chávez brothers carved the central altarpiece cross as covered with maize leaves and a round "jewel" at its center. Diego Chávez said that the jewel was the *k'ux* (heart) that gave the cross/maize plant its life as the "heart of the world" (fig. 90). Traditionalist Atitecos believe that all things that bear power

90. *Central altarpiece of the colonial-era church, Santiago Atitlán, 2008*

possess their own living *k'ux* that embodies the same life-sustaining presence that quickens the ancestors and saints of the community. The construction and subsequent decoration of the Monumento with living fruit, flowers, and evergreen boughs is conceptually linked to real mountains that produce new life along their slopes when the first rains fall soon after the Easter season. The Monumento is constructed in order to restore the "heart" of the altarpiece to its ancient original strength. From this center point the renewal of life extends outward to the four directions beyond the walls of the church following the successful completion of Holy Week rituals.

To emphasize the mountain aspect of the altarpiece, the artists carved other trees along the sides of the altarpiece as well as two traditional Tz'utujil *cofrades* climbing up each of the sides as if they were scaling its slopes. Both wear the *xkajkoj su't* headdress that is emblematic of their office. The one on the left holds the mask of Rilaj Mam with a cigar projecting from his mouth. The one on the right carries a Roman Catholic monstrance marked with a cross. Diego Chávez Petzey told me that he placed the two climbing figures at the same level on the altarpiece to show that they are equally valid forms of worship:

> Even though both climbers follow different paths toward the tree at the top of the altarpiece, they have the same destination, which is the *ruk'ux kaj, ruk'ux ruchiliew* [heart of the sky, heart of the earth]. Each works to bring about rain and abundance. Rilaj Mam and Christ both suffer and give their blood. For the Mam this blood is *psiwan ya'* [canyon water, a locally made fermented drink that forms a part of traditional Tz'utujil ceremonies]. For Christ it is wine. Both give life. I have heard some people say that the two climbers show the death of one religion and the life of the other. But I do not believe that one can replace the other. The Tz'utujil traditions will not end if we as a people do not end. (Christenson 2001, 64)

The decoration of the Holy Week Monumento represents the renewal of the earth, covered with fruit, flowers, and cypress boughs. The metallic paper on the fruit makes it shine with reflected light. Mendelson noted that in the 1950s Atitecos also hung a red velvet cloth with eight small mirrors sewn onto it (Mendelson 1957, 277f, n60), which would have accentuated the glowing effect when light struck it. Once the world has been reborn, symbolized by the raising of Christ's cross/tree on Friday afternoon, the Monumento is dismantled to reveal the great altarpiece behind it. Its physical permanence reassures the community that the world will continue under the protection of familiar saints and deities, safely sheltered in the niches of their mountain home.

RAISING THE TREE OF RILAJ MAM

> *In this year then they made an image or hollow figure of the god of clay, which they called Kan u Uayeyab [Yellow Wayeb' God, the southern B'akab'], and they carried it to the heaps of dry stone which they had raised at the southern side. . . . The image having been incensed, they cut off the head of a hen and presented or offered it to him. This having been done, they placed the statue upon a standard called kante [yellow tree].*
>
> LANDA 1941, 141

Until the mid-twentieth century Rilaj Mam accompanied the fruit up the steps of the church and occupied a position just to the right of the main doors on the church porch, remaining there until Friday afternoon. This is where Samuel Lothrop saw the Mam in 1927, the first recorded description of Holy Week in Santiago Atitlán (Lothrop 1929, 25). By occupying the space at the principal entryway to the church, the Mam symbolically controls access to the sacred space within, normally reserved for Christ and the saints. Elsie McDougall witnessed Holy Week in Santiago Atitlán in 1930. According to her account, the Mam was secured to an old post set into the floor of the church terrace between the wall of the church and the first pillar of the porch (fig. 91). The post was braced by a pile of boulders and smaller stones, including "Precolumbian club-heads in altar shape" (McDougall 1955, 66), per-

91. *Rilaj Mam on the church porch, 1930. Photograph by Elsie McDougall. Courtesy of the American Museum of Natural History, New York City*

haps similar to the "heaps of dry stone" mentioned by Landa. Worshippers come throughout the night to pray to the Mam and leave offerings of candles, incense, and other gifts.

Until recently the Mam's post was made from the wood of a tropical species of elderberry, known locally as *t'iney*. The post is now a more permanent concrete square column inside the *posa* chapel, although the original wooden version still exists and is kept in the home of a local traditionalist. Freshly cut branches of *t'iney* with their leaves still attached are secured to the top of the post, giving it the appearance of a living tree (fig. 92). An *alcalde* of Cofradía Santa Cruz once told me that the *t'iney* is a "life tree" that has medicinal powers. Tea made by boiling its leaves can alleviate the symptoms of diabetes, gastritis, and other stomach problems. The roots can also be boiled for medicine that is used to cure fevers, urinary infections, and prostate disease. A *telinel* said that *t'iney* leaves help eyesight and that when the Mam is hanging on his post surrounded by *t'iney* branches he is able to see far beyond the church plaza and know what the town's problems are that he needs to help with. The Mam's presence in the midst of the *t'iney* branches reinforces the belief that during Holy Week he is able to work miracles and heal sickness. It is said that a *t'iney* tree grew adjacent to the tree from which the Mam's body was first carved and that its healing powers gave him great strength to carry out his work during the year. The Mam is tied to the top of this leafy post, just as the ancient B'akab' deity was placed on the *k'ante'* (yellow tree) in Landa's description of the Yucatec New Year's rites, which he identified as a *palo* (standard, post) (Landa 1941, 140–141).

The positioning of the Mam on the church porch ended for the most part soon after 1950 as the result of a serious conflict with the Roman Catholic clergy. In that year a Dominican priest named Godofriedo Recinos arrived from San Lucas Tolimán to say Mass on Holy Wednesday. There was no resident priest in Santiago Atitlán at the time. According to a report by don Agustín Pop of the Instituto Indigenista published soon after the incident, Father Recinos was not invited by the town as a whole but by a single individual who had agreed to pay the priest 150 quetzals for administering the service (Mendelson 1957, 331). When Recinos arrived at the church, he became enraged at the sight of the Mam receiving offerings on the church porch. He broke down the wooden supports for the Mam's post and threw them over the porch railing:

> People got extremely angry and were about to set about killing the priest so someone fetched the literate boys and they were told to warn the priest to leave Maximon [Rilaj Mam] alone, for he was their god, and that he would

92. *Rilaj Mam on the "tree" post in his chapel, 1988*

> go mad and die. The priest answered that he did not give a fig about going mad, but that he would not allow them to worship the man who had been Christ's worst enemy before the crucifixion. The people's temper got considerably worse and some shouted that he should be put to death because he wasn't a Catholic but a Protestant. The priest ran over to the convent to get his pistol and made as if to shoot the people, shouting "I die for the truth but let's see that you go too, and to hell for a pack of idolators and savages that you are!" But when the priest went back to the convent, then the people set up the stones again and placed Maximon there with a golden incense-burner, litres of aguardiente and especially thick candles. When the priest came out he kicked the incense-burner and candles, but as he held his pistol the guardians endured this without moving. (Mendelson 1957, 332)

Press reports at the time said that the priest got off three shots before he could be subdued, although none harmed the Mam or any of his attendants. When asked about the incident later, Nicolás Chiviliu (one of the Mam's guardians during the conflict) said that Recinos was disarmed before he could fire his weapon, although one of the bullets did fall on the ground. Chiviliu put the bullet in the bottom of the Mam's chest of clothing as a relic (Tarn and Prechtel 1997, 3). A similar incident had occurred in 1912 or 1913 when a Roman Catholic bishop ordered that Rilaj Mam be burned. On that occasion an assembly of men armed with clubs and machetes protected the Mam and drove the bishop out of town (Lothrop 1929, 23).

After his altercation with the Mam's guardians in 1950, Father Recinos refused to say Mass unless the people stopped worshipping the idol. After much discussion a compromise was finally reached in which the *telinel* was allowed to keep the image of Rilaj Mam on the church porch, although no one could worship him publicly while the priest was around. Six weeks later Recinos returned with his father superior and another priest in a motor launch. After failing to enlist the town mayor's help in destroying the Mam, he and his fellow priests broke into the Cofradía Santa Cruz late at night. After exorcizing the sanctuary of "devils," the priests chopped off the image's head with a machete and confiscated two of his ancient masks before escaping across the lake. Although the *cofradía* soon fashioned a new head, the loss of the ancient masks was a blow. Those who came to pray and give offerings to the Mam were turned away without explanation. At first it was rumored that Rilaj Mam was absent because the pope himself had heard of his power and invited him to Rome for consultation (Mendelson 1965, 66). When the truth became evident traditionalists were outraged, harboring bitter feelings for years against orthodox Catholics in town who failed to condemn the theft. One of the masks somehow made its way to the Museé de l'Homme in Paris. After prolonged negotiations, the French government agreed to return the mask in 1979, sending a delegation from the French embassy in Guatemala City to deliver it to officials of the Cofradía Santa Cruz (Tarn and Prechtel 1997, 178–183). The other mask is still missing and was reportedly destroyed soon after it was taken.

In the following year, to avoid further difficulties, the Mam was placed in the *posa* chapel on the church plaza for the first time. The visiting priest at the time complained about the noise (his lodgings were directly across from the Mam's chapel), but otherwise Holy Week went smoothly without open hostilities (Mendelson 1957, 336–337). The positioning of the Mam became a battleground for the next few years. In 1952 he was set up in the marketplace near the municipal offices. The following year he was back on the church porch, although the priest requested that his post be placed further away from the main doorway, at the second pillar rather than the first. The conflict eventually was resolved by settling on the *posa* chapel as the Mam's designated sanctuary, and this has been his customary residence during Holy Week ever since. Despite initial resentment, traditionalists have grown comfortable with this situation. In 2002 a *cofrade* told me the following story about a time (about a decade before) when Rilaj Mam was returned to the church porch during Holy Week. This may have been in 1992, when it is known that the Mam occupied that position (Pieper 2002, 93–97):

> Years ago a former *cabecera* named Felipe Petzey tried to force the Cofradía Santa Cruz to put Rilaj Mam on the church porch like before. But the *alcalde* and the *cofrades* didn't want to change. The Catholic priest said that he wouldn't say Mass if he had to walk by the Mam into the church. It became a very dangerous thing. The ex-*cabeceras* became angry with Felipe. But he insisted and they put the Mam in the old place by the church doors and strung the entire porch with lights so that he could be seen better. Someone came along and told them that they weren't authorized but he didn't care. The church committee fought with him because he hadn't asked permission. Finally they decided to put the Mam back in his chapel in the plaza because he received more offerings there and the *cofrades* could drink in privacy without being criticized by the Catechists and Protestants. But the *cabecera* was still trying to keep the Mam up by the church. Soon after, Rilaj Mam appeared to him in a dream and told him that he wouldn't live long because he wouldn't listen. He said that he liked the chapel in the plaza and didn't want to be so close to the church anymore. On Friday

night, the *cabecera* became ill with fever and chills and told everyone that he had been cursed. The next day he couldn't walk. He died on Easter Sunday.

Rilaj Mam remains in his chapel until Friday afternoon, receiving worshippers who come to pray and give him gifts throughout the days and nights. These gifts include expensive scarves, alcohol, tobacco, candles, incense, and money. The *telinel* or one of the other attendants receives the gifts and touches them to various parts of the Mam's body, naming the giver and where he is from while calling on the god to bless the petitioner. It is believed that the Mam can work powerful miracles during this time, healing anyone who comes to visit him no matter how sick they are, as long as they come with a good heart. Nevertheless, the *telinel* has to watch over him to make sure that he carries out his traditional role. The *telinel* in 1998 told me the following while we sat with the Mam in the chapel:

> While the Mam is in his chapel he does not drink or smoke because he must take care of his responsibilities. He must watch over the town and protect it. Anciently he would sometimes convert into a person and come down from his post to go drinking. But he is now tied securely to the *t'iney* tree so that he will not leave. He must stay here in one place so that he can see the problems in the town and take care of the people who come to see him.

The dome of the Mam's chapel is painted on the inside with two wide concentric circles of blue color (fig. 93). Three vertical blue stripes link these two bands together. Between the blue circles on the east and west sides are red vegetal motifs with curling branches and flowers. Scattered about the dome are small angel faces with wings framing their heads. The *telinel* in 2010 gave the following description of the paintings while we sat together on a bench behind the Mam:

> The Mam's chapel is like the inside of a mountain, like a cave. Caves have power. The blue circles are water. Caves often have water in them because that is where rain comes from. Rainclouds are born in caves. The faces painted above us are the *nuwales*, powerful ancestors who live in the caves and watch over us. They help us when we are in trouble. The red plants are the tree of Rilaj Mam that gives life to people and heals them. They have the same leaves as the tree that the Mam hangs from. The Mam has power to heal people that are sick and that is why they come to see him during Holy Week. See how the plants have flowers? That is because they are growing and alive.

93. *Painted dome, interior of Rilaj Mam's chapel, 2010*

After centuries of persistent and sometimes brutal attempts to suppress even the smallest expression of indigenous worship, it may seem surprising that a traditional Maya deity like Rilaj Mam can continue to be worshipped so openly, even within the major centers of foreign power in Santiago Atitlán (the government offices of the city and the colonial-era Roman Catholic Church complex). This is all the more unexpected considering the unusual rituals that attend the Mam's worship during Holy Week, many of which represent a survival of Pre-Columbian Maya practices. For their part, traditionalists believe that to abandon these rituals would court disaster on a universal scale and are determined to carry them out despite threats from outsiders.

Notwithstanding their personal difficulties with various Roman Catholic priests over the years, many if not most traditionalists attend Mass, particularly during Holy Week. They consider themselves Catholic, as this is the only name for their religion that they've known over the past several centuries. Their Catholicism is a fusion of ancient Tz'utujil belief and European-derived Christianity. But where one ends and the other begins is largely irrelevant to them. In recent years there has been a growing movement among Maya activists and followers of the modern Maya Spirituality movement in Guatemala to divest traditional Maya ceremonies and beliefs of any perceived Christian influences, a process that C. James MacKenzie characterizes as "anti-syncretic" (MacKenzie 2009, 361).

Little of this is evident in traditional Atiteco ceremonialism. Christian saints and deities with Spanish names are revered alongside those with Maya names and attributes like Rilaj Mam. The process of weaving the two belief systems together has been going on for centuries. But at what time a particular choice was made to incorporate a new element of Christian or other foreign cultural tradition and the reasons for doing so have long since been forgotten. As Charles Wisdom writes:

> The early Catholic and native ideologies have become interwoven so that what we have is not a mere combining of two [or more] elements, a grafting of one upon the other, but rather what might be called a complete fusion to the extent that the Indians themselves are unaware that any such historical process has taken place. (Wisdom 1940, 120)

Traditionalists believe that *their* Catholicism is much older than that brought to Guatemala by the Europeans in the sixteenth century, extending back to the very beginning of time. They believe that they are not only Catholics but the only true Catholics. Oliver La Farge noted the same attitude among the Maya of Santa Eulalia, Guatemala: "The task confronting a priest who wished to revive true Christianity among these people is made almost overwhelming by the fact that they are not merely non-Christians but non-Christians who believe themselves to be the only maintainers of pure Christianity" (La Farge 1947, 81). If an orthodox Catholic priest exceeds his role in their society, as Father Recinos did in 1950 by threatening to destroy the Mam, Atitecos brand him a Protestant—not a complimentary term (Mendelson 1957, 332, 1958b, 3). Traditionalists believe that they alone understand the rituals that were handed down to them by their ancestors, rituals that are unique to their community and are not practiced anywhere else in the world. The situation is very much like that described by Nancy Farriss for Christianized Maya in the colonial era:

> No matter how much surveillance the parish priest might exercise over the finances of the cofradía, and I have suggested that it was fitful at best, the Maya leaders regarded themselves rather than the Catholic clergy as the guardians of the saints and all that belonged to them. The clergy could not be trusted with the responsibility. Curates came and went; they did not have the same stake in the community as the elite. And even if they had stayed permanently, they remained outsiders who never became integrated into Maya society, never shared the same values, and were therefore incapable of understanding the true significance of the saints in the world order. (Farriss 1984, 338)

Most of the time traditionalists and orthodox Roman Catholics reach an accommodation that keeps the peace. Atitecos recognize that there are certain ceremonies that only a Roman Catholic priest has the authority to do—celebrate Mass, perform baptisms, hear confessions, and oversee some important rituals linked with Holy Week. These are considered essential ordinances to both traditionalists and orthodox Catholics. John Early, an anthropologist who served as a Jesuit priest in Santiago Atitlán in the 1960s, writes that the efficacy of Roman Catholic rituals depended on the precise recitation of prayers, something that only the non-Maya priest could do until very recently:

> The non-Mayan Catholic priest is the only one who knows how to read or recite from memory the mass and baptismal prayers in Latin. Based on the similarity of purpose and structure between the traditional Mayan and imported Catholic rituals, the Maya view the Catholic priest as having a similar shamanic power in relation to the ladino saints as their own shamans have to the traditional gods. Both are seen as learning their prayer formulas from the gods themselves. (Early 2006, 224; see also Early 2012, 103–104)

But traditionalists also believe that the priest's role has boundaries, beyond which he has no right to go. During Holy Week ceremonies in 2002 the Roman Catholic priest was a Kaqchikel Maya who tried to curtail certain traditional ceremonies within the church. Although little came of his proposed restrictions, the attempt angered many in the community. In June of that year it was rumored that the priest saw a vision of Rilaj Mam looming in front of him while driving the church van to nearby Cerro de Oro and was so frightened that he lost control of the vehicle and hit a tree. Not long afterward he had a nightmare in which the Mam threatened to kill him if he didn't leave town. At least this was a common story repeated among traditionalists when the priest unexpectedly left soon after the car accident. He was replaced by a Tz'utujil priest from the coastal community of Chicacao, a member of Opus Dei who turned out to be far less tolerant of traditional Maya practices than his predecessor.

In the 1970s the priest assigned to Santiago Atitlán was an American from Oklahoma named Stanley Francis Rother. He commissioned a local sculptor, Nicolás Chávez Sojuel, to carve a pulpit and two ecclesiastical chairs. Chávez suggested that he be allowed to incorporate traditional Maya imagery into the designs to show that Tz'utujil beliefs were harmonious with those of orthodox Roman Catholicism: "Father Rother wanted me to show that words taught from the pulpit of the church are the bread of life. For us, this is maize and so I put a Maya maize god in the center of the pulpit as well as on the priest's chair" (Christenson 2001, 116). Despite initial misgivings, Father Rother allowed Chávez to proceed and over time became so impressed with the idea that he also had a special stole embroidered with Maya maize god images that he sometimes wore when presiding at the Eucharist.

The new priest from Chicacao was outraged when he saw these "pagan" images on the pulpit and the chair on which he was to sit during Mass. He immediately had the chair removed and arranged to have the pulpit's central maize god cut away and replaced with the image of a lamb. This and numerous subsequent actions angered traditionalists, who unsuccessfully petitioned the priest's superiors several times to have him removed for interfering with the practice of their faith. They considered the church and its adjacent buildings to be the property of the community as a whole, not of the priest. For his part it was the priest's belief that all traces of traditional Maya worship should be eliminated from the liturgical practices of the Roman Catholic Church, and he was merely following his conscience in these matters. Today traditionalists are equally adamant in their opposition to this policy. Over the years both sides have won skirmishes.

Some of the blending of ancient Maya and Christian theologies is heartfelt, such as the acceptance of Christ and the Roman Catholic saints as adopted Tz'utujil deities. This type of syncretism dates back to the very beginning of Spanish rule in the Maya world. But some of the links to Roman Catholic traditions are a conscious dissimulation. When criticized for engaging in traditional Maya ceremonies, some Atitecos use the New Testament to explain their actions. Rilaj Mam is Judas Iscariot: he is taken to the mayor's office just like Judas went to the authorities to betray Christ. The offerings given to the Mam are like the thirty pieces of silver that Judas received at the hands of the Jews. The Mam is hanged on a tree in his chapel just as Judas hanged himself when Christ was crucified. On the surface Holy Week in Santiago Atitlán can appear to outsiders as an elaborate Christian Passion Play. Roman Catholic authorities often chafe at the irregularities but generally overlook them in the same way that most Christians in the United States go along with Santa Claus and the Easter Bunny. It is only local tradition, after all.

But most traditionalist Atitecos are quick to emphasize that Rilaj Mam is not Judas Iscariot and are offended at the comparison. One *cofrade* assured me that the Mam has nothing to do with the Judas Iscariot that the Catholic priest preaches about in church, images of which are often hung and/or burned during Holy Week in other communities. "In Santiago Atitlan," he said, "he is not a traitor, he is our grandfather. We do not hang him or dishonor him. We respect him and he helps us with our needs." Some elements of the Mam's nature are undoubtedly syncretic with Roman Catholicism, although it is impossible to draw a clear line separating his Maya and Christian personalities.

As a "god-slayer," Rilaj Mam functions in a similar way to Judas, but only in the sense that he oversees the death of Christ. But he also becomes the temporary ruler of the world, a position that has nothing to do with European Christian tradition. Traditionalist Atitecos see the Mam as far more ancient than any Christian or Spanish character, having been present from the very foundation of the world. He does not kill Christ: he maintains the world by overseeing Christ's transition from death to rebirth. If the Mam in his chapel represents Judas, then why is he hanged on Wednesday rather than Friday? Why is he honored in the mayor's office as a supreme god-king, surrounded by women, fruit, and corozos? Why is he venerated after his "death" by hanging if he was just a human traitor who could be bought for thirty pieces of silver? And why were the Mam's keepers willing to die to protect him in 1950 if this was all just elaborate artifice? It is because this is not all just elaborate artifice. It is deadly serious. To abandon Holy Week observances or to neglect to carry them out in as authentic a way possible according to ancestral precedent is to invite the very real death of the world itself. An ex-*telinel* once told me:

> Sometimes the Catholic priest criticizes us because we honor Rilaj Mam. He calls him Judas Iscariot. He can call him whatever he likes. But we know better. We know that he is our Grandfather. He watches over us and protects us from the priest and everyone else that hates us. The Mam was here long before the Spanish speakers came and he will be here long after they are gone. I would serve as *telinel* again if they asked me, even though it is a heavy burden. I will never stop helping with Holy Week. I would rather die. It is all I know and all my ancestors knew. The crops would die if we stopped. The world would die if we stopped. How can we stop?

HOLY THURSDAY — *Chapter 8*

The guardians of Rilaj Mam passed the previous night in constant vigil. Despite many hours of ritual drinking and lack of sleep the *telinel* is usually quite functional on Thursday morning, although others attending the Mam are often overcome with it all by the time the sun comes up. The Mam remains in place atop his *t'iney* "tree" throughout the day. He may be seen through a single door on the southern side of his domed chapel and also through a glassless iron-barred window on the east. There is usually a small crowd of Atitecos around the Mam's shrine at all hours of the day and night. Some await their turn to approach the Mam, while others are content just to be nearby watching the proceedings. The main activity now shifts to the church and the town itself, where preparations are made for the culmination of Holy Week on Friday.

ADORNED ARCHWAYS

> *The lords and the priest and the men of the town assembled together and having cleaned and adorned with arches and green the road leading to the place of heaps of stone where the statue was, they went all together to it with great devotion.*
>
> LANDA 1941, 140

Early in the morning processional arches are set up along the route that Christ will take the following day. This is a counterclockwise circuit following the main streets that ring the central part of town, a square pathway roughly three blocks in length on each side. At each of the four corners of the route traditionalists set up a small shrine decorated with cypress boughs, fruit, and flowers. These shrines are occupied by images of saints brought from private *cofradías* to guard the processional route (fig. 94). Once the procession exits the west doors of the church on Friday afternoon, it will descend the steps to the plaza proceeding west toward the municipal offices. Here it will turn left and move south to the corner near the Banrural bank where the first of the four temporary shrines is set up, then east to the second shrine in front of

94. *First station of the processional route, 1998*

the fire department headquarters, north to the third shrine by a large house once occupied by the late artist Juan Sisay, west to the fourth shrine near the Alpha Omega Protestant church, and south to the municipal offices, where the procession turns east again to return to the church (fig. 95). This has been the established route for the Holy Week procession as far back as we have written accounts and is undoubtedly the same path taken when the town was established in the sixteenth century. When Mendelson witnessed Holy Week observances in 1953, six archways were set up along the processional way—one at the base of the church steps, one at the west end of the church plaza, and one at each of the corners where the shrines are set up (Mendelson 1957, 277e, n58). In recent years Atitecos have added many more, two additional archways in the church plaza as well as at each crossroad.

The arches consist of two wooden posts approximately twenty feet in height set into deep holes excavated on either side of the processional pathway (fig. 96). A crossbeam is bound to these posts spanning the street approximately fifteen feet above the ground. The construction and adornment of each arch is the responsibility of volunteers from the community, who recruit family members and neighbors to assist them. The arches are first covered with cypress. The crossbeam is hung with the same corozo flowers and fruit (also adorned with metallic paper) used to decorate the Monumento in the church. Atitecos often add other tropical flowers as well, particularly red bromeliads. They may also add colorful paper streamers and occasionally wild

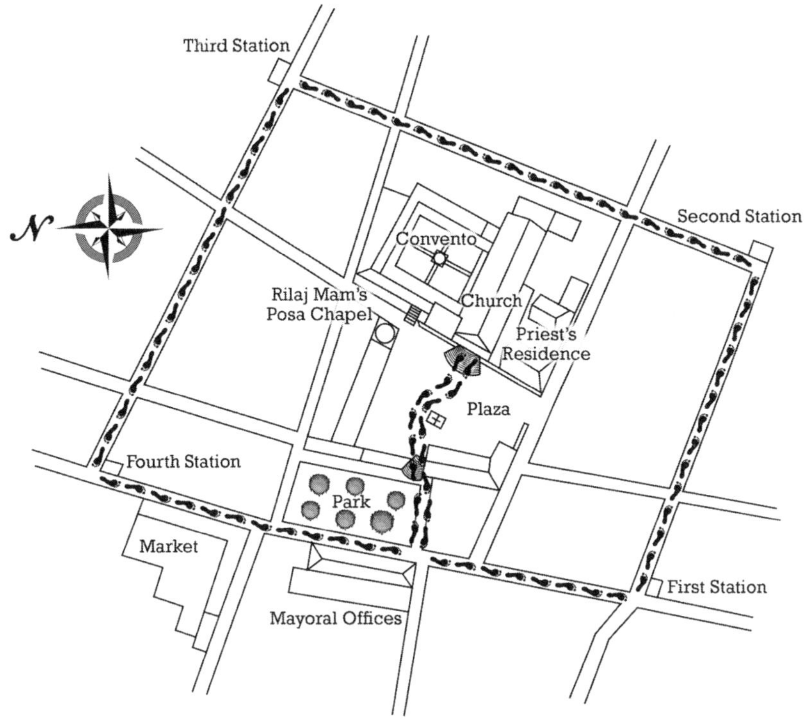

95. *Map of the central district of Santiago Atitlán with the processional route marked with footsteps. Drawn from satellite photographs, Allen and David Christenson*

animals. The animals are usually stuffed, but I have seen live coatimundis and raccoons tethered to the top of archways, huddled among the evergreen boughs. This is apparently a long-standing tradition. Lothrop wrote that the archway in front of the church had a stuffed raccoon and two live coatimundis tied to the archway among the cypress and pine boughs (Lothrop 1929, 25), and McDougall saw two stuffed "rodents," probably coatis, on an archway in 1930 (McDougall 1955, 66). I'm told that the animals are there to mark the archways as "wild" places, covered with vegetation like the mountains surrounding town. When the procession passes through the arches, it is symbolically passing through the world beyond the city, animating it with life-giving power. Although the animals are only there for two days, one considerate Atiteco provided his coatimundi with a large umbrella to shade it from the sun.

In addition to the archways, other important buildings are also adorned in the same way. This includes the buildings of the municipal complex (fig. 97), each of the corner shrines along the processional pathway, and the *cofradía* houses. McDougall noted that at the same time when the archways were

96. *Triumphal arches in the church plaza, 1998*

97. *Municipal offices adorned with evergreens and fruit, 2003*

adorned in 1930 the floor of the church was thickly strewn with pine needles, and evergreen boughs covered the pillars of the nave (McDougall 1955, 68). Although this is no longer done in the church, many Atitecos decorate their private homes and businesses with evergreens and scatter pine needles on the floor. The evergreens, fruit, and flowers represent renewed life following the death of the world at the beginning of the week. The first stirrings of rebirth took place when the Monumento was decorated on Wednesday afternoon. On Thursday this extends outward to the four cardinal directions to include the town and its inhabitants, a token of the new life beginning at this place, the center of the world. The power of Holy Week ceremonies to rebirth the world is a major reason why Atitecos refer to Santiago Atitlán as *rumuxux kaj, rumuxux uliw* (navel of the sky, navel of the earth).

PREPARATION OF THE WORLD CENTER HOLE

While the city is adorned with the tokens of rebirth on Thursday morning, special attention is given to the place that Atitecos consider to be the center of creation—the small hole in the nave of the church where Christ's cross will be raised on Friday afternoon. As noted before, this hole was first uncovered early on Monday morning. It is called *pa ruchi' jay xib'alb'a* (at the doorway of the underworld) or *rumuxux ruchuliw* (navel of the face of the earth). A *cofrade* told me in 1998 that the hole leads to the place of the dead and links to a network of underground passageways that extends to the fountain in the adjacent *convento* complex, to the lake, to the sacred cave of Paq'alib'al, and even to the sea, all watery places. He said that many years ago the ancient people of the town knew how to enter these underground tunnels when they traveled. They could take just a few steps and would be many kilometers away, "but now people are no longer powerful and they don't know how to enter these passageways. Now only the dead can go in and out through the world center hole."

Uncovering the hole frees both benevolent and malignant forces to enter the world of the living during Holy Week. These spirits prefer liminal places like crossroads, town entrances, doorways, shorelines, and stairways. They also continue to linger around the underworld hole in the church. This makes these places particularly dangerous. But it also provides an opportunity to restrict their power, because Atitecos know where spirits congregate and can perform ceremonies to counteract their potentially malignant influence. In 2003 the wife of the *alcalde* of Cofradía Santa Cruz went to the church at dawn on Thursday to light a white candle on the tile covering the hole. White candles are offerings to benevolent deities and ancestors and are a powerful means of warding off demons. She then laid out two pieces of cedar wood in the form of a cross, surrounded by yucca leaves. She told me that they had a sick baby in the family and feared that it might have been the result of a curse linked to the opening of the hole the previous Monday. Yucca leaves are believed to resist witchcraft and black curses, particularly those targeting children. For this reason yucca leaves are sometimes placed in the bottom of graves in the shape of a cross before the casket is lowered into it, especially if the deceased is young. The woman believed that her prayers would be more powerful here because this was not only the place where she could target bad forces with her talismans but also the place where good ancestors could be approached for help.

The most powerful object used to access the benevolent powers of the world center hole is also laid out Thursday morning. Members of the Cofradía Santa Cruz lay out a mat just to the west of the hole. On this mat they place the Ruk'ux Muxux, the ornate pillow marked with a gold cross that served as the Mam's pillow while he lay in the mayor's office the day before (fig. 98). The rest of the year it serves as Christ's pillow and represents the power of the center point where sky, earth, and the four cardinal directions come together. On Wednesday the Mam took possession of it as a token of his universal rule, the role normally played by Christ. In the absence of Jesus in the underworld, however, the pillow now rests on the mat by itself. Its presence not only marks the entrance to the realm of the dead (the nearby world center hole) but also empowers it with the ability to rebirth the world with Christ as its principal life deity when his cross is placed within it on Friday afternoon. Benches are placed on either side of the mat for those who keep vigil over the spot, one of whom maintains a censer of copal incense constantly burning.

At approximately 8:30 A.M., a procession bearing the Urna arrives at the church. This is a glass-enclosed coffin mounted on a massive platform that will eventually receive the body of Christ after his crucifixion. The procession of Christ in his Urna will be the climactic ceremony of Holy Week, representing his triumphant return from the underworld to take possession of the community once again. For now the empty Urna is placed in the far southwest corner of the church, the place associated with death and the entrance into the underworld. Members of the Cofradía Santa Cruz decorate it with flowers and colored lights in preparation for tomorrow's ceremony. It is also purified with incense smoke throughout the day by attendants who sit with it as guardians.

98. *Ruk'ux Muxux venerated at the World Center hole of the church, 2002*

A MAYA PASSION PLAY

> *They began to play their musical instruments, singing and dancing and performing plays and pantomimes, and other types of diversions and celebrations, as many as they could invent and could be carried out.*
>
> LAS CASAS 1958, CHAPTER 177, 151–152 (TRANSLATION BY AUTHOR)

One of the more curious traditions during Holy Week in Santiago Atitlán is an elaborate Passion Play performed by Maya actors from the coast on Thursday and Friday. Although this is a relatively recent introduction, it has become a recurring event since at least the early 1980s (Molina 1983, 29). The performers are not Atitecos but are familiar with at least some local traditions and tailor their performance accordingly. They generally arrive on Thursday morning, staging a parade of elaborately dressed young men through the main streets of the community. As they walk through town, they declare that they are looking for Jesus Christ to arrest and sacrifice him. But they are not dressed as Jews or Roman soldiers as in Roman Catholic Easter Passion Plays performed in other Guatemalan communities like Antigua or Guatemala City. All the costumes are uniquely Maya and represent the chaotic, dangerous nature of the five days of Holy Week. Leading the procession is a figure dressed all in red carrying a long wooden staff and the horn of a bull (fig. 99). The actors told me that this was Kaqi K'oxol. Throughout the Guatemalan highlands the Maya know him as a dangerous dwarf deity who lives in the mountains and other wild, uninhabited regions. His appearance is a sign of impending death in some traditions, although he also guards the land and protects the Maya from foreign invaders. He is especially invoked as a patron of *ajq'ijab'* who perform divination ceremonies based on the ancient Maya calendar. In the *Baile de la Conquista* (Dance of the Conquest) he appears as a little doll dressed in red held by a Maya prophet, a survivor of the Spanish invasion that killed the ancient kings and nobility. Both the prophet and Kaqi K'oxol represent the persistence of ancient Maya gods and traditions in opposition to foreign intrusion after the Spanish Conquest.

Behind Kaqi K'oxol other actors pose as death demons, dressed in black with skeleton designs and wearing skull masks (fig. 100). Others represent disease, their masks displaying bloody, bloated, or decomposing faces. In the midst of these, two columns of Maya lords or warriors march in more ordered unison wearing an odd combination of contemporary clothes and vaguely Pre-Columbian headdresses or skirts. Each is armed with a cudgel wrapped with colorful ribbons of the same size and shape as those carried by the *alguaciles* during Holy Week. Bringing up the rear are two or more per-

99. *Kaqi K'oxol leading the procession of Passion Play performers, 2010*

sons in the guise of modern Maya guerrillas complete with black ski masks and black woolen overgarments, characteristic of the Maya Zapatista fighters in Chiapas (fig. 101). These brandish disturbingly real-looking pistols in one hand and cans for collecting money in the other—this is after all expected to be a paid performance. In 2002 one of the guerrillas carried a stuffed mountain cat with which he threatened those who did not pay the actors. When I asked him about the wildcat, he said that he carried this "jaguar" because he was from the mountains. He added that Rilaj Mam was the lord of jaguars and that they were soldiers of the Mam, looking for Jesus Christ to kill him.

As they move rapidly through the streets, beating their drums, the actors pretend to be searching, ostensibly for Jesus Christ, peering through windows, storming shops, and even brazenly entering municipal and police offices. Atitecos enjoy the spectacle and officials seem to tolerate the annoyance and play along. But it is apparent that with their freedom to disrupt the normal life of the community the actors take the opportunity to playfully threaten nontraditionalists in particular—police in uniform, town officials, Protestant ministers, and tourists. For the most part they were less interested in Jesus than in the descendants of those who brought him from Spain. It is significant that the procession is led by Kaqi K'oxol, a survivor of the ancient Maya world who is a guardian of traditional Maya culture. The players are supposedly looking to capture and sacrifice Jesus Christ, consistent with Maya Holy Week beliefs concerning the death of the world and its deities.

100. *Death and disease demons, 2010*

101. *Maya performers dressed as guerrillas with a disease demon, 2010*

But the actors use the situation to rebel openly against imposed non-Maya institutions and influences under the guise of playacting. It is a thinly veiled threat carried out under the very noses of their perceived oppressors who smile at the whole thing as if it were just harmless entertainment. I doubt very much that this is all it is.

THE LAST SUPPER

> *And thus they made to it [the god of the Wayeb'] many offerings of food and drinks, of flesh and fish; and they divided these offerings among the strangers who were present and they gave the priest the leg of a deer.*
>
> LANDA 1941, 141

> *Returning to the subject at hand, on that day there were great feasts in which they ate many birds, and much game, and they drank diverse wines.*
>
> LAS CASAS 1958, CHAPTER 177, 152 (TRANSLATION BY AUTHOR)

The most elaborate ceremonial feast during Holy Week is linked to the Christian Last Supper. It is held in the *convento* complex of the town's colonial-era Roman Catholic church. This takes place early in the afternoon, timed so as to conclude before 3 o'clock Mass. As with most events during Holy Week, both participants and spectators alike arrive well before the time when the ritual is scheduled to begin. Having the community together in one place is a significant element of Tz'utujil religion, nearly as important as the ceremony itself. People come early and linger afterward. The ritual life of Santiago Atitlán is often characterized by long periods of patient waiting culminating in bursts of intense activity. Both are necessary.

Hours before the ceremony large numbers of people are already gathered in the courtyard. Teenaged girls generally sit together in groups and laugh at each other's stories. Old men congregate with other old men and elderly women with other elderly women. The ladies constantly adjust their clothes as they talk, cinching up their skirts, tucking in and straightening their *huipiles*, or winding and unwinding the elaborate halo headdresses that are now mostly worn on ceremonial occasions (fig. 102). It is only young couples who prefer to stay together, sitting close to one another engaged in low discussions, sometimes smiling or touching one another gently on the back or knee. Because it is a special occasion, babies and small children often have cookies, ice cream, or little plastic baggies filled with frozen juice, which is sipped through a straw as it melts. Vendors sell these from small refrigerated wooden carts in the church plaza during important festivals. But even without such distrac-

102. *Women gathered for the Last Supper, 2000*

tions, Atiteco babies are remarkably patient and don't seem to have learned the trick of looking for excuses to cry or pout for attention. Infants are generally carried on the back in a shawl or length of cloth tied across the breast. This is a comforting way to travel through town, because the child can sleep when it likes and peek out at the world when awake from a place of warm security. It is also ideal for breast feeding, as the child can simply be rotated to the front without having to remove it from its cloth cradle. Young girls learn to carry babies on their backs from a very early age. It is not uncommon to see children as young as six years old carrying little siblings on their backs as they go about their daily activities with no parents in sight.

Tz'utujil children are very independent and seem to be perfectly safe going wherever they please without fear. It is remarkable how patient and careful children are with infants, a bond that continues into older age, as young men and women are fiercely protective of their brothers and sisters. Older children love to run and don't seem to mind falling, even on the hard stone pavement of the streets and plazas. Children enjoy chasing each other but not really with the intention of catching anyone. When the pursued children eventually give up, the pursuers just wrap their arms around the other and the game is over. The joy is in the chase. It does not take much to entertain the young ones. Palm branches become playful clubs, or a pinecone can serve perfectly well as a soccer ball.

The ceremony of the Last Supper takes place in the *convento* complex adjacent to the church on its north side. This is an open-air cloistered space with a fountain at the center, bounded by covered aisles with a series of columns and archways on all four sides. There are three access points to the *convento* through large wooden doors leading to the interior of the church on the south and through gates located on the west and north sides. The plastered walls of the *convento* are cracked in many places, with peeling plaster and paint that exposes the underlying stone. Birds nest in larger crevices as well as atop the columns supporting the roof of the aisles. Yet the floors are neatly washed and swept throughout the year. Things are kept as left to them by their ancestors. Sweeping cleans away anything that does not belong and taints the sanctity of the place.

Although it is linked to the biblical account of the final Passover meal of Christ prior to his crucifixion, the organization and administration of the Last Supper is not done under the authority of the Roman Catholic Church. The sacristans and *cofradía* officials are completely in charge. Before the town had a resident priest the meal was administered by the *cabecera*, head of the *cofradía* system, but now the parish priest is expected to preside over the proceedings along with the town's mayor and the leaders of each of the *cofradías*. This is one of the first major ceremonies of Holy Week that requires the presence of the Catholic priest. In recent years this has caused some tension between orthodox Catholic participants and traditionalists, who are forced to work together in close proximity despite their mutual distrust.

In 2002 the *cabecera* asked the *rox* (third) *cofrade* of Santa Cruz to notify the mayor that everything was prepared and to bring him to the ceremony. As he ran through the *convento* toward the municipal offices he noticed me sitting by the fountain and stopped long enough to say that he had an important errand: "The *cabecera* just told me to get the mayor—me! He asked *me* to get the mayor. I'm going now to get the mayor. Yes, I'm going now to get the mayor." He excitedly told one or two others before he made it out of the gates of the *convento*. This small incident illustrates how emotionally energizing it is for *cofrades* when they are given new responsibilities. As they work their way up through the *cofradía* system they are given progressively more important tasks as they earn the trust of their leaders. Later the same man became a high official in the Cofradía Santiago, one of the most important in the community. In those few years he had become comfortable with authority, quietly delegating important duties to other *cofrades* and trusting them to work on their own. As *cofrades* rise through the ranks of the system they learn mostly by watching closely how their colleagues do things with an eye to doing the same when they reach that position. Generally this is done in an atmosphere of encouragement and trust, so that *cofrades* are comfortable in their tasks and enjoy working together.

At mid-afternoon members of the Cofradía Santa Cruz position the long table for the Last Supper in the southeast corner of the covered corridor of the *convento* and the participants take their places. Seated around the table are twelve young Atiteco boys representing the twelve apostles (fig. 103). They are chosen based on their sweetness of expression and manner by the *primer mayor*, who also oversees the activities of the *alguaciles*. It is customary for the *primer mayor* to go from door to door seeking out the best children in the community. Supposedly the *primer mayor* carries out his duties without any bias toward any particular family, although it is understood that at least some proud parents lobby on behalf of their sons. Rumor has it that bribery may occasionally come into play. The children's ages range from about six to ten years. The usual costume is a long white tunic with purple sashes worn over each shoulder and crisscrossed at the chest, with a tall headdress decorated with colorful artificial flowers. Six children sit on each side of the Last Supper table, holding their hands together in front of them as if praying. Fathers stand behind their sons. Mothers sit on the ground, each with a large basket covered with a cloth. The priest stands in the center of the south end of the table surrounded by the *cabecera*, the town mayor, the *alcalde* of Cofradía Santa Cruz, and both male and female representatives of all the *cofradías* (fig. 104).

The meal consists of twelve courses, each accompanied by two maize tortillas and a cup of maize *atole*. The food served for each course varies slightly from year to year but is mostly consistent. In 2002 the following courses were served: (1) rice with vegetables; (2) chicken in tomato sauce; (3) fish in tomato sauce; (4) turkey leg in tomato sauce; (5) white beans in tomato sauce; (6) crab in tomato sauce; (7) white fish; (8) garbanzos in brown sauce; (9) bread with honey; (10) rice with egg; (11) rice with a large fish; and (12) rice with a small fish. Mendelson listed the courses for the Last Supper observed in 1953 as (1) bread, (2) chocolate, (3) honey, (4) coot, (5) egg, (6) crab, (7) chickpeas, (8) white beans, (9) lizard, (10) dried fish, (11) black beans, and (12) chicken (Mendelson 1957, 277c, n45).

Each course is brought to the table by a line of twelve *alguaciles* led by the *primer mayor*, a sacristan, or the *cabecera*, from the opposite side of the *convento* where the food is prepared (fig. 105). The short procession is accom-

103. *Holy Week apostle, 1998*

104. *Roman Catholic priest presiding over the Last Supper with the apostles, 2002*

105. *Head sacristan leading the procession of the Last Supper, 2003*

panied by three beats of the great drum interspersed with flute music. Once the plates of food are arranged in front of each apostle, the priest identifies the food and declares it to be a sign of the Last Supper in token of the sacrificed Christ. This is perfectly consistent with Christian theology. Biblical tradition links the Last Supper before Christ's crucifixion with the institution of the Eucharist, in which the broken bread and wine of the meal represent the flesh and blood of Christ (Luke 22:19; 1 Corinthians 10:16). In Roman Catholic belief these are not symbolic tokens but literally become divine flesh and blood when consumed through transubstantiation. In Maya belief the maize tortillas and *atole* eaten at the Last Supper in Santiago Atitlán are also sacred, being the flesh and blood of a deity. An *ajq'ij* in Momostenango made the same comparison while we were conducting a ceremony in the mountains that involved an offering of maize:

> Have you ever noticed that Catholics when they go to Mass say that they are eating the flesh of Christ when they eat the Host? It is the same with us. Maize is the flesh of god. When we eat it we renew our own bodies and make it sacred. But we do this every meal instead of only once a week like the Catholics do.

Atitecos recognize the link between the Eucharist and sacred maize. As discussed earlier, in the 1970s the pastor in Santiago Atitlán, Father Stanley Francis Rother, commissioned Nicolás Chávez Sojuel, a Tz'utujil sculptor, to carve a new pulpit for the church (fig. 106). He suggested that the artist decorate it with sheaves of wheat to symbolize the wafers of the Eucharist as the "bread of life." Nicolás convinced Rother to allow him to carve the ancient Maya Maize God on the pulpit instead:

> Father Rother wanted me to carve wheat or bread on the pulpit to represent the Catholic Bread of Life. But for us, this is maize and so I put the Maize God in the center, surrounded by the four apostles who wrote the Bible. . . . This center part of the pulpit represents the church with its four corners and the altar as the Maize God in the middle. Around this I wanted to show the world. I put maize plants above and below to show that the source of life is maize. At the corners I put ears of maize to represent the four directions, and another two on the sides to represent the sky above and the underworld below the earth where the ancestors live.

The Atiteco Last Supper is consistent with eating sacred flesh in Christian terms but is also analogous to the great feast of the ancient Maya Wayeb' observances, in which a portion of each human sacrifice was eaten as a sacred

106. *Church pulpit, carved by Nicolás Chávez Sojuel, 1997*

meal. Both traditions emphasize the ritual consumption of sacrificial flesh as a sign of renewal (Landa 1941, 120; Las Casas 1958, chapter 177, 152).

Nicolás Chávez also participated in the reconstruction of the great central altarpiece in the church, although most of the work was carried out by his older brother, Diego Chávez Petzey. The Chávez brothers carved five new panels at the base of the altarpiece illustrating the most important traditional Atiteco ceremonies during the year. The largest of these panels is the third one, which depicts the Last Supper (fig. 107). It is also the only panel that focuses on a single ritual, the other four being divided into three parts, each with a separate subject. Because the third panel occupies the central position at the base of the altarpiece, it represents the *k'ux* (heart) of the monument,

107. *Third basal panel, central altarpiece*

the most powerful location. It is also situated immediately beneath the image of the town's patron saint, Santiago. Two pairs of Maya Maize Gods flank this center at the outer edges of the altarpiece just above the narrative panels. Together these represent the four cardinal directions of the world.

The top of the altarpiece would be the preeminent position in Western notions of hierarchy, and in fact the uppermost niche contains the image of God the Father holding up three fingers to represent the Trinity. But the Maya see the base of the altarpiece as being far more important. I once asked one of the church's Tz'utujil caretakers what the names of the saints were. He named each of them, beginning with Santiago, the largest of the saints and the one located at the bottom center of the monument. He did not even mention the image at the top of the altarpiece representing God the Father. When I asked what his name was, he shrugged his shoulders and said that he had no idea but "he couldn't be very important or he would have been closer to Santiago and the people that come to visit him." The Last Supper is depicted at the heart of the altarpiece because it is the pivotal act of Holy Week that brings life back into the world by means of the sacrifice and consumption of divine flesh provided by the *alguaciles*.

There is very little actual eating involved in the Last Supper in Santiago

Atitlán. After the food has been recognized and blessed by the priest, each child takes a single small bite and then hands the plate discreetly to his mother, who scoops it into her basket while the child eats a bit of tortilla and sips some of the *atole*. The food collected by the mothers will be distributed later among family members and eaten as the principal meal that evening with great ceremony. Similar feasts are held throughout the community as an extension of the Last Supper. Turkey or chicken is the traditional dish eaten on Thursday night, and the markets are crowded with vendors to meet the demand. Mendelson wrote that the Thursday of Holy Week marked the "beginning of food exchanges between kin: parents took bread and honey to their children's parents-in-law in the morning and chicken or turkey at lunchtime, while parents in general, if they wished to, exchanged similar food gifts" (Mendelson 1957, 256).

After all of the twelve courses of the Last Supper feast have been served, the Roman Catholic priest leads the apostles and *cofrades* in procession out the north exit of the *convento*, passing the Mam's chapel and then climbing the great stairway through the west doors of the church. There the priest washes the little apostles' feet before celebrating Mass.

When I attended the ceremony in 1998, the priest was a North American from Missouri named Father Michael. He had only recently arrived and knew little about what was expected of him, so the *cabecera* and other *cofrades* directed him where to stand, what to say, and when to say it. He later told me that the traditionalist *cofrades* were very kind to him and told him that he was the finest priest that they had had in many years because he respected them and did what tradition demanded without insulting them. This cordiality abruptly changed after Father Michael left and was replaced by native Guatemalan priests who were less tolerant of the unorthodox elements of *cofradía* worship. The situation in Santiago Atitlán is similar to the often tense relations between traditionalist Maya officials and their parish priests in other parts of the Maya world. Restall suggests that for the Yucatec Maya there is "a long-term struggle not to reject [Christianity's] beliefs but to control the expression of those beliefs; in other words, religious hostility took the form not of paganism but of anticlericalism" when the clergy refuses to be controlled by long-practiced local Maya customs even when they bear significant Christian elements (Restall 1997, 158).

In 2003 the Roman Catholic priest arrived more than an hour late for the Last Supper ceremony, leaving little time before Mass was to be celebrated. When he finally arrived, the *tixeles* gave him angry looks that are usually reserved for the deepest of offenses. He angered them further by giving a long speech on Roman Catholic doctrine in Spanish then tried to hurry the proceedings along once the traditionalists took over. After two courses the priest declared that he had had enough and tried to leave to celebrate Mass. The *alcalde* of Cofradía San Antonio and other *cofrades* immediately blocked his way and insisted that he finish the ceremony. An eight-minute discussion ensued in which the priest was jostled and finally pushed. Although the priest reluctantly returned to his place at the head of the table, he refused to bless the food, so the *cabecera* had to fill in. After the fourth course the *alcalde* of San Antonio took up his staff of office and angrily stormed out of the *convento* with his other *cofrades* following behind him.

In 2006 the priest refused to allow the Last Supper to be conducted at all. It was reinstituted in 2010 but celebrated concurrently with an outdoor Mass in the church plaza. The head of the church committee said that the priest had insisted on the combined ceremony because he complained that many people left after the Last Supper concluded in the *convento*. He did not want people to think that this local ceremony was more important than Mass and the reception of Communion. The apostles that year were not allowed to wear purple sashes or the flowery headdresses. They were also relegated to the first tier of steps leading up to the church rather than sitting at the customary Last Supper table. The *cofradías* mostly boycotted the proceedings as an insult to their traditions.

LIGHTING OF THE CANDELABRUM

In the evening traditionalists once again occupy the church for ancestral ceremonies, with no involvement of the orthodox Roman Catholic clergy. At about 8 P.M., when it is fully dark, most if not all the lights in the church are turned out. The *cabecera* and members of the Cofradía Santa Cruz bring out a large triangular wooden candelabrum, a wooden step stool with two risers, and a music stand, all of which are stored in the baptistery. These are set up at the west end of the nave, with the arms of the candelabrum oriented north to south. They also set up long benches on each side of the candelabrum where the leadership of each of the *cofradías* sit. The *alcaldes* wear their finest ceremonial clothes and hold their staffs of office erect in their right hands. The *xo*'s sit with the other *tixeles* on the floor east of the benches, each holding a tall white candle wrapped in banana leaves.

Once everyone is in position, the *alcalde* of Santa Cruz or one of his *cofrades* places eleven white candles of a type called *esterina* in the candelabrum—five to the north, five to the south, and one at the top in the center (fig. 108). *Cofradía* members attend these candles constantly, each taking a turn to stand on the wooden steps so that they can reach the highest candles. Whenever a

108. *Lighting the candelabrum, Holy Thursday, 1998*

small drip of wax forms along the side of one of the candles, it is instantly removed. After fifteen minutes or so the center candle is extinguished and taken out. The highest candle on the north is put in its place. Each of the candles on the north side is then moved up one place until finally a new candle is lit in the lowest position. The process is repeated with the candles on the south side of the candelabrum. Each candle is removed long before it is used up. This process is repeated for hours until approximately midnight. The total number of candles seems to vary, but I was told by the *cabecera* in 2002 that the tradition is to go through at least twelve sets of candles over the course of the evening. From my experience the *cofrades* seem to change the candles with greater frequency as the evening progresses.

In 1998 I sat with the Cofradía San Antonio for the ceremony. The *alcalde* told me that each candle represents life as it progresses from birth to death. The candles are changed frequently because they must burn as brightly as possible so as to give strength to the night. Once they become even the least bit "tired" they are removed in order to give a younger candle its turn. On other occasions I've been told that the candles represent the eleven good apostles, excluding Judas Iscariot. They stay up all night waiting for Christ, who is missing in the darkness. In Roman Catholic liturgy the lighting and extinguishing of the candles is called Tenebrae and is part of the Holy Office observed before the close of Holy Week.

109. *Sacristans on the evening of Holy Thursday, 2003*

In Santiago Atitlán the ceremony is accompanied by three or four sacristans, singing from a handwritten copy of the Divine Office, consisting mostly of psalms, placed on the music stand positioned to the west of the candelabrum (fig. 109). In orthodox Roman Catholicism the sacristan is the keeper of the sacristy, caring for the sacred vessels, vestments, the Host, holy oils, and sacred relics. He may also bear the responsibility for decorating the church for important feast days or ringing the church bells. In Santiago Atitlán sacristans hold a great deal of prestige and authority, although their duties no longer include caring for the sacristy or its contents. Before the town had a resident priest, the sacristans were responsible for conducting prayer and other church services. Now that there is a parish priest, the most visible duty of the sacristans is to sing hymns on special occasions, particularly during Holy Week. The sacristans in Santiago Atitlán are traditionalists and have no authority within the orthodox Roman Catholic hierarchy. Because of their prominence, sacristans are sometimes the targets of violence by factions within the *cofradía* system or by those who oppose the continued performance of ancient Maya traditions in town. At least two sacristans have been murdered in recent years, and another chose to give up his position for fear that he would be next. Both of the murdered sacristans were also prominent *ajkun*s. Until recently it was common for sacristans to hold positions in the *cofradía* system. Today the sacristans appear to be closely allied with the *cabecera*, accompanying him on his visits to the *cofradías* and going to his house to escort him to important activities such as processions.

On Thursday evening the sacristans sing in front of the candelabrum for hours, huddled around the music stand. The hymns are sung with an oddly hypnotic nasal tone that starts out soft and low, building in volume and emotion to a single powerful note that is held for a sustained length of time before dropping off to a brief silence. The process is then begun again and continues in cycles for the length of the song's performance. Little in the way of melody is involved, making it more like a monophonic chant. At one time the sacristans were accompanied by an ancient violin but this went missing twenty or so years ago.

The first sacristan in 2010 was sixty-one years old and had served as a sacristan for most of his life. In 1969 he took his turn as an *alguacil*, making the trip to the coast to obtain the Holy Week fruit less than a year after he was married, as was the tradition. Both his father and grandfather were sacristans before him. He is devoted to his work and unusually given to expressing his feelings, a rare trait among most Tz'utujil men. During major festivals he seemed to be everywhere. At times he appeared to submit easily to the authority of the *cabecera* and other *cofradía* officials. At other times he was openly confrontational, particularly when he felt that traditions were not respected or followed properly. At such times even high officials within the *cofradía* system treated him with some deference. It is difficult to know where the sacristans stand within the traditionalist hierarchy.

We sat together on Thursday evening one year, waiting for the candle lighting ceremony to begin. He said that he was only happy when singing. The rest of the time his life was filled with sadness and poverty. Singing was the only thing that made him forget his problems: "When I sing I don't know anyone—my friends, my family, anyone. I am with God. These are not my songs, they are God's songs, but he sings through me. I feel him. We are the same blood as Christ. We have the same mother. We are the same flesh as God. We are separate, but of the same flesh."

Relatively few Atitecos participate in the lighting of the candles. It is reserved mostly for *cofradía* officials, who preside over the proceedings patiently with little conversation. This makes the sonorous voices of the sacristans all the more hypnotic and powerful. The waning hours of Thursday evening are thus spent in watchful vigil, the final moments of the world's death before its rebirth the following day. Non-*cofrades* come and go during the long hours of the candle-lighting ceremony, inspecting the Urna, looking over the shoulders of the sacristans as they sing, or simply standing behind the *cofrade* officials. The inside of the church is dark, illuminated mostly by candlelight. The air is fragrant with copal incense that billows up from braziers kept constantly burning at both the world center hole at the east end of the nave and the empty glass coffin of Christ in the southwest corner. The clouds of heavy smoke drifts through the church, softly illuminated when passing near the candles held by the *tixeles* or burning on the candelabrum. In 1998 a bat flew back and forth across the nave during the entire evening, though no one seemed to pay much attention to it.

SAN JUAN RACES

At the same time when the candelabrum is set up at the west end of the church's nave five wooden images of saints are lined up on litters just east of the world center hole (fig. 110). These will be the deities that participate in the San Juan "races" held throughout the early morning hours after midnight. The purpose of the races is to reanimate the world in preparation for the triumphant return of Christ as the principal life deity on Good Friday. The five saints are (from north to south) San Juan (St. John), who usually occupies the second basal niche of the church's central altarpiece; María Andolor (the

110. *St. John in procession, 1968. Photograph by Jude Pansini*

Atiteco pronunciation of María Dolores, "Mary of Sorrows") who usually occupies the first basal niche of the central altarpiece; Jesús Nazareno (an image of Jesus bearing his cross), who generally stands to the left of the central altarpiece; San Nicolás, who was brought from the Cofradía San Nicolás; and Domingo Ramos (Palm Sunday: an image of Jesus riding a donkey, referring to the entry of Christ into Jerusalem on a donkey on the Sunday before his crucifixion), who belongs to the Cofradía San Francisco and occupies the third position in the line of saints at the northeast corner of the church's nave. Each saint is lashed to his or her litter with artfully knotted cords. In recent years only one man in the community has been fully trusted to tie the saints down properly. He is called upon not only to secure the saints to their litters in the church but also to make any necessary readjustments once they have taken up their positions in the street later that night. If this is done in a slipshod manner the heavy saints could easily come loose from their moorings and tumble to the ground. San Juan in particular bears the scars of several such unfortunate incidents that have required repairs over the years. As a result his lashings receive the closest attention. One year the cord expert held out for more money on Thursday evening. The *cofrades* eventually agreed to pay, but the negotiations delayed the procession's departure until after 1 A.M., a testament to the *cofrades*' respect for his skills.

At about midnight the candles are slowly snuffed out one by one, darkening the nave further. Once the last of the candles is extinguished, one of the *cofrades* blows on a large conch shell, a long plaintive note that when done properly can be very loud in the enclosed space of the church. Nicolás Chávez Sojuel told me that even if you are not in the church you can still hear the faint sound of otherworldly conch shells in the distance:

> At midnight on Holy Thursday the dead who drowned in Lake Atitlán rise up out of the water and blow conch shells at the same time as the one in the church. The sound of three other conch shells can also be heard—from the ruins of the ancient capital of the Tz'utujils at Chutinamit across the bay to the northwest, from the place where Rilaj Mam was born above town to the east, and from the mountains above Xetuc [the direction of the sacred cave of Paq'alib'al to the southwest].

The single note from the conch shell is answered by several beats of the great drum, interspersed with flute music as well as the rattling sound of several *matracas*. Those assigned to carry the saints immediately lift the litters to their shoulders, four bearers for each of the first four saints. A procession quickly forms with the great drum in the lead, then the women bearing candles, then the sacristans, the *cabecera*, and other male *cofradía* officials, followed in turn by Cristo Nazareno, San Nicolás, María Andolor, and San Juan bringing up the rear. Domingo Ramos is left behind in the church to stand guard.

The procession follows the same path that Christ's Urna will take on Friday afternoon and evening—out the main doors of the church heading west to the municipal offices then left to the first shrine near the Banrural bank. Here María Andolor takes up her station at the southwest corner of the processional route. Southwest is the direction most associated with death, linked to the setting of the sun at its southernmost point on the horizon. The ancient Maya also associated the south with death, particularly the destruction of the world by flood (Vail and Hernández 2014, 99). The "races" are timed to fall at or soon after midnight, the lowest point of the sun in the underworld. But it is also the time when the sun begins its slow rise toward the eastern horizon and thus is often chosen for ceremonies intended to regenerate life, as this one is. All of the *tixeles* and other female participants remain with María throughout the evening. The sacristans also remain with her, singing as often as they can stand during the night, fueled by a constant stream of drinks as well as maize *atole*.

The rest of the procession then continues along the ceremonial route to the fourth station at the northwest corner. Here Cristo Nazareno takes up a position in the middle of the street, looking south with San Nicolás immediately to his left. The *cabecera* and other male *cofradía* officials surround them on both sides. San Juan continues another ten feet or so and then turns around to face the other saints. His bearers lift him high in the air three times while saying the single world *junam* (together, united). He is then turned around again and the bearers run quickly southward down the street (fig. 111) toward María Andolor. When they reach her station, San Juan is again lifted three times in front of her, while saying *junam* each time. He is then run back to the northwest station as fast as the bearers can go. This process is repeated again and again throughout the remainder of the night until dawn. For the races San Juan is fitted with a conical hat of palm fronds crested by a spray of long leaves that fan out like a fountain. This cap is made for the saint on Thursday evening so that it is fresh and green for the races, plaited by one of the *cofrades* right up until the time when it is needed. One of Mendelson's informants told him in 1953 that "he wore a cap because when he had gone looking for the spirit of Jesus in the mountain, the sun was so strong that it had burned his hat off and he had to make himself a crown of pecaya leaves" (Mendelson 1957, 236). This hat invariably slides to the side at a rakish angle during the course of the night as the saint is jostled and bounced up and down the street. The *rukab'* (second) *cofrade* of Santa Cruz told me that María An-

111. *St. John run through the streets, predawn Holy Friday, 2010*

dolor stands in the underworld at the south end of the street and that San Juan is delivering messages on behalf of Rilaj Mam, going back and forth from the upper world to María's place among the dead. On this night María Andolor's slightly downturned head and sad expression is made all the more melancholy by a wig of long, disheveled black hair.

The oldest traditions concerning the races have sexual overtones: San Juan symbolically impregnates María in order to give birth to Jesus as the "new sun" the following day at dawn (Carlsen 1997, 155; Christenson 2001, 130). One of Tarn's informants said that María Andolor is the "full moon of Holy Thursday," the mother of Jesus as the sun (Tarn and Prechtel 1986, 180). A number of local myths link María Andolor with the moon, a concept reinforced by the numerous depictions of the Virgin Mary standing on a crescent moon in Roman Catholic iconography. A life-size image of María Concepción on the traditional sliver of a moon stands in a glass case near the front of the church in Santiago Atitlán. In Maya cosmology, both ancient and modern, the young moon goddess is associated with regenerative sexual power (Thompson 1970, 164; Miller and Taube 1993, 147). It is clear that the sexual nature of this ceremony has been recognized by non-Tz'utujils in Santiago Atitlán for more than a century, and at times they have tried to suppress it. Early in the twentieth century Samuel Lothrop wrote that authorities imprisoned the images of María Andolor and San Juan in separate cells of the town jail to keep them from committing adultery while Jesus was dead: "To prevent the annual repetition of this scandalous divertissement strong measures are necessary. Hence the image of each was locked up in separate cells with the usual crowd of inebriates" (Lothrop 1929, 25). In order to free them from jail the following morning, *cofradía* officials had to pay a fine of 200 pesos. Although officials ceased to imprison the saints soon after Lothrop's description, the practice was remembered long afterward. Mendelson wrote:

> I found greater difficulty in getting anything solid on the rumoured custom concerning the imprisonment by the Alcalde municipal of Juan and the Virgin on Thursday night. This was said to depend on a belief concerning the prevention of sexual intercourse between Juan and María who were in love with each other. The above informant on being pressed admitted that Juan used to be put in prison and had to be extracted by the cofrades on payment of 2–3 pesos. "Why?—Because of a sin. What sin?—I do not know, we weren't there.—With María?—Yes that is it." (Mendelson 1957, 262)

Most Tz'utujils prefer not to talk about the sexual nature of the races with outsiders. This is partly the result of a tendency to reticence in speaking about sexual matters among many Atitecos, but it is also to avoid accusations of unorthodoxy by nontraditionalists. When asked about the meaning of the races, a common response is that San Juan is announcing the death of Christ to Mary or alternatively that he is running to tell her that Christ has been resurrected. Neither of these explanations makes much sense, because the crucifixion takes place the following day. It also does not explain San Juan's well-known nickname, Carajo—a crude Spanish term for male genitals or for coitus itself. While observing the races, I once asked a young man that I had known for many years why San Juan is run through the streets all night. He said that the saint was God's messenger. I asked why, then, did people call him Carajo. He immediately blushed visibly, admitting that people call him that and that old grandfathers and grandmothers say that he lies with María on Thursday night. But he was shocked that I knew of such things and refused to say anything more about it.

In the *Popol Vuh* account the principal life deity is named Hun Hunahpu, a deity linked with Christ soon after the Spanish Conquest (Ximénez 1929–1931, 1:57). In highland Maya mythology Hun Hunahpu descended into the underworld realm of Xibalba where he was sacrificed by the Lords of Death who hung his head in the branches of a dead tree. The tree immediately sprang to life when it received the head of Hun Hunahpu, bearing fruit that mimicked the appearance of his skull (Christenson 2007, 125–127). As suggested in the last chapter, the Holy Week Monumento in the church is the modern equivalent of this tree, bearing sacrificial heads in the form of fruit. Life was restored to the world when an underworld maiden, Xkik' (Lady Blood), visited the tree and was miraculously impregnated by Hun Hunahpu's skull. She eventually climbed up to the surface of the earth, where she gave birth to twin sons, Hunahpu and Xbalanqueh. These gods eventually defeated the Death Lords and restored their father to his former position of authority as the object of prayers and veneration. The twins then entered the sky as the sun and moon (ibid., 189–191).

The Post-Conquest highland Maya associated Xkik' with the Virgin Mary, a logical association because both became mothers of powerful life deities by means of a miraculous "virgin birth." It is a fair assumption that the races of San Juan represent a symbolic reenactment of the impregnation of María Andolor in the underworld, giving rise to the rebirth of Christ. San Juan's hat of freshly plaited leaves gives him tree-like attributes, although it is unclear why the Tz'utujils chose this particular saint to play the role of María's lover. Linda O'Brien-Rothe (personal communication, 2015) quite plausibly suggests that the two are linked together because St. John became responsible for Mary after the death of Christ (John 19:26–27). They are often depicted together at the base of the cross, although there is no orthodox Roman Catholic foundation for their romantic involvement. The two saints occupy adjacent niches in the church's central altarpiece during the year.

The young men who bear San Juan through the streets are nearly always traditionalists, and many are *ajkun*s in training. It is considered a great privilege to carry San Juan during the races, but it is also a grueling experience, a test of their strength and purity of heart. The intention is to carry him the entire night, up to five or six hours straight, although most are unable to endure that long. It is also tradition to run barefoot. Mendelson wrote that in the early 1950s *alguaciles* ran behind San Juan's bearers, goading and striking them with their batons, yet the runners could not cry out or get angry but "must run faster to avoid being struck" (Mendelson 1957, 259–260).

I've been told that *ajkuns* try to test the strength and endurance of the runners by casting *ch'ay* into the streets when San Juan approaches. *Ch'ay* literally means "obsidian" or "broken glass." Most often in the context of the San Juan races this is simply a metaphor for obstacles or dangers placed in the way of a person. It is therefore a ritual curse to test their ability to overcome supernatural power. But many runners insist that real glass shards are sometimes thrown out into the street. In 2003 a group of young men arrived at the church on Thursday evening offering to carry San Juan. Several had run the saint the year before and almost dropped him, so they were told that it was better to have others bear San Juan. After a brief argument, they were forced to leave. As they turned to go one of them told the bearers: "We'll see who will be able to endure the night." The rejected group sat on the curb together to watch the races and intimidate those chosen to carry San Juan. One of the runners was only able to make three rounds before he had to drop out. Afterward one of the runners said that the young man had been cursed:

> One of our companions was only able to run three times. He said that he saw snakes and spiders and his feet began to bleed. If someone has a good heart, no harm can come to him. But if his heart is not pure, the street will slice his feet apart. It is common to see blood smears in the street the next day. People say that it is easy to curse someone but very difficult to cure. This is why it is a very dangerous thing to curse people. Only bad people do this. To curse someone you only have to take some string or cord, roll it up like a snake, and throw it into the street. This becomes a snake that bewitches the runners. Some people say that the *telinel* made the Mam too small this year by putting too few scarves on him. Another man who had wanted to be *telinel* is now trying to curse him so that he will fall down in the streets while carrying the Mam. But such is the city of the Tz'utujils.

In Mendelson's day the runners were expected to remain celibate for fifteen days before the races in order to ensure their purity and strength (Mendelson 1957, 260). This tradition is no longer current. Prayers and ceremonies are often performed on behalf of the runners the day before the races to protect them from witchcraft and evil spirits, as they are conceptually passing the night in the realm of the dead. That year only one young man was able to run the entire night. Surprisingly, he seemed to have been the least tired of the lot and had gone barefoot. Two of the bearers collapsed from exhaustion once they put down San Juan's litter in the church.

At about 4 A.M. the saints at each end of the street are carried a block or so toward one another. From then on, after every few circuits by San Juan, the saints are moved incrementally closer together. At about dawn María Andolor and her attendants meet the delegation surrounding Cristo Nazareno and San Nicolás in front of the mayor's office. At a signal from the *cabecera*, the two groups come together to form a single procession and return to the church, except for San Nicolás, who is carried back to his own *cofradía*. The long-awaited moment seems oddly anticlimactic, with little fanfare or even acknowledgment that the exhausting races are finally over. The participants simply return the saints to the church without comment or celebration. Nevertheless, with the dawn on Friday morning, the races are said to have done their job in giving the sun power to be reborn.

GOOD FRIDAY *Chapter 9*

Dawn on Friday morning is linked to the rebirth of Christ as the sun, bringing light back into the world following the long dark night of the San Juan races. Light is a major theme of Good Friday observances, the more elaborate and colorful the better. At about 6 A.M. when the sky above the mountains to the east of town first begins to brighten, the world navel hole in the church is reopened, a ceremony customarily carried out by the *cabecera* and other leading officials of the *cofradía* system. This hole will receive the base of Christ's cross when it is raised later in the day. Traditionalist Atitecos say that the heavy cross is "planted" in the world navel hole like a tree, not "set." To reinforce the identification of the cross with a tree, the cross-piece near Christ's head is adorned with artificial leaves, fruits, and flowers. In keeping with this belief, the *cofrades* who open the hole on Friday morning pour water into it to nourish Christ's "tree." The *cabecera* in 1998 told me that long ago they used the blood of a sacrificed turkey to prepare the hole but that this hadn't been done in decades. When I asked an *ajkun* about this that same year, he said that a chicken had been sacrificed at the navel hole only three years earlier. If that is true, then it is possible that blood is still used at least in some years, perhaps related to the turkey sacrifices linked to the World Tree as depicted on the Dresden New Year's pages (fig. 8). Once the hole is opened, *cofradía* officials lower a smoking brazier of copal incense deep inside to purify it. This is followed by copious amounts of cologne from aerosol spray cans.

Soon thereafter the first Atitecos arrive bearing great candles decorated with brightly colored metallic ribbons or artificial flowers. These candles are expensive and are meant to last for several days or even weeks. Most are four or five feet in height and heavy, requiring the bearer to carry the candle against the chest with both arms. Families that can afford to do so purchase at least one of these elaborate candles and sometimes more so that each individual can have one, a significant financial burden for many households. The real sacrifice is in time and effort. Although it is a burden, most Atitecos rather enjoy it.

The candles must be specially blessed in the church before lighting them. Each Atiteco brings a candle to the east end of the nave, some approaching on

112. *Blessing candles within the World Center hole of the church, 2002*

their knees for the length of the church. There a *cofrade* censes the candle with copal while others spray it with cologne. The *cofrade* lays each candle briefly atop Christ's pillow, the Ruk'ux Muxux, first oriented north to south and then east to west, mirroring the arms of the pillow's embroidered cross. Often the *cofrade* recites a brief prayer while doing this, calling on the power of earth and sky, lake and sea, to come together at this center place. Each candle is then placed inside the world navel hole, either individually if they are large or in small groups of three or four (fig. 112). The *cofrade* blesses the candle to give light and life to the family of its owner. This is one of the prayers given in 1998:

> This candle is offered to bring light, to bring life to the family of this man. It rises up out of darkness from the earth. It gives light in the night and the day. It comes from the earth, from the place of death. It emerges from the ground like the sun at dawn. May it give to the family of this man life; may it bless them with health; may it bless them with strength; may it bless them with food and water; may it bless them with wealth and abundance. Take away their sins and shine for them in the darkness. It is Christ's light. He is the light. He is with us.

The candle is then lifted out of the hole. Its owner immediately lights it from the flame of other candles that have already been blessed. Once the candle has been blessed, the bearer finds a place with friends or family members along the sides of the church or on the steps leading to the altar where they wait for the raising of the cross (fig. 113). The process is repeated again and again until the nave is filled with people tending their candles and watching the preparations for the crucifixion ceremony. The floor, not to mention the clothes, skin, and hair of anyone who holds a candle or who even stands nearby, soon becomes dappled with candle wax drippings. The combination of early morning daylight filtering into the church with the slowly multiplying glow of hundreds of candles illuminates the church well beyond its usual dim lighting.

After all the candles have been blessed, the world navel hole is again censed with copal smoke and sprayed with cologne before it is covered with two long strips of narrow cloth with a pattern of purple stripes, the same colors used on traditional Atiteco women's blouses and men's pants. These are laid crisscross over each other with the arms oriented to the cardinal directions. Three candles in glass cups are then placed atop the cloths to keep them in place

113. *Women with Holy Week candles, 2002*

and to "feed" the space with light (fig. 114). The *cabecera* who opened the hole in 1998 told me that if the cloths were not placed over the hole its power would escape, resulting in earthquakes, winds, or a flood that would destroy the world. Once Holy Week is over, the cloths are kept in the glass chest of the left altarpiece beneath the body of Christ, where they continue to prevent such calamities.

LAYING OF THE *ALFOMBRAS*

> *They made a statue to the god called Kinich Ahau [Sun God], and they placed it in the house of the* principal *in a suitable place, and from there by a path which was very clean and ornamented, they went all together with their accustomed devotion.*
>
> LANDA 1941, 144

As soon as the St. John races are concluded, teams of Atitecos block off the streets that will be used for Christ's procession later in the day in order to sweep them clean of all debris and cover them with *alfombras* (carpets). Until a few decades ago these consisted of a layer of pine needles and flowers scattered over the streets (fig. 115). Occasionally some of them still are, but most are now composed of brightly colored sawdust laid out with elaborate designs that require most of the day to complete (fig. 116). Individual Atitecos volunteer to organize the decoration of a certain length of the processional way (usually no more than a block, as they are very time-consuming and expensive to produce). Nicolás Chávez Sojuel oversees the *alfombras* along the northwest corner of the processional way, extending from the fourth station to the end of the indoor market. He often asks me to help with his section of the *alfombra*, a task that requires all the help that he can get. Sometimes I draw out a few of the patterns on the street, but mostly he enlists me to participate along with a team of family members and friends in the backbreaking work of laying down the sawdust.

The sawdust is hand-dyed the week before. Nicolás draws out the designs to be used in a small notebook. Some are based on Tz'utujil Maya traditions while others are more recognizably European Christian in origin. He seldom repeats these designs from year to year, preferring to try more detailed and imaginative images each time. Nicolás or one of his associates transfers the patterns onto the paving stones of the street using chalk, beginning early Friday morning. These are then "painted" with a thick layer of colored sawdust. Because the patterns are often intricate, this requires a great deal of care, sprinkling one handful of sawdust at a time, often using only the thumb and

114. *World Center hole covered with cloths, 2002*

115. *(Above) Pine needles and flowers on the processional route, ca. 1968. Photograph by John D. Early*

116. *(Left) Laying an* alfombra, *1998*

forefinger to avoid going over the lines. The border between one color and another is supposed to be sharply delineated, with no Rothko-like bleeding from one section to another. The work is hot, tedious, time-consuming, and ultimately heartbreaking (at least for me) because it is all doomed to be trampled underfoot by the procession that evening.

This process has two great enemies. The first is wind, which can easily destroy hours of work with a single gust. To avoid this, most teams obtain a pump-action pressurized metal canister filled with water. These are normally used for spraying pesticides on crops but also work well for spraying an even mist of water over the *alfombras*, making them heavy enough to resist being blown away. The other danger is from dogs, hundreds of which wander the streets of the city unimpeded. Most years dogs appear seemingly out of nowhere to stroll across the *alfombra*-covered streets. Unfortunately nothing can be done to prevent this. Once a dog enters the *alfombra*, it is best to let it cross unmolested, as shooing it away serves only to increase the damage. Canine-damaged sections must be painstakingly repaired or, in the worst cases, cleared away in order to start the process over again.

Although technically the teams of *alfombra* makers do not engage in a competition, they take a certain amount of pride in having their *alfombra* complimented. Most people in town take an hour or so to walk the processional route at some point during the day to watch the progress of the *alfombras* and choose their favorites. Church officials are in charge of organizing the *alfombra* decoration leading from the church steps across the plaza to the west. This is done quickly and efficiently, using stencils for many of the border designs and even some of the principal panels, repeating the same patterns from year to year (fig. 117). Atitecos who design the *alfombras* for the city streets are generally disdainful of this approach. Nicolás compared his designs with those on the church plaza while drawing out a pattern on the street:

> The *alfombra* makers hired by the church use stencils rather than using their own hands. Their designs have no *k'ux* [heart]. They don't mean anything because they didn't come from the mind, or the soul, or the hands of human beings. They're pretty, but there's no life in them and that is what is most important.

For traditionalists it is important that the *alfombras* have a powerful "heart." As the procession bearing the image of Christ and the saints who accompany him passes over an *alfombra*, they are not so much destroying it as releasing its essence to strengthen both the deities and those who carry them.

117. Alfombra *in the church plaza, 2010*

PLACING THE BODY OF THE SACRIFICED CHRIST ON THE WORLD TREE

> *Now when [the Lords of Death] went to place the head [of Hun Hunahpu] in the midst of the tree, the tree bore fruit. The tree had never borne fruit until the head of One Hunahpu was placed in it. . . . This was seen by all Xibalba when they came to look at it. In their hearts they perceived the greatness of the essence of that tree, for it was accomplished immediately when the head of One Hunahpu entered into its midst.*
>
> *POPOL VUH*, IN CHRISTENSON 2007, 126–127

In the *Popol Vuh*, the foundational myth that addresses the universal mystery of the endless cycles of death and rebirth in the world centers on the god Hun Hunahpu, the father of the ancestral gods of the Guatemalan highlands. Soon after Spanish missionaries and conquerors introduced Jesus Christ as the new principal life god, the Maya conflated him with Hun Hunahpu (Ximénez 1929–1931, 1:57). The two play very similar roles in regenerating life from death.

Christianity resonated with long-held Maya beliefs that often used the same or very similar symbols linked to the sacrifice of deity as a precursor to the regeneration of life. The Maya did not have to abandon sacred ceremonies that had sustained their ancestors for untold generations. They had only to repaint the scenery a bit, alter the costumes, and call some of the actors by different names. This is not to say that modern Tz'utujils consciously practice pristine Maya ceremonies under a false façade of Christianity in order to fool the authorities. They venerate Christ with just as much heartfelt passion as their ancestors once honored their old gods. They know him by no other name. When they call themselves Christians, they mean it. They believe that Christ's resurrection is the only means whereby the world itself can be regenerated to new life. Unlike most Christians, however, they believe that they play an essential role as human mediators in wrenching Jesus from the clutches of death and the underworld. It is apparent, therefore, that the five days of Holy Week as practiced in Santiago Atitlán echo core ancient Maya concepts that have no precedent in Western biblical tradition.

At about 8 A.M. the great cross is taken down from the north wall of the apse, just to the right of the door leading to the sacristy. It is approximately thirty feet in height. During the year the cross is wrapped in white linen and bound with colorful plastic cords, generally orange and blue. The cross is never seen without its cloth wrapping except on Good Friday. Other important crosses in Santiago Atitlán are also wrapped. The cross borne by Cristo Nazareno on the evening of the San Juan races is wrapped in a white cloth during the year and customarily hangs on a wall in the Cofradía Santiago. A much smaller cross is used in Day of the Dead processions, the only time during the year when it is unwrapped and adorned with evergreen boughs.

Members of the Cofradía Santa Cruz carry the heavy cross to the east end of the nave next to the world center hole, where it is laid on a plaited reed mat with the head pointing toward the altar. The cords are untied and the cloth wrapping is taken away. As soon as the cross is revealed, the twelve little apostle boys arrange themselves on the floor around its lower shaft as guardians. The cross is painted with a pattern of green lines over a gold background that winds back and forth diagonally around the shaft and arms, ending with a wide band of solid green at its base (fig. 118). Where the green lines intersect on the front of the cross are green disks with a pale lavender center. Lavender-colored four-pointed stars occupy the diamond-shaped spaces formed by the green lines. To the right and left of each disk are other eight-pointed stars. The cross was given a fresh coat of paint in 1983 by a local artist, Miguel Chávez Petzey, who said that he followed precisely the pattern and colors that were there before. The *cabecera* told me that the cross is actually a tree with green vines winding around it. The disks where the vines come together are flowers. The stars show that when the cross is lifted up with the body of

118. *Painted design on the Holy Week cross, 1998*

Christ it reaches into the sky to give light to the darkness of the night sky. Most traditionalist Atitecos give a similar interpretation: the cross is a tree decorated with stars that make it shine, even if the church were completely dark. Nicolás Chávez Sojuel identified the star pattern as symbolic of the Morning Star.

Many traditionalists, including an elderly *ajkun* who helped to prepare the cross in 1998, said that the diamond pattern on the cross shows that it is not only a tree but a snake and linked it with the twisted cords on the Monumento behind the altar as well as the traditional winding headdress worn by Atiteca women. He said that all of these are "like snakes." In Tz'utujil belief the halo-like female headdress is often called a "rainbow serpent." It was first worn by the creator deity Yaxper as patroness of the moon, weaving, childbirth, and midwives. Diego Chávez Petzey gave the following account while the cords of the Monumento were being knotted:

> Yaxper helped in the creation of the world. She along with María Castellana and other ancestral women wove together the framework of the world on their backstrap looms. Their headdresses were like those worn by women in Santiago Atitlán today except that they didn't have any designs on them, only a series of colors in the same order as the rainbow. This is why we call the headdress "rainbow serpent." This serpent ties holy women to the sky like an umbilical cord. The twisted ropes of the Monumento are like ser-

pents, but they are also like umbilical cords because they give life to the fruit hung from its cords and help the world to be reborn with the coming of the rains.

This is one of the principal reasons why the hole in the nave is called the *muxux* (navel). When the cross is placed in the world navel hole, it forms the umbilicus of the newborn Christ at the center, linking the underworld to the sky as well as to the four cardinal directions of the earth. In ancient Yucatec tradition the World Trees depicted on the New Year's pages of the Dresden Codex are adorned with leafy branches as well as snakes (fig. 8), the same combination seen on the Holy Week cross at Santiago Atitlán. Both are associated with world renewal. The World Trees pictured in the Dresden Codex are analogous to the Akantuns, described by Landa as monuments erected at the climax of the Wayeb' period.

After the cross has been unwrapped, it is sprayed with the entire contents of six or seven cans of cologne. Three attendants also wave braziers of copal incense over and around the cross continuously for the next several hours. While the cross is being prepared, other members of the Cofradía Santa Cruz lift the white cloth away from the north altarpiece in the apse of the church, revealing the glass case containing the principal image of Christ. This image has been hidden from view since Monday as a sign that Christ was absent in the underworld. The carved wooden Christ is lifted from the case and his waistcloth and wrappings are removed, although he keeps his wig of unkempt shoulder length black hair. Once uncovered, the image is carried to the cross in a shroud to ensure that his disrobed body is not seen by the crowd gathering in the church. The arms of the Christ image are articulated at the shoulders, allowing them to be extended into a crucifixion posture. *Cofrades* drive nails through the holes in the hands and feet in order to secure the image on the cross, while crowds of Atitecos wedge themselves as close as possible to watch. After the nails are inserted, the *cofrades* tie cords around the wrists, ankles, and body of the statue to ensure that it does not slip.

After the image of Christ is securely affixed to the cross, *cofradía* officials dress him with two or three layers of cloth around his waist. The color of Christ's clothing varies from year to year. The first layer is generally pure white with gold tassels around the edges, but the outer layer is often more colorful. In 1988 it was green, in 2000 purple, in 2002 and 2003 turquoise, in 2008 a deep royal blue, and in 2010 crimson with an embroidered pattern of gold vines and flowers. After Christ's skirt is wrapped around his waist, the outer layer is decorated with dozens of colorful metallic flowers, each individually sewn onto the cloth while the image reclines on the cross. Once Christ re-

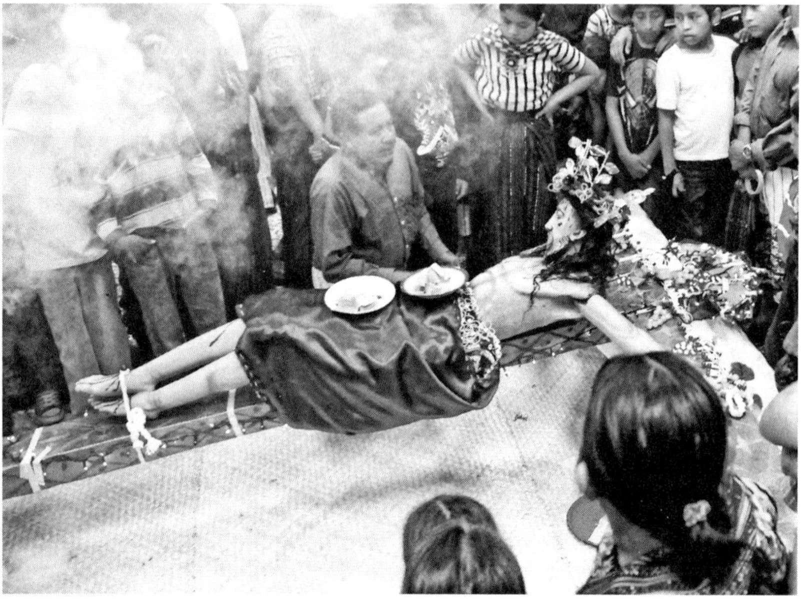

119. *Christ on the cross, adorned with foliage, fruit, and lights, 2010*

turns to his glass case at the close of Holy Week, he will retain this adorned waistcloth throughout the year. The flowers from the old garment are considered powerful talismans and are distributed among the *cofrades* to give away to friends and family members. At the same time, other *cofrades* attach a carved wooden crown of thorns to Christ's head, partly obscured by layers of artificial flowers and leaves. McDougall wrote that the head and apron of Christ were adorned with actual "greenery and flowers" in 1930 (McDougall 1955, 70). The cross behind Christ's head is further adorned with an abundance of plastic and metal flowers, leaves, and fruit, particularly clusters of grapes equipped with tiny electric lights (fig. 119).

Before being placed on the body of Christ or on his cross, each adornment is sprayed with copious amounts of cologne and enveloped in clouds of incense smoke. In 2003 the crown of thorns alone received five full minutes of continuous spraying from ten men with aerosol cans of Kent cologne. The crown was held by an elderly *cofrade* who cradled it on a cloth to avoid touching it directly. The thick cloud of acrid cologne must have been excruciating for his unprotected eyes and nose, but he bore it stoically. The cross is further illuminated with a string of Christmas tree lights of various colors that wrap around both arms of the cross as well as down the shaft to a point just below Christ's feet, essentially surrounding the image with light. When the whole assemblage is switched on later, it glows brightly with an array of colors that reflects off the metal flowers and leaves like dozens of colored mirrors. As people move about the nave, the colors shift as the angle of the light changes. The symbolism of Christ's cross as a fruitful tree is further reinforced when seen directly from the front after it is raised. From this vantage point the cross and the body of Christ are framed completely by the cacao, bananas, *melocotones*, and other fruits hanging from the framework of the Monumento behind them.

By 10:30 or so Christ and the cross are fully prepared. Crowds of Atitecos approach him to pray, bring offerings, and welcome him back to their community. While Christ and his cross are being venerated in the center of the nave, *cofrades* work on the Urna, an ornate glass chest with a wooden framework attached to a much larger bier or catafalque. This has occupied the southwest corner of the church since Thursday morning. Following Christ's crucifixion, his image will be placed in the Urna and borne through the city in a grand procession. Both the chest and bier are adorned with flowers, both real and artificial, as well as long strings of colored lights. Once these have been arranged, the interior of the chest is prepared. During the year the sculpted image of Christ rests on a mattress in the glass case at the base of the left altarpiece, wrapped in a white sheet and two or three blankets. The head is also wrapped with scarves, leaving only the face of the image uncovered. One by one *cofrades* bring these articles from the altarpiece to the southwest corner of the church, where they are censed with copal and sprayed with cologne before being placed within the Urna.

RAISING CHRIST'S CROSS

At noon the cross bearing the image of Christ is raised (fig. 120). By this time the interior of the church is packed solid with more than a thousand people, as many as can possibly force their way in with more spilling out onto the porch and into the plaza, making it very difficult to move. The air soon becomes nearly unbreathable from the heat, candle smoke, incense, and cologne, not to mention the lack of oxygen from the throngs of people breathing in the enclosed space of the church. The cross bearing the image of Christ is raised with eight long bamboo poles, each with a padded V-shaped fork at the ends to support the arms of the cross, four on each side. As the cross is raised, several men guide the base of the shaft into the world navel hole. Once in place it is wedged firmly with sticks of wood and bound with ropes to prevent it from leaning. The reed mat bearing the Ruk'ux Muxux pillow is then positioned on the floor in front of the cross to mark the place as the center of the world.

This all takes place to the accompaniment of a din of sound. A snare drum

120. *Raising of Christ's cross, 2010*

keeps up a constant rolling beat while the *cofrades* shout commands to one another in order to lift the heavy cross in unison. Many of those gathered in the church weep openly during the raising of the cross, an outpouring of emotion that is relatively rare in its depth of expression and intensity. One side or the other of the cross invariably tilts a bit during the process, eliciting a collective gasp of horror from the crowd gathered in the church. As the great cross is slowly muscled into the air, people react audibly, beginning with a low rumble that builds in intensity, reaching a climax when the base of the shaft drops heavily into the navel hole. Christ will remain on the cross for the next three hours. Few leave after the cross is in position, content to stand patiently in the hot, dense air within the church, staring at the resplendently adorned image of Christ raised high above them.

For traditionalists the raising of Christ's cross does not represent his death (that took place on Monday with the shrouding of his image) but rather his triumphant return from a five-day sojourn in the underworld. Now he is lifted up to new life within the boughs of a flowering tree, resplendent with blinking lights, foliage, and fruit. The raising of the cross is linked with the rebirth of maize, inaugurating the wet season and the first planting of the maize fields (Tarn and Prechtel 1997, 276). There is a certain sense of relief that the ceremonies of the past week have turned out well (if indeed they have) and their god has returned to his temple.

DEPOSITION FROM THE CROSS AND THE PROCESSION OF THE URNA

> *They decorated and adorned their idols for these fiestas and sacrifices with gold, precious stones, and mantles of the finest materials that they had and could use. They placed them on litters and carried them in procession with inestimable devotion with drums and trumpets and other musical instruments.*
>
> LAS CASAS 1958, CHAPTER 177, 149 (TRANSLATION BY AUTHOR)

> *They had some litters, richly prepared with many jewels of gold, silver, and stones, arranged with roses and flowers upon which they placed the idols, dressed in a careful and curious manner. With these they walked in procession around the patio of the temple with great songs, music, diversions, dances, and eminent persons, all arranged in order without a hint of confusion.*
>
> LAS CASAS 1958, CHAPTER 177, 151–152 (TRANSLATION BY AUTHOR)

After hanging on the cross for three hours, Christ is carefully taken down and placed in the Urna for his triumphal procession through the streets of the city. A tall wooden ladder is placed behind each of the arms of the cross and two sacristans climb up to carry out the deposition (fig. 121). The sacristans are dressed in long white robes with purple stripes. Their faces are obscured by ill-fitting blond wigs and beards. Apparently this costume has a measure of antiquity. Eleanor Lothrop described the sacristans that she saw in the 1920s as wearing "blonde curly wigs and beards, dressed in white ceremonial robes. . . . They looked like sunburned unshaven Harpo Marxes" (Lothrop 1948, 124). The two sacristans who lower Christ from his cross are probably meant to represent Joseph of Arimathea and Nicodemus, although Atitecos only know them as "the Jews." First they wind a long cloth several times about Christ's upper body, crisscrossed at his back and looped around the top of the cross to support his weight. The nails and cords are then removed from each of his arms and legs. Finally the body is slowly lowered to waiting *cofrades* below, who place it gently in the Urna, which had been carried to the center of the nave. The Ruk'ux Muxux pillow is placed under his head, and his body is wrapped in the white sheet and blankets. Christ's image is then censed with copal smoke and sprayed with the contents of more than a dozen aerosol cans of cologne. When Christ is sufficiently enveloped with fragrant mist, the lid is quickly placed on the chest to prevent the cloud from dissipating. All of this is accompanied by a steady, rhythmic beat from the great drum.

When everything is ready, the Urna and its much larger bier are lifted onto

121. *Christ lowered from the cross by sacristans, 2013. Photograph by Andrew Weeks*

the shoulders of fifty young men, three in front, three in back, and twenty-two along each side (fig. 122). Until at least the 1970s they used a much smaller bier, just slightly larger than the Urna itself, but the trend in many ways is to expend ever-increasing amounts of money to create more lavish displays where possible. Although the procession route is relatively short (only sixteen blocks or so), it takes nearly fifteen hours to complete the circuit and return to the church, timed to arrive at sunrise. Bearing the Urna is a great honor, and each of the young men pays for the privilege. Most of the bearers pay for half the route, switching with another team around midnight when the Urna reaches the area at the back of the church compound. It is not uncommon for some to pay double in order to carry the Urna along the entire processional route. It is considered a test of endurance to carry the Urna, but it also brings good fortune in the coming year. In 2002 a brief scuffle broke out because one of the bearers did not want to relinquish his place at the designated time. He looked exhausted, covered with sweat, but he claimed that he could carry the heavy Urna for days because Christ had given him strength. His replacement, however, insisted that he had paid for the honor and needed the blessings as well. The exchange was soon made with the intervention of some in the crowd, and the Urna continued on its way without further difficulty.

As always the procession is led by the great drum, followed closely by the principal women of the *cofradías* all carrying candles. Next come the sacristans, still dressed as Jews, who will sing continuously throughout the night. They are followed by the male *cofradía* officials holding their staffs of office. The bearers of the Urna come next. For many years the Urna was followed by a separate small litter for the portable generator that powered the ornamental lights. The generator had four bearers who carried the little machine with as

122. *Procession of the Urna containing Christ's image, 2010*

much solemnity as if it were one of the saints. In 2002 the generator broke down during the procession. Soon volunteers appeared with about fifty meters of extension cords. These were plugged into outlets in homes and businesses along the processional route to power the Urna's lights. As soon as the Urna reached the limit of the cord's length, it was unplugged and run as quickly as possible to another outlet ahead of the procession.

Most years the strings of colorful lights are of the type used on Christmas trees and play tinny versions of Christmas carols over and over again. The selections that played the year the generator broke down included *Rudolph the Red-Nosed Reindeer* and *Santa Claus Is Coming to Town*. To an outsider the blinking lights and unsophisticated Christmas music might detract from what otherwise is a beautiful and solemn ceremony. But that is a misconception. For Atitecos Christ has returned to their community bathed in light, color, and sound. Few if any know the words or meaning of the tunes—it is simply music that animates the air around the Urna in much the same way that the strings of colorful lights illuminate and give life to the darkness of the night.

The pace is glacial, forward progress being nearly imperceptible from moment to moment. At first glance it seems that the bearers mostly shift from one foot to the other, causing the Urna to sway gently from side to side. Just when it seems that the Urna has advanced significantly, the bearers backtrack several paces—not enough to negate all their progress but enough to make the prospect of advancing through sixteen blocks of city streets seem nearly impossible even with the entire night ahead of them. In 2002 the procession began at 3:20 P.M. when the lid of the Urna was closed. It did not reach the doors of the church until 4:25 P.M. It took until 4:40 P.M. for the Urna to advance another six feet or so to the top of the steps leading down into the plaza.

Once the Urna has reached the center of the church's nave, María Andolor joins the procession on a litter born by four young men. When these have advanced another nine feet or so, San Juan (still wearing his leafy headdress) is carried into the line, bringing up the rear. Those directly behind the Urna have to be very careful not to approach too closely. Its bearers surge backward without any warning and are completely unpredictable. It is not uncommon for people to be toppled by the crowd following the Urna when it is forced to change direction suddenly. While the Urna is making its way slowly westward through the nave of the church, the apostle children and hundreds of others wait patiently on the steps until the Urna reaches them and they join the procession as it passes. Over a thousand more fill the plaza.

THE DEPARTURE OF RILAJ MAM

> *They had a wooden idol which they placed on a bench over a mat, and offered him things to eat and other gifts in a festival called Uayeyab [Wayeb']. And at the end of the festival, they undressed him and threw the pieces of wood to the ground without giving him any more reverence. And this idol they called Mam.*
>
> COGOLLUDO 1957, BOOK 4, CHAPTER 8, 197 (TRANSLATION BY AUTHOR)

About the time when the procession of the Urna reaches the doors of the church, Rilaj Mam's attendants take him down from his tree and set him on the porch of his chapel, where he can observe Christ's progress as he exits the church. Traditionalists often prefer to gather around the Mam rather than to accompany the Urna in the church, so there is a rather large crowd surrounding him. These are the final few hours of the Mam's reign during Holy Week and the only time that he and Christ are within sight of one another. When Rilaj Mam left his *cofradía* to take possession of the mayor's office and settle into his sanctuary on the plaza on Wednesday, the image of Christ on the left altarpiece of the church had already been hidden behind a shroud-like curtain for two days, conceptually absent in the underworld. Now that Christ has returned to take possession of Santiago Atitlán, Rilaj Mam will soon lose the power that he briefly held. When the Mam lay in the mayor's office his head rested on the Ruk'ux Muxux pillow, a token of his authority to rule at the center of the world. That pillow now once again supports the head of Christ in his Urna.

The most difficult part of the Urna's journey through town, at least for the bearers, is undoubtedly its precarious descent down the uneven flight of steps leading from the church porch to the plaza below. Only three young men are at the front end of the Urna, although the first of those assigned to the sides shift around to help brace it during the descent. Those at the front have the honor of taking the first steps onto the pristine *alfombras*, which begin at the base of the church steps. By the time the last bearer reaches the plaza and the Urna is back on level ground, the pattern of the first section of the *alfombra* is completely obliterated, churned into multicolored piles of sawdust like the wake of a slow-moving ship.

About the time when San Juan at the tail end of the procession reaches the plaza the *telinel* lifts Rilaj Mam onto his shoulder and boosts him three times into the air facing each of the cardinal directions. In 2003 the sequence was east, west, south, north. He then carries the Mam toward the procession of the Urna, attended by hundreds of his traditionalist supporters. In con-

123. *Rilaj Mam joins the procession of the Urna in the church plaza, 1988*

trast to the orderly and slow movement of the Urna, the *telinel* dances Rilaj Mam animatedly, turning him this way and that to look out over the people thronging the plaza (fig. 123). This is the final journey that the Mam will make during Holy Week and is considered a major test of the *telinel*'s strength. An ex-*telinel* told me that it is very dangerous to carry the Mam in the presence of Christ's Urna:

> During the year the Mam gets thirsty and we give him drinks throughout the day, wiping his face with a cloth afterward. This cloth becomes powerful because it is soaked with the Mam's drink. *Telinel*s cover their shoulders with one of these cloths when they carry the Mam during Holy Week to give them strength. Otherwise they would not be able to endure the weight. Nevertheless, sometimes people put curses on the *telinel* to make him faint or cause him to stumble. When I was *telinel*, it felt like there were knives cutting into my shoulder when I first lifted the Mam on Friday afternoon during Holy Week because someone had tried to curse me. But the Mam soon gave me strength and I ignored the pain until it went away. It is best to carry the Mam on the left shoulder to show strength. If a *telinel* carries him on the right shoulder it means that he is weak. The left side is the weak side, so if you can carry him there everyone knows that you are strong. I carry him with my left fingers locked into the Mam's *faja* [a traditional woven belt], my right hand held over my head to hold onto the

> *faja* on the other side. Many *telinels* just walk with the Mam because they are tired. But I danced with him the whole way, and the more I danced the lighter he became.

Once he reaches the base of the church steps, the *telinel* again lifts the Mam three times to the cardinal directions before merging into the wake of the procession. The crowd that surrounds the Mam and the crowd accompanying Christ's Urna meet and surge around one another, reminiscent of tributaries coming together to form a single great river. The two groups move more or less in unison until the Urna reaches the west end of the church plaza around sunset. At this point the tradition is for the Mam and his entourage to surge forward to the left of Christ (fig. 124). As he passes the Urna and attendant saints, the *telinel* again lifts Rilaj Mam up and down three times facing each of the cardinal directions. The bearers of the Urna lift Christ three times in response, after which the Mam quickly descends the steps leading to the town center. He is bounced up and down to the cardinal directions at three other locations—at the base of the plaza steps, in front of the mayor's offices, and finally in front of the entrance to his *cofradía* house. Rilaj Mam is accompanied by a crowd of his devotees back to Cofradía Santa Cruz, with the *telinel* often dancing his way through the darkened streets to the degree that his stamina and enthusiasm allow.

Some years, particularly if there has been contention with the Roman

124. *Rilaj Mam passes Christ's Urna on the way back to his* cofradía, *1988*

Catholic authorities, the Mam's keepers are loath to cede the stage to Christ's procession until it is absolutely necessary. According to long-established custom, the Urna should not descend the west plaza steps into the center of the city until Rilaj Mam has departed. This should be when it starts getting dark after sunset. In 2003, when the new priest had spoken out against what he perceived to be non-Catholic irregularities in the Holy Week observances and refused to participate in some of the ceremonies, the *telinel* delayed the Mam's departure until well after dark, dancing and turning the Mam this way and that through the crowds with no sign of leaving. The Urna had long since reached the top of the plaza steps, so its bearers were forced to march in place for more than an hour waiting for Rilaj Mam to depart. Orthodox Catholics were outraged by the delay, while traditionalists reveled in their brief ability to discomfit those who had opposed them during the week.

Until the late 1980s Rilaj Mam was taken apart once he arrived at the Cofradía Santa Cruz on Friday night. The disarticulated pieces of his body were then wrapped in reed mats and returned to the rafters for the remainder of the year, with his head turned backward so that he could not "cause harm" (Mendelson 1957, 265). Bill Douglas wrote that in the 1960s the Mam's head was separated from his body, which was securely wrapped in a mat and bound to the trellis with ropes so that he would not leave or "walk about" (Douglas 1969, 103, 123). This tradition is no longer followed. Instead the Mam is received at the *cofradía* house in triumph, surrounded by his supporters and feted late into the night before returning him to his mattress in the rafters for the night. Each morning thereafter he is brought down soon after sunrise in order to receive those who venerate him during the year. Although he is given a great deal of respect, the Mam is not allowed to leave the confines of the Cofradía Santa Cruz and is watched over constantly by an image of Christ in a glass Urna nearly identical to the one making its way around the city on Friday night. The presence of Christ is meant to ensure that Rilaj Mam comports himself appropriately. His wooden image will not see the sun or breathe open air again for the next 362 days.

Once the Mam has departed, the Urna containing the image of Christ continues on throughout the night, circumambulating through the streets that ring the center of the city before returning to the church at dawn. The movement of Christ's procession follows a counterclockwise circuit that recapitulates his journey through the underworld realm of the dead toward rebirth. Thus the Urna initially moves west out of the church toward the mayoral offices. It then turns south, the direction associated with the entrance into the underworld. At the first station at the southwest corner of the pro-

125. *Procession of the Urna, Holy Friday, 1968. Photograph by Jude Pansini*

cessional route the procession turns east and then north, ultimately reentering the church on an easterly pathway timed to the rising of the sun.

After the departure of Rilaj Mam at sunset, the procession of Christ takes place in darkness. The entire route is lined with people who wait patiently for the passage of the Urna through their section of the city. Other than those actually in the procession, relatively few accompany Christ along the streets as he progresses through the city. For the most part people are content to spend the night waiting for him to come to them. It is difficult to explain how oddly fascinating it is to watch the Urna's slow journey through the dark streets of Santiago Atitlán. It is hypnotic without the somnolence. A certain thrill goes through the crowds when, after hours of patient vigil, the Urna finally reaches their corner of the world.

There is always a bit of drama as well. When borne on the shoulders of its carriers, the Urna atop its massive bier is taller than the crosspieces of the decorated archways, not to mention many of the power lines and telephone wires strung back and forth above the streets. As the night wears on, the bearers appear to be exhausted. Sweat streams from their bodies and their heads often rest on the shoulders of those ahead of them (fig. 125). There is always the question of how they will be able to endure the night, much less have the strength to navigate around all the obstacles in their way. The young men like to play on these doubts. They will slowly approach an arch or low-hanging wire, then, just when it looks as if they will collide with it they back up rapidly and start over, making another unsuccessful run at it. After they repeat this several times, the crowds wonder if they will be able to get beyond the obstruction. Low murmurs build to nervous oohs and aahs and finally to shouts when it appears that there will be a collision. But it's all theater. After frightening the crowds a bit, the bearers simply bend their knees or lower their shoulders and pass through quickly before resuming their slow, stately pace. One Good Friday night I asked one of the bearers why they went backward so often. His response was elegant in its simplicity: "to go slower."

AFTERMATH AND CONCLUSIONS *Chapter 10*

The rate of the procession is timed so as to arrive back at the church around dawn on Saturday morning. The earlier tradition was to return Christ to his place beneath the left altarpiece immediately after his return to the church so as to be there when the sun rises (Mendelson 1957, 266). In more recent years the bearers have placed the Urna in the center of the nave near the world navel hole surrounded by several rows of white candles. It isn't until later that afternoon or early evening that the image of Christ is returned to the left altarpiece in the apse of the church where he will remain during the year until the following Holy Week (fig. 126). The empty Urna and its palanquin are left in the nave through Sunday with its lid open as a symbol that Christ has returned to his customary place. The empty Urna in the church on Saturday contrasts with orthodox Christian tradition in which Christ does not rise from death until Sunday morning, leaving behind the empty "tomb" as a token of his resurrection.

Both the Urna and the chest beneath Christ's altarpiece in the church's apse appear to be glass-enclosed coffins, and this is undoubtedly what they are intended to be. The most common name for the sculpted image of Christ in the Urna is Santo Entierro (Holy Buried One). Yet traditionalist Atitecos do not consider him to be dead when he is carried through the streets on Good Friday, at least not in the usual sense. Except when hidden behind the white cloth draped across the left altarpiece of the church during Holy Week, this sculpted image of Christ is the preeminent tangible manifestation of the god's presence in the community. Douglas was told that Santo Entierro was the eldest of the holy family and "the most powerful in the world" (Douglas 1969, 75). He hears prayers and grants favors to those who approach him during the year. His closed eyes and slightly turned head do make him appear to be at least sleeping, an impression made all the more evident as his body is wrapped in blankets and his head rests on a pillow, often the Ruk'ux Muxux. As a result, those who come to pray before him frequently tap on the glass with a coin to wake him up so that he will pay attention to their petitions and see that an offering has been brought to him. Traditionalist Atitecos perceive

126. *Image of Christ below the left altarpiece, 2005*

Christ as being in a liminal state after his rebirth at the close of Holy Week—neither fully alive in the heavens nor fully dead in the underworld.

This is consistent with Maya texts with regard to Hun Hunahpu, the god that the Maya linked with Christ soon after the Spanish Conquest of highland Guatemala. The *Popol Vuh* asserts that after Hun Hunahpu's sacrifice by the Lords of Death in the underworld his skull retained the ability to hear and to speak. The great mystery of Maya cosmology is that death bears within itself the seeds of its own rebirth. The underworld is both tomb and womb. Maize plants wither and die on an annual basis, their seeds becoming dry and hard. In most Maya languages, including Tz'utujil, maize kernels are often called "little skulls," the bony remnants of the maize plant after its death in the fields (Carlsen 1996, 148). When these are buried in the earth, symbolically entering the underworld, they germinate in season and grow into a new living plant, continuing an endless cycle of dissolution and regeneration.

But Hun Hunahpu was not fully dead. His skull, hanging within the branches of a fruit-bearing tree, had the power to miraculously impregnate an underworld maiden named Xkik', who eventually gave birth to twin sons. These in turn also descended into the underworld realm, where they were sacrificed, rose from death, and ultimately defeated the underworld gods who had killed their father. The *Popol Vuh* explicitly links the death and rebirth of the Hero Twins in the underworld to the life cycle of maize (Christenson 2007, 160, 188–189). Having sacrificed the Lords of Death, the Hero Twins then elevated their father as the "first" deity to be worshipped in perpetuity, although he remained in the underworld realm of Xibalba as a partially animated corpse near the ballcourt where he died:

> They now went, therefore, to see the face of their father there at Xibalba. Their father spoke to them when Xibalba was defeated.
>
> Here now is the adornment of their father by them, along with the adornment of Seven Hunahpu. For they went to adorn them at Crushing Ballcourt.
>
> They merely wanted his face to be restored. Thus they asked him to name everything—his mouth, his nose, and his eyes. He was able to recover the first name, but then little more was said. He did not say the corresponding names for that which is above the mouth. Still, this had been said, and thus they honored him.
>
> Thus the heart of their father was left behind at Crushing Ballcourt. His sons then said to him:
>
> "Here you will be called upon. It shall be so." Thus his heart was comforted. "The child who is born in the light, and the son who is begotten in the light shall go out to you first. They shall worship you first. Your name shall not be forgotten. Thus be it so," they said to their father when they comforted his heart. (Christenson 2007, 190–191)

Hun Hunahpu's inability to identify his nose and his eyes undoubtedly alludes to the fact that he was still a skull. He would have had a mouth with which to speak, but there would only have been empty cavities where his nose and eyes once existed. In a similar way Christ in Tz'utujil thought resides within his coffin during the year, appearing to all the world to be dead and buried. The church itself is considered to be an underworld location, the interior of a sacred mountain.

But he is not really dead. He hears and answers prayers directed to him. His death and resurrection during Holy Week are tied to the coming of the first rains of the year, animating the world after months of sterility and allowing the sown maize fields to germinate and produce new life-giving crops. For this reason the first plantings of maize take place immediately after Holy Week (Tarn and Prechtel 1997, 276). The emergence of new life from sacrificial death is a fundamental tenet of both ancient Maya belief and Roman Catholicism.

RETURN TO NORMALCY

If an entire town can be exhausted, then this is the atmosphere that hangs over Santiago Atitlán on Saturday morning following the all-night vigil of the Urna's procession. The once beautiful arches along the processional route are spent, with the posts often leaning precariously to one side or another. Many of the crosspieces hang askew. Most of their cypress boughs have already fallen to the streets. Those that still cling halfheartedly to the posts are dried out and lifeless. Each arch had been adorned with hanging fruit and large corozo flowers. Most of the fruit is now gone. Remnants of many of the large purple *melocotón* gourds litter the streets where they fell, smashed like pumpkins after Halloween. The fleshy petals of the corozo flowers are considered good luck, so young men and children with long sticks go from arch to arch striking them as if they were piñatas until only the stems remain. They gather up the petals and take them to their homes where they are scattered at the four corners to bless their families for the coming year. The colored sawdust of the *alfombras* is also considered lucky. Hordes of children scour the streets for the remnants, scooping them up into little plastic bags to take home.

By 7 in the morning men assemble in the streets to dismantle the archways and sweep away whatever remains of the *alfombras* and other debris (fig. 127). The shrines at the four corners of the processional way are now gone, the saints having been returned to their customary places after the Urna passed them during the night. The greenery and flowers are also taken down from public buildings and private homes. A group of women sweeps the church plaza and *convento* complex. Within the church teams of men and women scrape the floors of the nave and porch to remove wax drippings and sweep everything clean. The great cross used in Christ's crucifixion was removed from the world navel hole soon after the procession of the Urna began the previous day. It was quickly rewrapped and hung in its place by the sacristy door. At the same time the hole was briefly censed with copal smoke before being covered with its floor tile, effectively ending the five-day period in which the portal allowed underworld influences to escape into the world of the living.

The Monumento and its fruit are usually taken down on Saturday as well, although some years it remains in place until after Sunday morning Mass.

127. *Dismantling the arches and sweeping the streets on Saturday morning, 2010*

The fruit had given a wonderful sweet odor to the church that complemented the copal incense, but by now it has grown overripe and is beginning to smell and attract flies. According to Mendelson, writing in the 1950s, the fruit was taken to the town center to be distributed among municipal officials, beginning with the mayor (Mendelson 1957, 277f, n63). Today the fruit is gathered into baskets and taken back to the Cofradía Santa Cruz, where the best fruit is hung from the rafters for a day or two. The corozo flowers are given to children, who shake the petals free from their stems onto the floor of the church in front of the central altarpiece. Like those gleaned from the archways, the petals are gathered up into sacks to be used in rituals to bless homes in the community.

During the day the saints that belong within the church will all return to their customary places. St. John returned with the procession of the Urna at dawn. Early on Saturday morning a dagger is placed blade-first over the chest of María Andolor in a ceremony in the church plaza that is presided over by the Cofradía Santiago. This is undoubtedly a reference to the statement given by Simeon to the Virgin Mary on the occasion of Jesus's circumcision in the temple: "(Yea, a sword shall pierce through thy own soul also,) that the thoughts of many hearts may be revealed" (Luke 2:35). Although based on biblical tradition, the ceremony is carried out by traditionalists with no orthodox Roman Catholic clergy involved. The image of María is then carried to the Cofradía Santiago accompanied by that *cofradía*'s cult image of Santiago, the patron saint of the community. In Atiteco belief Santiago is a close relative of María (either her brother or uncle), and she spends the day at his house. She and the image of Santiago are danced there before he accompanies her back to the church around sunset.

NEW FIRE CEREMONY

> *Once having expelled the evil spirit, all began to pray with great devotion, and the Chacs kindled the new fire, and lighted the brazier for in the feasts in which all joined in common, they burned incense to the idol with new fire.*
>
> LANDA 1941, 152–153

The major ceremony observed on Saturday is the creation of new fire. Mendelson wrote that in the early 1950s this took place early in the morning, about 7 A.M., no doubt timed to coincide with the dawn following Christ's return to the church (Mendelson 1957, 277f, n64). This first dawn after the procession of the Urna is considered the "first sunrise of the year" (Tarn and Prechtel 1997, 269), analogous to the first dawn of the ancient New Year's rites. It is called "new fire" because it must be newly created rather than lit from a preexisting flame. In the past this was done with flint and cotton (ibid.), although in recent years the tradition may or may not be strictly followed. The newly ignited flame is then used to light all the candles and incense burners in the church. The creation of new fire symbolizes Christ's rebirth and the restoration of light and life in the world. In recent years, however, the ritual usually takes place Saturday evening, perhaps in order to bring the ceremony closer to the orthodox tradition of Christ's resurrection early Sunday morning.

About 8:30 or 9:00 P.M., when it is fully dark, all the electric lights are turned off in the church and plaza area—the only time during the year that the area is cast into absolute darkness. A large pile of wood is assembled midway between the plaza cross and the steps of the church. A bonfire is lit with new fire in the presence of a Roman Catholic priest if one is available (fig. 128). When the town had no resident priest in the past the *cabecera* or one of the sacristans presided over the ritual. Once the fire is burning well, the priest blesses a large candle as a symbol of the body of Christ. Before lighting it, he inserts five pins, each with a black globular head, to form a cross in the

128. *New Fire ceremony, Santiago Atitlán, 2010. Photograph by Nicolás Chávez Sojuel*

center of the candle. He then addresses the candle as Alpha and Omega—God as "the beginning and the end." This great candle is lit from the flames of the bonfire, after which the priest carries it up the stairs of the church, stopping in front of the west doors, which have been closed for this part of the ceremony. As many people as possible follow the priest up the stairs holding unlit candles, filling the stairway as well as the eastern end of the plaza. Once everyone has found a place near the church, the priest uses his candle to light those held by the Atitecos closest to him. They in turn light the candles of those below them on the steps, creating the illusion of a cascade of light slowly flowing down into the plaza below.

Once all the candles have been lit, the doors of the church are opened and the people stream inside, lighting more candles within the darkened interior. They use the same new fire to light numerous incense braziers prepared beforehand for this purpose. Soon the nave is filled once again with candlelight and a thick cloud of copal smoke. The priest sets the great candle in an elaborately carved wooden holder near the dais of the altar. When everyone has entered the nave, all the electric lights of the church are illuminated simultaneously, nearly blinding the participants, whose eyes have become accustomed to the darkness. Most years the priest then gives a brief sermon on the resurrection, focusing on Christ as the "light of the world," illuminating the darkness (John 8:12; 9:5).

Dozens of water jars have been placed at the east end of the church. These are blessed by the priest, who uses an aspergillum made of cypress branches to sprinkle the crowds to sanctify them. In 2003 the priest used the occasion to perform a number of late-night baptisms, linking the ritual rebirth of the children with the rebirth of the world, so that "all things are now made new" (2 Corinthians 5:17; Revelation 21:1–8).

The New Fire ceremony is a beautiful expression of the syncretic blending of traditional Maya rituals tied to world regeneration with Roman Catholic belief in the resurrection of Jesus Christ. Among the Pre-Columbian Maya, New Fire ceremonies were performed at the close of New Year's observances as a symbol that life and light had been restored to the world following a period of ritual death, a concept that is consistent with both modern Atiteco belief as well as orthodox Christianity. The major adaptation in Santiago Atitlán involves the timing of these ceremonial observances. For traditionalist Tz'utujils the climax of Holy Week occurs on Friday with the raising of the cross as a symbol of their ancient World Tree, adorned with the body of Christ as a life deity newly returned from the realm of the dead after a five-day absence.

Easter Sunday, the day of Christ's resurrection in orthodox Christian belief, is far less important in Santiago Atitlán, at least among those who adhere to traditionalist Atiteco religious practices. In their view Christ has already made his triumphal circuit of the city and returned to his customary place in the church the day before. Other than a procession to return Santiago to his *cofradía* house, no major traditionalist ceremonies are held on Easter Sunday. Elsie McDougall was surprised that after all the pageantry and elaborate rituals carried out during Holy Week in Santiago Atitlán in 1930 Sunday was not celebrated with any ceremonial activity in the church or plaza (McDougall 1955, 73). Mendelson concurs, noting that other than returning Santiago to his *cofradía*, life in Santiago Atitlán returns to normal on Easter Sunday with no significant ceremonies on the part of traditionalist Tz'utujils (Mendelson 1957, 268). Tarn and Prechtel characterize Sunday as "dismantling day," in which everything that remains of the materials used during Holy Week is dismantled and put away (Tarn and Prechtel 1997, 270).

After a week of anger and frustration over what he perceived to be remnants of paganism in the course of Holy Week observances, the Roman Catholic priest in 2003 gave a homily at Saturday Mass in which he accused traditionalists in Santiago Atitlán of misunderstanding the true meaning of the crucifixion reenacted the previous day. He was particularly upset that Atitecos paid far more attention to Friday observances commemorating the crucifixion of Christ than to Easter Sunday:

> Christ was born in a stable among donkeys and oxen, not pigs. But pigs are what you are when you continue to practice these pagan rituals, celebrating when you should be mourning Christ's death on the cross on Friday. If a beloved relative was shot to death, or hit by a truck, would you celebrate? Would you honor the one who killed him? Would you worship the rifle or truck that was the instrument of his death? No. You would mourn. You would sorrow over his death and look forward to his resurrection in Christ, whose victory over the tomb we as good Christians will celebrate tomorrow on Easter Sunday. I am sorry that I ever came to Santiago Atitlán to see this.

An elderly woman, offended at the priest's misunderstanding of traditional Tz'utujil belief, could be heard to say in response: "If you're sorry, then there's the door."

At some point, probably soon after the Spanish Conquest, ancient Maya rituals of world renewal were transferred to Holy Week, the principal Christian festival marking the resurrection of God and the rebirth of life. In highland Guatemala this period marks the beginning of the rainy season when crops are planted, particularly maize. In most important respects the two traditions dovetail perfectly, with little need to abandon the core elements of either. Farriss writes that Christian evangelization among the Maya after the Spanish Conquest was not so much a process of conversion from one religion to another as an "interchange" whereby Maya religion and Christianity "merged into a syncretistic cult of the saints, which enabled the Maya elite, through the development of *cofradías* and the annual round of village fiestas, to recapture their control of public ritual and thus validate their continued control of wealth and power" (Farriss 1984, 10). But she also notes that this created a problem in most Maya areas:

> To worship their deities provoked punishment from the Spaniards; not to worship them courted perhaps less immediate but more terrifying consequences. This dilemma produced a split within the public or corporate sphere of religion between open observance of Christian ritual and clandestine adherence to the old religion. The Christian ritual took over the towns, just as the churches took over the temple sites. . . . The Maya ritual remained as a parallel system driven underground—often literally, into sacred caves. There, in the bush, or in the houses of the principals, the idols were hidden and when possible worshiped and fed with copal incense, maize gruel, and the blood of sacrificial victims. (ibid., 290)

The Tz'utujils in Santiago Atitlán have found a way to celebrate their ancient traditions in a more public way than in any other Maya community in Guatemala, at least during Holy Week. They have been able to weave the most valued threads of both traditional Maya and Roman Catholic ceremonialism together into a new cloth that seamlessly harmonizes the two theologies. This process of syncretism wasn't passive. The Maya controlled whatever elements of Roman Catholicism they chose to adopt, ignoring others or rejecting them outright. Robert Carlsen wrote concerning the Tz'utujils of Santiago Atitlán that, "far from integrating elements of Spanish culture in order to emulate the foreigners, the Mayas did so in ways that preserved important aspects of their own culture. The net result was gradual evolutionary change" (Carlsen 1997, 99). It is therefore legitimate to say that Atitecos converted the Roman Catholic saints to their traditional Maya belief system to at least the same degree that they were converted to Roman Catholicism. As Garry Sparks recently asserted, the "highland Maya were neither merely victims of nor simply reactionary resistors to Hispano-Catholic and Imperial Spanish hegemony, but rather agents and co-authors in the reconfiguration of Maya religiosity" (Sparks 2011b, 6).

During Holy Week elements of both ancient Maya ritual and Roman Catholic practices are played out together on the public stage. Modern Tz'utujils view the Christian elements of their traditions not as an imposed religion of occupation but as a concept that can be interpreted from the perspective of their own unique understanding of the world. Their ancestral heritage enjoins them to renew the world at periodic intervals because in Maya belief all things, including gods, weaken and die in annual cycles. It is the role of humans to perpetuate these cycles through ritual, periodically rebirthing their gods from the dead at annual times of crisis. Not to do so according to ancient precedent would have devastating consequences for the world. The ceremonial life of Santiago Atitlán is a social necessity, bound up with the everyday life of the community, giving it meaning, purpose, and structure. Modern North American and European cultures could not exist without their computers and currency. Traditional Tz'utujil society could not exist without its ancestral rituals.

At times the Tz'utujils have suffered terrible persecution because of their beliefs and ceremonial practices. Yet despite centuries of opposition and pressure to conform to Western notions of Christian orthodoxy, traditionalists insist on performing the rituals passed on to them by their ancestors. They are never carried out precisely as they were the year before, because Atitecos know that they must continually adapt to ever-changing economic and social circumstances. Yet the core elements of Holy Week in Santiago Atitlán have remained remarkably consistent over at least the last century, when written accounts by Western observers were first published. Considering how similar they are to Pre-Columbian antecedents, it is probable that the blending of Christian and Tz'utujil traditions now seen during Holy Week took place soon after the Spanish Conquest, establishing the basic ritual framework that survives today. I once asked a young Tz'utujil named Xuan, who was then training to become an *ajkun*, why it was so important for him to carry on the old traditions. He replied:

> As the old people say, when the Spaniards came, they broke off the branches of our world. They even burned the trunk. But the roots remain, and they can never reach the roots. We will never die because the roots have power. They draw strength from our ancestors.
>
> Today our future is in doubt. *Cofrades* have children that are Catechists [orthodox Roman Catholics] or Evangelicals. We are no longer united. People who abandon the past lose their history, their ancestors, the ones who live in their blood. They ignore their roots, and this causes them to die as Tz'utujils. We must be united. We must teach our children or we will lose our future. Everything will pass away.
>
> But the ancestors are still present with us. They are all around us. They are alive in our blood. They calm our hearts and give us strength. Understanding comes from the simple words of the heart. We must be honest. We must endure because everything comes from within ourselves, from our blood. Outsiders try to manipulate us and our words, but we cannot allow this.
>
> My daughter is a flower. Flowers die, but they leave their seed. Each of us has our time on earth and then we pass away, but our seed remains to create other flowers. Each flower is different, but they are also all the same. We must remember this. If we do, we will never die.

BIBLIOGRAPHY

ACUÑA, RENÉ

1975 "Problemas del *Popol Vuh*." *Mester* 5 (2): 123–132.

1982 *Relaciones geográficas del siglo XVI: Guatemala*. Mexico City: Universidad Nacional Autónoma de México.

1983 "El *Popol Vuh*, Vico y la *Theologia Indorum*." In *Nuevas perspectivas sobre el Popol Vuh*, Robert M. Carmack and Francisco Morales Santos, eds., 1–16. Guatemala City: Piedra Santa.

1984 *Relaciones geográficas del siglo XVI: Tlaxcala*. Vol. 1. Mexico City: Universidad Nacional Autónoma de México.

1985 "La *Theologia Indorum* de Fray Domingo de Vico." *Tlalocan* 10: 281–307.

ADORNO, ROLENA

1993 "La censura y su evasión: Jerónimo Román y Bartolomé de las Casas." *Estudios de Cultura Náhuatl* 23: 263–294.

AGUILERA, MIGUEL ASTOR

2002 *Survey of Talking Crosses in Yucatán and Quintana Roo*. Foundation for the Advancement of Mesoamerican Studies. famsi.org/reports/99034/index.html.

ALVARADO, PEDRO DE

1924 *An Account of the Conquest of Guatemala in 1524 by Pedro de Alvarado*. Sedley J. Mackie, ed. New York: Cortes Society.

1946 *Relación hecha por Pedro de Alvarado a Hernando Cortes (1524)*. Biblioteca de Autores Españoles, Vol. 22. Madrid: Biblioteca de Autores Españoles.

ANONYMOUS

1935 [ca. 1700] *Isagoge histórica apologética de las Indias Occidentales*. Vol. 8. Guatemala City: Biblioteca "Goathemala."

1952 "Relación de los caciques y principales del pueblo de Atitlán (1571)." *Anales de la Sociedad de Geografía e Historia de Guatemala* 26: 435–438.

1985 *Los códices Mayas*. Tuxtla Gutiérrez: Universidad Autónoma de Chiapas.

AVENDAÑO Y LOYOLA, FRAY ANDRÉS DE

1987 *Relation of Two Trips to Peten: Made for the Conversion of the Heathen Ytzaex and Cehaches*. Charles P. Bowditch and Guillermo Rivera, trans. Culver City: Labyrinthos.

AVENI, ANTHONY F.

2000 "Out of Teotihuacan: Origins of the Celestial Canon in Mesoamerica." In *Mesoamerica's Classic Heritage*, Davíd Carrasco, Lindsay Jones, and Scott Sessions, eds., 253–268. Boulder: University of Colorado Press.

BARRERA VÁSQUEZ, ALFREDO

1995 *Diccionario Maya*. Mexico City: Editorial Porrúa.

BASSIE-SWEET, KAREN

2008 *Maya Sacred Geography and the Creator Deities*. Norman: University of Oklahoma Press.

BETANCOR, ALONSO PÁEZ, AND FRAY PEDRO DE ARBOLEDA

1964 "Relación de Santiago Atitlán, año de 1585. *Anales de la Sociedad de Geografía e Historia de Guatemala* 37: 87–106.

BOSSÚZ, ENNIO MARÍA

1990 *Un manuscrito K'ekchi' del siglo XVI*. Guatemala City: Ediciones Comisión Interuniversitaria Guatemalteca de Conmemoración del V Centenario del Descrubrimiento de América.

BRASSEUR DE BOURBOURG, CHARLES ÉTIENNE

1869 *Manuscrit Troano: Études sur le système graphique et la langue des Mayas*. Paris: Imprimerie Impériale.

BRICKER, VICTORIA REIFLER

1981 *The Indian Christ, the Indian King: The Historical Substrate of Maya Myth and Ritual*. Austin: University of Texas Press.

BRICKER, VICTORIA REIFLER, AND HELGA-MARIA MIRAM

2002 *An Encounter of Two Worlds: The Book of Chilam Balam of Kaua*. Middle American Research Institute Publication 68. New Orleans: Tulane University.

BRINTON, DANIEL G.

1884 "A Grammar of the Cakchiquel Language of Guatemala." *Proceedings of the American Philosophical Society* 21 (115): 345–412.

BUNZEL, RUTH LEAH

1952 *Chichicastenango*. American Ethnological Society Publication 22. Seattle: University of Washington Press.

CAMPBELL, LYLE R.

1983 "Préstamos lingüísticos en el Popol Vuh." In *Nuevas perspectivas sobre el Popol Vuh*, Robert M. Carmack and Francisco Morales Santos, eds., 81–86. Guatemala City: Piedra Santa.

CARLSEN, ROBERT S.

1996 "Social Organization and Disorganization in Santiago Atitlán, Guatemala." *Ethnology* 35 (2) (Spring 1996): 141–159.

1997 *The War for the Heart and Soul of a Highland Maya Town.* Austin: University of Texas Press.

2001 "Judas." In *The Oxford Encyclopedia of Mesoamerican Cultures: The Civilizations of Mexico and Central America,* Davíd Carrasco, ed., 179–181. Oxford: Oxford University Press.

CARLSEN, ROBERT S., AND MARTÍN PRECHTEL

1991 "The Flowering of the Dead: An Interpretation of Highland Maya Culture." *Man* 26: 23–42.

1994 "Walking on Two Legs: Shamanism in Santiago Atitlán, Guatemala." In *Ancient Traditions: Culture and Shamanism in Central Asia and the Americas,* Gary Seaman and Jane Day, eds., 77–111. Niwot: University Press of Colorado.

CARLSON, JOHN B.

2011 "Anticipating the Maya Apocalypse: What Might the Ancient Day-Keepers Have Envisioned for December 21, 2012?" *Archaeoastronomy* 24: 143–182.

CARMACK, ROBERT M.

1973 *Quichean Civilization.* Berkeley: University of California Press.

1981 *The Quiché Mayas of Utatlán: The Evolution of a Highland Guatemala Kingdom.* Norman: University of Oklahoma Press.

1995 *Rebels of Highland Guatemala: The Quiché-Mayas of Momostenango.* Norman: University of Oklahoma Press.

2011 "Bartolomé de las Casas y etnología de Indígenas de Guatemala." In *Cosmovisión Mesoamericana,* 17–34. Guatemala City: Universidad Mesoamericana.

CARMACK, ROBERT M., AND JAMES L. MONDLOCH

1983 *Título de Totonicapán.* Mexico City: Universidad Nacional Autónoma de México.

1989 *Título de Yax, y otros documentos quichés de Totonicapán, Guatemala.* Mexico City: Centro de Estudios Mayas, Universidad Nacional Autónoma de México.

2007 *Uwujil Kulewal aj Chwi Miq'ina': El Título de Totonicapán.* Guatemala City: Cholsamaj.

CARRASCO, PEDRO

1967 "Don Juan Cortés, Cacique de Santa Cruz Quiché." *Estudios de Cultura Maya* 6: 251–266.

CERVANTES, FERNANDO

1994 *The Devil in the New World: The Impact of Diabolism in New Spain.* New Haven: Yale University Press.

CHAVERO, ALFREDO

1892 *Homenaje a Cristóbal Colón: Antigüedades.* Mexico City: Junta Colombina.

CHINCHILLA MAZARIEGOS, OSWALDO

2013 "Tecum, the Fallen Sun: Mesoamerican Cosmogony and the Spanish Conquest of Guatemala." *Ethnohistory* 60 (4) (Fall 2013): 693–719.

CHRISTENSON, ALLEN J.

2001 *Art and Society in a Highland Maya Community*. Austin: University of Texas Press.

2003 *Popol Vuh: Literal Poetic Version*. Winchester, UK: O Books.

2007 *Popol Vuh: The Sacred Book of the Maya*. Norman: University of Oklahoma Press.

CHUCHIAK, JOHN

2005 "In Servitio Dei: Fray Diego de Landa, the Franciscan Order, and the Return of the Extirpation of Idolatry in the Colonial Diocese of Yucatán, 1573–1579." *The Americas* 61 (4) (April 2005): 611–646.

2012 *The Inquisition in New Spain, 1536–1820: A Documentary History*. Baltimore: Johns Hopkins University Press.

CLENDINNEN, INGA

1987 *Ambivalent Conquests: Maya and Spaniard in Yucatan, 1517–1570*. Cambridge: Cambridge University Press.

1991 *Aztecs: An Interpretation*. Cambridge: Cambridge University Press.

COE, MICHAEL D.

2011 *The Maya*. New York: Thames and Hudson.

COGOLLUDO, FRAY DIEGO LÓPEZ DE

1957 *Historia de Yucatán*. 2 vols. Mexico City: Editorial Academia Literaria.

2006 *Historia de Yucatán*. Barcelona: Linkgua Ediciones.

COOK, GARRETT

1986 "Quichean Folk Theology and Southern Maya Supernaturalism." In *Symbol and Meaning Beyond the Closed Community: Essays in Mesoamerican Ideas*, Gary H. Gossen, ed., 138–153. Albany: Institute for Mesoamerican Studies, University of Albany.

2000 *Renewing the Maya World: Expressive Culture in a Highland Town*. Austin: University of Texas Press.

COOK, GARRETT, THOMAS OFFIT, AND RHONDA TAUBE

2013 *Indigenous Religion and Cultural Performance in the New Maya World*. Albuquerque: University of New Mexico Press.

CORTÉS Y LARRAZ, PEDRO

1958 [1770] *Descripción geográfico-moral de la Diócesis de Goathemala*. 2 vols. Guatemala City: Biblioteca de la Sociedad de Geografía e Historia de Guatemala.

COTO, FRAY THOMÁS DE

1983 *Thesaurus Verboru: Vocabulario de la lengua cakchiquel v [el] Guatemalteca*. René Acuña, ed. Mexico City: Universidad Nacional Autónoma de México.

CRAINE, EUGENE R., AND REGINALD C. REINDORP

1979 *The Codex Pérez and the Book of Chilam Balam of Mani.* Norman: University of Oklahoma Press.

DÍAZ DEL CASTILLO, BERNAL

1963 *The Conquest of New Spain.* J. M. Cohen, trans. London: Penguin.

1984 *Historia verdadera de la conquista de la Nueva España.* 2 vols. Miguel León-Portilla, ed. Madrid: n.p.

DOUGLAS, BILL

1969 "Illness and Curing in Santiago Atitlán." PhD dissertation, Stanford University.

DURÁN, FRAY DIEGO

1867–1880 *Historia de las Indias de Nueva-España y Islas de Tierra Firme.* 2 vols. Mexico City: Escalante.

EARLY, JOHN D.

2006 *The Maya and Catholicism: An Encounter of Worldviews.* Gainesville: University Press of Florida.

2012 *Maya and Catholic Cultures in Crisis.* Gainesville: University Press of Florida.

EDMONSON, MUNRO S.

1982 *The Ancient Future of the Itza: The Book of Chilam Balam of Tizimin.* Austin: University of Texas Press.

1986 *Heaven Born Mérida and Its Destiny: The Book of Chilam Balam of Chumayel.* Austin: University of Texas Press.

ESTRADA MONROY, AGUSTÍN

1979 *El Mundo K'ekchi' de la Vera Paz.* Guatemala City: Editorial del Ejército.

FARRISS, NANCY M.

1984 *Maya Society under Colonial Rule: The Collective Enterprise of Survival.* Princeton: Princeton University Press.

FASH, WILLIAM.

1991 *Scribes, Warriors and Kings.* London: Thames and Hudson.

FÉRÉAL, VICTOR DE

1844 *Les mystères de l'inquisition et autres sociétés d'Espagne.* Paris: Librairie, Rue Visconti 22.

FÖRSTEMANN, ERNST WILHELM

1880 *Die Maya Handschrift der königlichen öffentlichen bibliothek zu Dresden.* Leipzig: Verlag der A. Naumannschen Lichtdruckeret.

FREIDEL, DAVID, LINDA SCHELE, AND JOY PARKER

1993 *Maya Cosmos: Three Thousand Years on the Shaman's Path.* New York: William Morrow and Company.

FUENTES Y GUZMÁN, FRANCISCO DE

1932–1933 [1699] *Recordación Florida.* 3 vols. Guatemala City: Biblioteca Goathemala.

1972 [1690] *Obras históricas de don Francisco Antonio de Fuentes y Guzmán.* 3 vols. Carmelo Sáenz de Santa María, ed. Madrid: Biblioteca de Autores Españoles.

GAGE, THOMAS

1958 *Travels in the New World.* J. Eric S. Thompson, ed. Westport: Greenwood Press.

GARCÍA ICAZBALCETA, JOAQUÍN, ED.

1889–1892 *Nueva colección de documentos para la historia de México.* 5 vols. Mexico City: Andrade y Morales.

GARCÍA PELÁEZ, FRANCISCO DE PAULA

1943 [1851] *Memorias para la historia del antiguo reino de Guatemala.* Guatemala City: Biblioteca "Payo de Rivera."

GARZA, MERCEDES DE LA

1983 *Relaciones histórico-geográficas de la gobernación de Yucatán.* 2 vols. Mexico City: Universidad Nacional Autónoma de México.

GRUBE, NIKOLAI

2001 "Die Errichtung von Stelen: Entzifferung einer Verbhieroglyphe auf Monumenten der klassischen Mayakultur." In *The Decipherment of Ancient Maya Writing*, Stephen Houston, Oswaldo Chinchilla Mazariegos, and David Stuart, eds., 486–504. Norman: University of Oklahoma Press.

HANKE, LEWIS

1949 *The Spanish Struggle for Justice in the Conquest of America.* Philadelphia: University of Pennsylvania Press.

1951 *Las Casas, historiador, estudio preliminar a la Historia de las Indias.* Mexico City: Fondo de Cultura Económica.

1952 *Bartolomé de las Casas, Bookman, Scholar & Propagandist.* Philadelphia: University of Pennsylvania Press.

HANKE, LEWIS, AND MANUEL GIMÉNEZ FERNÁNDEZ

1954 *Bartolomé de las Casas, 1474–1566: Bibliografía crítica.* Santiago, Chile: Fondo Histórico y Bibliográfico José Toribio Medina.

HANKS, WILLIAM F.

2010 *Converting Words: Maya in the Age of the Cross.* Berkeley: University of California Press.

HERRERA Y TORDESILLAS, ANTONIO DE

1726 *Historia general de los hechos de los castellanos en las islas y tierra firma del Mar Océano.* Madrid: n.p.

HILL, ROBERT M.

1992 *Colonial Cakchiquels: Highland Maya Adaptation to Spanish Rule, 1600–1700.* Fort Worth: Harcourt Brace Jovanovich.

HOUSTON, STEPHEN

2014 *The Life Within: Classic Maya and the Matter of Permanence.* New Haven: Yale University Press.

HOUSTON, STEPHEN, AND DAVID STUART

1996 "Of Gods, Glyphs and Kings: Divinity and Rulership among the Classic Maya." *Antiquity* 70: 289–312.

HOUSTON, STEPHEN, DAVID STUART, AND KARL TAUBE

2006 *The Memory of Bones: Body, Being, and Experience among the Classic Maya.* Austin: University of Texas Press.

JONES, GRANT D.

1998 *The Conquest of the Last Maya Kingdom.* Stanford: Stanford University Press.

JONES, OAKAH L., JR.

1994 *Guatemala in the Spanish Colonial Period.* Norman: University of Oklahoma Press.

KARTTUNEN, FRANCES E.

1994 *Between Worlds: Interpreters, Guides, and Survivors.* New Brunswick: Rutgers University Press.

KLEIN, CECELIA F.

1990 "Editor's Statement: Depictions of the Dispossessed." *Art Journal* 49 (2): 106–109.

KNOWLTON, TIMOTHY W.

2004 "Dialogism in the Languages of Colonial Maya Creation Myths." PhD dissertation. Department of Anthropology, Tulane University, New Orleans.

2010 *Maya Creation Myths: Words and Worlds of the Chilam Balam.* Boulder: University Press of Colorado.

KNOWLTON, TIMOTHY W., AND GABRIELLE VAIL

2010 "Hybrid Cosmologies in Mesoamerica: A Reevaluation of the *Yax Cheel Cab*, a Maya World Tree." *Ethnohistory* 57 (4): 709–739.

KUBLER, GEORGE

1948 *Mexican Architecture of the Sixteenth Century.* 2 vols. New Haven: Yale University Press.

LA FARGE, OLIVER

1947 *Santa Eulalia: The Religion of a Cuchumatan Indian Town.* Chicago: University of Chicago Press.

LA FARGE, OLIVER, AND DOUGLAS BYERS

1931 *The Year Bearer's People.* Middle American Research Institute, Publication 3. New Orleans: Tulane University.

LANDA, FRAY DIEGO DE

1941 *Landa's Relación de las cosas de Yucatán*. Alfred M. Tozzer, trans. Cambridge, MA: Peabody Museum of Archaeology and Ethnology, Harvard University.

LAS CASAS, FRAY BARTOLOMÉ DE

1909 *Apologética historia de las Indias, Bartolomé de las Casas*. Manuel Serrano y Sanz, ed. Nueva Biblioteca de Autores Españoles no. 13. Madrid: Bailly, Bailliére é Hijos.

1957 *Historia de las Indias*. 2 vols. Juan Pérez de Tudela y Emilio López Oto, eds. Madrid: Biblioteca de Autores Españoles.

1958 *Apologética historia*. Juan Pérez de Tudela Bueso, ed. Madrid: Biblioteca de Autores Españoles.

1967 *Apologética historia sumaria*. 2 vols. Edmundo O'Gorman, ed. Mexico City: Universidad Nacional Autónoma de México.

1971 *Bartolomé de Las Casas: A Selection of His Writings*. George Sanderlin, ed. New York: Alfred A. Knopf.

1992 *In Defense of the Indians*. Stafford Poole, trans. DeKalb: Northern Illinois University Press.

LEÓN-PORTILLA, MIGUEL

1980 *Native Mesoamerican Spirituality*. New York: Paulist Press.

LIZANA, BERNARDO DE

1893 *Historia de Yucatán: Devocionario de Nuestra Señora de Izamal y conquista spiritual de Yucatán*. Mexico City: Imprenta del Museo Nacional.

LÓPEZ DE GÓMARA, FRANCISCO

1554 *La historia general de las Indias: Con todos los descubrimientos, y cosas notables que han acaescido enellas, dende que se ganaron hasta agora*. Madrid: n.p.

LOTHROP, ELEANOR

1948 *Throw Me a Bone*. New York: Whittlesey House.

LOTHROP, SAMUEL K.

1928 "Santiago Atitlán, Guatemala." *Indian Notes* 5: 370–395.

1929 "Further Notes on Indian Ceremonies in Guatemala." *Indian Notes* 6: 1–25.

MACKENZIE, C. JAMES

2009 "Judas off the Noose: Sacerdotes Mayas, Costumbristas, and the Politics of Purity in the Tradition of San Simón in Guatemala." *Journal of Latin American and Caribbean Anthropology* 14 (2): 355–381.

MACLEOD, BARBARA

1989 "The 819-Day-Count: A Soulful Mechanism." In *Word and Image in Maya Culture: Explorations in Language, Writing, and Representation*, William F. Hanks and Don S. Rice, eds., 112–126. Salt Lake City: University of Utah Press.

MAXWELL, JUDITH M., AND ROBERT M. HILL II

2006 *Kaqchikel Chronicles*. Austin: University of Texas Press.

MCDOUGALL, ELSIE

1955 "Easter Ceremonies at Santiago Atitlán in 1930." *Notes on Middle American Archaeology and Ethnology* 123: 63–74. Washington, DC: Carnegie Institution of Washington.

MENDELSON, E. MICHAEL

1956 "Religion and World-View in Santiago Atitlán." PhD dissertation, University of Chicago.

1957 *Religion and World-View in a Guatemalan Village.* Microfilm Collection of Manuscripts on Middle American Cultural Anthropology no. 52. Chicago: University of Chicago Library.

1958a "A Guatemalan Sacred Bundle." *Man* 58: 121–126.

1958b "The King, the Traitor, and the Cross: An Interpretation of a Highland Maya Religious Conflict." *Diogenes* 21: 1–10.

1959 "Maximon: An Iconographical Introduction." *Man* 59: 57–60.

1965 *Las escándolas de Maximon.* Publication 19. Guatemala City: Seminario de Integración Social Guatemalteca.

MENDIETA, FRAY GERÓNIMO DE

1993 *Historia eclesiástica Indiana.* Mexico City: Editorial Porrúa.

MENDOZA, RUBEN G.

2008 "The Divine Gourd Tree, Tzompantli Skull Racks, Decapitation Rituals, and Human Trophies in Ancient Mesoamerica." In *The Taking and Displaying of Human Body Parts as Trophied by Amerindians*, Richard Chacon and David Dye, eds., 396–439. New York: Springer.

MILLER, MARY

2001 "The Maya Ballgame: Rebirth in the Court of Life and Death." In *The Sport of Life and Death: The Mesoamerican Ballgame*, E. Michael Whittington, ed., 78–87. New York: Thames and Hudson.

MILLER, MARY, AND STEPHEN HOUSTON

1987 "Stairways and Ballcourt Glyphs." *RES: Anthropology and Aesthetics* 14: 47–66.

MILLER, MARY, AND KARL TAUBE

1993 *The Gods and Symbols of Ancient Mexico and the Maya.* London: Thames and Hudson.

MOLINA, DIEGO

1983 *Las confesiones de Maximón.* Guatemala City: Artemis y Edinter.

MORLEY, SYLVANUS G., GEORGE W. BRAINERD, AND ROBERT SHARER

1983 *The Ancient Maya.* Stanford: Stanford University Press.

NASH, JUNE

1968 "The Passion Play in Maya Indian Communities." *Comparative Studies in Society and History* 10 (3): 318–327.

NAVARRETE, CARLOS

1982 *San Pascualito Rey y el culto a la muerte en Chiapas*. Mexico City: Universidad Nacional Autónoma de México.

NEWSOME, ELIZABETH A.

2001 *Trees of Paradise and Pillars of the World: The Serial Stela Cycle of "18-Rabbit-God K," King of Copan*. Austin: University of Texas Press.

NICHOLSON, HENRY B.

2001 *Topiltzin Quetzalcoatl: The Once and Future Lord of the Toltecs*. Boulder: University Press of Colorado.

O'BRIEN-ROTHE, LINDA

1975 "Songs of the Face of the Earth: Ancestor Songs of the Tzutuhil Maya of Santiago Atitlán, Guatemala." PhD dissertation, University of California at Los Angeles.

2015 *Songs That Make the Road Dance: Courtship and Fertility Music of the Tz'utujil Maya*. Austin: University of Texas Press.

O'FLAHERTY, EDWARD MARTIN

1979 "Institutionalization of the Catholic Church in the Americas: The Case of Colonial Guatemala, 1524–1563." PhD dissertation, University of Pennsylvania, Philadelphia.

O'NEIL, MEGAN

2012 *Engaging Ancient Maya Sculpture at Piedras Negras, Guatemala*. Norman: University of Oklahoma Press.

ORDOÑEZ CHIPIN, MARTÍN

1973 "La figura de Judas Iscariote en el medio Guatemalteco." *Guatemala Indígena* 7 (1): 143–172.

ORELLANA, SANDRA L.

1981 "Idols and Idolatry in Highland Guatemala." *Ethnohistory* 28 (2) (Spring 1981): 157–177.

1984 *The Tzutujil Mayas: Continuity and Change, 1250–1630*. Norman: University of Oklahoma Press.

PAXTON, MERIDETH

2009 "The Map of the Province of Maní: A Record of Landscape and Northern Maya Lowland Concepts of Origin." In *Landscapes of Origin in the Americas*, Jessica Joyce Christie, ed., 77–97. Tuscaloosa: University of Alabama Press.

2011 *The Cosmos of the Yucatec Maya: Cycles and Steps from the Madrid Codex*. Albuquerque: University of New Mexico Press.

PETERSON, JEANETTE FAVROT

1993 *The Paradise Garden Murals of Malinalco*. Austin: University of Texas Press.

PIEPER, JIM

2002 *Guatemala's Folk Saints*. Los Angeles: Pieper and Associates.

PRECHTEL, MARTÍN

1998 *Secrets of the Talking Jaguar: Memoirs From the Living Heart of a Mayan Village.* New York: Tarcher/Putnam.

PRECHTEL, MARTÍN, AND ROBERT S. CARLSEN

1988 "Weaving and Cosmos amongst the Tzutujil Maya." *RES* 15: 122–132.

RECINOS, ADRIÁN

1950 *Popol Vuh: The Sacred Book of the Ancient Quiche Maya.* Delia Goetz and Sylvanus G. Morley, trans. Norman: University of Oklahoma Press.

1957 *Crónicas indígenas de Guatemala.* Guatemala City: Editorial Universitaria.

RECINOS, ADRIÁN, AND DELIA GOETZ

1953 *The Annals of the Cakchiquels.* Norman: University of Oklahoma Press.

REMESAL, FRAY ANTONIO DE

1964 [1619] *Historia general de las Indias Occidentales y particular de la gobernación de Chiapa y Guatemala.* Vol. 1. P. Carmelo Sáenz de Santa María, ed. Madrid: Biblioteca de Autores Españoles.

1966 *Historia general de las Indias Occidentales y particular de la gobernación de Chiapa y Guatemala.* Vol. 2. P. Carmelo Sáenz de Santa María, ed. Madrid: Biblioteca de Autores Españoles.

RESTALL, MATTHEW

1997 *The Maya World: Yucatec Culture and Society, 1550–1850.* Stanford: Stanford University Press.

1998 *Maya Conquistador.* Boston: Beacon Press.

RESTALL, MATTHEW, AND JOHN F. CHUCHIAK IV

2002 "A Reevaluation of the Authenticity of Fray Diego de Landa's *Relación de las cosas de Yucatán.*" *Ethnohistory* 49 (3): 651–669.

RICE, PRUDENCE

1985 "Reptilian Imagery and Vessel Function in Petén Postclassic Pottery: A Preliminary Review." In *Fifth Palenque Round Table, 1983,* Merle Greene Robertson, ed., 115–122. San Francisco: Pre-Columbian Art Research Institute.

ROMÁN Y ZAMORA, FRAY JERÓNIMO

1897 *Repúblicas de Indias: Idolatrías y gobierno en México y Perú antes de la Conquista.* 2 vols. Madrid: n.p.

ROSNY, LÉON DE

1887 *Codex Peresianus: Manuscrit hiératique des anciens Indiens de l'Amérique Centrale, conservé à la Bibliothèque Nationale de Paris.* Paris: Bureau de la Société Américaine.

ROYS, RALPH L.

1965 *Ritual of the Bacabs: A Book of Maya Incantations.* Norman: University of Oklahoma Press.

1967 *The Book of Chilam Balam of Chumayel.* Norman: University of Oklahoma Press.

SACHSE, FRAUKE

2008 "Over Distant Waters: Places of Origin and Creation in Colonial K'iche'an Sources." In *Pre-Columbian Landscapes of Origin*, John Edward Staller, ed., 123–160. New York: Springer.

SAHAGÚN, FRAY BERNARDINO DE

1953 *Florentine Codex.* Arthur J. O. Anderson and Charles E. Dibble, trans. 13 vols. Santa Fe: School of American Research.

1956 *Historia general de las cosas de Nueva España.* 4 vols. Mexico City: Editorial Porrúa.

1997 *Primeros memoriales.* Thelma D. Sullivan and Henry B. Nicholson, trans. Norman: University of Oklahoma Press.

2002 *El Calepino de Sahagún, un acercamiento.* Pilar Máynez y Miguel León-Portilla, eds. Mexico City: Universidad Nacional Autónoma de México.

SATURNO, WILLIAM A., KARL A. TAUBE, AND DAVID STUART

2005 *The Murals of San Bartolo, El Petén, Guatemala, Part 1: The North Wall.* Ancient America, Publication 7. Barnardsville, NC: Center for Ancient American Studies.

SAVILLE, MARSHALL H.

1921 *Reports on the Maya Indians of Yucatan by Santiago Méndez, Antonio García y Cubas, Pedro Sánchez de Aguilar and Francisco Hernández.* Indian Notes and Monographs 9. New York: Museum of the American Indian, Heye Foundation.

SCARBOROUGH, VERNON L., AND DAVID R. WILCOX

1991 *The Mesoamerican Ballgame.* Tucson: University of Arizona Press.

SCHOLES, FRANCE V., AND ELEANOR B. ADAMS

1938 *Don Diego Quijada, alcalde mayor de Yucatán, 1561–1565.* 2 vols. Mexico City: Antigua Librería Robredo, de José Porrúa e Hijos.

SHARER, ROBERT J.

1994 *The Ancient Maya.* Stanford: Stanford University Press.

SPARKS, GARRY

2011a "Fill in the Middle Ground: Intertextuality and Interreligious Dialogue in 16th-Century Guatemala." *Journal of Inter-Religious Dialogue* 5 (2) (February 2011): 1–30.

2011b "Xalqat B'e and the Theologia Indorum: Crossroads between Maya Spirituality and the Americas' First Theology." PhD dissertation, University of Chicago.

STANZIONE, VINCENT JAMES

2003 *Rituals of Sacrifice: Walking the Face of the Earth on the Sacred Path of the Sun.* Albuquerque: University of New Mexico Press.

STEPHENS, JOHN LLOYD

1963 *Incidents of Travel in Yucatan*. 2 vols. New York: Dover Publications.

1969 *Incidents of Travel in Central America, Chiapas, and Yucatan*. 2 vols. New York: Dover Publications.

STONE, ANDREA J., AND MARC ZENDER

2011 *Reading Maya Art: A Hieroglyphic Guide to Ancient Maya Painting and Sculpture*. New York: Thames and Hudson.

STUART, DAVID

1988 "Blood Symbolism in Maya Iconography." In *Maya Iconography*, Elizabeth P. Benson and Gillett G. Griffin, eds., 175–221. Princeton: Princeton University Press, 175–221.

1996 "Kings of Stone: A Consideration of Stelae in Classic Maya Ritual and Representation." RES: *Anthropology and Aesthetics* 29–30: 148–171.

2004 "New Year Records in Classic Maya Inscriptions." PARI *Journal* 5 (2) (Fall 2004): 1–6.

2005 *The Inscriptions from Temple XIX at Palenque*. San Francisco: Pre-Columbian Art Research Institute.

STUART, DAVID, AND GEORGE STUART

2008 *Palenque: Eternal City of the Maya*. London: Thames and Hudson.

TARN, NATHANIEL, AND MARTÍN PRECHTEL

1986 "Constant Inconstancy: The Feminine Principle in Atiteco Mythology." In *Symbol and Meaning beyond the Closed Community: Essays in Mesoamerican Ideas*, Gary H. Gossen, ed., 173–184. Albany: Institute for Mesoamerican Studies, University at Albany, SUNY.

1990 "Comiéndose la fruta: Metáforos sexuales e iniciaciones en Santiago Atitlán." *Mesoamérica* 19: 73–82.

1997 *Scandals in the House of Birds: Shamans and Priests on Lake Atitlán*. New York: Marsilio Publishers.

TAUBE, KARL A.

1988 "The Ancient Yucatec New Year Festival: The Liminal Period in Maya Ritual and Cosmology." PhD dissertation, Yale University, New Haven, CT.

1992 *The Major Gods of Ancient Yucatan*. Studies in Pre-Columbian Art and Archaeology no. 32. Washington, DC: Dumbarton Oaks Research Library and Collection.

1994 "The Birth Vase: Natal Imagery in Ancient Maya Myth and Ritual." In *The Maya Vase Book*, vol. 4, Justin Kerr, ed., 652–685. New York: Kerr Associates.

2004 "Flower Mountain: Concepts of Life, Beauty, and Paradise among the Classic Maya." RES: *Anthropology and Aesthetics* 45 (Spring 2004): 69–98.

TAUBE, KARL, WILLIAM A. SATURNO, DAVID STUART, AND HEATHER HURST

2010 "The Murals of San Bartolo, El Petén, Guatemala. Part 2: The West Wall." *Ancient America* 10: 3–107.

TEDLOCK, BARBARA

1982 *Time and the Highland Maya.* Albuquerque: University of New Mexico Press.

TEDLOCK, DENNIS E.

1986 "Creation in the *Popol Vuh*: A Hermeneutical Approach." In *Symbol and Meaning Beyond the Closed Community: Essays in Mesoamerican Ideas*, Gary H. Gossen, ed., 77–82. Albany: Institute for Mesoamerican Studies, SUNY.

1993 "Torture in the Archives: Mayans Meet Europeans." *American Anthropologist* 95 (1) (March 1993): 139–152.

1996 *Popol Vuh.* New York: Simon and Schuster.

TERMER, FRANZ

1957 *Etnología y etnografía de Guatemala.* Publicación 5, Seminario de Integración Social Guatemalteca. Guatemala City: Ministerio de Educación Pública.

THOMPSON, SIR J. ERIC S.

1970 *Maya History and Religion.* Norman: University of Oklahoma Press.

1972 *Commentary on the Dresden Codex: A Maya Hieroglyphic Book.* Philadelphia: American Philosophical Society.

TIMMER, DAVID E.

1997 "Providence and Perdition: Fray Diego de Landa Justifies His Inquisition against the Yucatecan Maya." *Church History* 66 (33) (September 1997): 477–488.

TORQUEMADA, FRAY JUAN DE

1723 *Monarchia Indiana: Con el origen y guerras de los Indios Occidentales de sus poblaçiones, descubrimento, conquista, conversión y otras cosas marauillosas de la mesma tierra distribuydos en tres tomos.* Andrés Gonzáles de Barcia Carballido y Zuñaga, ed. 3 vols. Madrid: n.p.

VAIL, GABRIELLE, AND CHRISTINE HERNÁNDEZ

2014 *Re-Creating Primordial Time: Foundation Rituals and Mythology in the Postclassic Maya Codices.* Boulder: University Press of Colorado.

VAN AKKEREN, RUUD

2011 "Fray Domingo de Vico, maestro de autores indígenas." In *Cosmovisión Mesoamericana*, Horacio Cabezas Carcache, ed., 83–118. Guatemala City: Publicaciones Mesoamericanas.

VÁZQUEZ, FRAY FRANCISCO

1937–1944 [1714] *Crónica del Santísimo Nombre de Jesús de Guatemala.* 4 vols. Guatemala City: Biblioteca "Goathemala" de la Sociedad de Geografía e Historia.

VÁZQUEZ DE ESPINOSA, FRAY ANTONIO

1944 *Descripción de la Nueva España en el siglo XVII.* Mariano Cuevas, ed. Mexico City: Editorial Patria.

VOGT, EVON Z.

1969 *Zinacantan: A Maya Community in the Highlands of Chiapas*. Cambridge, MA: Harvard University Press.

1970 *The Zinacantecos of Mexico: A Modern Maya Way of Life*. New York: Holt, Rinehart, and Winston.

1993 *Tortillas for the Gods: A Symbolic Analysis of Zinacanteco Rituals*. New edition. Norman: University of Oklahoma Press.

WAGNER, EUGENE LOGAN

1997 "Open Space as a Tool of Conversion: The Syncretism of Sacred Courts and Plazas in Post Conquest Mexico." PhD dissertation, University of Texas at Austin.

WATANABE, JOHN M.

1990 "From Saints to Shibboleths: Image, Structure, and Identity in Maya Religious Syncretism." *American Ethnologist* 17 (1): 131–150.

1992 *Maya Saints and Souls in a Changing World*. Austin: University of Texas Press.

WHITTINGTON, E. MICHAEL

2001 *The Sport of Life and Death: The Mesoamerican Ballgame*. New York: Thames and Hudson.

WISDOM, CHARLES

1940 *The Chorti Indians of Guatemala*. Chicago: University of Chicago Press.

XIMÉNEZ, FRAY FRANCISCO

1701 "Arte de las tres lenguas 3a3chiquel, quiche y 4'utuhil." Manuscript in the Ayer collection at the Newberry Library, Chicago, Illinois.

1926 *Las historias del origen de los indios de esta Provincia de Guatemala*. San Salvador.

1929–1931 [1722] *Historia de la provincia de San Vicente de Chiapa y Guatemala*. 3 vols. Guatemala City: Biblioteca "Goathemala."

1967 [1722] *Escolios a las historias de origen de los indios*. Sociedad de Geografía e Historia de Guatemala Special Publication no. 13. Guatemala City: n.p.

1985 *Primera parte del tesoro de las lenguas cakchiquel, quiche y zutuhil, en que las dichas lenguas se traducen a la nuestra española*. Special Publication no. 30. Guatemala City: Academia de Geografía e Historia.

ZORITA, ALONSO DE

1963 *Life and Labor in Ancient Mexico: The Brief and Summary Relation of the Lords of New Spain*. Benjamin Keen, trans. New Brunswick, NJ: Rutgers University Press.

INDEX

Page numbers in italics denote illustrations.